Sermons
and
Teachings
of
Billy R. Brown

Sermons
and
Teachings
of
Billy R. Brown

Senior Pastor
Houston Area Gospel Assembly
Humble, Texas

Volume 1

Acclaim Press
— Your Next Great Book —
P.O. Box 238
Morley, MO 63767
(573) 472-9800
www.acclaimpress.com

Book & Cover Design: M. Frene Melton

ISBN: 978-1-942613-48-0 / 1-942613-48-2
Library of Congress Control Number: 2016909382

First Printing: 2016
Printed in the United States of America
10 9 8 7 6 5 4 3 2 1

Contents

This is a random collection of sermons spanning several years. Subject Titles for each chapter generally focus on one or two topics. Other subjects may be addressed throughout the chapter. Although effort was made to minimize repetition of topics, some may be discussed in various chapters. Scripture references are from the King James Version and most are italicized whether directly quoted or paraphrased. Some people who speak from the audience are not named because comments or questions are not clear and identification of the person speaking was not possible.

Brother Billy Brown and his wife, Sister Sonja Brown

The sermons in this book are transcribed with Brother Brown's permission. He was reluctant to give permission because of his viewpoint about the writing of doctrines in books. The following excerpt from one of the sermons expresses his view.

> "The problem in writing a book is, when you write it down on paper it's hard to change it. After you've published a book you can't erase the error out of that book you've published. So many men have tied themselves down or boxed themselves into a corner by writing books prematurely. People wonder why we don't write books. Why don't we write this doctrine down? Why don't we print it where people can study it? Well, we might write an error down and you would study the error. Do you realize that error is damning? Error is destructive. Error is fatal. It will keep you from entering into everlasting life. The error must finally be wiped out of our minds. We must see clearly the truth. It's the truth that sets you free.
>
> We've got to be taught the truth about God. We have to learn the true interpretation of the Word of God because it takes that to set us free. Until we hear the truth we can't be judged by it, but neither can we be saved by it. We can't be set free by it until we hear the truth.
>
> We must receive the proper interpretation. That's the reason we are holding out, the reason we study so much and consider different ideas trying to improve on what we've got. We want the truth, the whole truth and nothing but the truth."
>
> *April 17, 1988*

It is the glory of God to conceal a thing:
but the honour of kings is to search out a matter.
Proverbs 25:2

Recognition

In the tradition of giving honor where honor is due, or in this case, credit where credit is due, these transcribed sermons would not have been produced had it not been for our Deaf brothers, Chris Orta and Chad Hanna. They desired written sermons in order to be able to study the doctrines and messages in depth and to supplement and enforce their understanding of the interpreted messages in the church services.

Chris and Chad came to the Houston church as young men in 1999 and have remained faithful workers in the church. They married in the church and are now raising their children in the nurture and admonition of the Lord. Their songs, testimonies and preaching in American Sign Language, interpreted for the hearing people, have blessed the church, inspired us and touched our hearts many times.

Sermons and Teachings of Billy R. Brown

Senior Pastor
Houston Area Gospel Assembly
Humble, Texas

Volume 1

Chapter 1

The Mark of the Beast

1970's
(no exact date)

I want to direct your attention to a scripture in Hebrews 6. I invite you to open your Bible to Hebrews 6 because the first few verses of this chapter show us that there are some things basic in the Bible, some things basic in the Christian life; other things follow after that. We have to build on a foundation. Paul said, *"Other foundation can no man lay but that which is laid, Jesus Christ. I built you on the foundation of the apostles and prophets, Jesus Christ himself being the chief cornerstone."* He said, *"I've laid the foundation and another man builds thereon. Let every man take heed how he builds."*

There are some things that are our foundation in the Word of God, and other things follow on top of that. When you get these basic understandings, they're what we call key scriptures in the Bible. Those scriptures unlock whole mysteries throughout the Bible. You get one of these key scriptures and the next time you read the Bible, you'll see it unraveling, scripture after scripture, verse after verse, as you go down through the Bible. Let's watch for these keys as we study the Word of God.

"Therefore leaving the principles of the doctrine of Christ...." Why would we want to leave any of these doctrines? His thought is to not have to be forever dwelling on this, on these first principles, *"not laying again the foundation of repentance,"* he said later in that verse, *"let us go on to perfection."* If we can get these foundation truths, then we can go on using those for keys and using them to help perfect our lives. We can go on to perfection! And, we can advance toward that hidden manna I was talking about. Remember, that is hidden way back in the holiest place. You have to go in there to get it. You'll never see the hidden manna unless you go in to the mercy seat, where the hidden manna is.

We have a long way to go before we get there. We have to come by the altar of sacrifice, have to go by the laver and wash up, have to go on through the hanging for the door of the tabernacle and eat some of that shew bread; twelve loaves of bread on the table of shew bread. You have to live by the light of the seven-branch candlestick in there. Then you have to go on between them until you come by the altar of incense and offer your life as a sacrifice for a sweet smell, a sweet savor to God, and then go through the veil to get to the mercy seat. On that mercy seat was the Ark of the Covenant. In that ark was laid up the hidden manna. That's where we've got to go to get to the hidden manna.

Well, let's consider this foundation: "*Leaving the principles of the doctrine of Christ, let us go on to perfection not laying again...*," not having to do it over and over. I believe Paul said this in another place that some people were "*ever learning and never able to come to the knowledge of the truth.*" They're trying to learn the same thing over and over, never able to come to a knowledge of the truth. We need to come to knowledge of these basic things so that we can go on to other things. "*Not laying again the foundation of repentance from dead works....*" That's what you did when you got saved. You repented from the works of the flesh. Those are dead works. "*Not laying again the foundation of .... faith toward God.*"

That's part of the foundation: faith toward God. You have to repent; you have to believe. Then what do you do? You get baptized, don't you? Here's some more of the foundation: ".... *of the doctrine of baptisms and of laying on of hands and of resurrection of the dead and of eternal judgment.*" If you're the kind of person that makes marks in your Bible, you ought to draw a ring around that second verse there. Ring that up! Those are the four major doctrines of the Christian faith. They're the four—somebody called them the four horns on the altar. I'm more inclined to call them the four feet on the altar.

Question from Congregation

That's one thing that laying on of hands is used for. See, 'Laying on of Hands' is one of the four major doctrines, and we'll try to get into that sometimes; go through the doctrine of Laying on of Hands. Just briefly, it includes healing, ordination to the ministry and it's done sometimes for Holy Ghost baptism. Remember, at times in the New Testament they laid hands on people to receive the Holy Ghost. And, sometimes it figured in judgment. I believe this is back in Numbers also. Somewhere back there, they had a man that cursed and broke the law against swearing. The witnesses heard him curse. They took him out and, to identify him, they laid hands on his head. Then, the whole congregation stoned him to death. That's in Leviticus 24. They stoned him to death after they laid hands on his head and identified him.

Then again, you'll notice when you read through the sacrifices that the priest would lay hands on the head of the sacrifice, the animal they brought to kill for a sacrifice. They laid hands on his head, at least in certain cases. All that is part of the doctrine of Laying on of Hands. That sounded like a simple one, didn't it? The doctrine of Baptisms—what could be simpler than baptism? But, it's a whole doctrine.

First of all, are you aware that there are three baptisms? There are three baptisms: Water Baptism, Spirit Baptism and Fire Baptism. When I first got saved, I testified like this because everybody else did: "I praise God for the Holy Ghost and fire, because John said I baptize you with water, but he that comes after me will baptize you with the Holy Ghost and with fire!" I didn't realize that I had got the Holy Ghost but I hadn't got the fire, yet. Well, that's another doctrine in itself. Holy Ghost baptism is one thing and Fire Baptism is another, but both are part of the Doctrine of Baptisms. That's why he puts it in the plural: Baptisms—plural.

Comment from Congregation: "I guess all the Pentecostal people thought if you were baptized with fire that you were real fiery. You know, someone would get up and go like a house was afire, and they'd say "Boy he's really got the fire!"

Yes, that's where we got that.

Comment from Congregation: "But then we find out that's really not the fire."

Yes, that's something entirely different. My mother always testified and argued "I got the fire when I got mine! Some people may not get the fire when they get the Holy Ghost, but I got the fire with mine because I saw it!" She had a vision when she got the Holy Ghost. Mother was alone in a closet, praying her heart out, seeking for the Holy Ghost. There wasn't even a church in that part of the country. She just heard about the Holy Ghost somehow and started seeking for it at home alone. She took the Bible literally, so she went into the closet. We had a rather large walk-in closet where we had a big pine chest that we stored the quilts in, and on top of that we'd pile the dirty clothes. We didn't have these modern rods that you hang your clothes up on. We didn't even have such a thing as a coat hanger in our house. Anything that we had to hang up, we just hung it up on a nail. Drive a nail in the wall and hang your shirt up on a nail by the collar. We didn't hang up very many things. Those were pioneer days.

Mother would enter into that walk-in closet, shut the door and get on her knees and pray! She prayed so hard that when she finally got the Holy Ghost she had a vision! She saw, literally, in her vision, flames coming down upon her out of heaven, kind of like what they saw on the day of Pentecost. It took us a long time (and I don't know if we've done it, yet) to talk Mother out of saying, "I got the fire when I got mine!"

It's like Brother Nelson said. We just thought, "He's got a fiery testimony; he preaches real fast; he's a fiery preacher!" But that's not the baptism of fire. That's not what John was talking about. Sometime, we'll go into that. Could do it tonight if we had time, but I wanted to go ahead and answer this question that was handed to me first. I just wanted to point out some of these things to you here and while I'm on this, my purpose is to show you how involved it can get. Don't expect any of these to clear up in one teaching service. Don't be surprised if you go away with more questions than you came with. This will stir your mind to thinking and I may take a scripture and prove something to you that contradicts what you've always believed and really cause the questions to whirl around in your head. But that's how we get the truth; that's how we learn.

We have a saying that, if you can't see it, if you don't believe what the preacher's teaching, if you can't see this teaching yet, on one certain point, well—lay it up on the shelf! That means to not say, "I believe it," or "I don't believe it." Just say, "I don't see it, yet." Just lay it up there and leave it for a while and a week or two or a month later, after you see some more things, then you pick that one up off the shelf, "I remember Brother Brown, or Brother Nelson, said so and so." It may look different to you after you take it off the shelf the next time, look at it again and think about it some more in the light of your recently acquired knowledge.

We have to keep our hearts open to get the truth out of the Word of God. And in connection with that, I wanted to show how it's impossible to thoroughly go through one of these subjects in one teaching service. That's why you should pay attention. Every time a preacher gets up and goes down a line of teaching you've heard before, you should pay attention because, in all probability, he'll say something that you haven't heard before on that subject. He'll say something he didn't say the last time. You can't cover it all in one service.

For example, when we would get on the Doctrine of Baptisms, we would have three baptisms to talk about first of all. When we would get to talking about Water Baptism (the first one), to make it clear and show all about water baptism, we'd have to deal with the subject of the Name of Jesus, doing things in the name of Jesus. Then, when we would get too far out on the name of Jesus, it led us on to the Godhead. Everything's tied together in the scriptures and it's hard to keep them separated. That's why one thing I say will bring a lot of other questions up in your mind because they touch on these other subjects. It's true, the whole Bible is related. It's one unit; it's one chain from start to finish. Everything's tied together.

Take the 'Resurrection of the Dead' or 'Eternal Judgment' subjects, either one of them. If we talked on it very long, we would end up on the subject of Hell. We would have to deal with the different kinds of hells. So just be patient and remember you're free to stop me to clear up a point anytime, like Sister Darlene did. Anytime you want a point cleared up that I'm going over and you think I'm not covering it clearly, ask me to clear it up. Tell me your question and don't be bashful about your questions because, remember, the question you want to ask, most likely there's somebody else wanting to ask it too, but they're just too bashful to ask. So, every question you ask will bring things to light. And, these questions are really inspirational.

God led the church into this many years ago before I got into the ministry. Before I was born, I guess, God gave this to Brother Sowders. He came into church one time and sat down behind the pulpit. It was his church; he was pastoring, teaching it. He didn't know what to do that night, didn't feel any inspiration. God suddenly spoke to him and said, "Invite the people to ask questions." He had never done that before. He just kept his seat and said, "Anybody have a Bible question, ask it and maybe we'll talk on it."

So, somebody asked him a question about something. He felt the Spirit hit him! He got up and really fed their souls for the rest of the service just from the inspiration he got from talking on that one question! One of the most inspiring things to anybody that has a gift of teaching is to find out what people's questions are, what's bothering them. That pulls something out of our hearts, pulls something out of the teacher. He wants to immediately go to work to resolve that doubt, to clear up that confusion, to answer that question! That's just a part of his makeup.

One question I received tonight concerned the Mark of the Beast in Revelation 13. You can turn over there now if you want to. Now, let me confuse you real quick and good to start with. There are four beasts in this chapter; count them for yourself. I went through that with different colored pencils and painted every beast a different color. Every time it mentioned a beast in a verse in Revelation 13, I colored it in a certain color. And I colored that beast the same color every time I found him. I colored the other beasts different colors so I could look in there and spot immediately where those four beasts all are.

One of them, the first one, not the first one mentioned in the chapter, but the first one we run into coming up to the chapter, started back in chapter 12. That's the Red Dragon, the old red dragon which the ninth verse says, *"The great dragon was cast out, that old serpent."* Remember, you that were here last Wednesday, we talked a little on the serpent; started with him all the way back in the Garden of Eden. Remember that? That old serpent! We found him for the first time in the Garden of Eden in Genesis 3. And here he is still over here in the last book of the Bible! That old serpent called *'the devil and Satan'*. Why do you reckon he has so many names? Four different names in one verse there! Well, each one means something; each one is significant.

Comment from congregation—unclear

I believe that, but a lot of the brethren in this Body don't believe that. There's a division over that and so, since it's that way, I don't want to do much teaching on the personality of the devil until we get it thrashed out. But see, both sides in this controversy reckon with these scriptures and have a way of explaining them and so we all can talk about Revelation 12:9: *The great dragon*. I explain it one way and they explain it a little different way. So, we're not that far off and I'm going to emphasize the points where we are together. I'm going to teach it like I see it, but I might not teach all of it. See, I might not teach everything I see, but I won't teach anything I don't see unless I clarify that point.

This is the way some of the brethren believe it, but to this extent, we're together on this, the great red dragon in Revelation 12, *"having seven heads and ten horns."* Those seven heads signify the devil working in seven great world empires. Whatever you say the devil is, we all agree that he worked in those seven great world empires. You know what they are? The seven great world empires of history: Egypt, Assyria, Babylon, Persia, Greece and Rome. That's six. We still need one more for seven. Well, the seventh one is papal Rome, the Catholic Church. That's the seventh great world empire because the pope reigned over the kings of the earth during the Dark Ages. The Catholic Church was a world empire during those dark ages.

Those were seven great world empires that affected the people of God. You notice that we don't deal with Chinese history or Indian history or Japanese history, the Mongols, the Huns and all of those that you can find in the history books because they didn't rule over the people of God. Remember, the Jews, God's chosen people naturally speaking, have been in captivity in every one of those seven empires that I named.

Moses led them out of Egypt when they were in bondage in Egypt. The Assyrians took ten tribes into captivity and some people say they're still lost to this day; they're still looking for them. Then, Babylon took the other two tribes into captivity. And then Persia took over before Daniel died. Persia let the Jews come back home out of captivity but they still governed them; they still ruled over them. After Persia, Alexander the Great came through and conquered the Persians. He took over and ruled over the Jews for a short space of time and his empire, after he died, kept on doing that. After that, after the Grecian Empire, came the Romans. They came in and ruled over the Jews. They were ruling when Jesus came. After the church had been in existence for some time, some hundreds of years, it fell away and the pope of Rome rose up. The pagan Roman kingdom weakened, crumbled and split up, lost its power and the pope rose to authority over the kings of the earth. That was the seventh kingdom. That's the seventh head on the dragon.

The dragon (the devil) worked in every one of those kingdoms. He was the moving force, the moving power in every one of those kingdoms and each kingdom was a manifestation of the devil. Wasn't a manifestation of God! You couldn't say the nation of Egypt was a manifestation of God, could you, even though God sometimes came along and had his way and showed his power? He said to Pharaoh, *"For this cause have I raised you up to show my power in you."* How did he do that? He drowned him in the Red Sea after he worked ten plagues on him.

You couldn't say that Babylon under Nebuchadnezzar was a manifestation of the kingdom of God. It was a kingdom of the devil even though God raised Nebuchadnezzar to the throne.

God made sure the one he wanted on the throne got there. And when he got tired of him, he took him away and put another one on the throne, but they didn't worship God. They didn't serve God; they served their idols.

Nebuchadnezzar set up an image out there and commanded everybody to fall down and worship it. He wanted to cast the three Hebrew children into the fiery furnace because they wouldn't fall down and worship it. Did you know that's a type of the beast? See, I'm leading up to Revelation 13 now and to the beast in our day. Nebuchadnezzar set up that image out there on the plains of Shinar and said, "*When you hear the band strike up, boys, hear all these instruments play, every musician hitting the same tune, you better fall down and worship this image!*"

That was the beast back there in Babylon. One of the heads of the *Dragon* was in power right then. See, the dragon's seven heads weren't here all at the same time. They rose up one after the other. First Egypt, then Assyria, then Babylon; each head had its day. That was the head on the dragon. There's an image being set up and you find that word 'image' here in Revelation 13:14. There's an image in there, and it talks about that image for the next three verses. An image—the same thing Nebuchadnezzar raised up and commanded everybody to worship and was going to kill them if they wouldn't worship it.

This chapter in Revelation prophesies a day coming when there is going to be another image set up, but not like the one Nebuchadnezzar set up. It's a spiritual, symbolic image, but it's an image all the same. It's an image, a likeness of something that happened before. You know what the word 'image' means, don't you? We're made in God's image. What does that mean? Why it means that we look like him. We're shaped like him; we're built like him. You say, "Does God have ears and a nose?" Why sure! It's not made out of flesh and blood. It's not something you can see with fleshly eyes, but he's got them all the same. He's made out of spirit. God has a form.

This kind of preaching is what modern educated theologians call anthropomorphism. That means talking like God looks like man. They say we've created God in man's image, but that's not right! The Bible said God created us in his image! See, God said that before we said it. God said we looked like him before we said it. Nowadays, if you say we look like God, they say, "You're an anthropomorphist; you're trying to make God look like you." No, I'm not trying to make God look like me, I'm just admitting the fact that I look like God! God told me I did! That's scripture! I'm an image of God; I look like him.

An image is something that looks like something else. God told the Jews not to make any image of four-footed beasts or anything like that to worship because, he said, "*You didn't see any likeness when you heard me thunder out the law from Mount Sinai. You didn't see anything, so don't make an image of anything.*"

Well, we're going to lead up to that image. I told you there are four beasts in this chapter. The first one is the dragon himself, the devil himself. And immediately, as we go into chapter 13, the first verse, you see another beast rise out of the sea. It's a beast, and he has seven heads and ten horns. Lo, and behold! He looks like the devil! Seven heads and ten horns! Well, those seven heads and ten horns mean the same thing. Those seven heads just represent the fact that this is another kingdom of Satan rising out of the earth and it really is one of the heads on the devil. This is one of the heads on the dragon! Here is this kingdom that the devil himself heads up.

'Head', you remember, means government. The head is the governor of the body. The head gives the orders and the hands and the mouth obey. The head is the governor. So that devil had seven heads, seven governments. Well, this beast that comes up out of the sea in Revelation 13 having seven heads and ten horns just means he patterned after the devil. It's not a move of God; it's a move of the devil and it's got all the ingredients of these seven kingdoms in it. In fact, it is one of these seven kingdoms, and the one it is, is the seventh one. This beast *is* the seventh head, the seventh kingdom. That is papal Rome. What you see this beast doing... "*And the dragon gave him his power and his seat and great authority.*" See, the devil gave all his power over to that kingdom during the Dark Ages and they persecuted the saints of God. You know that from history.

Now, unless you want me to talk on all of these details through here, I'll skip over the deadly wound and all of that and just go down through the beasts, trying to summarize the four beasts. That first beast continued a certain space of time, forty and two months, but down in verse 11 you find another beast coming up out of the earth because that first beast didn't last forever. The beast that came out of the sea, having seven heads and ten horns, one of his heads was wounded to death, but his wound was healed. So he didn't die but he did lose his government, lose his power. That beast no longer could govern the earth. At one time the Catholic Church governed the world. It doesn't govern today, but it's still here. It's not dead, is it?

All of those other beasts faded away. They died. You don't even find the Egyptian kingdom here anymore in its form. It's an entirely different group of people that live in Egypt now from what was back there. Those kingdoms all died, but this beast had a deadly wound but it didn't die. It didn't fall apart; it didn't cease to exist. Alexander's empire fell apart and ceased to exist and it's not here anymore. This one is still here but it is not ruling anymore. The world is temporarily without a world empire, and the red dragon, the devil, is without a head to manifest himself through.

He's in bad shape, isn't he? He's in a bad fix. He won't put up with that very long. So what happens? Another beast in verse 11, coming up out of the earth, had two horns like a lamb. Two of these beasts had ten horns. This beast just has two horns. Any time you read about horns in the Bible—I'll give you a key now. Every time you read about a horn in the Bible, you'll know what it represents. It's power. A horn is power. When you read about a horn, it's something powerful. We've agreed on that for many years in this Body of people. It was discussed many times, back and forth, in the camp meetings and three day schools. We came to the agreement that these two horns represent Civil and Ecclesiastical power, two different kinds of power. That's the two different kinds of powers, primarily, that exist today.

You can add military power, but that's governed by civil power. The civil power sends the armies around the world. This is part of civil power. You can name all the ten gods of Egypt and call them powers, but they all head up under one of these or the other: either Civil, which is worldly power, governmental power here in the earth or Ecclesiastical, which means church power, religious power. We've got lots of both kinds around today. And so, this beast is an organization of people.

I should throw this in for your benefit to help you understand the word 'beast'. Just hold your thumb here in chapter 13 and turn over to Revelation 17:1. "*And there came one of the seven angels which had the seven vials, and talked with me, saying unto me, come hither*; (remember we're trying to find out what a beast is, exactly.) *I will shew unto thee the judgment of the great whore that sitteth upon many waters.*" Notice that '*many waters*'. Skip the second verse. Verse 3: "*So he carried me away in the spirit into the wilderness and I saw a woman,*" (That's the great whore that he mentioned in the first verse) "… *sitting upon* (what?)…*a scarlet colored beast*"

The angel said to John, "*Come and I'll show you this woman sitting on many waters.*" But when he came and saw, he didn't see her sitting on many waters, he saw her sitting on a scarlet colored beast. So this lets you know that the many waters and the beast are the same thing. Well, we still haven't figured it out, have we? Let's keep going. Let's look on down through the chapter and see if we can find the explanation. All the way down to verse 15. We're looking for what the waters are. We found out that a beast is many waters. Now, what is '*many waters*'? Verse 15: "*And he saith unto me, the waters which thou sawest, where the whore sitteth, are peoples, and multitudes, and nations and tongues.*" In other words, it's a BIG bunch of people. A beast is a bunch of people and the only way you can keep a bunch of people together is with some kind of government. Isn't that right? That's why every beast has at least one head on it. Some of our beasts have seven heads on it, but a beast has got to have a head.

A group of people, if they're united in a group, have got a government somewhere. Every lodge, every club in this world has a governmental structure. They elect their officials in some way. Every nation on earth has some kind of government, either a dictator or a king; or a president, or a congress or parliament. They've got to have some kind of government or they're not a nation; they're not a group of people.

So every beast has a head on it, a government. And the two horns on this beast here in verse 11 are the kinds of power that the government of this beast has. Since it's both civil and ecclesiastical, it signifies cooperation between church and state, doesn't it? Oh, how the Baptists have preached against church and state! And so do we, by the way; we preach hard against it. We say it's an abomination for church and state to be united on the only kind of basis that they can be united under today.

I believe that God will finally unite church and state under Jesus Christ. But as long as they are united any other way than under Jesus Christ, then it's an abomination! It's wrong and it becomes a Biblical beast when that happens.

We found our third beast in verse 11. And what does he do? He exercises the power the first beast had. Remember, the first beast is still there. What do you see out here today beginning to exercise power over people world-wide like, religiously speaking now, like the Catholic Church used to in the dark ages? What you see pointing that way now is an ecclesiastical, what they call 'ecumenical', movement. They are seeking the backing of civil powers.

Every church that organizes and secures a charter from the government, the worldly government, seeks the backing of civil power. See, they erect that civil horn right there. They already are a religious horn. The preacher and all the elders and deacons and whatever kind of government they have in the church is the ecclesiastical horn; they're a power. They dictate to their people in some fashion or another. They make plans. They say, "We're going to send missionaries to this country; we're going to build churches over here; we're going to pay our preacher so much; we're going to dis-fellowship this preacher because he doesn't preach right. There's a government in every church, every church organization. So that's a horn; that's religious power. But most churches nowadays, just as soon as they get set up, they've got to get the state government and the national government to back them. So, they organize and secure a charter and get a lawyer to draw up papers and get a stamp of governmental approval on their having church.

Then there goes that civil horn, that civil power sticking up! When you go into a church like that, that church has two horns. It's got some civil power behind it. You can't exercise too much freedom in that church. If you cross something, do something they don't want done, they can try you in the courts of the land downtown. They won't necessarily have to try you in their own court, their religious court; they can try you in the civil courts. They've got the government behind them, and the government authorizes them and protects them. That's the kind of beast this is.

But that's not all he does. In verse14, *"He deceived them that dwell on the earth by means of those miracles which he had power to do in the sight of the beast."* That means the same beast in the first verse with seven heads and ten horns, papal Rome, and *"...saying unto them that dwell on the earth, that they should make an image to the beast,* " (That is the first beast.) *"Make an image, make something like him; let's build something like it."*

Isn't that what the ecumenical movement is doing today? They're saying, "We've got to have a one-world church. We've got to unite all Christianity under one head, the World Council of Churches or some such head." They're still trying to agree on the head, trying to get everything together. They haven't got it all done yet. They haven't gotten the image built. They're working on an image. They are looking back to the hundreds of years in which the papal Roman government, the Roman church government, was able to keep peace in the earth, keep any major war from breaking out because the pope was the boss. If a king wanted to go to war he couldn't go to war without the permission of the pope.

It wasn't always that way, but there were times when it was that way. And that was the power he always tried to keep. He couldn't always keep it, but part of the time he had that power during the Dark Ages. And now they're saying we need a government just like that. It's been said for many years now. F.D. Roosevelt said, "Let's have another world church," and people have been saying it ever since. Preachers are saying it now. They're saying that we've got to get together.

We've got communism facing us out here, and they are about to take the world. They point the finger of scorn at the Christians, "You Christians that think you've got the answer to the world, you can't even agree among yourselves. Look how divided up you are! You can't get together. What can you do?" That's become an embarrassment to Christian people, Christian preachers. So they're saying, "Let's get together and erase that embarrassment; we don't want to be embarrassed any more. Let's get together." And so, they're trying to build an image of united Christianity like it was united in the Dark Ages, build something like that, an image to the beast.

Now what about that image? *"And he,"* (this beast with two horns) *"had power to give life unto the image of the beast,"* after he got it built. Now this is something that's going to happen. It won't be very far off when it happens. This is what we're facing. He had power to give life to the image of the beast that, *"the image of the beast should both speak and cause that as many as would not worship the image of the beast...,"* (shades of Nebuchadnezzar!) *"...should be killed."* In other words, we'll throw you into a burning fiery furnace, heated seven times hotter than it was wont to be heated! This is what that typifies. We're talking in spiritual symbols now. If they ever get this image built and get all the Christian world united under one head, then they won't allow people like you and me to have church the way we're having it. If we don't get a charter and get the government stamp on our papers, we won't come to these church doors and open up and turn the lights on when it gets that way. That's what is going to happen.

Isaiah said, *"They lay house to house, join house to house, lay field to field,"* Is that the way it goes? *"And join house to house and lay field to field until there be no place left in the earth."* That means no place left for anybody like us that doesn't do it that way. We don't build that kind of house. We don't farm their kind of field. We're doing something different and they're going to crowd us out. They fill up the whole earth, tighten everything down, organize it, legalize it, until it will be against the law to have church free like we're having it now.

Someone asks question—not understood

Yes, that is the fourth beast because he comes alive. See, he gave life to the image and when he comes alive, it is a real live beast. That's the fourth beast in that chapter. *"And he causeth all, both small and great, rich and poor, free and bond, to receive a mark in their right hand or in their forehead."* That's everybody, no exceptions! No exceptions allowed! If you refuse to take that mark, you're breaking the law! So, what's your judgment in verse 15? *"Should be killed!"* Be killed!

What do you think a mark is? Have you ever studied on the subject of marks? I think the first mark we find in the Bible is way back in Genesis. It's surprising how many important things you can trace all the way back to Genesis. Genesis is full of beginnings. It is the book of beginnings. The first mark was the mark that God set upon Cain. Cain killed his brother and God said, *"Where is your brother? His blood cries out of the ground to me."* Cain said, *"Am I my brother's keeper?"*

God said, *"Why have you done this? Because you have done this, you're going to be a fugitive and a vagabond in the earth."*

Cain said, *"That's too much. I can't take all that. It's too dangerous because everybody will know about it and the first one I run into will kill me. Everybody that finds me will slay me."*

Well how many times could they slay him? He just meant, "I'll be in danger of my life every time I meet somebody. I'll have to disguise myself or I'll have to run for my life every time I meet somebody or they'll kill me." So to keep anybody from killing Cain, God set a mark on him and said, *"Don't anybody kill this man. He killed his brother, but don't you kill him."* Remember this was before the flood, and there was no law of retribution spoken before the flood. They weren't allowed to kill a murderer, weren't allowed to have capital punishment before the flood. God wouldn't let them kill Cain. In our day in time they would have arrested him and tried him and given him the electric chair.

God said, *"If anybody tries to kill Cain, I'll kill him seven times,"* in words to that effect. He said vengeance will be taken on him sevenfold if anybody bothers Cain. This is my child; this is my son. I'll punish him. "*Vengeance is mine saith God; I will repay.*" So, he set a mark on him. What do you think that mark was? Ever wonder about that? What does that mean? God got out a pencil and marked a "V" check on his forehead or his cheek or somewhere? And everybody that met Cain, they saw a man with a check mark on his forehead and said, "Ah, that's Cain! Better not bother him! The Lord will bother us sevenfold!" No, you don't really believe that, do you? I don't guess anybody believes that.

Some people have got weird ideas about it. Some think he was the first black man; some think this, that and the other, but that's not the point. The point is that God identified him. That's what a mark is, an identification, an identity. And it boils down to a reputation.

When you come to this church, you're marked. Everybody in town knows you've been here. When you get the Holy Ghost, you're marked. Everybody hears about it. "Aha! One of them 'postolics!" That's what they did to me when I got the Holy Ghost at ten years old. I knew I was going to face it as soon as I got back with my old playmates! I was prepared for it; I had my heart fixed. They weren't going to take my salvation away! Well, my elders warned me about it. "Your little friends and playmates will tease you and make fun of you and they'll call you names. But you be a Christian now, and don't lose your salvation!"

So I was fixed. I went back around my playmates and, immediately, my bosom buddy began to tease me and laugh at me, "Billy is one of them 'postolics now. Little 'postolic! Little 'postolic!"

I'd say, "Yeah, don't you wish you were?"

But, I was marked. Not with a check mark, but I had a reputation, a reputation as a 'postolic, as a saved little boy. A reputation can be hard to live down, you know that? Everybody wants a good name in town. You want a good name, don't you? Well, why don't you go down to the court house and change your name? That's not the point. That good name you want is a good reputation. You want to be known as a good person.

So, this is the kind of mark that Cain had. He had a reputation as a murderer, not only a murderer, but a fratricide. Isn't that what we call it? Killing your brother is a fratricide. Cain was a fratricide. Everywhere he went they were pointing at him, they recognized him. They all knew him. Somebody said his reputation preceded his face. Ever hear that expression "His reputation preceded his face?" That means they heard about him before he got there. Before they ever saw his face, they had heard of his story. They heard, "You know there's a fellow across town that killed his brother? Oh, why would any man do that? Wonder what kind of fellow he his? What does he look like?" Well the next day you see him walking down the sidewalk and everybody is pointing him out to you. "See, that's him! That's the one that you heard about yesterday. He killed his brother!" He's marked, a marked man from then on. Everywhere he goes his story will go ahead of him. He's marked.

In Psalms, it says, "*Mark the perfect man. Behold the upright, for the end of that man is peace.*" How are you going to mark the perfect man? What's he's trying to get you to do is look at him. Observe that perfect man; keep your eye on him because he's somebody to follow. He's somebody to watch. Keep your eye on that perfect man. You'll see something good will happen to him. You watch and see. God will bless him, you watch and see! Watch him! Mark him! Take notice of him.

Paul said, "*Mark them that cause divisions among you and avoid them.*" Mark them! If anybody tries to split this church, let's mark him! Let's identify him, point him out! Everybody watch out for that fellow now! He's trying to split this church! Don't let him come around and pull you off from this ministry, pull you out of this church and turn you against the Body of Christ! Don't let anybody do that to you!" You're marking that fellow when you do that. He's a marked man from then on.

When the preacher gets up and says something like that, everybody hears it. They all know who he's talking about and that man's marked from then on. Everybody knows him. He's the one that's trying to split this church. He's trying to pull off and start another church over on the next corner. A marked man!

"*He causeth all, both small and great, rich and poor, free and bond, to receive a mark in their right hand or in their foreheads.*" Remember, 'mark' means identification. "No *man might buy or sell, save he that had the mark or the name of the beast, or the number of the name.*" The mark—The Mark of the Beast! That's an awful sounding phrase, isn't it? The Mark of the Beast! I've heard that all my life. "Watch out for the Mark of the Beast! Don't take the Mark of the Beast! Don't ever take the Mark of the Beast!"

What is the Mark of the Beast? We've discussed it. I heard Pentecostal preachers preach on it when I was a little boy. The Mark of the Beast! It just boils down to being identified with the beast, lumped together with them. See, when you join the Holy Ghost people, they mark you. They lump you with all the rest of the Holy Ghost people and some of the Holy Ghost people are not worth being lumped with. I guess you're aware of that! Some Holy Ghost people we'd rather not be identified with, but we're all lumped together. And whoever knows that we've got the Holy Ghost may know some Holy Ghost people who are not what they ought to be. They lump us with them and we're marked with that. There's nothing we can do about it except just live it down.

The Mark of the Beast: Identified with the beast, joined up with the beast, is all it means. Doing the things the beast does. The mark of the beast is a characteristic of the beast. A characteristic of the beast is to organize religion under civil power and then try to make religion the boss of the civil power. That's the mark of the beast.

That'll bear some studying, won't it? That'll bear some meditation. The mark of the beast, the characteristic of the beast! If you do like the beast does, you're identified with them. You may say "I never did join the Catholic Church, or I never did join the World Council of Churches. I never did join up with the ecumenical movement." But, are you doing what they did? How is your church set up? What kind of government have you got? Do you have two horns? Be careful, you may have one of the characteristics of the beast. That's the Mark of the Beast.

"That no man might buy or sell...." Not literally. They used to scare me with that, although it could happen literally. When I say 'not literally', that's not what this means, but it could happen literally. People have lost their jobs before over religion. I guess you've heard about some of that. *"No man might buy or sell,"* that's the same thing as *"join house to house and field to field, until there be no place left,"* no room for us to operate in, no room for us to function.

We're buying and selling here tonight. I'm selling; you're buying. I hope you are! You're looking it over anyway, sizing it up. Maybe you'll buy some of it. Buy and sell! *"Buy the truth and sell it not,"* Solomon said. In Proverbs isn't it? *"Buy the truth and sell it not."* That means when you buy it, don't get rid of it. Don't ever let anyone trade you out of it anymore. You buy the truth by coming to church and studying these things and listening and being hammered on by the preacher and having your old doctrines crossed, having to give up some things to get the truth and then going through fire to live it, put it in practice, overcome the flesh, struggle and pay and sacrifice and sit through hours of meetings when your body is uncomfortable. It would be nicer to be at home in bed maybe, as far as the body is concerned, but you're paying a price for this. Paying a price to get this! So, you're buying it. Now, don't sell it! The way you'd sell it would be to give it up for what it was you gave for it in the first place.

You buy something with money. If you sell it, you trade it back for money. See, you trade your money for the goods. If you don't like the goods, you can trade the goods back for the money and get your money back. Well, you have to give up the world to get God. *"Buy the truth and sell it not." "And that no man might buy or sell."* See, I'm selling, in a sense, this scripture because somebody's got to sell before you can buy it. You've got to find somebody that's selling.

In the parable of the ten virgins, when the wise virgins trimmed their lamps and were ready to go into the wedding feast, the foolish virgins ran out of oil because they didn't have any extra. They said, *"Give us some more; let us borrow some from you."* They said, *"Not so, lest we run out too. There would not be enough for both of us. Here's what you do. You go out here to the market place where they buy and sell and get you some more."* While they were gone, the door was opened; the wedding feast started and the door was shut again before they got back. So, there's some buying and selling going on.

But, you be careful you buy in time! Buy in plenty of time! Buy when you have a chance, when it's in season! There's a season for everything. There's going to come an end to this season. This is what is meant where it says, some place in Revelation, that *"an angel stood with one foot on land and one foot on sea, lifted his hand to the heavens and swore by him that lives forever and ever that time should be no more."* That means there shall be no more time for what we've been doing. There's going to come an end to this time we're living in and it's going to change and it will be time for something else.

That signals a change of dispensation; not just a little change of dispensation like we've experienced several times already, but a big major change in the world scheme. In God's universe a big change is going to take place. After that, it's too late to go and buy. You may go out there in the market place and find they're still buying and selling, but it's out of season. It's too late to make the wedding feast, too late to get married to Jesus. That's the interpretation of that.

"Save he that had the mark or the name of the beast or the number of his name." That's three different ways you can be associated with that image of the beast that had life. Three

ways to be associated with it: You can have the mark, you can have that characteristic of it and do things like it does and associate with it, or you can have the name of the beast in your forehead. See, they receive a mark in two different places: in the right hand or in the forehead. You can take the mark either one of those places. 'In your forehead' is to believe it. When somebody converts to the Catholic Church, the Baptist Church or the Pentecostal Church that happens ***in*** their forehead. The change takes place in their mind; they believe it.

And when somebody joins up with that system, they are throwing in with it. They believe it, "I believe that's the way it ought to be! I believe we ought to have a world church. That's what I thought all the time. That's the best thing that ever happened!" Well, that's taking it in your forehead.

To take it *'in your hand'*, (right hand, he said) that's the right hand of fellowship. Shake, old buddy. Shake and we'll walk together. We'll agree together. You go to your church and I'll go to mine, but we'll walk along together. Shake! Right hand of fellowship with the beast! Never cry out against it; never speak against it. Say, "We'll support each other. We'll come together and have our big evangelistic campaigns in the Astrodome all together and I'll take my share of the converts and you take your share: and we'll all just work together." That's taking it in the right hand. And, you can just take the *'number of the name'*. You may say, "I'm staying out of that. I don't like these big campaigns."

You have a question?

Question—not clear

There's just one thing I'd add to that to make it a little clearer. Since you brought this up, I think we ought to throw in this parable in Mathew 13 that you're referring to with this subject. What I think helps clear it up a little is in Matthew 13:30. This is the parable of the wheat and the tares. The master sowed good seed in the field and he was sowing wheat and after a while somebody looked out and there was wheat and tares both out there. He said to the master, *"Where did these tares come from? You didn't plant them did you?"* *"No,"* he said, *"an enemy has done this."*

Well you know who the enemy is. But, they wanted to go out and pull them up like I used to go out and pull suckers off the corn. He said, "*No, lest you pull up the wheat along with them. The roots are all tangled together right now; let them grow until they mature and when we get ready to reap, we'll take care of this. We'll reap and we'll separate them while we're reaping.*" And here's what he said, "*Let both grow together until the harvest and at the time of harvest, I will say to the reapers, gather ye together first the tares.*" (Notice that 'first'.) "*And bind them in bundles to burn them.*" This, to me, is what clears up the picture a great deal.

When the separation comes, this is how it comes. When the tares are separated out of the church, they are bound in bundles. Does that sound like a denomination, some organized church? That's a bundle. It's a group of people with a string tied around it. That's what a bundle is and that's what a church organization is. That's exactly what a denomination is. It's a group of people with a fence around them, a string around them. They're tied together; they're bound together and they can't get out. You think they can get out? Well, you go talk to them and see if they can!

"No, my preacher told me not to go down to that church. They told me they preach false doctrine down there. Don't even go around those people." They're keeping a string tied around them.

They can't get out. It's what Jesus called a prison house, spirits in prison. That's not down under the earth somewhere. That's up here in church houses. '*Spirits of men*'. Remember the expression "*spirits of just men made perfect?*" Spirits of just men. That's here on the earth in the church. We've all got spirits. We are spirits. I'll put it that way. Spirits in prison are just people that are bound in church houses. They are bound in those churches and denominations.

Thank God we're free! Aren't you glad to be free? You're not bound here, as far as I'm concerned. Go visit every church in town! I used to do a lot of that; don't have time anymore. Now, Wednesday night is taken up. Don't have any nights left to go visit. We're getting too busy! We're working for God and we don't have time to look over the fence anymore. But the time was when I went and visited churches, looked around to see what was going on. We always say if you find something better than this, come back and tell us about it because we're looking for more truth. We're looking for more good. We're looking for more of God.

But finally, in the parable of the wheat and the tares, he gathered the tares into the bundles to be burned, because that's what is going to happen to the church world. The religious world is going to be burned up in Armageddon. He said we gather the wheat into the barn. What we're trying to get set in order right now is the barn, the garner. John the Baptist called it a garner, didn't he? Talking about Jesus, John the Baptist said, "*His fan is in his hand.*" His fan is something to stir up a breeze with in case there is no natural wind blowing. The Word of God will really do that, won't it? It'll start people talking; the hot air will fly and make a breeze blow. Sometimes it's winds of doctrine that's stirred up by it, but Jesus' fan is in his 'Hand'. It's the word of God and he'll thoroughly purge his floor. That means cleanse the chaff out of it. The wheat he'll gather into the garner and the chaff he'll burn with unquenchable fire. Praise God! I'd rather be wheat in the garner than be chaff in the fire, wouldn't you? Glory to God! Amen!

I like this!

Chapter 2

Job

June 1, 1997

I made some statements here last night about—how shall I put it?—God's tolerance of human suffering. God is not particularly concerned with alleviating our suffering at the present time, although I didn't say that to discourage people from seeking relief. The note here says, "Please explain further your statement last night that God is not moved or concerned with our physical suffering. That statement is difficult to harmonize with the scripture *'God is love.'* One of the most widely quoted, most frequently preached-on Bible verses in this religious world is *'God is love'.*"

The questioner commented at the end, "I understand that God is more than love but that isn't all he is. I could more easily understand it if God knew a person had a very short time left and that person needed some fine tuning to possibly reach maturity."

That reminds me of a comment Brother Don Patton made to me many years ago when I was a young man starting out in the ministry. He was just giving me some fatherly comments. He had an old brother, an old retired minister in this Body, living there in the Fort Worth church at that time, old Brother Sherman. How many of you remember Brother Sherman? He was a good old brother, but of course, at that stage in his life, he was very old and was having lots of sickness, lots of health problems, having to see the doctor frequently, going to the hospital; in and out of the hospital.

Brother Don got to talking to me about that case and other cases like that. He said, "I think that when we get to that stage of life, God uses those things to bring to our attention, to remind us of what we might otherwise ignore." We don't like to face unpleasant facts, do we? But God will keep reminding you that you're born to die. In this natural life, you're born to die. And, you need to get ready to die. We need to spend our time here getting ready to die right. We've got to die, so let's die right. There's a right way to die. And he said, "I just think that every time something like this happens to Brother Sherman, it's God saying to him, 'You're going to die, Brother Sherman.'" He kept reminding him, again and again, "You're going to die, Brother Sherman," to keep him pressing on. Too, as I think I said here last night, when you fall, fall forward to draw a little closer to God in the end of your days.

The final point to this question was "Should we ever call on God for a healing touch"? Jesus did a lot of healing, maybe more than anything else in his ministry. This morning, I taught about the woman that was sick for twelve years, who just believed. She had so much faith in Jesus that if she could just touch his clothes she'd get well. If she could just touch the clothes of that holy man, she believed she would get well. She believed it so strong she got through that crowd of hundreds of people that were surrounding him. She elbowed her way through there until she could reach through and around somebody and touch the hem of his garment.

Low and behold, she got healed right then! So, healing was a big part of the ministry of Jesus and the apostles. He put that burden on the apostles. That was one of the main assignments he gave to them. Let me show you a scripture in Mark where Jesus commissioned the apostles, what he told them to do. This is in some of the other gospels but Mark boiled it down the lowest, to three requirements, three assignments that God gave to the apostles. Some of the others listed four, but Mark kept boiling it on down until he got it down to three principles.

Mark 3:14: *"Jesus ordained twelve that they should be with him and that he might send them forth to preach."* That's number one. That's the first thing an apostle is supposed to do: preach. Preach Jesus; preach the Gospel!

Number two: *"To have power to heal sicknesses."* That was the second thing in the apostles' commission.

Number three was to cast out devils. If a man wanted to be considered an apostle in that early church, he had to cast out devils. Healing sicknesses and casting out devils are just ways of helping people and alleviating their suffering. People that have demons are suffering. There're uncomfortable. They may be mean as the devil, and it may be the devil that is making them mean, but they are unhappy being that way. They are uncomfortable with that and it's a great deliverance and a great freedom when somebody like that gets free from their bondage.

But, my point last night was that God will let you suffer a lot longer than you want to, a lot longer than you think you deserve to. Sometimes there are reasons that we are totally unaware of and it's really none of our business at the time. The classic example of that is Job in the Old Testament. I had a note here requesting help on understanding the Book of Job. Evidently this person is reading the Bible through this year as we encourage everybody to do. So, about this time of the year we come up on the book of Job. Actually, if you're just going into Job right now, you're several weeks behind. And that's where I am; I'm running behind.

Job has been one of the hardest books of the Old Testament to understand. It's so easy to get the wrong lesson out of it. For generations, even in this body of people, we have mainly drawn the conclusion from Job that he was self-righteous and that the book of Job is a story of how God corrected Job's self-righteousness. But that totally misses the point of Job.

Let's look at a few points in there. I might be able to help you get more out of it the next time you read it. The story opens with a list of Job's wealth. He was a very wealthy man; God had blessed him richly. Then there arose a testing. You've got to get this setting here to understand why Job was going through so much suffering. It's because he was being tested. There's a very exotic and obscure source about the reason for the testing. It's described in here as controversy between God and Satan over whether Job's righteousness was real and how deep it was. The result was God turned Job over to Satan to test him, to find out if his righteousness was as real as it was supposed to be.

And so, in the first two chapters you have the story of Job being brought down and stripped of his wealth; not only his wealth, but of his children, his family. The worse thing that happened to him was the loss of his ten children, seven sons and three daughters he had. All ten of them got killed in a tornado like what blew through Jarrell, Texas up here a few days ago. It razed houses right down to the foundation. That's what happened to Job's children. They were all in one house having a party. The family all got together and had a party and at that moment a storm came by and blew the house down on that family, killed all those ten sons and three daughters of Job.

That's one of the most terrible calamities that could happen to anybody. And in all of this, it says that Job sinned not. Now in the last two verses, last three verses, of the first chapter, after all of those calamities struck him, here's the result: Job arose and rent his mantle. That means he tore his clothes and shaved his head and fell down upon the ground and worshipped. Can you believe that?

Is that what you'd do if your family was wiped out in the tornado and all of your wealth was gone and your business destroyed in various ways at the same time? Would you get down on your knees and worship? I told you Job was a righteous man. We're trying to find out just how righteous he was. It's what God and Satan were trying to find out here. Just how righteous was Job, anyway?

He fell down and worshipped. Here's what he said, "*Naked came I out of my mother's womb, and naked shall I return thither*". Of course, he's not going back into his mother's womb, but he's going back into the oblivion he came out of. He knows he's going to die one of these days. You're going to die Job! You're going to die Job, get ready! "*Naked shall I return thither into oblivion. The Lord gave and the Lord hath taken away, blessed be the name of the Lord!*"

Is that what you would say when you lose everything, go broke and have to take bankruptcy? You bury your children. Do you say, "*The Lord gave and the Lord hath taken away. Blessed be the name of the Lord.*"? How many people would say that? *"But in all this, Job sinned not nor charged God foolishly."* We're probing the depths of Job's righteousness. He was a real saint of God.

The next chapter is about him being beset with sickness and suffering and pain and the threat of death. He was threatened with approaching death; looks like he was sick enough to die. Not only had he lost everything, but then he got sick. Apparently he had some skin disease. It says, in one of the later chapters, *"If after my skin worms go ahead and destroy my body, yet in my flesh I'll see God."* He still kept his faith. His skin probably was afflicted with some kind of parasites; swelling and boils breaking out and itching constantly. He went out and camped on the garbage dump of the city. He spent his days out there and took a piece of broken pottery, broken clay pottery, to scrape himself with. That's what he scratched with. All he could do was sit out there and scratch. All the man had left that he could do was scratch where it itched.

So he spent his days scratching and mourning, enduring and waiting, praying and waiting. He was praying and waiting, but the days stretched into weeks, the weeks stretched into months. There was no relief. It went on so long that some of Job's acquaintances (supposed to be his friends, and I guess they were) in other countries, heard about his condition. They got together and said *"Let's go and see Job, go visit that man. Some terrible calamities have happened to him. We'll at least visit him."* They got over there... By the way, before we get to that, let's close out this second chapter. Well, it closes out with those men coming.

I wanted you to see how Job reacted when he got sick like that. Verse 8 of chapter 2 says he took him a potsherd, a piece of broken pottery, to scrap himself with and sat down among the ashes. *"Then said his wife unto him, Dost thou still retain thy integrity?"* (What's wrong with you?) *"Curse God and die"*. (Get out of this!) Do you much blame her? Remember this is the woman that had just buried ten kids. And it really wasn't her righteousness that was being tested. It was her husband's righteousness being tested. That mother had to suffer the loss of those children, the loss of her wealth and luxury and comfort and her security for old age; all that was gone from her.

Still Job said unto her, *"Thou speakest as one of the foolish women speakest. What? Shall we receive good of the Lord and not receive evil? In all this did not Job sin with his lips."* You're not quite sure of all the thoughts that were running through his heart and his mind, but he kept the right words in his mouth. We're still searching the depths of Job's righteousness.

Someone asks a question.

What verse is that? You mean the last one I just read, Verse 10? *"Shall we receive good at the hand of the Lord and not receive evil?"* Is that what your question is about? Well, how many people understand that like Job understood it? He accepted that you can expect good and evil from God but we don't really accept that. We don't expect evil from God, because God is love. That's what we've heard about him. *"Every good and perfect gift comes down from above from the Father of lights."* We don't expect any evil from God.

But do you see yet, in this story, why this evil came upon Job? It was for the glory of God. God was bragging on Job when somebody challenged Job's integrity. Somebody said to God, "You think he's such a good fellow; you're proud of him, but you're paying him to be good like we pay the preachers to be good and everybody else is good for nothing." He didn't think Job would be good for nothing. So God said, "All right." God's glory was at stake then. God was being challenged. "You think you're so good at managing people and developing saints, Job may not be as good a saint as you think he is. If you weren't paying him to be good, he might not be so good." So that challenged God's glory.

This was really a test of God's philosophies and his methods to see whether God's ways really work in producing righteous people. That was the reason for Job's testing. It wasn't just so much that they were curious about Job, but it was to establish God's authority in telling us how to live and helping us to learn to live that way. You have to see that as the foundation for the story of Job. It was a test of whether God could produce a righteous man, or not, in that day and time. And so, every test was put to him. Finally, he was threatened with the loss of his life, *"but in all this did not Job sin with his lips."*

But here came his three friends; three visitors come into the hospital to visit the sick. His hospital was out there on the city dump. They came out there and sat down with him. Verse 13, Chapter 2: *"They sat down with him on the ground seven days and seven nights. None spake a word to him for they saw that his grief was very great."*

Don't misunderstand that. They weren't being cold and callous by sitting silently there for seven days. That was an expression of their sympathy and their awe and their feeling of the gravity of the situation, "How great a calamity has struck our friend here!" They were left speechless by it. That was their point in remaining silent for seven days. All that was to the good. But the first verse of chapter 3 says, *"After this Job opened his mouth,"* and here's where he may have started to sin with his lips. But up to this point he hadn't sinned with his lips. He hadn't blamed God for anything; he hadn't complained about how God treated him.

Now, here's where we miss it a lot. We may not blame God. We may be mature enough not to blame God, but we can still complain very loudly about the sufferings we're going through. When you do that, you're implying criticism of the God who let you endure that suffering. We're not supposed to even complain about our suffering, our pressures and our discomforts. Don't even complain about those things, because that implies criticism of the God that lets us suffer that way.

So at this point, Job may have begun to sin with his lips. He cursed his day. But, I don't want to go through all the details of his complaint. I just want to point out these principles for you to watch as you read them. But in complaining... See, when you complain, you imply, "I don't deserve this. It's wrong for me to have to suffer this. It's wrong for me to be treated this way. There's something wrong. It ought not to be this way," and that reflects upon God.

That's what Job began to do. He began to complain about the suffering he was going through. Chapter 3, Verse 26 says, *"I was not in safety"*. He was talking about back there when he was wealthy and sitting comfortably in his house with his children around him. "I was not in safety". Because he just said, *"The thing which I greatly feared has come upon me."* That which I was afraid of is come upon me. That shows that he was cautious all that time. He didn't take anything for granted. He knew all along that he could lose his wealth; that anything can happen, that comfort and wealth and money in the bank may be temporary. So he wasn't arrogant about his position when he was wealthy.

"I was not in safety, neither had I rest, neither was I quiet," meaning, sitting around at peace and not worrying about anything. Yet trouble came anyhow. A little complaint there! He's justifying himself at this point, and this is why people call him self-righteous. He did, several times through here, justify and defend himself. Up to this point he hadn't been under attack so he didn't justify himself very hard. Immediately his friends pick up on that and they see Job is not repenting. He hadn't learned anything! He needs to repent and get right with God! They automatically assumed that if any trouble happened to a saint of God, it was God punishing him and correcting him.

Now part of the lesson in the book of Job is to defeat that misimpression. Don't get the delusion that everybody that gets sick around here is under the judgment of God. You can't assume that. There are many other reasons why people can be in trouble. There were other very obscure reasons why Job was in trouble. It wasn't obvious at all why Job was in trouble, but they just took the obvious view that, "He's in trouble because God's mad at him. If he would just repent and straighten up, well things would get better immediately," and they began to tell him that.

Paul quoted something in the New Testament that Eliphaz said, two or three things, I think, as scripture. It's written in the scripture. These things are true, but they were misapplied to Job. These righteous Bible teachers were misjudging Job. None of these things applied to him.

Eliphaz, in the fourth and fifth chapters, began to advise him to make things right. *"Humble yourself under the mighty hand of God."* They quoted platitudes and scriptures and proverbs like that, which are all true. Nearly everything they said was true except they were wrong in applying it to Job; that wasn't the condition Job was in. Those weren't the things Job needed to be told; those weren't the things that would help him. In fact, a lot of things they said, or some of the things they said, are actually quoted in other parts of the Bible.

But, Job began to defend himself as he went along and they kept turning up the pressure. He kept fighting back harder and maintaining that he was innocent; he didn't deserve any of this. The more he defended himself, the more they attacked him. Isn't that the way human nature works? When someone jumps on you, the more you defend yourself the more they work on you, the harder they work on you. Most of the time, if you'll just realize, shut your mouth, take it and quit defending yourself, they'll run out of steam pretty quick and quit running you down. Maybe somebody will come along and take up for you. But if everybody that comes along finds you taking up for yourself and they can't get a word in edgewise, then nobody's going to take up for you much. You just have to defend yourself when you get started on that. If you get started down that trail, you can't quit.

Well, that's basically what Job was doing by implication. He began to blame his troubles on God. His troubles did lie at the feet of God. It was God that let those things happen to him. You might read the story back there and say it was the devil that did that to him, but only by God's permission. And each time God gave him permission, he said, *"Only so far. You can go just so far, but not farther. You can't take his life."*

When you're reading the story of Job, you've got to remember that Job and his three comforters, nobody in town had read the first two chapters of Job. None of them knew about that meeting, wherever it was, between God and Satan. That revelation came out later. If Job had known about that, he might have borne the test more easily.

You could stand your suffering a whole lot better if you knew that God wasn't blaming you for something but was proving something to somebody else through your suffering. You might take it more patiently. You'd say, "Well, God's getting glory out of my suffering." That would make you get glory out of it, wouldn't it? But that would nullify the test. The real test was whether he could bear all this without knowing the reason for it. You don't have to know the reason for everything. How does that song go, "I don't need to understand; I just need to hold his hand"? You won't always know what God's doing and why he's doing it. You'll suffer some things without knowing the reason why.

A lot of times I hear this complaint and sometimes, I say it myself, "If God's whipping me, if I just knew what he was whipping me about, I'd straighten up. But he won't even tell me what he's whipping me for." And we criticize God for that. But God was Job's adversary. Somebody get your Bible computer and look up the verse in there where he said, *"Oh that my enemy or adversary had written a book."* He was talking about God. God was his adversary; God was his persecutor.

By the way, there are several clues in this book, as to how old and ancient this story is. The book of Job is one of the oldest books in the Bible. It was set way back there, probably in the days between Abraham and Moses, in that period when men lived a long time. Job, it said, lived 140 years so he was one of those old timers. And it was in the days before there was very much writing of the Word of God. It was hard to find any written word of God. There may have been some histories written down from the days of Adam and Noah and Abraham but there wasn't much word of God written that a man could get hold of.

Where was that verse now, 19:31, 31 and 35? This is Job talking in chapter 31. *"Oh that one would hear me."* (Will somebody please listen to me?) *"Behold my desire is that the Almighty,"* (Get that.) *"...would answer me."* (I wish God would answer me when I complain. Why doesn't God give me an explanation? Surely He owes me an explanation.) *"My de-*

sire is that the Almighty would answer me, and that mine adversary (the Almighty) *had written a book."*

Well aren't you glad that God has finally written a book? If you can find somebody's book, you can kind of get around him and get the edge on him and see where he's coming from, maybe find his mistakes. That's why it's so dangerous for preachers to write books. As soon as they write books, you can clue in on their mistakes. You can zero in on their mistakes and trap them after that.

Of course, God didn't make any mistakes, so it didn't help much that way to find the book that he wrote if you're in trouble; except it helps you understand, maybe, how to get out of trouble, how to please God. There wasn't anything Job could do to get out of this trouble except wait until the test was over, just endure it patiently to the end.

But these brethren of his kept on persecuting him. Each time he answered them, they would come back and hit him a little harder. Look in your computer now and find the one where, I think, Bildad the Shuhite said something about his children having sinned. *"If your children have sinned...."* That was twisting the knife in the wound. What he was saying there was, "I know you had to bury all your ten kids, but you know, if they got their just punishment, if they sinned and God took them out of the world, you just have to accept that. But if you'll repent of your sins, straighten up what you've been doing, God will let you off."

Where is that? Chapter 8:4. Bildad didn't waste much time getting to that point, did he? He brought it up early in the debate. *"Then answered Bildad the Shuhite, and said, How long wilt thou speak these things?"* They didn't like Job's self-righteousness.

Now remember, if you accuse Job of being self-righteous, you're joining in with his three comforters and they are the men that God said in the last chapter, didn't tell it right. They didn't have the answer. They totally misunderstood Job's troubles but they believed he was self-righteous. *"How long will you speak these things? And how long shall the words of thy mouth be like a strong wind?"* That's just a cute way of calling him a windbag, wasn't it?

"Doth God pervert judgment?" Everybody feels like he's got to take up for God; even I do that. If you come around saying things that run God down, I'll take up for him right quick! So, they were taking up for God. They thought Job was discrediting God. *"Doth God pervert judgment? Or doth the Almighty pervert justice? If thy children have sinned against him, then it is justice and he has cast them away for their transgression."*

Don't you know how that twisted the knife in Job's wound! His heart was broken about the loss of his children and here comes somebody telling him they've died and gone to hell because they deserved to! They died and went to the grave, went into their punishment because they deserved to! No wonder he said later on, *"Miserable comforters are you all."* Poor set of comforters, but they got caught up in trying to save Job. They were trying to save Job out of his troubles, get him to repent and see it right.

You'll notice some famous and outstanding expressions of faith on Job's part and these are important as you read through here, like in Chapter 14, I believe it is—Chapter 13 Job said, *"Though he slay me,"* talking about God, *"I'm still going to trust Him."* Don't you like that? Don't you appreciate that? I'll trust God if he kills me! And he might very well do that; God just may kill you!

You know you're going to die somehow. Who do you want to kill you? How do you want to die? Maybe God will take you out easy. *"But though he slay me, yet will I trust him."* Keep your faith in God and keep yourself in God's hands and on his hands. We're in his hands and on his hands. That was 13:15, *"Though he slay me, yet will I trust him."*

However, here's a little self-righteousness bleeding through, *"I will maintain mine own ways before him."* Maybe we shouldn't call it self-righteousness, just call it righteousness. Job knew that he had been living right. There wasn't any use in trying to get him to confess, "I haven't been living right." He would have been lying if he repented that way, "I'm sorry,

Lord, I haven't been living right. I deserve all this." No, he *had* been living right! He didn't deserve all this. Job was right. We need to get that through our head. Job did not deserve all this. God never said he deserved all this.

Let me show you what God said about him before all this debate with his friends. Back in the second chapter—this was after he lost his wealth and his children, but before he got sick. At another meeting between the Lord and Satan, in verse 3 of chapter 2, the Lord said unto Satan—went to bragging again! It's dangerous when God brags on you. The Lord said unto Satan, *"Hast thou considered my servant Job, that there is none like him in the earth?"*

Same thing he said the first time. That got Job in trouble. *"A perfect and an upright man,"* (This is what God said about Job) *"one that fears God and eschews* (or abhors*) evil, and still he holds fast his integrity* (or his right way of living) *although you moved me against him to destroy him without cause."* I want you to get that *"without cause"* in there. See, there was no reason, no good reason, to persecute Job and make him suffer. The only reason was the challenge that Satan issued to God. They were destroying Job without any cause on Job's part. Job did not cause his own troubles. Unusual case, I think. We mostly cause our own troubles, don't we? But not in every case. Job was perfect in his time. He did all that God required of him in that day.

Over in the fourteenth chapter, Job is still talking like he did in the thirteenth chapter; he's talking about man dying in verse 10. *"Man dieth and wasteth away. Yea, man giveth up the ghost."* You know what it means to give up the ghost? It means to give up the spirit of life, the spirit of natural life that you've got. That was all Job had. The only spirit he had was the spirit of natural life that Adam had left after he lost the Holy Ghost. Adam gave up the Holy Ghost when he sinned, but he gave up the natural ghost nine hundred, thirty years later when he died.

All his descendants were born without the Holy Ghost, just with that natural ghost, the natural spirit of life. When somebody dies, they say he 'gave up the ghost'. Abraham gave up the ghost and was gathered to his fathers. He gave up that spirit of natural life. That spirit of natural life returned to God who gave it. Abraham's body returned to the dust from whence it came. Where did Abraham's soul go? But that's another subject.

He says here in 14:10: "*Man dieth, and wasteth away.*" Job is philosophizing. "*Yea man giveth up the ghost and where is he?*" Where is he after that? He's not anywhere. "*As the waters fail from the sea, and the flood decayeth and drieth up, so man lieth down and riseth not.*" He is just like evaporated water—it's gone. You can't get it back. So man lies down in death and rises not, "*till the heavens be no more, they shall not awake nor be raised out of their sleep.*" Now that's talking about the ungodly. That's the average man's condition. "*Till the heavens be no more, they won't awake.*" But Job still believes it's going to be different for him.

In Verse 13, he says, "*O that thou wouldest hide me in the grave, that thou wouldest keep me secret until thy wrath be past, that thou wouldest appoint me a set time, and remember me!*" That's everybody's hope that dies with faith in God, that you'll be appointed a set time and remembered in the resurrection. You want God to keep your name in his book, don't you? And you'll wake up before the heavens '*be no more*'. God's going to bring you back in a resurrection and give you another existence.

Verse 14: "*If a man die, shall he live again?*" Good question. And the answer is: Job believed he could live again. "*All the days of my appointed time will I wait, till my change come.*" Listen to this: "*Thou shalt call and I will answer thee. Thou wilt have a desire to the work of thine hands.*" That's nice. God loves and wants to see again the things that he made back here thousands of years ago. He doesn't forget his people. He may forget the mountains and the things he made thousands of years ago, but he won't forget his people that he made thousands of years ago. The works of his hands—he spent our life time working on us to get us ready for a better life. He's not going to forget that. He'll have a desire to see us again. God will want to see us again. Good thing, because if we're in the grave, we can't want anything! We can't want to see him again.

But while we're in the grave, dead and really in oblivion, *God will be wanting to see us again! Praise God! Doesn't that make you feel good?* Think of the loved ones that you have buried, but you're still alive! How you'd like to see them again! God feels the same way. He'd like to see them again too. He can do something about it.

The debate rages on here for several cycles: four men arguing with each other; each of the four would have his turn. Finally, the three comforters, Eliphaz, Bildad and Zophar gave up on Job. They couldn't convince him. They were convinced that he had done something mean and he ought to repent, but they couldn't convince him. They couldn't make him admit it. They had no witnesses, no evidence, except that he was sick. So they finally gave up and Job went into a long soliloquy, from chapter 26 on down through chapter 31, complaining about his condition, describing his former condition, wishing he could be that way again.

Question: "Do you want to comment on 15:15? This is Eliphaz talking."

Well, yeah, he was using that to try to shake Job's confidence. Job was firmly maintaining his innocence and his righteousness, so Eliphaz comes up with this argument that nobody's as righteous as God. *"He put no trust in his saints. Yea the heavens are not clean in his sight."* Whatever he meant by that, he's just saying that God can find something wrong with anybody. God's like the IRS. The IRS brags that they can find a fault in anybody's tax return. Probably can! They can interpret the law to make a flaw show up on your tax return.

But I'm sure if God looked too closely at us—and seems like Job said this somewhere in here himself. Was it Job or David or somebody else that said, *"If thou, Lord, shouldest mark iniquities who shall....?"* That wasn't Job's words, but he said something like that in here. He as much admitted that, *"If I've sinned,"* he said, *"My sin remains with myself."* Nobody but God knows about it and he said to God, *"Why don't you for-*

give me for it, why don't you give me some grace?" But he hadn't done anything that he was conscious of; his conscience was not condemning him.

We have a good lesson in I John about how you have *"confidence before God and in the day of judgment"* if your conscience doesn't condemn you. That was the condition Job was in. His conscience did not condemn him. There was no evil on his conscience. He hadn't done anything that he could remember, that he could think of, to repent for. Here these preachers were around him, trying to talk him into repenting, trying to preach him under conviction. They had to give up because he didn't know of anything to repent of.

But after they gave up and Job gave his soliloquy, along comes another preacher in Chapter 32, (and this is one of the most difficult parts of Job) Elihu, apparently a young man. He commented on his own position as a youth in the presence of the aged men who should be wise, but he criticized those three comforters for not being able to find anything wrong with Job and he criticized Job for being self-righteous. He took that much of the part of the three comforters. They all four agreed that Job was self-righteous; he was discrediting and accusing God and deserved to suffer.

That was something I don't think the first three comforters had thought up. Elihu thought of that argument: Job deserves to suffer for the way he's talking against God! It's been traditional in our Ministry to take the position that Job's three comforters couldn't pin him down, but Elihu, the young fellow, the young preacher, came along and pinned him down.

I was standing around a group of our preachers at a minister's meeting some years back. They got to talking about Job. Finally one of them said, "Well Elihu got him told, didn't he?" I had already begun to study this case and was already seeing the weakness of Elihu's position. I asked them, "What did Elihu say that the rest of them didn't say?" They really couldn't answer that. We just kind of took it for granted and accepted it that Elihu got him told. Our position has been (for most of us) that Elihu finally got through to Job, shut his mouth for him, and got him in a mood to listen to God who began to talk in chapter thirty-eight.

Finally God began to talk to Job in chapter 38. Elihu got Job ready for that. But I just invite you—now I challenge you—to study Elihu's comments and see how well founded they are. I found a lot of weaknesses and false accusations in Elihu's words. Here's one place where his arrogance and what you might call in a young person, a smart aleck spirit, shows up in chapter 33 in verse 6, where Elihu is inviting Job to counsel with him. "*You counsel with me. If you can answer me,*" in verse 5, "*set your words in order before me; stand up and answer me.*"

Now Job had already been answering those old gray-bearded men, and here's this young whippersnapper challenging him, "*You stand up and answer me! Behold I am according to thy wish in God's stead,*" because Job had complained that God wouldn't talk to him. "*It's just ignorant people around here talking to me and God won't talk to me. I wish God would come talk to me. I wish somebody that understood God's position would talk to me.*" So Elihu said, "*Okay here I am. I'm here in the place of God. You talk to me.*" That didn't satisfy Job. He didn't think Elihu was in the stead of God.

He begins to accuse Job, like in verse 9, "*You're saying I am clean without transgression. I am innocent, neither is there iniquity in me. Behold God findeth occasions against me, he counteth me for his enemy. He puts my feet in the stocks, he marketh all my paths. Listen, Job, in all this you're not just. I will answer you that God is greater than man.*" Well that's beside the point. Job had never claimed that he was as great as God. He had just claimed that God was letting him suffer things that he didn't deserve.

It's just hard for people to believe and accept that God will let people suffer things they don't deserve. Elihu couldn't stomach that; the other three comforters couldn't stomach that. They kept trying to talk Job out of that, but it was the truth that God admitted back in chapter 2 where I showed you a while ago. God said to Satan, "*You moved me against him without cause."* He was suffering things he didn't deserve. The world doesn't believe that, if they believe in God at all.

In 34:9, Elihu accuses Job of saying, *"He hath said it profiteth a man nothing that he should delight himself with God."* Job did not exactly say that, but by implication he was saying that was his experience. He had served God faithfully. He did make that plain. And here he had had all his blessings taken away from him, getting no reward for it. He was making those complaints alright, but at that moment in his life, he was telling the truth. He was in that condition.

Over in verse 18, Elihu makes this criticism. *"Is it fit or right to say to a king thou art wicked? And to princes ye are ungodly? How much less to him that accepteth not the persons of princes, nor regardeth the rich more than the poor."* He's accusing Job of saying to God what is not even fit to say to a king and princes. But Job hadn't actually called God wicked. It's just that people think it's wicked to let somebody suffer what they don't deserve to suffer.

That's human opinion. Human philosophy is that it would be wrong of God; it would be wicked of God to let people suffer what they don't deserve to suffer. That's how little we understand God. Job didn't understand it either. He just knew it happened to him. He felt the same way, really, but he refused to blame God for it. He refused to call God wicked but he was pointing out the facts of the case. God was letting him suffer unjustly. People just couldn't swallow that. Elihu couldn't swallow it.

Now here's where Elihu's rank, youthful, inexperienced spirit shows up the worst, in my opinion. In Chapter 34, verse 36, after he's spent a chapter or two there running Job down, he lets his feelings come out. *"Here's what I'd like to see happen. My desire is that Job may be tried unto the end."* Pour it on him, Lord! Chapter 34:36. *"Pour it on him, Lord! Let him suffer some more because of his answers for wicked men!"*

That's not the kind of preacher you want praying for you in a prayer line! Don't pray for me if you've got that spirit!

Down in chapter 35:3, he accuses Job again. *"You said what advantage will it be unto thee and what profit shall I have if I be cleansed from my sin?"* Where did Job say that? I searched in vain for anything he could have based that on in Job's words. And in verse 15 of that chapter, he makes again the same mistake the three comforters had made, "*...but now because it is not so, God hath visited in his anger."* God wasn't angry with Job. Read the story again. Go back and read the first two chapters again. God wasn't mad at Job. That wasn't what this story was about.

But you really can't blame all these men for not knowing that. Nobody told them what God was doing. They hadn't read the book of Job yet. We have the advantage over them. We can read the story there in the first two chapters and then the final chapter which we need to get to about how it finally came out.

I just wanted to show you some of these things. I made up a list one time, a long list of mistakes that Elihu made here in his judgment of Job, just to show that he didn't understand the case any better than the rest of them did. He couldn't; he hadn't read the first two chapters of Job. No passerby coming along could properly explain what had happened to Job. It finally took God to explain it. And you'd have to say when you read it, he didn't explain it very well. Not so anybody could understand it.

After Elihu finally ran down, God began to talk. After all the men quit talking, God began to talk in chapter 38. The Lord answered Job out of a whirlwind and began to re-emphasize his own greatness. I suppose Job understood that. "*As great as God is, he can be trusted even if I'm hurting."* Like Brother Lacy Hawkins said, "Even when I'm hurting, God can be trusted." That's what the whole thing is about. You can still trust God even when you're hurting and don't deserve to hurt and don't know why you're hurting. You don't have to know why. I don't have to understand; I just need to hold his hand. God just emphasized his own greatness to Job.

He began to bless Job again. Now we read the last chapter. Don't give up until you get to the last chapter. As somebody said, God's not finished with me yet. And in the last chapter, God began to bless Job again. But first, God judged his three friends, his critics. In verse 7 of Chapter 42, after the Lord had spoken these words unto Job, the Lord said to Eliphaz, the Temanite, *"My wrath is kindled against you and against your two friends, for you have not spoken of me the thing that is right as my servant Job hath."*

I want you to get this now. All those right things those men said that the wicked can't prosper forever and God will finally judge the wicked, that was their main point in all of their arguments. That's the truth. But they were applying it wrongly in judging Job. And here Job is complaining about how God's treating him, letting him suffer unfairly and people trying to take up for God, and then God said Job's telling the truth! Job spoke the thing that's right about God.

So let's quit calling Job self-righteous, saying he brought it on himself! There's a lesson in here! Don't jump on other people when they're down! It might be some other reason for it. Note though that God totally ignored Elihu in this chapter; he made no mention of him after all that long speech the young fellow made back there, God completely overlooked it, as much as to say, "These older men should have known better. They're supposed to be old and wise. They should have known better than what they did. That young fellow though, who can blame him? He'll learn. Give him time; he'll finally learn. You don't expect him to know the true situation," so he didn't even judge him.

But then after that, in the last half of that chapter, you want to compare it with the first chapter which lists all of Job's wealth, the wealth that he lost. And when you compare it here in the last chapter, his 14,000 sheep, in verse 12 and his 6,000 camels, and his 1,000 yoke of oxen and 1,000 she asses and all that, that he got in the latter part of his life, now you observe that is twice as much as what he started out with in the first chapter. God gave him back twice as much as he took away from him when he finally did get around to blessing him again, except one thing, his children. He gave him again seven sons and three daughters.

Now, people that don't understand God can criticize that. I read a lecture by Robert Ingersoll who used to lecture against religion back in the 1800's. He used this example as an example of the ignorance of religious people to even make up a story like this, because who thinks that you can be paid back after you've buried seven sons and three daughters; that you can be paid back and compensated with a new set of seven sons and three daughters? Anybody that's ever stood by the graveside of a little child that they've buried understands that those parents don't want another child. They want that child. There's not much comfort to tell them they can have some more children. That doesn't make them feel any better. They don't want more children that day. They want that child.

Well God's no fool either. He knows all that. And that's the reason he didn't give Job twenty children back. He didn't try to double his children and pay him back that way. He just gave him another set of ten kids to finish his life with, with a promise of the first ten back in the resurrection. See, that's something Job's comforters never thought of when they said, "*God has judged your children and cast them away from you. You repent and let him bless you again.*"

No, God didn't kill those kids because they sinned and deserved it any more than he made Job sick because he deserved it. That wasn't the issue. We just think God couldn't let ten kids get killed unless they deserved to die. You don't understand God or kids either. This little interruption in our existence means little to God. It looms so large to us, but give us ten or fifteen thousand years of life on the other side and we will hardly remember what we've been through back here or how many years we were asleep in the grave. It won't even matter after fifty million years. You probably won't even remember it happened after fifty million years. How much can you remember now out of what happened fifty years ago?

Question—not understood.

Sure, he understood that even if his comforters didn't. Job understood that and he understood why God just gave him ten more kids. He's just going to be patient again.

You've heard of the patience of Job. James said, "*You've heard of the patience of Job.*" Job is still being patient today, waiting for his twenty kids. Down in the Resurrection he'll finally have twenty kids, twice as many as he lost. He'll get the first ten back. That'll help you in reading the book of Job a little bit the next time you read it.

Question: "Who wrote the book of Job?"

Don't you wish you knew! (Laughter) Fact is, nobody knows, but might as well blame it on Moses as anybody. Undoubtedly he got hold of a copy of it and included it in the scriptures.

Question: "In Matthew 5:25, can the adversary be the Lord?"

Let's take a look at that one. Matthew 5:25. Is that where he said if you bring your gift to the altar, agree with your adversary quickly while you're in the way with him? "*Agree with thine adversary quickly whiles thou art in the way with him.*" Well you could use it that way, I guess. You could use the principle that way, but that wasn't the thought in Jesus' mind, because the thought in his mind in the parable he made up here is, God is the judge.

Your adversary is your brother or sister. It's whoever you're having a problem with in church. It might be wife or husband. Agree with your adversary. Your adversary is whoever is giving you trouble. '*Agree with them*', means to make peace with them. Get together, talk it over, and reach a working agreement that is acceptable to both sides. "*...lest at any time...*" Here's what the adversary is liable to do if you don't finally make peace: the adversary may deliver you to the judge. That's God. Your adversary, if you keep treating him wrong, offending him, he finally turns you over to God.

Your adversary will cry to God because his feelings are hurt. You hurt somebody's feelings and when they pray, that bleeds through, whether or not they complain about you. They may not say, "Oh, God will you take care of my brother there that keeps hurting me? Will you curse him some way, punish him for hurting me?" They probably won't say that, but while they're praying to God, they're praying out of a broken heart and God knows why that heart is broken, and so, that's the adversary delivering you to the judge.

And here's what the judge can do: "*Deliver thee to the officer....*" He's got more than one officer. Whatever officer God has in your town, is who that is, "*and thou be cast into prison.*"

Now God can cast you into a spiritual prison. He can put you in the prison of sickness. He can put you in the prison of poverty. What's worse than that, he can put you in the prison of deception, but he'll have to be pretty desperate to do that. That's radical treatment to put you in the prison of deception. But he can turn you over to one of his officers that are gifted at deceiving. He can let him lock you up in a church house and threaten you with the judgment of God if you ever go visit anywhere else or ever go back where you came from. You'll be locked up in a prison house, the kind of prison house Jesus came to set us free from.

Here's what happens to you: "*Verily I say unto thee, thou shalt by no means come out thence, till you've paid the fine, paid the uttermost farthing.*" You can't pay half of it and say, "Lord that's the best I can do. I don't think I'll ever get the rest." You can't wait it out and get out on probation, get off on good behavior or get off early for good behavior. Jesus said you won't get out of that prison until you've served your time. You'll have to serve your time and pay your fine before God will let you out of there, because you've been hurting some of his children.

God wants to take you to heaven but he's not going to take you there until you quit hurting his children. God can't have people up in heaven that hurt his children, people that make other people suffer, make people hurt, wound and injure, criticize and say spiteful things. We can't have that up there in heaven where God wants to wipe away all tears from every eye. He can't keep wiping away tears from eyes that are being hurt by spite and envy and jealousy and anger or just cold contempt. All those things are hurtful, painful. God would be drying up tears for eternity if he had people in heaven that would do those things.

So, he's not going to have people like that. If they don't quit being like that down here, they won't ever get up to heaven.

Does everybody see that? You can't, somebody said, live a hog, die a cow and resurrect a horse. The grave won't make that kind of change in you. You can't live here a spiteful sinner, mean spirited, cold and hard-hearted, go down in the grave and spend a few thousand years in the graveyard and come out of there a beautiful angel, a saint, kind spirited, soft-spoken and gentle to everybody. Nothing like that takes place in the graveyard. There are no preachers in the graveyard. Who said that? But they're not doing any preaching there! (Laughter) Alright, where are we? Praise God!

Question: "Why did God listen to Satan? Why did God want to prove Job to Satan? Why did God not just ignore Satan?"

You're getting in deep theology there. I don't know if we can satisfy you on those points. We just have to take the story as factual; that it is what happened. God's reputation is worth a great deal to you and me. It's not just God being selfish, jealous of his own reputation because he wants to be admired.

No, it's partly this, that God wants his reputation to be safe so you and I can believe him. Who's going to believe him? Who's going to believe him if he tells lies or if he fails in his projects; if he tries to save people and can't save them? Then who's going to believe him when he promised, "*Come unto me all ye that labor and are heavy laden and I'll give you rest.*"

So, God does a lot of things to defend his reputation. He'll take up for his name. His reputation is synonymous with the subject of the name of God. The name of God is not just a handle that people call him by, but it's his reputation, his good name in the community, his good name in this world. God has a good name because he's always kept his promises. He's always done what he said he would do. His word is his bond. That gives him a good name and he will defend his name.

There's a scripture in the Psalms somewhere that says, "*He has magnified his word above his name.*" Isn't that how it goes? The explanation for that, the reason why he magnifies his word so highly is because his name depends on his word. His name depends on him keeping his word. God will shake heaven and earth to keep his word. God will send floods, tornados, and hurricanes or atom bombs if need be to keep his promises. God will make radical moves and changes to keep his promises because he wants us to believe he will keep his promises. He wants us to believe that he'll keep his promise to bring us out of the grave. So, God has gone far out of his way to magnify his word.

He's a truthful God. He claims to be a truthful God and this is why the scripture says God cannot lie. It doesn't mean that God's not smart enough to think up a big one. It's just that he can't lie and still be the truthful God that he claims to be. It would destroy his reputation. He wouldn't be the God that he presents himself as if he ever told a lie. So, he's bound by his own choice. He chooses to be a truthful God that people can believe; consequently, he cannot lie. That puts a constraint upon his behavior. Maybe that helps with some of these confused questions:

Question: "Is God so desperate for glory that he causes those that love him to suffer for his ego?"

No it's not as simple as that.

Question: "Why is it wrong to complain about God's allowing us to suffer?"

Well, I guess I haven't emphasized that point enough. It's wrong to complain because it implies criticism of the person that's letting you suffer. In the first place, we are assuming that it's wrong for us to suffer. Quit assuming that! Whoever wrote this question—quit assuming that! It's not wrong for you to suffer. It is not wicked for you to suffer. No blame attaches to God for letting you suffer. It really isn't harmful to suffer. It's good for you, good medicine lots of time to suffer. If we suffer with Jesus, we'll also reign with Jesus. Do you want to reign with Jesus? Then suffer with him! It's as simple as that.

Question: "Are we to lose our sense of fairness? Just accept anything?"

From God, you're to just accept anything. That's what Job did. Don't look for fairness. Life is not fair. Life cannot really be made fair. There's too much difference between people. We can't all be treated alike. We can't all have the same thing. Fairness is not what God promises. He did promise us justice. God promises justice, not fairness. So let's have our confidence in his justice and forget about fairness.

Comment: "If most of us didn't question things, we wouldn't have turned against the false religious system and seen this Body."

Well, God doesn't blame you for questioning things. In fact, he takes pride in our searching for answers. God approves of us searching for answers. As Solomon said, "I*t's the glory of God to conceal things, but the honor of kings is to search out a matter.*" God lets us receive honor by searching out answers to these questions. God won't blame you for having these questions, but he wants you to try to find the right answer. Try to figure out why it's this way, why God's like this.

See, the scripture tells us, God told us many times, "*My ways,*" he said, "*are higher than your ways.*" Do you believe that? Do you believe God's ways are higher? That means better than your ways. God lets people suffer? You wouldn't let them suffer. You'd get them out of their suffering. They wouldn't learn a thing. God's ways are better than yours.

Comment from audience—not understood.

Yeah, those that God... God won't let them suffer. We want them to suffer. See, God's ways are better than our ways. He said, "*My thoughts are higher than your thoughts.*" Believe that. Accept what he said. Try to learn to think like God thinks. Try to learn to act like God acts. Of course, you won't ever be able to send a hurricane. Don't try. But treat people as honestly and justly as God does, then you can be in the same category. You can be perfect as your Father in heaven. So quit criticizing God and start justifying God. That way, you're thinking like God. Think along with God. Try to think what he thinks. Approve what he approves. Bless the people he blesses, and dis-fellowship the people he dis-fellowships. Amen! Amen!

Comment from audience—not understood.

When we complain about it, we're simply postponing the good we could get out of it. If you're going to complain, then you're going to need a lot more patience. You make the trial last longer.

Question: "Today, when the sons of God come together, does Satan still come?"

I'm afraid so.

Question: "I've heard several ministers tell the story of a shepherd breaking the leg of a sheep who strayed. Do you know where this came from and if it's fact?"

Well, I've read that in several analyses of Psalms 23. I don't know it for a fact myself. But informed people have written that some shepherd might do that sometimes to keep a sheep from straying away and being lost. This person says I've tried several resources, but I found nothing about it. Well, I haven't found anything authentic either; just read that in some books. Well, we've got a lot of good things here.

Question: "In Chapter 1, Verses 4 and 5, it says Job, after his children had feasted, that Job would sacrifice for his children because he was afraid that his children may have sinned in their heart. Could that imply that Job didn't trust God enough regarding their spiritual walk? Our children are lent to us by God. Shouldn't we give them the chance to show that God has a hold on their life?"

Sure, but I think the point of that comment in the story was just how careful Job was to raise his children right. You couldn't even accuse Job of carelessly bringing up his children. A man that would offer sacrifice for his children just in case they had sinned is certainly not a man that neglected to teach them about God. The comment is in there just to sew up the story to make it plain that Job hadn't neglected anything. His children weren't bad children. There's no hint in there that his children were bad children. They didn't die because they were bad children and if you've lost some children, they may not have died because they were bad children. Consider other possible explanations. Well, that's probably enough of this today.

Chapter 3

Daniel's Prayer

September 5, 1998, Camp Meeting

I sense God trying to speak to us in this meeting. We need to get what he is saying and get it right. Sometimes people don't understand what God says. Some of you fellows will say, "God told me this, that and the other." I have to wonder: Did you understand what God told you? Maybe he did tell you something, but did you hear it right? There is an undercurrent here lately; it's been building up for a good while. God is trying to contact our spirits. It's coming out in some of the messages. I guess the trend of the world today is making us get more sober.

The subject yesterday was imposing, wasn't it? It will make you stop and think. If those dangers are facing the world, it behooves God's ministers to, as Brother Angelo said, read the newspaper, follow trends and see what God is doing. That's one source of information. Some of our information comes from the world, just watching God work with the world. But, information is hard to put together from those sources. It's unreliable and misinterpreted; people get overboard, stampeded, as Brother Rader said. We don't want to go off the deep end, but there's a lot of machinery in place to shake this world if God wants to shake it. Somebody pointed out yesterday that there are several loose ends and shaky aspects of the economic world today. Y2K might just be 'the straw that breaks the camel's back'.

The programmer that sent up the encouraging note yesterday—I'd love to talk with you if you'd hunt me up sometime before this meeting is over. I value your input and your opinion. I've been following this subject closely for a few months and what I'm observing is that the programmers whose projects are on time are getting it under control. They're relaxing now and telling us not to worry. Those programmers whose projects are falling behind and see they don't have a prayer of meeting the deadline, are telling us civilization is going to collapse. The truth may fall somewhere between. Business runs in cycles. We can't forever stay in a bull market or a productive cycle in business.

Things are bound to change. Things have always changed. We've lived through depressions before. As I said, the machinery is in place for a severe one if God wants it to be severe. I, for one, will probably have a few extra cans of hominy in the pantry when that day comes.

That's what you call buying insurance. When you buy insurance you hope you just wasted that money. That's the whole point—you hope you wasted the money that you spent on insurance. But, nobody will know what's going to happen until it happens. Maybe it would be better to just trust God from the start.

I want to talk to you a little bit. When God comes to your rescue, he may not do it until your faith has been tested. He doesn't know if you've got faith or not until it's stretched a little bit, sees how elastic your faith is, how long it lasts, how far it will stretch. When the children of Israel were in the wilderness, God allowed them to get to their extremity at times. He never let them starve to death, but he let them be afraid they might if they didn't have pretty strong faith. Now, those that had enough faith never seemed to worry about it. You never heard Moses complain about being thirsty or hungry or wondering where the next water was coming from until the people got too heavy on him. They leaned on him pretty hard and then he would maybe complain to God, "*Why are you putting me through this*"? *I can't make the water come out of the rock. What are you going to do?*"

It's up to God, isn't it? And this is what we see about things coming on the world today. How bad it will get depends on how bad God wants it to get. And, if he wants to shake the world or try the faith of his people, he'll let it happen and we don't want to be alarmed about that. Neither do I want you to be shocked if it comes to that. That's why we're talking along these lines to get prepared for anything. Be prepared for anything because God is impressing us with the need to draw close to him and live more in the Spirit. He may put pressure on us to do that sometimes. I felt to point out to you that the way God answers prayer sometimes is not the way we expect it.

I have lots of examples on how trusting God, a lot of times, depends on the times and seasons, what's going on in history, so to speak. Trusting God may mean not living in luxury. It depends on the times and the seasons. I'm not saying that we've missed God by living in luxury. The times and the seasons have allowed for that. But there are times when it doesn't allow for that. To follow God means to be led through some trying times.

A good example of that principle is the days of Jeremiah. In the days of Jeremiah, God was preparing judgment for the nation of Israel. Most of the people in the nation deserved it, but some didn't. Not everybody was backslid in Israel. Jeremiah wasn't the only faithful man that God had. God made promises to those people, to some of them, through the mouth of Jeremiah that he would take care of them and spare them in the trouble that was coming. But what he could not do was promise them ease and luxury particularly.

There is a short chapter in Jeremiah devoted to the promise he made to the man who was Jeremiah's stenographer, the man who was taking down his prophesies and recording them. Jeremiah 45 is God's word to Baruch, who was sticking by Jeremiah. He was writing down all these bad things Jeremiah was saying were going to happen. It made him feel bad. It's depressing to read prophesies about destruction and wrath and collapse of civilization. Things like that will depress you if you spend too much time on it. He was spending a lot of time on that. He was hearing everything Jeremiah said, and so he got under depression. God gave him a promise in that little chapter there.

He said in there, "*...seeketh thou great things for thyself? Seek them not because, behold, I bring trouble on all the land.*" You can read that for yourself when you have time to get the exact words, but the message, the implication, was that if it had been another day in time he might have been justified in seeking a great position. Baruch apparently was an educated man.

He could have expected to get a good government job, work hard, build up a pension and retire with a house in the city and a house in the country and maybe two or three chariots in his garage. He could have expected good times because he had the means to do it.

If he had lived in the days of Isaiah that's the way it would have worked. But he wasn't lucky enough to live in that time. He was unfortunate enough to be born in Jeremiah's days, in the end of that world. It *was* the end of that world, so it just wasn't the time for him to be blessed that way financially and made to prosper. But God did promise him this: He said, *"I'll give your life to you for a prey* (that is a reward) *in any place where you go. Wherever you wander throughout your captivity, I'll watch over you and spare your life."*

I'm not saying this is that kind of time. I'm using this for an example of how God deals with people according to the time that they live in and his rewards are not always equal. Things don't come out equal. Sometimes, some generations have it easy; some generations have it hard. It's not always the fault of the people of God living in those generations, but we're instructed, as they were, to pray for the peace of the city you live in. Jeremiah sent that message to the people who were already in captivity while he was still preaching back there in Jerusalem.

There were some people already taken into captivity in Babylon while the main body of the people stayed behind in Jerusalem before the destruction of the temple and the destruction of the city in 586 B.C. There were people already over in Babylon and they were disheartened and discouraged about it. Let me read some of that to you because Jeremiah wrote them a letter and it was a blessing of God and a promise of God to them, but it wasn't what they wanted to hear.

The point I'm making to you is that what God says may not always be what you want to hear. Jeremiah 29, I believe it is. These are the words of the letter that Jeremiah the prophet sent from Jerusalem unto the residue of the elders which were carried away captives. Skipping on down to the 4th verse, this is what the letter said: *"Thus saith the Lord of hosts, the God of Israel, unto all that are carried away captives, whom I have caused to be carried away from Jerusalem unto Babylon. Build ye houses, and dwell in them; and plant gardens and eat the fruit of them. Take ye wives, and beget sons and daughters; and take wives for your sons, and give your daughters to husbands, that they may bear sons and daughters; that ye may be increased there, and not diminished. And seek the peace of the city whither I have caused you to be carried away captives and pray unto the Lord for it; for in the peace thereof shall ye have peace."*

On down in the tenth verse he told them seventy years they would be there. This is not what those people wanted to hear. They had been carried away from their homeland and they were taught (like we are taught) to pray *"Deliver us from evil."* Those people carried away captive had just been delivered from evil, but they didn't know it. They thought their captivity was evil and they were praying to be sent back home. They wanted to go home and they thought, "Any day...," and, they had prophets telling them, promising them, "Any day now you'll be allowed to go back home." They thought they would get away from evil.

In the previous chapter, you'll read about a case like that where a prophet there in Jerusalem prophesied that within two years God will bring everybody back. That was encouraging! That was an encouraging message! Within two years, God will let everybody come home! And here comes Jeremiah writing a letter saying it will be seventy years before you get to come home! They had been delivered from evil and didn't know it because they didn't know the evil God was going to bring on their homeland. God said those things about the people in captivity that I just read to you.

Down farther in that chapter, he spoke about the people that remained behind in Jerusalem. I'll start with verse 16 in chapter 29. *"Know that thus saith the Lord of the king that sittteth upon the throne of David, and of all the people that dwelleth in this city, and of your brethren that are not gone forth with you into captivity; thus saith the Lord of hosts; Behold, I will send upon them the sword, the famine, and the pestilence, and will make them like vile figs, that cannot be eaten, they are so evil. And I will persecute them* (How would you like for God to be persecuting you?) *with the sword, with the famine, and with the pestilence, and will deliver them to be removed to all the kingdoms of the earth, to be a curse, and an astonishment, and an hissing, and a reproach among all the nations whither I have driven them."*

This was the evil that those early captives had been delivered from. God had heard their prayers and had provided for them. I just wanted you to see the point there that it's not always pleasant to the flesh; it's not always pleasant to the natural mind, to endure God's protection, but it's better than the alternative. It was far better than the alternative! We are to trust God whatever comes! If trouble happens in this country, we are to not be surprised and we are to trust God and accept our deprivations. When those cans of hominy run out, God will send some more! Expect God to come to your rescue and keep you alive! You've never seen the righteous forsaken nor his seed begging for bread!

Well, as I said, we don't know how bad it will get and it doesn't have to get as bad as it could. The machinery is in place for it to get very bad if God wants to use it, if He wants to crank up all that machinery. But it's only as bad as God wants it to happen.

Now, do you feel like you can influence what God wants? Yes, to a degree you can have an influence on what God wants to happen. People have prayed their way out of trouble before. This is why God said to pray for the peace of the city that you are in.

We ought to be praying for the peace and prosperity of our nation. Its prosperity has made us prosperous. All the luxury we live in is because of the prosperity God has blessed this nation with. We ought to be thankful for it and pray for the peace of our country. There are always preachers and prophets rising up out here in the religious world trying to get America to bow down and pray. They quote that scripture in II Chronicles where God said, *"If my people that are called by my name will humble themselves and turn from their wicked ways and pray, I'll forgive their sin and heal their land."* And there are always people rising up trying to get us as a nation to break and humble ourselves and repent and pray. But, you can't get this nation to do that. There are just too many people that weren't even raised Christian, who don't believe in Christianity in this country now.

This is no longer a Christian nation. There are too many Muslims, Hindus, atheists and all kinds of unbelievers in the land. So, we can't get this country to humble itself and repent and pray. But we can still pray, ourselves, for the peace of the land. I feel God has been dealing with us along that line for some time now.

It's been brought to my attention that Brother Mears preached on this subject of the ninth chapter of Daniel. Some time back, Brother Daves preached on it. In fact, he referred to it and dealt with some of it here in the opening of this meeting. It's a time like that when God wants his people to consider their sins, not only of the present, but of the past.

I want to talk to you a little bit about repenting for the sins of the past, repenting for the sins of generations gone by. We had—we refer to it constantly—an outstanding camp meeting here many years ago. It's been 45 years ago now since something special happened and God forgave the sins of this body. I hardly ever hear anybody say that, but that's the way it was presented to us, and I believe it. I believed it then and I still believe that God cleaned the slate for us. We left from that meeting with a clean slate. It didn't stay clean very long, but we had a fresh start when God actually forgave our sins. Our step was lighter. There was a spring in our heel and we felt a load gone off our shoulders because God gave us a fresh start. That applied particularly to this movement, this group, this body of people.

That wasn't for the Pentecostal people; it wasn't for the whole religious world. It was something God did here on this hilltop for this group of people. But, that's been 45 years ago.

Lots of things have happened since then; there have been lots of unpleasant, unrighteous things happen. Our tendency, everybody's tendency, is to blame somebody else: "It was somebody else that did that." We blame our leader or we blame the particular sinners that we know about and let them bear the burden. We don't see anything we can do about it.

Here sometime ago, a few months ago, the idea, suggestion, was raised in the nation out here that we should maybe consider, as a nation, repenting or apologizing for slavery. Do you remember that? It didn't go very far. I brushed it off like you did because I didn't persecute the slaves; I wasn't back there. It wasn't anything I did, so what can I do about it now? I can't apologize for what my forefathers did.

But after reading Daniel's prayer, I reconsidered that subject. It might indeed be a good thing for the U.S.A. to apologize for slavery if we could come at it in the spirit of Daniel in Daniel 9. I'm not going to pursue that thought; I'm just using that for an example of how we can repent for things that we didn't do. But our group, our family, our body, what we're a part of, did those things.

I'm going to show you; I'm going to read this whole chapter. Brother Daves read some of it the other day but I want to read to you the whole prayer here that Daniel prayed in Daniel 9. If we are ever going to do this... and we've been brought right up to it by some of these other brethren. Brother Wright had us right out on the diving board last night. We need to actually do this. We need to pray this kind of prayer. So if you're going to pray it, here's how you have to do it. You've got to accept some responsibility, take some guilt upon yourself that doesn't necessarily belong to you.

Let me show you here how Daniel approached this. In Daniel 9:3, he said, "*And I set my face unto the Lord God, to seek by prayer and supplications, with fasting, and sackcloth, and ashes.*" That's weighty right there! Daniel didn't just pray! He put on sackcloth and ashes, and fasted and prayed! That had a lot of affect. He was a righteous man. You know the kind of man Daniel was from his youth up. Somebody mentioned here already that, no doubt, he was just a teenager when he turned down the king's meat and said, *"I won't defile myself, I won't break the law of my fathers and my God. Let me just get by on vegetables and clean food."*

He stood that test. Then shortly after that, he interpreted the king's vision while he was still a young man. Daniel was a great man of God and his three friends were great men. They suffered the fiery furnace, endured being cast into the fire, facing certain annihilation, certain death. They accepted certain death, just trusting in God. And I don't suppose they expected to be delivered. Hardly anybody has ever been delivered in a case like that. A lot of people have died in those very circumstances, trusting in God. Don't forget that, because God's going to let you die some way, some day. The attitude of the three Hebrew children was: If it's our day to die, fine, we'll go out trusting in God. So, they had no assurance, no promise that the angel was going to be there when they were cast into the fire. Those were great men.

Daniel was a righteous man, beloved of the Lord. God didn't have any complaint against him. But here's how he prayed in verse 4: *"And I prayed unto the Lord my God, and made my confession,* (We need to make our confession.) *and said, Oh Lord, the great and dreadful God, keeping the covenant and mercy to them that love him, and to them that keep his commandments; We have sinned..."*

Brother Daves got to say that the other night. We need to say that. We need to be praying that. We need to, all together, pray that. It would have been good and he would have been happy if he could have had the whole crowd praying with him here this day. But his means of communications didn't make it easy to do that. So, he just took it on himself and prayed. But he said, "We have sinned."

And when he said that, he was speaking for the whole crowd. He hadn't sinned. That was not the sins he was talking about. No doubt he had sinned some way, but the sins he was confessing were not sins he had committed. He was confessing and accepting guilt for the rest of the crowd, the rest of the people.

"*We have sinned, and have committed iniquity.*" Can you say that as a crowd? As a people today, can we say that? We have sinned and have committed iniquity. It has certainly happened in our midst. Somebody in here has done it, somebody in our midst. Some of them are dead and buried now, but those things happened in our midst, in our company. It was our brothers and sisters. It was our family members that committed those sins. We need to repent.

"*I have done wickedly.*" Imagine Daniel saying ***we*** have done wickedly. He hadn't done wickedly! He had stood the lions' den. He had been a faithful man of God. He kept the law. He obeyed the word of God. But he stood there before God and humbled himself and spoke on behalf of his brethren. "*We have done wickedly and have rebelled, even by departing from thy precepts and from thy judgment. Neither have we harkened unto thy servants the preachers* (prophets) *which spake in thy name to our kings, our princes, and our fathers, and to all the people of the land. Oh Lord, righteousness belongeth unto thee, but unto us* (belongs) *confusion of faces, as at this day.*"

You can get the picture here. Remember, these people were scattered in Babylonian captivity. They were confused. "*To the men of Judah, and to the inhabitants of Jerusalem, and unto all Israel, that are near, and that are far off, through all the countries whither thou hast driven them, because of their trespass that they have trespassed against thee. Oh Lord, to us belongeth confusion of face, to our kings, to our princes, and to our fathers.*" In other words, confusion belongs to our leadership, because we have sinned against thee.

"*To the Lord our God belong mercies and forgiveness, though we have rebelled against him;*

Neither have we obeyed the voice of the Lord our God, to walk in his laws, which he set before us by his servants the prophets.

Yea, all Israel have transgressed thy law, even by departing, that they might not obey thy voice; therefore the curse is poured upon us, and the oath that is written in the law of Moses the servant of God, because we have sinned against him.

And he hath confirmed his words, which he spake against us, and against our judges that judged us, by bringing upon us a great evil: for under the whole heaven hath not been done as hath been done upon Jerusalem.

As it is written in the law of Moses, all this evil is come upon us: yet made we not our prayer before the Lord our God, that we might turn from our iniquities, and understand thy truth.

Therefore hath the Lord watched upon the evil, and brought it upon us: for the Lord our God is righteous in all his works which he doeth: for we obeyed not his voice.

*And now, O Lord our God that hast brought thy people forth out of the land of Egypt with a mighty hand, and hast gotten thee renown, as at this day. (*He confesses again) *"We have sinned, we have done wickedly.*

Oh Lord, according to all thy righteousness, I beseech thee, let thine anger and thy fury be turned away from thy city Jerusalem, thy holy mountain: because for our sins, and for the iniquities of our fathers, Jerusalem and thy people are become a reproach to all that are about us.

Now therefore, O our God, hear the prayer of thy servant, and his supplications, and cause thy face to shine upon thy sanctuary that is desolate, for the Lord's sake.

O my God, incline thine ear, and hear; open thine eyes, and behold our desolations, and the city which is called by thy name: for we do not present our supplications before thee for our righteousness, but for thy great mercies.

O Lord, hear; O Lord, forgive; O Lord, hearken and do; defer not, for thine own sake, O my God for thy city and thy people are called by thy name."

Daniel was an eloquent pray-er. The time setting here, of course, is at the end of the captivity when it was time for God to bless the people again and let them return home. He was ready to pour out a blessing upon them. But I just wondered if some of that evil could have been spared, could have been escaped, if Daniel or somebody like Daniel, could have prayed a prayer like that before the captivity, before things got so bad, before God's wrath was confirmed upon his people, before it got to where he said that, *"if old Noah, Job and Daniel stood before him, my face couldn't be toward this people"*. Before it got that bad, if somebody could have prayed like this, maybe it could have been forestalled and held back and so much trouble wouldn't have had to happen.

We need to touch God. It's possible I could incur the displeasure of these brethren here by taking too much on myself. There are not but two or three preachers here with the authority to do what I'm wanting to do and I'm not one of them. But brethren, grant me a dispensation of grace and back me up here. If we could get this whole crowd of people to pray like Daniel prayed...I'll be frank with you, I can't pray like Daniel, but there are some prayer warriors in this crowd. There are some people in here that are skilled at praying.

And, we certainly have things to pray about. There's a load and weight of iniquity and evil that has stacked up over our heads. There's been too much dissension! There's been too much rebellion, too much rivalry, too much jealousy and envy in our ranks! There have been too many preachers' reputations torn down by false reports! There have been too many saints brow-beaten by their pastors, discouraged and driven out of church! There's been too much sin and evil, too much child-molesting! And adulteries! And divorce! And broken homes! And children suffering! There's too much turning to the world and pursuit of pleasure and accepting evil into our ranks! There are too many televisions babysitting for the children in our front rooms, our family rooms! We need to repent of those things!

Some of you, though, are sitting out there and saying, "I haven't done that. I didn't do those things! That isn't my fault!" Maybe not, maybe so. Will you pray for the rest of us? If you don't feel any guilt today for what's happened, will you pray Daniel's prayer and join with the group, be a part of the group and say *WE* have sinned? And you that do feel burdened with guilt—you know you're guilty! You know you've done things that offended God!

You know you've departed from these principles that Brother Wright preached here last night! You know you need to turn to God! Pray as eloquently as you can!

You may be a backwoods country hick, not know any great words, you may not be fluent in speech, but be honest and sincere and that's what touches the heart of God! A broken and contrite spirit he said he would not despise! He told those people, *"You'll find me when you seek me with your whole heart."* Will you help me pray today? Will you help me pray the prayer of Daniel today? Right now? In these four walls here? How about standing right now and everybody pray and confess the sins of the people. Ask God to forgive us!

Father in Heaven, we have sinned! We've done wickedly. We've committed iniquity. We've departed from thy precepts and thy truths. We confess our sins, O Lord. We ask for mercy. We ask forgiveness and cleansing. We ask you, Lord, for comfort and healing for the lives of the people. Heal our souls! Heal our spirits! Pour out upon us the spirit of repentance! Pour out on us the spirit of prayer! Pour out into our bosoms, Lord, a spirit of faith, sincerity, humility; all the beatitudes!

> O God, give us a clean slate; let us start over again! Cleanse this people from their sins! Forgive us, Lord, for all the sins of our fathers, all the sins of the past, all the mistakes and the evil! Deliver us, oh God, from the evil that's headed this way! We see evil coming upon the world.
>
> You're justified in judging the nations and judging your people. You're justified, Lord! You're holy and just in all your ways! O God, pardon our transgressions! Heal us of our iniquities! Deliver us, Lord, from the wrath that is stored up against us! Give us a clean slate to move on into the latter rain! Lift the burden of guilt from us, Lord! Let us rise up into the Spirit and live pure and holy!
>
> O God, inspire us with that desire and that vision and the conviction that we can live right; we can overcome; we can press on to perfection; we can stay together; we

can stand for unity; we can stand for holiness; we can produce what you're working on in the earth!

The seed can grow! The seed can sprout and grow! You can have a tree of righteousness! Praise the great God of heaven! Bless your wonderful name! Feed your people, Lord, in this meeting! Lift us out of our flesh condition! Lift us out of the flesh! Oh God, set us free from the bondage of the flesh! Teach us to live in the Spirit! Help us rise above the wickedness of this world, the spirit of the day, the entertainment world and its hold upon us.

Save us from deception, Lord! Don't let us be deceived! Don't let us miss what you're saying to us! Don't let us fail to obey the truth! Lord, don't let our vision pass away! Praise the great God! Hallelujah! Thank you, Jesus. Amen!

Chapter 4

Judgment

February 9, 1999, Ministers Meeting, Tyler, Texas

Thank you for that good prayer. That makes me feel better, already! Without the Lord, we can do nothing. We must never forget that. Don't try to do anything without him. I understand how Brother Kennedy feels. I feel like he's proved himself already, at least on the level he's been working on. I guess you do, to a degree, have to prove yourself when you get booted up to a new position. But, we've got confidence in Brother Kennedy and he's doing a good job.

We want to welcome all the ministers back to Texas. I'm sorry we couldn't have a meeting in Houston this year, but this is a good place for this meeting, and it's a good crowd here. It would be hard to get any more preachers in here, wouldn't it? We've got a lot of the wives and local saints coming in toward the end of the meeting. It's just good to see a packed-out house. It's a sign of our interest. We, at least, are interested in the work of God.

I want to welcome Brother Glen Goodwin here to our midst. I think this is the first general meeting of ours that he's been in. I told him, "If you can come sit here and hear your doctrine insulted and stay good-natured about it, come on." He chuckled and said, "We ought to be able to tolerate each other's opinions."

I reminded him we have to do that when we go to his meetings. It's getting to where that, when we go to his meetings and when we come to our meetings, I hope we can all be mannerly and good-natured. We do, sometimes, have to disagree about doctrines, but can we criticize a man's doctrine without criticizing the man?

We're to remember that we're brethren. You've heard (You that were back there to see it, I wasn't) many times how Brother Sowders used to deal with different sides of an opinion and a doctrine during the time when the Godhead doctrine was so hot among us and for a long time thereafter. The different sides of that doctrine would come up in the meetings and, they tell me, he would sit a oneness preacher on one side of him and a trinity preacher on the other side.

In those days, they didn't have a break for the diabetics to go get anything to eat. He would bring an apple to the meeting with him and in the heat of the day he would be sitting there with a pocket knife, peeling his apple. When he got it all peeled, he would slice it in half and hand one half to the trinity brother and half to the oneness brother. That was his demonstration that they were brethren.

When preachers got too heated on the threshing floor, he would sometimes remind them of that. "Remember brethren, this is your brother you are talking to," or, "Don't forget this is your brother you are talking to." It's easy to forget, when you are heated up, that he is your brother. You tend to think of him as an opponent. We don't want to be each other's opponents. We're all on the same team; we're trying to get to the same goal. We're trying to accomplish the same purpose. We're trying to work for God, work with Jesus Christ. Every one of us is!

We don't see everything alike in detail but we can be friendly and good-natured about that while we talk about it. Down the line somewhere, we will have the unity of the faith, but this work of the ministry is important in the overall plan of God. Leadership is necessary.

I made a controversial point one time and may make it again someday, and it will still be controversial, that God's will for Israel was not to have a king. The order that they lived under, the judges, was God's plan for them. It didn't work too well because they didn't have the Holy Ghost. They weren't in the Spirit and they didn't know how to live under that kind of order. They weren't ready to work under divine order. But even in that period there was leadership. God raised up judges. And, there was the priesthood. Prophets would come on the scene. In every generation, there was somebody to speak for God and to lead the people. There's always been a need for that and there always will be.

He could just as well have chosen the death of Christ, that year of the death and resurrection of Christ and the inauguration of the church. He might just as well have chosen the martyrdom of Stephen as the end of the seventieth week of Daniel. Good cases could be made for those dates just as well as 4 BC. If this doesn't throw you too sharp a curve, a case could even be made for 70 AD just as well as 4 BC. I'm not going to try to make it; I'm just throwing out these things here to show there are other options. There are other possibilities but the world is, right now, caught up with the year 2000. That's in their concepts.

There's a lot of prophecy going forth out there in the Pentecostal world. Groups of prophets and apostles are meeting together and holding meetings in strategic places. The big names and the bigwigs are coming together with meetings, sharing their views and prophecies for the next year or two. So, it's an important time, whether it's God's date or not. It's important to the world's people and we don't want to be behind in discerning the signs of the times, to see what God is really doing at this hour and what we're supposed to do to fit in with it.

This is what the Bride of Christ, or the Man Child, (those two things we call it) is chosen for. The one hundred, forty-four thousand is the rulership. That's God's government for the future. He'll always need a government. We've harped on its use during the thousand years, but I don't think it's limited to the thousand years. I don't think God's government will come to an end at the end of the thousand years. It'll just be promoted to go on. My take on that is, it's to become the government of the universe (whatever that means). We're here working as well as we can, as much as we can see how to, trying to find and do the will of God. We need the Lord to be with us.

We're living in momentous times. Even the world is excited about the calendar dates. This year, 1999, and next year, 2000, are drawing a lot of attention, not only in the religious world, but even in the secular world. I, personally, am not convinced that is such a significant date because that is a date chosen by men. In the first place, it is man's established date. Some preacher or Bible scholar chose to start the calendar at what he thought was the birth of Christ and he missed that. Maybe that was the wisdom of God, just to show him he was out of his will. But I discern no Bible reason, no certain reason, for choosing the birth of Christ to start history over, to have that as a rollover point.

Last year looked like a major year in our history. Our experience was of some important events. Several people let me know that they sensed a judgment spirit during the past year. And, I felt led personally to talk along those lines at the last camp meeting. It seems like God has been dealing with that subject of judgment. It was an important event to us when Brother Angelo was taken from us. He passed away without warning in a moment of time. It was hard to relate that to the subject of judgment. We didn't see anything in his life that would call for judgment.

The same point could be made perhaps about Brother Nick Gruick who is a central figure in the history of this church right here. It ought to be noted that this church is here because of Brother Nick Gruick. He led Brother Goforth to see some of this vision and to share and work with us for a while. He got this church started here in Tyler. I remember coming up to one of his services when they were meeting in what had been a garage. Yeah! A diesel garage, wasn't it? That was where, I think, I first met Brother Goforth, or maybe it was the first time I saw him in Tyler. I saw him in some other meetings in East Texas when he came and visited in our services. He came down to Sebastopol one time. What was that other place, Holly Grove? Yeah, close to Nacogdoches.

I don't know what you'll think about this, but this was the insight I felt God gave me in that case. You know, Isaiah told us that God sometimes takes the righteous away from the evil to come. Isaiah didn't say this part, but it leaves the implication that he leaves the rest of us here to face the evil to come without the help and assistance of those righteous people.

He *was a preacher!* He made an impression wherever he went and he put some of his spirit on his people. I came to another meeting when Brother Nick Gruick was holding a meeting here and they had a little church house. I don't think they owned it. I think they had borrowed it or rented it, or something. We were in a church building, and I remember one brother in that service who would jump up and down. He would get excited and jump up and down like a jumping jack. He would just jump as high as he could, up and down, up and down for five minutes.

After the service was over he was out on the front sidewalk jumping up and down like a jumping jack. Every time you'd say something to him and talk about the good service we had, he would go into his jumping-jack routine. Where is that brother? I wish we had him back; I wish we had him in our midst. We need some people to add life, spice and activity, not let us get stale and settled on our lees, get too comfortable, too dignified. The Lord may stand you on your head sometimes, shake you around. Yeah! Somebody say, "Amen!" The Lord can take your dignity away from you!

Brother Nick Gruick was taken away from us too early. We felt we needed him. It was hard to live without him. The work down in Haiti has continued to thrive, but they sure did miss him. They didn't know whether they would make it or not when he was gone. I know the church here felt that way about Brother Angelo. These men were too good for this world.

How did Paul put that in Hebrews 11? *"Of whom the world was not worthy."* Maybe we weren't worthy, but we're striving to be. We're not going to quit striving. We believe in improving, going further with God. So, I recognize and honor the importance of the ministry. I think these men gathered here tonight are the main part of the ministry that the Lord Jesus is leading in these last days.

I talked the other night at home about our need for humility. We must not get exalted and lifted up with pride. I said that the man in the white dress that was up in St. Louis recently, he may not be called to be humble. Humility may not be a required qualification for his position, but for our position, it is.

Humility is a prerequisite to this ministry. Lack of it can cause a person to lose his ministry, among other things. There are other things that can do that also.

But, we need to be aware of where we are and conscious of the world around us. The world is confused right now, in turmoil about the Y2K problem. There are so many things. The world's economy is still strong in the United States but it's weak in most of the rest of the world. Nobody is certain; everybody is uncertain. Nobody knows what to expect.

All the experts don't have any expert advice about this situation. They will all, almost without exception, if they have any knowledge, will tell you, "We don't know what to expect. It may be bad; it may not be. We don't know what to prepare for." It almost sounds like the four winds of the heavens striving upon the great sea. Do you know what happens when that happens? The results of that is a beast that comes up out of the sea. We are living in that kind of time period and it behooves us to stay close to God and be conscious of his judgments.

With your indulgence, I would like to take some time tonight to talk on the subject of judgment because it's a perpetual, unending task. Judgment will never cease in our midst until we get into the next world. We can never cease to practice and exercise judgment. The higher in God you go, the more you're called on to decide cases and make decisions. I don't think I can cover the subject. I won't even try to touch on all of the scriptures, but I'm going to approach it tonight from the angle of things that interfere with righteous judgment, attitudes and mistakes we make that can prevent us from reaching a righteous decision. We are to approach things from a Biblical standpoint. There are a lot of detailed instructions given. God considered this subject important enough to go into detail about it in the Bible. He gave a lot of the qualifications. David said, "*He that ruleth over men must be just.*" He must be just because he has to practice judgment. If you're not just, your judgment won't be just.

The higher in God you go, as I said, the more authority you are called upon to exercise and the more you need to work at being just. He gave a lot of rules in the Old Testament about how to be a righteous judge. I'm going to start in Exodus 23. The second verse says, *"Thou shalt not follow a multitude to do evil."* This is one way that people miss it, by being influenced by the crowd. You can let yourself be influenced by the crowd. Public opinion weighs a lot. You have to have a pretty thick hide; you have to have alligator hide. I keep telling brethren that, to work in the ministry and stand the opposition and criticism that you have to take, you've got to be almost impervious to public opinion when you sit in judgment on a case. You cannot allow public opinion to influence your decision.

"Neither shalt thou speak in a cause to decline after many," (That word 'many' is synonymous with a multitude.) *"...to wrest judgment."* If we're not careful, the opinion of 'the many' can cause us to wrest our judgment. The next verse: *"Neither shalt thou countenance a poor man in his cause."* The significance of that is, a lot of us just naturally tend to take up for the underdog. We think the poor man is the underdog. We sympathize with him. We're working from sympathy when we approach a case like that. You can't let sympathy sway your judgment.

If you are going to be a righteous judge you can't judge out of sympathy to this person or to that person, what you consider the underdog. You know, he may have been the top dog in the incident created, but you'll forget that because he becomes the underdog the moment he becomes accused when his victims turn on him. They become the accusers and he becomes the accused. You will see him as the underdog, but the victims were the underdog to begin with. They were harmed; they were wounded. They were hurt, but we'll forget them and just take up the cause of the poor man that's being accused and persecuted.

Verse 6 goes along with that same thought: *"Thou shalt not wrest the judgment of thy poor in his cause."* Now when you read that, you automatically think that's saying, "You shall not be hard on the poor." But, he's talking about either way. Don't wrest it either way. Don't be hard on him; don't be easy on him. Be just! Be righteous! Righteous judgment! Don't wrest the judgment of the poor in his cause either way.

Now, the eighth verse is a good one, but I'm going to save it to go with another verse later. I just want to make this statement here that you might want to write down as a key thought: "Sympathy is not the key to justice!" That is not how you decide what just judgment is. Sympathy for anybody does not determine what is right in a case. We will sympathize with people in our condition, if we're not careful, because we identify with them.

It's hard to judge a minister because we are ministers and we want to have an easy judgment, if I can use that term. We want people to be easy on us when they judge us. I'll admit, up front, there is a place for mercy in judgment but we must have judgment before we can have mercy and so, sympathy is not the key to judgment.

People will work on you. They will tell a sorrowful story and make such a plausible case they will influence you. Once they've got your sympathy, they will sway you. They will sway your opinion because they see they've got your attention and you feel for them. We will say, "Well, I've known this man a long time, I don't believe he would do anything like that. I don't believe he would be capable of that," and forget the admonition in Jeremiah. I'll just throw this one in for good measure: Jeremiah 17:9: *"The heart of man is deceitful above all things and desperately wicked. Who can know it?* I don't know of hardly anybody who can know it. Very few people know their own heart.

I used to hear a preacher get up and criticize people for testifying and saying, "If I know my heart, I'm going all the way with God." He would say, "You know your heart! Don't say that! You know whether your heart's with God or not!"

But, a lot of people don't know their heart. They think they're ready to go all the way with God until they run into some of the problems and difficulties that are involved in going on with God. Paul said to the Corinthian church (I believe it was) one time, "*What, know ye not your own selves?*" Evidently he had just figured out they didn't know their own selves. That's a very common condition. A lot of people don't know their own selves. If you're ever going to know other people, you've got to know yourself. That's the only way you'll ever know other people.

"*What man knoweth the things of a man but the spirit of a man that is in him?*" You had better study your own spirit. When you see what's in your own spirit, then you will understand other men, too. But just remember, "*The heart of man is deceitful above all things.*" We're all flesh and anybody is capable of any kind of sin. Any human being living in the flesh is capable of any kind of sin. Not everyone is going to do all of those things, but they could if circumstances were right and they gave over to a certain spirit. It could happen to anybody; it's human nature.

So, let's go on to Leviticus 19:15 where it says, "*Ye shall do no unrighteousness in judgment. Thou shalt not respect the person of the poor nor honor the person of the mighty.*" Neither one! Some people are swayed by sympathy for the poor and others are swayed by respect for the mighty, honor, respect and prestige, and that influences their judgment and disqualifies them from being a judge. "*But in righteousness shalt thou judge thy neighbor.*" To be a righteous judge you've got to put those things out of the picture. The only question at issue in the case you're dealing with is either 'Guilt' or 'Innocence'. Are the accusations true? Is this true? That's what you are called upon to decide. We will come to some instructions about how to do that.

Money, position, reputation or influence cannot decide your judgment. Those things have to be laid aside when you sit in judgment on a case to be able to judge righteously. Going back to Exodus 23:8, we will read that verse and put it with another one in Deuteronomy: "*Thou shalt take no gift, for the gift blindeth the wise,*" (W-I-S-E—WISE! I want everybody to get that!) "*...and perverteth the words of the righteous.*" Putting that together with Deuteronomy 16:19 which makes the same point in practically the same words, "*Thou shalt not wrest judgment.*

Thou shalt not respect persons, neither take a gift for a gift doth blind the eyes of the wise and pervert the words of the righteous."

You've got to lay some emphasis on that, brethren, on that word 'wise'. We all think we're wise; we don't think we can be swayed. We're too smart for that! We can see through the ruses, but a gift, little favors that have been done over the years, all the good that a person has done in your church or to you personally, or to other people, those things have to be laid aside in judgment or they will pervert the words of the righteous; they will blind the eyes of the wise.

You say, "I know him too well. He's done too much good; he's never done me any harm. You will forget the people that have been done harm because of all the favors and good things and help that person has given. That translates as a gift. We have all received gifts from one another; we have been receiving gifts from one another. I appreciate all the help that I have received from different brethren in here, but if judgment comes up, we cannot consider that in the judgment when trying to arrive at a verdict, a conclusion, because *"A gift blinds the eyes of the wise."*

Now, we come to the investigation. Deuteronomy 13:14 says, (This is about idolatry, but the advice applies to any kind of investigation.) *"Then shalt thou enquire and make search and ask diligently and behold, if it be truth and the thing certain..."* See how much emphasis he lays on finding out the truth! Don't take anything for granted! Don't fall for the first accusation or the first denial, but consider and investigate and search out; ask questions. Make sure, because you are handling people's lives; souls are at stake. This burden is heavy! If you don't have to judge, don't do it if you can let somebody else do it! If there is somebody else that can do it, let them do it!

Judgment is dangerous! You can get in trouble exercising judgment! You've got to find out if the thing is certain or not. The same thought is in Deuteronomy 17:4. This seventeenth chapter has a lot of good things in it about judgment. *"...and it be told thee and thou hast heard of it."* First, you heard of it and inquired diligently and asked questions and checked it out; pursued leads, investigated. You've got to do some detective work. "*...and behold, if it be true and the thing certain...,*" That's what you are looking for: to make sure that the thing is certain. You've got to be clear; you've got to be certain. You've got to have good evidence.

Down in verse 6 he said, "*At the mouth of two witnesses or three witnesses shall he that is worthy of death be put to death.*" This may not apply to us directly but the point I want to show is that the number of witnesses makes the difference. "*At the mouth of one witness he shall not be put to death.*" They couldn't put anyone to death, give them a death sentence on the strength of just one testimony.

There had to be more than one witness for that. You look for several witnesses and then when the thing is decided, when the judges—and this may be good advice to do it in the plural in serious cases. You are bearing a heavy burden if you judge a serious case alone, all by yourself, because your judgment may be called into question. You need some support. It's good to have advice, not trust altogether to your own judgment, but share the case with somebody else. The plurality of judges is a safety for everybody.

When the judgment is made—we're going to skip down to verse 10, "*When the judgment is made,*" he says, "*Thou shalt do according to the sentence which they of that place which the Lord shall choose shall shew thee and thou shalt observe to do according to all that they inform thee.*" See, everybody in the congregation is not going to get to investigate these things. Not everybody gets to search out these cases. Somebody is faced with that responsibility and he deserves the support and trust and confidence of the people that are behind him and the other people out in the populace.

Brother Kennedy here is going to have to judge cases occasionally in this church. It will fall his lot to make a decision about somebody's life, somebody's position, somebody's place in the church. And when he's done these investigations, he will have searched it out; he will have talked to the people involved.

He's the one that heard the testimony. Nobody else has any right to form a different opinion unless they get to hear the same testimonies that he heard! Do you get that point? Nobody has the right to challenge the judges and criticize their decision unless they've heard the same people, the same witnesses, and the same accusers as the judge has heard.

Of course, most of us will never get to do that in any particular case. We will have to take it from somebody else. Most of the time, we have to accept somebody else's word for what happened. Everybody can't check it out. Everybody is not called on; everybody doesn't have the opportunity. The people have to accept the word of the one that did.

Don't just talk to one person involved and then form an opinion that wrong judgment was handed down; that somebody was misjudged, somebody was abused or somebody was mistreated just because they denied their guilt. Do you understand that you do not have to extract a confession in order to convict somebody? They don't have to admit what they did to be judged if you've got enough evidence. You've got to weigh the evidence. You can pass judgment without a confession if you've got enough evidence. You've got to weigh and consider the witnesses. Instruction to the rest of the crowd is to do according to that sentence that the judge has handed down. In verse 12, he says, *"And the man that will do presumptuously,"* Presumptuously means self-willed and rebellious, independent minded. *"...and will not hearken unto the priest or the judge, even that man shall die."* That's how serious this is!

This is not talking about the criminal; it's talking about the people that sympathize with the criminal! They can lose their soul over it! And sometimes, do! Sadly, sometimes they do lose their soul over sympathizing with the wrongdoer. So, you see how serious this is. You have no right to disagree with the people who heard the evidence and made the decision because you are not going to get to hear the evidence. You're not going to get to make the investigation.

Now, we want to come to Matthew; we'll come to the New Testament now and deal with a few thoughts and scriptures in the New Testament. There is not near as much on judgment in the New Testament as there is in the Old Testament because the foundation of the subject had already been laid down in the Old Testament. Nothing in the New Testament negates those detailed instructions in the Old Testament. That was just; that was good advice. Those were excellent rules that were given by Moses and are not discarded or overruled in the New Testament.

But, the Spirit is added and some more thoughts on mercy and forgiveness and love. There is more emphasis laid on these things in the New Testament and yet, the thought of judgment runs through the New Testament. "*Judgment must begin at the house of God,*" and "*We shall all stand before the judgment seat of Christ,*" and "*Ye shall be judged according to the things written in the books and the deeds done in the body,*" and even for every idle word. He says you are going to give an account. So, the thought of judgment is strong throughout the New Testament.

Matthew 18 is frequently brought up, beginning in verse 15. But really, this passage is not primarily a judgment passage; it's about reconciliation. This is not talking to the judge. This passage is not to the judge; it's to the aggrieved parties, the parties that are having a conflict with each other. It's the way for them to achieve reconciliation and make peace, if they can, without going before a judge. It does, finally, end up in judgment when it goes before the church. Of course, it ends up in judgment if reconciliation cannot be effected because of intransigence of one or more parties. This is a reconciliation passage where, "*If your brother trespass against thee, go and tell him his fault between thee and him alone.*" See, the judge is not the party trespassed against. He has another job, another purpose in mind.

I wanted to make that clear about how to use that passage if we bring it in on judgment. I won't turn to this one; I'll just remind you of the judgment that fell in Acts 5 on Ananias and Sapphira. There was no investigation made; there was no mercy shown. That was an outstanding case wasn't it? It was a severe case. It was judged severely and yet it doesn't look that bad to us. These two people brought an offering and fell dead!

Who could help but sympathize with them? *Be careful! I told you, sympathy is not the key to judgment!*

It's hard not to sympathize with Ananias and Sapphira when you consider their circumstances. Surely, they didn't realize fully the enormity of their crime. They didn't expect God to judge them that way for what they did. It seemed like a little thing to them. Most sinners commonly do minimize their sins. They are not willing, it seems, to see the enormity of their crimes. It may be that Peter got a little criticism from people in the town. I've run into people in my time that actually criticized Peter for killing those people!

Look what a trauma that was to the church! Two people fell dead right there before the altar, before the pulpit in the church! All they were doing was trying to give an offering and that old Bigshot Peter, just looked down and pronounced judgment on them! They fell dead! Some people might have been tempted to get mad at Peter over that. I have heard people point out that Peter created a problem in the church; he was cruel and unmerciful. They fail to recognize that Peter did not kill those people. God killed those people!

You know, the same thing happened in the wilderness when Moses had all the people separate themselves from the tents of Korah, Dathan and Abiram. The earth opened up and swallowed those people. A few days later, you have the crowd rising up, criticizing Moses, saying, "*You've killed the people of the Lord, you rascal you!*" as if Moses made the ground open up! Boy! They gave him credit for a lot of power that day! Other days, they didn't think he had any power when they were thirsty and hungry, didn't think he could do anything to feed them! But, they gave him credit for a lot of power when they were mad at him and were jealous and critical of his power! I think another plague broke out as a result of that criticism.

So, there are times when there is no chance to investigate; it just doesn't figure in the case. Another similar example, but a different kind of case was in I Corinthians where Paul ruled on a case from a distance. He didn't go over there and investigate it. Of course, no investigation was needed. This was a public case; everybody knew the circumstances. The argument was not over guilt or innocence, it was over whether it deserved any punishment, or not. Paul just ruled from a distance. He took the word of the people that brought it to him and said, "*Go back over there and put that man out of the church.*" That probably brings up the question of penalties.

This is where the questions are most likely to come up: "What is a just penalty?" I don't think I can answer that, but just suggest that we must do things in the Spirit and pray and seek the will of God. We must go by precedence and other cases we know about, cases in the Bible. But, ultimately, every case stands on its own merits. You can't go around comparing cases and trying to do everything the same way. It's like trying to treat everybody just alike.

Aren't you glad that God doesn't treat us all just alike? God has to get rough with some people. Aren't you glad he doesn't get rough with you? You don't want him to treat you like that, do you? So, we want God to treat everybody just alike. But, you can't treat everybody just alike. You can't judge two cases just alike because there will be different circumstances; there will be different motives.

There will be different degrees of understanding. You know God looks at that, don't you? He considers how far a person has come. And finally, if a person has come to the full knowledge of the truth, He said, "*There remaineth no more repentance but a certain fearful looking for of wrath and fiery indignation which shall devour the adversaries.*" It gets hot close to God and he's a consuming fire! He devours the adversaries!

Yet, God is merciful, loving and kind and he treats... You know penalties may be mitigated by the attitude of the guilty person, whether he is truly, properly, fully repentant, or not. This seems to figure in the case of David. David committed a grave sin, a terrible sin. It wasn't just a case of adultery; it was a case of murder to cover-up adultery and to try to extricate himself from the situation. He just made it worse.

Sometimes, that is what you do when you try to fix it up. You've made a mistake; you've committed a sin and you try to find some way to hide it. It's like we used to say when we were little kids when somebody told what we thought was a whopper. We would say, "You'd better tell another one to prop that one up." One lie calls for another; one lie leads to another one, calls forth another one.

David's efforts to hide his sin—look at the trouble he went to; look at all the efforts he made to hide his sin. He sent a messenger of the army and called for that woman's husband to be sent home and thought, "Surely he will come home and go straight to his wife because he's been away from her for a long time. They are young and in love. They will want to be together and that'll fix everything!" But, he didn't count on the particular degree of dedication that was in this soldier. This man had high principles.

You have to admire Uriah. I don't guess he was even an Israelite. He was a Hittite, a foreigner that had immigrated to Israel and joined David's army. But he, I guess, had become a proselyte and accepted the Israelite religion. He was associating and living together with them. He had high principles.

Sometimes, people that come from out in the world may have higher principles than we who were raised in here. If you don't watch out, we've always been warned, people are going to come in here and go around you. You hold onto your seat! Somebody may get it away from you just because you don't qualify for it, don't any longer deserve it.

That man had high principles and rather than take personal advantage of his mission, called to deliver a message to the king. When the rest of his buddies in the army couldn't take that advantage, they didn't have that opportunity to go home; he would not take that advantage but slept with the palace guard that night. David found out about that the next day and so he called him in for a banquet. He fed him up with wine and strong food, made him sleepy and half drunk and thought, "Surely, that will befuddle his mind until he will end up at home." But, that didn't work, either. That man had too much principle.

Also, I guess God was in it. You have to look for God in everything, don't you? No doubt, God was setting that up. He would not let David's sin get covered up. He was determined for it to be exposed. There are some people that God wants their sins exposed. There comes a time when he wants to have it exposed and make an example out of it. So, he made a public example out of David's case. It was humiliating; it was tragic and it was embarrassing. It was shameful, but David repented. He never denied his guilt after that effort to cover it up failed.

When the prophet approached him, he threw up his hands and gave up and quit denying; he just cast himself on the mercy of God. If God was ready to put him out of the ministry, he was ready to quit the ministry right then. That was a good spirit David had. He showed that again, years later, while he was still paying the price for his sin. When his son, Absalom, was seeking his life, he had to flee for his life, take his family with him and leave Jerusalem, hoofing it down a dusty road. The priest brought out the Ark of the Covenant and said, "*We'll go with you and take this with us.*" That was something precious to have the Ark of the Covenant with you. It was almost like having that pillar of cloud and pillar of fire with you. David, undoubtedly, was tempted with that. It would have felt good to have the Ark of the Covenant traveling with him, but he thought it over and said, "*Take it back to the city. If God has any pleasure in me, he will bring me back again and show me the Ark and his habitation, both it and his habitation. But if he thus say, I have no delight in you, here am I. Let him do with me as seemeth good unto him.*"

It's hard to find anybody that will say that. He was ready to suffer judgment and justify God in it. That calls a scripture to my mind from somewhere in the Psalms and it's quoted somewhere in Romans, something like this, "*That thou mightest be justified in thy sayings.*" Is that the fifty-first Psalm? "*Overcome when thou are judged.*" Somebody look up the version of it in Romans. I guess this is part of David's confession. Psalms 51:4: "*Against thee, thee only have I sinned and done this evil in thy sight that thou mightest be justified when thou speakest and be clear when thou judgest.*"

Has anybody found that one in Romans? Romans 3:4. I want to see Paul's New Testament version of it. *"God forbid. Yea, let God be true but every man a liar as it is written, that thou* (meaning God) *mightest be justified in thy saying and mightest overcome when thou art judged."* Did you ever think that God would get judged? Who judges God? Who qualifies to judge him? Well, nobody, but people do it all the time. You may have done it a time or two. Did you ever criticize God? Say, "God shouldn't have done that. God shouldn't have let my little baby die. God shouldn't have taken my mother away. God shouldn't have taken Brother Angelo away so soon!" If we're not careful, we will judge God.

David's position was to admit that he was wrong and God was right. That's how you justify God. We admit that God was right so God will be justified before the world. The world won't be tempted to join us in criticizing God. You're always hearing this question: "If there's a good God, then why do so many bad things happen to good people?" I read an article in an editorial page one time that asked, "Where are all these good people that bad things are happening to?"

We've all sinned and come short of the glory of God. There is none good but God. There are not so many good people around so it's not hard to find a good person that bad things are happening to. Bad things do happen to people that don't deserve it. The story of Job is an example of that, but I'm not going any further into that. I just wanted to use this to show that David gave glory to God. He confessed his weakness, his faults and flaws, his humanness, shall we call it, that God might be justified. He put himself in the hands of God, even to accept being set aside if that would be God's will.

Don't you admire David for that? Is there anybody in here that could say what David said, *"Here am I. If he find no delight in me, Here am I, let him do with me as seemeth good unto him."*

Another point I want to make in connection with that—I don't have a scripture on the tip of my tongue, but several times in the book of Psalms, it says, *"Judge me."* Have you ever prayed for judgment? Did you ever ask God for judgment? We're scared to. We don't want to be judged. We're saying, "Lord, don't judge me." We've got to get to the place where we can say, "Judge me, Lord, judge me." You've got to have a lot of confidence toward God, as John said, to do that and not be afraid in the day of judgment.

Not in his wrath—I don't mean to ask him to judge me without mercy. Judge me, but not in your wrath; with mercy. *"Not in your hot displeasure lest you bring me to nothing."* But, we do want to get to that place where we're not afraid to say, "Judge me." That's really what John, the point he was making there in chapter 3 or 4, maybe. Chapter 2, verse 28 says, "*... and now little children abide in him that, when he shall appear we may have confidence and not be ashamed before him at his coming.*"

How will you have confidence? Well, if you've been abiding in him, then you haven't been sinning; you don't have anything to be ashamed of. You can have confidence he will accept you and won't have wrath to place upon you. Chapter 3, verses 19, 20: *"And hereby we know that we are of the truth and shall assure our hearts before him."* I would like to have my heart assured before the Lord. I would like to feel that blessed assurance that all is right between me and God, that he hasn't got anything against me.

If God's holding something against you, then you have to be afraid in his presence. *"For if our heart condemn us, God is greater than our heart and knoweth all things."* The point of that is, if my heart is condemning me, it's because it knows something I've done wrong. My heart knows what I've been doing. There's somebody greater than my heart that knows what I've been doing. If my heart condemns me, God will condemn me, too. He knows the same thing my heart knows, so I'll be in trouble. I won't feel comfortable in the presence of God.

Verse 21: *"Beloved, if our heart condemn us not, then have we confidence toward God."* We won't be afraid in his presence because our heart doesn't condemn us. Now, I'll admit that my heart might be ignorant of something but this is the kind of thing that Paul said, *"God shall reveal even this unto us."* If we've gotten to the point where our heart doesn't know anything to condemn us of, if God's still got anything to condemn us of, he'll let us know about it. He'll give us a chance to fix it up, send those sins on beforehand to judgment. So, we can have confidence in him.

Finally, in 4:17, he said, *"Herein is our love made perfect, that we may have boldness in the day of judgment."* Do you want to have boldness in the day of judgment, or do you want to come up to the judgment bar of Christ trembling, fearful, shaking and afraid? There's a way you can come boldly to the throne of grace. We may have boldness in the day of judgment because, *"As he is, so are we in this world."* That's an interesting comment right there. The reason we can have boldness in the day of judgment is because we have become like him. Jesus said, *"Be perfect as your Father in heaven is perfect."*

The illustration he gave of that was in being good to people, loving people. God makes it rain on the just and the unjust; makes the sun rise on the evil and on the good. That's a measure of his perfection. John said here, if we're in this condition "*as he is* (as God is), *so are we in this world.*"

Well, how is he? How is God? Your answer is up in the previous verse. Verse 16 says, *"God is love, and he that dwelleth in love dwelleth in God."* So, God is love up there in the heavens, and as he is, so are we in this world. Are you love? You say God is love. Can you say, "I am love?" Why can't we? If we can, we can have boldness in the day of judgment.

That was a digression I got onto there. I never did finish up on repentance and pardon and penalties and stuff like that. There's another point or two I want to make before I quit. A lot of people, when they repent and receive forgiveness, expect to be exempted from any penalty. That doesn't always follow. You can be forgiven and still be penalized.

I think this is in Numbers 14. This is where the twelve spies went out and came back and the crowd offended God by refusing to go take the land. To top it off, they threatened to stone Moses and Joshua and Caleb, saying, *"Let's elect us another captain to lead us back into Egypt. We'll rebel against Moses. We're tired of this leadership. He hasn't led us into a land that flows with milk and honey. We'll choose another leader and let him lead us back to Egypt."* God got so offended over that he said, *"I'll wipe them all out, Moses, and let you have children and raise up another generation to follow me."*

But Moses interceded there and asked God to pardon the people. It wasn't the people themselves repenting in this case, but Moses repented for them and begged God to pardon the people. God said, *"I have pardoned according to your word. Nevertheless, all the earth shall be filled with my glory and not one of these people that have rebelled against me here will ever see the Promised Land. They'll all die in this wilderness."* He pardoned, but he placed a heavy penalty on them.

Look at poor old Moses himself. Wasn't that something? Such a little thing; such a simple mistake! It looked like God was expecting perfection out of Moses. Another point to be made on that is, this was down toward the end of Moses' life when God was expecting more of him than he did earlier in his life. Now, Moses put up a big argument with God back there when he was starting out in the ministry. God was calling him at the burning bush and Moses brought up every objection; he invented every kind of excuse. Finally, he ran out of excuses and just backed out anyway and said, "I can't do it. Get somebody else." God got mad at him but didn't penalize him there because he was young and green. He was a beginner in the ministry and God was tolerant and patient with him.

But years later, after Moses had grown old in God, He expected more of him. He expected more faith, more obedience. When Moses slipped up that time by striking the rock when he was told to speak to it, God said, *"Your penalty is, you won't get to see the Promised Land."* Oh, that was heartbreaking to Moses! That would have capped his career if he could have led the children of Israel across that river! That was what he lived for. That was the crowning glory of his vision, his ministry, and he had to give it up.

He tried, a time or two, to change God's mind on that. He

tried to talk him out of it. He reminded him just before he died, *"Lord, couldn't you let me go over there and see that land?"* and God said, *"No, don't speak to me anymore about that. Don't ask me again. That's all I'm going to hear about it."* There was no chance of changing God's mind about that. But it was such a little thing that it's hard for us not to sympathize with Moses. If we had been there, we wouldn't have had the patience and faith that he had, most of us. And, most of the time, Moses' faith was firm. I guess his faith wavered a little bit that one time.

If you were called on to perform as many miracles as Moses did, yours might waver now and then. He had helped work all those miracles down in the land of Egypt. He waved his rod over the Red Sea and divided it. He struck a rock and water came out of it. He did miracle after miracle after miracle at the command of God.

After a while, even your faith gets tired and you get to wondering, "Will it work this time?" Don't you have that problem? God stood by you so many times, but when you get in a jam again you wonder, "Is it gonna work this time? Will he stand by me this time?" Lord, help us!

Question from audience—not understood.

Well, that's one thing all right, but the comment that God made there, I forget how he worded it when he rebuked Moses. It implied that he failed to believe: *"Because you believed me not...."* That suggests to me that Moses' faith weakened right there and he remembered. So, you have to wonder: Why did he smite the rock? Was it because he wondered is it going to work this time? God just told him to speak to it. He remembered the last time he had to bring water out of a rock that he had hit it with a stick and it worked. Maybe it would be all right to speak and hit it with a stick, too, this time.

We sure don't want to fail. That's the way you'll feel when your faith gets weak. You forget how many times God has stood by you if you did it *JUST HIS WAY!* When you do it your way, things go wrong. God still may bring it out to where the people's needs are met, but you'll pay a penalty. Moses paid a price for that, for not sanctifying God with faith that one time. Then, there's one more passage that's really depressing. It's in Ezekiel 3 and warns us what can happen if we miss God and don't straighten it up.

Verse 20: "*When a righteous man doth turn from his righteousness...,*" Oh, that's a sad saying! That's depressing already, to think of a righteous man turning from his righteousness! "*Again, when a righteous man doth turn from his righteousness and commit iniquity and I lay a stumbling block before him...,*" That's what follows. When a righteous man turns from his righteousness and commits iniquity too long, too many times, God will finally lay a stumbling block in front of him to cause him to fall and be exposed. That's the result that God brings about. He causes those things to happen. God will lay a stumbling block before him and he shall die, he said, "*... because thou has not given him warning.*"

This is a passage about warning the wicked. He shall die in his sin if you didn't warn him. And here's what's so heavy and hard to accept: "*His righteousness which he hath done shall not be remembered.*" See, you can lose all your history, all your record, all the things you've done for God and God's people if you don't stand firm to the end. Stand fast! Hold fast that which you have! Don't let anything steal your testimony!

It's been done. You can lose all the credit you had built up. All those favors and gifts that you did for God's people can be forgotten, wasted, lost because of not responding correctly to some temptation.

That's about all I have to say tonight and I don't intend for this necessarily to be the subject for the meeting. I wasn't trying to establish a theme for the meeting. I just felt like this was relevant. It's pertinent to our times and, in fact, it's pertinent to all times. These things keep coming up over and over and over and we have to remind ourselves how to handle them. Any points I've made, if the brethren want to discuss, feel free to do it, or any different subject can be brought up on a different line.

Thank you for your attention.

Chapter 5

Personal History; Early Pentecost

July 4, 1999

Sadly, what happened to Pentecost was, before a score of years went by, they were building prison houses. We Holy Ghost people went to building prison houses and organizing things against each other. The controversy arose back there in the teens of this century between the different positions on the godhead. Then that brought, I guess, the first big division on how to baptize in water. Those two subjects brought big divisions between the Holy Ghost people. They started churches to organize against each other and to protect their membership from one another. They sometimes formed raiding parties and went to steal somebody out of another church, splitting that church wide open, taking half the people down the street a few blocks and starting another church, building another jail house. They warned their people, "Don't you go anywhere else! Don't you go visit those other people!"

I thank God! I guess I call myself lucky, if that's a valid term. Is that a spiritual term? Is the word fortunate acceptable? Are we fortunate? I'll accept 'blessed'. I feel like I was blessed to be born spiritually outside of those walls. I got the Holy Ghost out in what we used to call 'Free Pentecost'. It was in a backward part of the country, about as east as you could get in East Texas. That was pretty backward in those days in the middle Forties. Somebody used to say we were so far back in the woods that we didn't hear the Saturday night Grand Old Opry until Wednesday night!

We hadn't heard about all the arguments and divisions in Pentecost when I got the Holy Ghost. About all we were hearing was about the Holy Ghost. Preachers came through there preaching the Holy Ghost and baptizing us in the Sabine River or Palo Gaucho Creek. We got the Holy Ghost and talked in tongues and loved each other. We loved our brothers and sisters in those days. There were only a few of us; we needed each other bad. We had lots of opposition and enemies in the country and we sure needed some friends.

When we would get a rumor that another apostolic family had moved in up across the creek, we would get excited. We didn't think to ask, "What do they believe about the godhead? How do they baptize in water?" We didn't know there was any controversy over that. We just heard they were apostolic people and knew that meant they talked in tongues; they had the Holy Ghost. They were somebody we could fellowship with.

About the only kind of fellowship we had for a while was to walk a mile or two down to the creek and meet a neighbor family from across the creek. We met there on the bank of the creek and had a picnic and a prayer meeting. That was our fellowship meeting, two families getting together and having a prayer meeting.

All the people who came to the prayer meeting didn't believe. Ovie's parents-in-law, they didn't believe this stuff! They were ashamed of their daughter-in-law, but they came to the picnic anyhow to dip snuff, eat pie and criticize. They did their share of criticizing! When Ovie got full of the Spirit, shut her eyes and took a running fit, she ran straight toward a pine tree. You would think she had busted her nose open on the pine tree, but just as she got to the pine tree, she did a circle. She danced a circle around that pine tree and came back with her eyes still shut. Her mother-in-law mumbled behind her snuff box, "She saw that tree!" But, she didn't; she had her eyes closed.

We thought, in those days, you couldn't get in the Spirit if you had your eyes open, so we clinched our eyes tight shut when the Spirit came on us. No telling what could have happened to us. It's a wonder we didn't run off down the creek bank into the creek.

We were hungry for the family of God. We were hungry for fellowship. We enticed preachers to come to our community and hold revival meetings. We prayed people through to the

Holy Ghost. We enjoyed the people of God. It was just Pentecostal people. That's all we had heard of. There weren't any organizations to separate us at the time, but there was a rumor about this Godhead problem.

Dad would load up the old, single-seater, 1937 Chevrolet, prop up the turtle hull and fill it full with about five people. Three or four people would be hanging on the running board and sitting on the front fenders. We went to a fellowship meeting one time with thirteen people in and on that single-seater car. We arrived at church and people came spilling out of that car. It was like, in more recent times, when college kids would see how many people they could pack into a Volkswagen or telephone booth. We would see how many people we could pack into that Chevrolet and go to a fellowship meeting.

We moved off down to Beaumont for six months when I was a little boy. We were already hearing about those trinity churches and we didn't dare go visit any of them. Once in a while, we would meet one of them somewhere and get into an argument. Any time a Oneness met a Trinitarian, the fur flew; the sparks flew! We couldn't keep from getting into a verbal fight. But, we didn't stay in Beaumont long enough to get acquainted with all the ways of the Pentecostal people. Dad lost his job at the shipyard and we went back to the farm and carried on like we did before.

Dad finally became pastor of a little church over in Louisiana. He pastored there for several years. I guess I had already gone away to college when the organizing preachers began to come through our part of the country trying to round up all the free churches, enticing them into the organization. That became a big issue, the new thing. That was the new move. The big question in everybody's minds was, "Should we join the organization, or not?" Now, I don't remember which organization it was that was trying to take up our country churches.

Dad heard about a certain preacher from the organization that was going to be at a wedding at the house of one of our friends who lived about twenty miles away. He decided to go to the wedding and meet that preacher and find out more about it. He wanted to size the thing up. He was praying about what to do. Should he join the organization, or not?

So, he went to the wedding and that preacher from the organization was there. Dad listened to the conversation. They were talking about religious affairs and church affairs all around that county and the neighboring county. Somebody finally asked that preacher, "Have you been to the church down at Quicksand?"

Dad said that preacher reared back in his chair and said, "No, I haven't been down there, yet. Fact is, those people are not in fellowship yet." Dad pricked up his ears. He thought, "What? Not in fellowship? Why are they not in fellowship? Do you mean because they have not joined the organization you can't fellowship people like that?!" He began to get a bad taste in his mouth and left that wedding. He was driving home alone through the black of the night, one of those dark East Texas nights. There were no street lights; I don't know if there was a moon out that night, or not. While he was driving down those country roads, it was boiling in his mind, "Not in fellowship, yet!" He was bothered by that.

All at once a voice spoke into his head, or a thought came from somewhere, and these words came to him: *"Dead flies cause the ointment of the apothecary to send forth a stinking savor; so doth a little folly him that is in reputation for wisdom and honor."* Dad thought, "What is that? Where did that come from? Is it a quotation from Shakespeare, or is that from some poem? Is that in the Bible?"

He made it on home and got out his Sears and Roebuck mail order Cruden's Concordance and began to look for it. Sure enough, he found it in Ecclesiastes 10 where it said exactly those words: *"Dead flies cause the ointment of the apothecary to send forth a stinking savor; so doth a little folly him that is in reputation for wisdom and honor."*

Dad began to see that there was a little folly in that big preacher. That big preacher from the organization was in reputation for wisdom and honor. He had a big name, a big fellowship, but he showed a little folly there that Dad picked up on. Not everybody else saw it.

You know, you can be foolish and somebody may think you're smart. They may think you're smart when you are being foolish. The wisdom of this world is foolishness with God anyway and the wisdom of God is foolishness to the world. You've got to learn how to measure wisdom and foolishness.

That man may have thought he was being smart, showing his power or something in saying he would not soil his hands by visiting a church somewhere that wasn't a member of his organization, but that came across as folly to Dad. That is one of the things that convinced my dad to stay out of the organization. We stayed free until God led us to this Body of people. We found that there were people that God was moving on, talking to, giving revelations to and had never formed an organization.

We have a strong fellowship, but it is a voluntary fellowship. You can get in it or get out of it any time you want to. There is no test that you have to pass. If you speak in tongues, if you have the Holy Ghost, you're one of us. If you don't speak in tongues, you haven't got the Holy Ghost. You are welcome here. We will try to help you get the Holy Ghost, but you're not yet one of us because that is how you get into it. You are born into it. The birth of the Spirit is what puts you in the kingdom of Heaven. Until that time, you can be accepted as a member of the family of God in the flesh, just like every Jew for 1,500 years was in the family of God.

That was God's family in the earth, but they were in the flesh, and flesh and blood don't inherit the kingdom of Heaven. Every Jew needed to get born again. His natural birth that made him a full-blood Jew wasn't sufficient to put him in the kingdom of Heaven; he needed another birth. They began to get it in the second chapter of Acts. After Jesus went back to the Father in Heaven, he shed forth this which you've been seeing and hearing. Thank God for what we can see and hear! Amen! You can pick it up; you can detect it.

Don't come here expecting to sit by quietly and have a solemn service where you can hear a pin drop, where the preacher doesn't dare raise his voice and nobody will testify! Don't expect a service like that! You can see and hear something here! And if your spiritual senses are alert, you can feel something. You can feel something when the power of God comes into these meetings!

That's the kind of freedom we're looking for, the freedom from deception, false religion; freedom from sin, carnality and lust, all these things. Jesus set people free from a lot of things. They are not all the same, but it all comes under that freedom that you get with the Holy Ghost. With the Holy Ghost, you get born into the kingdom of Heaven. You don't need somebody to vote on you, to enroll your name on a church book for you to be a member, for you to be in. People sometimes ask us, "How do we join your church? How do you get to be a member?"

Well, we say, "Just come, the doors are open. If we see you out there every service, we will decide you're a member.

Sometimes, preachers want to know, "How can I get in this ministry? I would like to have one of your churches." One preacher came by here and said, "Brother Patton, I'd like to have a church in this fellowship. I wouldn't want one this big; I couldn't handle it. There's too much work to it, but I'd like to have a little church like this."

We don't have any machinery where we can provide that. You just come and God decides. The Lord Jesus is the head of the church. God has made him that. God has made Jesus both Lord and Christ. Jesus said, one time, *"All power in Heaven and earth is given unto me."* He was recognizing someone greater than himself when he said somebody gave it to him. You might be able to argue that Jesus can be called 'Almighty' because he's got all power, but he didn't invent it; somebody gave it to him. Whoever gave it to him has all power, too. Whoever gave it to him has all power because he didn't give it away when he gave it.

When God gives you power, he doesn't lose any. It doesn't weaken him a bit to give you some power. He can give you plenty of power and still have all the power he had to start with. Praise God for the power we get when we get the Holy

Ghost! Jesus told them that way back there, "*You shall receive power when the Holy Ghost is come upon you.*" That power was the power to overcome self, mainly. It's the power to stay on that cross. If you don't have a lot of power, you won't stay on your cross; you won't bear your cross without a lot of power. If you are too weak, you will lay it down and run off. You will come down off that cross.

Jesus could have come down off the cross. He had enough power to do that, but he also had enough power to stay up there. God bless him for staying up there! We're glad he didn't come down off the cross! He stayed there until he died on his cross. That's what you've got to do spiritually; you've got to put the old man to death.

Chapter 6

The Church Through the Ages

June 2000, Camp Meeting

I think all the things that happen at this camp meeting are important. The prayer lines, the songs, the teachings, I think God's in all of it. I just feel the honor and privilege of being a part of this. It keeps us in the middle of the road, keeps us from missing God many times. Listening to each other keeps us from missing God. So, I'm glad for all that's going on here in this camp meeting.

By the way, I was glad to see us here on the platform, sitting down in time to listen to the band play a while ago. A lot of the time we are so busy talking when we get in here, we've got so much business to conduct and so many conferences to have here on the platform that we don't get to listen to the band. They're finished before we all get through and quieted down.

Years ago, I had a record of classical music in my collection. It was an album of overtures they described (I'm not a musical expert) and defined on the jacket the record was in, as being frequently used to introduce an opera, a short piece of orchestral music. That would be used as the introduction to a program of music. They said that an overture frequently begins with loud, crashing chords to get the crowd's attention. That's to signal that it's time to stop visiting, sit down and quiet down. They call that 'Sit-down-and-be-quiet' chords.

The band plays our 'sit-down-and-be-quiet' music. We're supposed to sit down and get our minds on the Lord and settle down for the service, unless it's a signal to get up and shout. Sometimes, it turns into that, doesn't it? It can be a signal to get up and shout.

I was especially struck by the performance of the band in one of the services in our Houston meeting back in February. Brother Charles Gray was conducting. I thought the Lord brought in a special spirit that night. Some of you will remember it. Some people don't notice music, but those of us that do, notice when the Lord moves in the music. I thought there was something special about that spirit, something we seldom feel. It reminded me of the spirit that moved in here at the camp meeting where we had the repenting service. That was a spirit that we didn't know how to continue in.

Maybe there isn't any way; maybe we can't stay up on that level. It may be just a high point, a peak experience that God gives us once in a while. But, it does suggest to me that God wants to take us deeper in the Spirit. I sense something coming. I want God's people to be encouraged. God is moving us on. He isn't going to let us stay on the level we've been on. We've got to be prepared to go deeper with God and let him deal with us in spiritual ways.

We've had some deep experiences on this campground. It was—what?—forty-seven years ago when the 'New Experience' (We called it that; we didn't know what else to call it.) came in such a special move of God? It continued for a long time. It went on for days at a time. That was my first trip to the campground. I was brand new to this body. I sat up there in the balcony, stood up a lot of times, and looked out over this platform full of great ministers. I watched as people were slain under the Spirit of God, the power of God moving.

I remember one young man who was so carried away he was turning somersaults continually up there in the balcony. His father was trying to explain to everybody, "He's a very demonstrative young man; he's a cheerleader." His point was, you've got to look over him. He was a little embarrassed about it.

A lot of people were demonstrative in that meeting because God was doing something for us in the Spirit. Sadly, after that, the Lord let us go through shakings and hard experiences, unpleasant things; and has many times since. We've seen cycles, moves and waves of the Glory of God and we've seen times of trials and testing. I just want to remind us that God was with us all the time. He was with us in all of those experiences and he's still with us today.

There are new people here. This is brand new to them like it was for me in 1953. Everything is tasty; everything is exciting. Even the bad things that were happening in the '50s were interesting to me. I was just eating it up! I was watching the warfare take place, watching the fights, spiritual fights on the platform and that was just feeding my soul. I didn't know any better; I didn't know the danger.

They say that's why they send young men into battle; they're too ignorant to know the danger. They're not as frightened by bullets and shells as more mature people are. There are people here today that this is new to. Everything looks good, perhaps, to you. The longer you stay around, the more you'll begin to pick out the weak points and the problems in the people of God. You've got to take that and keep your faith strong. You've got to be able to see things done wrong, see moves made wrong, see times when we miss God and you've got to take that and not let your faith be shaken by it. You've got to be able to see the battles break out and the wrong spirits show up.

It can happen at any time. It could come through me if I'm not careful. I could show a wrong spirit on the threshing floor or anywhere else on the grounds here. Somebody may mistreat you. It won't take you long in these meetings, now, to have your seat stolen. Lord, help us!

Thank God for the crowd! Isn't it a blessing to have to scramble for a seat? Isn't it wonderful to have such a hard time getting a seat? Isn't that great? It's because God has blessed us. We're to look at it that way and see the favor of God showing through, not let that affect your faith in God and faith in the move of God. Every move of God has been riddled with problems.

Let me talk to you for a minute about the church in the Garden. You've heard about the church on the rock, the church in the house of Priscilla and Aquila, the church in Jerusalem. What about that church in the Garden of Eden? It only had two human members, but God was in that church. That was a move of God. It was something that God did and it was great. I don't know how comfortable we would be in the Garden of Eden.

This morning, some of us were talking in the dining room about how spoiled we are and about modern technology. To have had to live in the Garden of Eden with no clothes, no mattress, no electricity, no running water, (Running water was down at the creek.) most of us wouldn't be happy. But nevertheless, there was a church in the Garden and God was in it. God was moving in that church; he was talking to people.

But, the wrong spirit came to the front; a bad spirit broke out in that church in the Garden. Half the church couldn't tell that was the wrong spirit. Here's what I want to point out to you: there can be things wrong that are deceptive; they are not easy to spot. When you get experienced enough to spot those things, you'll want to criticize the rest of us for not being able to see it. We may not all see everything that you see.

Half of that church was deceived by the wrong spirit. It led the rest of the church astray. And of course, when sin broke out, judgment broke out; there had to be action taken. There were unpleasant consequences. But even then, it was the best church in the whole world; that was the best there was. You couldn't leave and go somewhere else and find anything better. You just might as well stay where God's working. Even when he's working in judgment, you might as well stay with God and work along with him.

Then, we can talk about the church in the wilderness, the church that Moses led out of Egypt and led for 40 years in the wilderness. It was a move of God. It was one of the greatest things that had ever happened; there had been nothing like it in history. A whole nation of slaves were delivered out of their slavery and led out under the rulership of God. A covenant was made with them, a law given to them and a method of worship prescribed to them.

Mighty miracles! It looked like miracles on the wholesale plan happened in that church and yet, it was full of doubt and contention, dissention, rivalry, criticism and complaining. The Bible says God '*suffered their manners 40 years in the wilderness*'. Oh! How bad their manners were! I know that 'manners' there didn't mean what we mean by 'manners' today. We need to talk some about what we mean by 'manners' today. All you preachers get up a sermon on manners, morals and ethics and come preach it here! You can do it better than I can!

God had to put up with the ways of those people and they had to put up with it. There were people like Korah, Dathan and Abiram in that church, *'men of renown'*, it says. They were great men in that church. The reason they were such a problem is because they were influential. They probably were great preachers, great leaders. They were active men, captains. They would be pastors in the church today. They would have been pastors of local churches and they had a following. They were influential and powerful until they challenged Moses. They were successful; God kept backing them.

See, just because a man has a bad spirit that he's wrestling with, that doesn't mean that God is not using him. There is something wrong with all of us. God hasn't got anything but people to build a church out of. Don't you expect anything better! You just expect that of all of the preachers, all the leaders, all the musicians, all the cooks. They're people. Fights can break out in the kitchen. We've got a history on this campground I wouldn't want to tell you about right now. Lots of things have happened. They can happen everywhere else in our local churches. It's still the move of God. That was the move of God back there in the wilderness.

By the way, that was not the only thing God was doing in the earth. I was pleased to hear Brother Leniger, I believe it was, who pointed out that Job and his friends, no doubt, were descendants of Esau. That's the best deduction we can make. They were mighty men of God. This probably took place during the time when the nation of Israel was slaving its life away under the Egyptian taskmasters.

God was doing mighty things with Job and other men like him at that time. But, they were dwindling away; their dispensation was running down. A move of God was over there in Egypt where the Israelites were having their back beaten by the Egyptian taskmasters. That's where the real move of God was, in Egypt. That was the place to be if you wanted to move on with God.

Before the wilderness period was over, Balaam the prophet and his church showed up on the scene. God had been working with him in another part of the country to the degree that Balaam would allow God to work with him. His religion was very primitive; his approach to God was flawed and weak but God responded to him and used him on the level that he was capable of being used.

But when he came up on that mountain top, hired to curse Israel, and looked out over the tents of Israel spread out over the valley below, God wouldn't let him pronounce a curse. Every time he opened his mouth a blessing would come out. By the way, this is one of the things that prove he was a prophet, that he was a prophet of God. He was used to letting God speak through him. That's why he had a reputation for accuracy and veracity. Here, he wanted something bad to come out but it wouldn't come out.

Finally, one time at the end, it says that he didn't go to get in touch with God that last time. He just decided he would say what he wanted to say. But God wouldn't let him say it against those people, against anybody else. He might have been able to do that but God wouldn't let him say it against those people. Here's where Balaam missed God, the worst time in his life that he missed God.

When he looked out over the tents of Israel and pronounced that blessing over them, the best thing he could have done was run down the back side of that mountain in the camp of tents and asked to rent a tent among them. Then he could have been named among the heroes of faith like Rahab, the harlot. Those people God let him see were the move of God with all its faults, all of its flaws and difficulties.

Next, we have the history of the church in Canaan. That church had two phases: the period of the judges and the period under the kings. Both of those had their highs and lows. The period of the kings turned out worse, although its high points were higher than anything that happened under the judges. But the problem with the kings lay in their opportunities while being king. The problem was leadership. When the leadership was good, they led the people to God. They built the temple and brought the Ark into Jerusalem. All those things were mighty things.

They held great feasts and times of fellowship among the people of God when the leaders were good and righteous. But when the leaders were evil and wicked, they led the whole nation away swiftly, which was worse than the period under the judges. Under the judges, people just drifted away into idolatry. The period of the judges ended with the great prophet Samuel anointing the first king of Israel and inaugurating that period.

The period of the kings ended with the whole nation destroyed, taken into captivity and scattered under the wrath of God because that period was so riddled with wickedness and evil in the church. Still, it was the move of God. When Manasseh was filling Jerusalem with blood, you might have been well advised to get out of the city and move to one of the smaller churches in Judea. But, there wasn't any other country in the world that you could go to and find God more than you could there.

We have this outstanding example when Elijah the prophet of the northern kingdom complained to God, *"I'm the only one you've got left,"* God spoke to him and said, *"I've got seven thousand hid away in that idolatrous kingdom."* That was the place to be. Those were people that were in touch with God. They were part of the move of God and they knew it. Their faith never failed. Some of those names are listed in places like Hebrews 11, men that died in faith. Men, and women too, died in faith believing that God was going to give them something better.

Then, we have the Church of the Return when God began to bless Israel again and restore them to their homeland. There were great leaders given to them, great preachers and builders that could lead the people to cooperate in rebuilding Jerusalem and the temple. There's an outstanding instance in there: the story of the time when the preachers read the Law to the people gathered together one day. They heard the word of God read and people's hearts were smitten. Their sense of guilt was aroused and they took on a repentant spirit.

That's always a good thing for people to do. Accept that we have missed God, when we have, and be willing to straighten things up with God. That's good for any people at any time, especially though, when God is moving in that spirit. It was peculiar that day. It is recorded in *Nehemiah* that the preachers told them that this is the feast day; this is the day for rejoicing. The people were starting to weep and cry in a spirit of repentance but the leaders told them, *"This is a day for rejoicing."* It says, *"The joy of the Lord is your strength."* What that means is, there's a time, as Solomon said, for all things.

There's a time for repentance and there's a time for rejoicing. But, in all cases, we're to remember that the joy of the Lord is our strength, even when we're sorry for the mistakes that have been made and we're conscious of (maybe some of us are) mistakes being made all the time. If you can see the mistakes that are being made, don't let that sap your joy, because the joy of the Lord is your strength. You're going to need that. You're going to need this rejoicing. You get all you can when the power is falling around here. Come down in the prayer line and let these brethren lay hands on your head and pray over you. Get all the joy that you can in your heart.

Praise God for these healings. That ought to stir up joy within us when we get a testimony of a healing. It does something to stimulate our gratitude and our good feeling, our happiness and our joy. It strengthens us to go on. Thank God! We can go on and meet the test, meet the opposition that's on the outside. There's plenty of criticism and there's plenty of enemies on the outside, many of them.

Some of those enemies we've made, or they've been made in our midst, and they've got justifiable complaints and criticism. But, we're to rise above that. Repent for whatever our connection with it was and go on with the move of God. It's still the move of God, the Church of Israel! It's a fact of religious history that God cured the Jews of their idolatry by the Babylonian captivity. During that one thousand years or so, he had been dealing with them. Before then, they were prone continually to fall away into idolatry. They would drift away into worshipping the gods of their neighbors and they couldn't seem to stop.

It was the main failure of the period of the judges and it kept recurring under the kings. God's people turning to idols! It's just a work of the flesh. It's common to humanity. It's part of human nature to worship idols, false gods. And yet, after the return from Babylon, you don't see the Jews ever turning to idolatry again. What went with that work of the flesh?

They were still humans; they still had human nature. That work of the flesh is prone to crop up among everybody at all times and everywhere. How did it manifest itself after the captivity? It was in sectarianism. Before the days of the captivity, Israel wasn't divided into denominations. Everybody respected everybody else's idols. That's the way they looked at God in those days. They might have said, "My god can whip your god," but they didn't say, "Yours is not a god." They granted everybody their god.

After the Babylonian captivity the Jews began to divide into denominations, sectarian movements. The Pharisees and the Sadducees sprang up during that time period. They were strong when Jesus and the apostles were preaching. They had the faith, those denominational movements in Israel! It was the old work of the flesh, the spirit of idolatry still manifesting itself.

It happens today, doesn't it? If we're not careful, it'll happen among us because it's the work of the flesh. We can choose our captain and choose our champions and worship our particular local leaders. That's the spirit of sectarianism, the spirit of idolatry, the work of the flesh. Watch out for it! It's something that we have to fight. We have to keep it down. You have to overcome it. You have to kill it out in your own nature.

So, that brings us to the church of the New Testament. It had its flaws from the beginning. The disciples of Jesus were relatively ignorant; they were untaught in many ways. Jesus spent three and one-half years intensely teaching them. Yet, he was teaching people with carnal minds. Jesus didn't have a Holy Ghost person to talk to among his followers. He didn't have any really spiritual-minded people among his followers. And, there was a Judas even among the twelve apostles! He was there by design. I think that's a point that has been pointed out already in this meeting. He was there by the will of God; he was there for a purpose, a reason.

It wasn't easy to pick out who, or what, Judas was. I want to issue this for a warning: There can be wrong spirits in the camp! And they may not be obvious! We tend to automatically assume that if there is anybody with a bad spirit, we will know it, "I can see it; I won't follow it; I won't pay attention to it." But, Judas could preach with the rest of them. He cast out devils; he healed the sick like the rest of the apostles did. The power and the anointing were upon him. It was only when his time came to do the evil work he was ordained to do that it became obvious who he was. Even Peter had to signal to John at the last supper, make signs to him, *"Ask Him who it is."*

Jesus was saying, *"Somebody is going to betray me. One of you is going to betray me."*

John was next to him where they could share secrets. John whispered to him, "*Who is it, Lord?*" Jesus could whisper back, *"I'll give you the sign: whoever I give the sop to."* Only John could hear it. Peter was over there signaling to John, *"Ask Him who it is!"* Then, John got the answer: "*Watch!*" He, no doubt, signaled back to Peter, *"That was him!"* That was the only way they had of knowing who the traitor in the camp was.

These things are so deceptive. The point is, good men can go wrong. Good men can fail you. Good men can let you down. Good men, used of God for a while, can miss God. So, we want to be careful, every one of us, that we don't let ourselves go astray, or don't let ourselves be led astray by the wrong spirit in the camp.

Those problems were throughout the New Testament Church. Paul had enemies and contestants and adversaries inside the church throughout his ministry. It wasn't always an outsider that he had to strike blind; he had to brand great preachers, strong influential preachers who had churches and followings. Hymenaeus and Philetus he rebuked for forsaking the faith, overthrowing the faith of some and teaching the wrong doctrine. Finally, he wrote back to Timothy, I believe it was, and said, *"All Asia has turned against me."*

That was a sad thing for Paul to say. And, that was in the church! This was the Christian church! This was a move of God! Asia was really where the cloud had settled by that time. I guess John got in there and straightened things out after that. He got things back together for a while in Asia. That was a move of God, but it had its problems.

The most outstanding example of it is in the book of Jude. If you read that (I know we've chosen that book for our day) but that was the condition of the church in Jude's day when he wrote it. What I'm telling you is..., I'd like to tell you...I wish I could tell you..., "Give us a little more time. We'll get this platform cleaned up. There won't be anything left up here except pure-minded, clean-handed, self-sacrificial men of God." But, I can't tell you that.

All I can tell you is, it's going to get worse! Let me show you how bad it can get by using the book of Jude. I guess it's not this bad, yet. We're probably not perfect enough to have men like this around, yet. But, they had them back there and they will come down here when we get into that condition. We will have people around that you've got to be alert to, like those that Jude spoke of. He said, *"There are certain men crept in unawares..."* Notice that: *Unawares*. That's the first signal that they're hard to spot. Nobody knew what they were when they came in. It was hard for the people to figure out what they were. Because of the way he described these things, we think, "Well, who would listen to anybody like that!"

They weren't that obvious. He was trying to make them obvious. *"Men of old, ordained to this condemnation, ungodly men..."* But, these were Holy Ghost men, tongue-talking preachers. By 'ungodly', he just meant 'not God-like'. These were not godly men, but they acted like it. They presented themselves and sold themselves to the people as godly men. Doesn't this happen in the Christian world today? Don't you see a lot of that taking place?

It's obvious to us because we've been taught about those things. But, it's not obvious to the people that are following them. It can come in, creep in unawares and people won't know it because they don't know how to recognize it. *"Turning the grace of our God into lasciviousness and denying the only Lord God and our Lord Jesus Christ."* The way they deny him is by denying his lordship and his right to govern their lives and his right to have the leadership in the church, his position, his lifestyle. They rejected his lifestyle by rejecting the cross of Christ. They deny the Lord Jesus Christ.

I want you to skip on over to the twelfth verse. He says people like that are *"spots in your feasts of charity when they feast with you."* A feast of charity, by the way, is not like a feast of barbeque or a feast of fruit and vegetables. Isn't charity good? Doesn't it taste good? Don't you like to eat at a feast of charity? But, *"There are spots in your feast of charity,"* he said, *"when they feast with you, feeding themselves* (that means feeding their egos) *without fear, clouds without water, carried about of wind; trees whose fruit withereth, without fruit...etc."* These are progressive and it ends up this way: they end up *"twice dead and plucked up by the root."* But, they don't start out that way, necessarily. It's not that easy to see when it's taking place.

That's why you'll see this ministry tolerating things that you wouldn't tolerate. You'll criticize us for tolerating it. You may sit out there and wonder, "Could this be the move of God? Could this really be the people of God? How do they let things like that go on?" It's hard to tell when the line has been crossed over, when we have borne long enough. As somebody said, "Put about fourteen *o's* in there when you spell it: "L-o-o-o-o-o-o-o-o-o-o-o-o-o-ong suffering!" That's fourteen o's! But, it's hard to count those o's and say when we've reached the limit. So, things are tolerated that will cause your faith in this ministry to weaken. You'll think that we don't see it. You will think, "If I can see it, why can't they see it?"

Finally, verse 16: *"These are murmurers, complainers...* (that is, criticizers) *...walking after their own lusts and their mouths speaking great swelling words."* These are good preachers.

They can bring a crowd to its feet. They speak a lot of truth. That makes them deceptive and a lot of the people can't tell the difference. They can't separate out any better than the disciples could Judas. They couldn't tell the difference when Judas was mingling with the other twelve apostles. It was hard to see and easy to be deceived.

"Having men's persons in admiration because of advantage," That's what we call politics, I guess. It goes on. It's part of human nature. That should have been included as one of the works of the flesh, shouldn't it? Politics! That's just one of the things we have to endure and live with. Because people have influence, you can't easily remove them from their place. I still see this as significant.

The trouble that David had with Joab was, David had to put up with Joab for forty years. He kept wanting to get rid of him, but couldn't; Joab was too slick, too powerful. He had too big a following; he had too many people backing him, too many people taking up for him. So, David never could get rid of him. David died before he could get rid of Joab. He left it to somebody else to judge that case.

You may not think preachers, now-a-days, in the kingdom of God have to consider things like that. But, you had better be as smart as David and put up with what you have to put up with. Otherwise, you just end up.... You think you're standing for the truth and righteousness, standing on principle, but all you'll do is divide the people of God, split the church, split the campground, split the Body of Christ by not being willing to suffer long! Lo-o-o-o-o-o-o-o-o-o-o-o-o-ong! With fourteen o's!

It's tiresome! You get tired of it! But, this is what's going to come! That's why I said it's going to get worse. There'll be men like this show up, but you be prepared for them! That'll happen in the Latter Rain. We'll have things like that in the Latter Rain! Now, this may sound like a bleak picture. I don't want to leave it like this. There are better times coming. We will finally get things cleaned up. There are times prophesied about in Revelation in which we won't have to endure things like that. We'll get power above it. And, I don't think we're far away from a time like that. We're approaching the end time. We're living in the buildup to the end of this world.

We're approaching a crucial time in history. I think it's described in Revelation 9 as the time when the four angels are loosed out of the great River Euphrates that are prepared for, what did he say? *"...for an hour and a day and a month and a year."* That can be read as an hour of a day of a month of a year. In fact, I've got one translation that says this hour of this day of this month of this year. The point being, that the time is at hand. That's what he's signaling to us there. The time has come! This is the moment that we've been waiting for!

When you look at it that way, you don't have to try to figure out time values for those terms. It's all signifying that the time has come! This last hour of Gentile times is at hand and the time is ready for this to break out! It's an end of some things! It's the end of some things and the beginning of others! It's a time when, as he says in Revelation 11, *"the nations were angry and God's wrath has come..."* and all that in the nineteenth verse. He says, *"The temple of God was opened in heaven."* Don't you want to see that? The reason it's finally opened is because it's a grand opening! It has never been opened before because it hasn't been built, yet.

Solomon's temple finally opened because they finished building it. They put it together on the hilltop without the sound of a hammer. They got it completed, ready to show off and ready for the glory of God to move into. They had the opening of the temple on Mount Moriah, or wherever it was.

The temple of God is going to be opened in heaven when we put it together, when 144,000 stand on Mount Zion, having their Father's name written in their foreheads. They are *"they that followed the lamb wheresoever he goes."* When they get up there to the top of the mountain, how do they get there? They have to climb! There are no helicopters or ski lifts going up that mountain! You have to climb Mount Zion! It's a long, hard climb! It's a difficult, trudging climb, but there's a peak up there and there's a Lamb up there! When you get there, you can follow that Lamb wheresoever he goes! He goes a lot of places; going to go a lot of places!

The temple of God is going to be open in heaven. *"There was seen in his temple the ark of his testament, the Word of God."* That's the Ark of the Covenant. It's the covenant that God made with his people. The word of God is contained in that temple. That temple, by the way, is made out of people, built up of lively stones, hewn out down here in this valley. They're worked on down here. There are hammers and saws and all kinds of tools down here in the valley, but there won't be up there when he takes us up to Third Heaven. We're talking now about the church in Third Heaven.

We've come all the way from the church in the Garden of Eden to the church in Third Heaven. It's going to have people in it and they won't have any flaws in their character. By that time, they won't need any hammering on or beating on to beat them into shape because that has all been completed. The same thing is described in chapter fifteen when he says in verse five, *"I looked and behold, the temple of the tabernacle of the testimony in heaven was opened."* The 'tabernacle' there must mean the same thing as the ark, the ark of the testimony, or the covenant.

But, the temple was opened and seven angels came out of that temple with seven plagues. All of that takes place after the temple is opened. In the eighth verse, *"The temple was filled with smoke from the glory of God."* This is still describing the Grand Opening. The initial opening, when he has gotten it ready and now can show it off to everybody that can see it. *"Filled with smoke from the glory of God and his power…and no man was able to enter into the temple after that until these seven plagues are fulfilled."*

When God gets the Bride, what we call the Bride or the Man Child, completed and put together, the one hundred, forty-four thousand overcomers have completed their process. They're put together as a temple in heaven. Then, it won't be possible for anybody else to reap that condition. That's what it takes to enter into the temple after it's built. You have to be an overcomer, to begin with, to make up the temple. But after that, to enter into that temple and be part of the worship there requires overcomers. During the short period of time while the seven plagues are being poured out and the wrath of God is falling on the world, no man is able to enter into that condition. Nobody is able to do that but by the grace of God.

To overcome, you have to have help from God. You can't just make up your mind and say, "I'm going to do this. I've fooled around long enough; I'm going to perfect myself, now. Next camp meeting, you will look at a walking overcomer on this hilltop!" You can't do that! Only God can help you do that! Somebody might be able to do that. I hope, by the grace of God, you will. But, it will be by the grace of God if you do! God will have to help you! All it takes to render someone helpless to do it, to be unable to enter in, is for God to quit

For that seven-and-one-half-year period, God will quit helping people overcome but he will start again after that. He's going to start helping people overcome again after that and there is going to be *"a world wherein dwelleth righteousness."* By the time God gets through with what he has described as a temple, and later on describes as a city, and tells us the kind of people that are in it, in Revelation 21 he says, *"There shall in no wise enter into it anything that defileth."*

You can't say that about the church today. You can't say that about any move of God in this earth until that time comes. But when that time comes, there *"shall in no wise enter into it anything that defileth, neither whatsoever worketh abomination."* You must watch what abominations you work. Study the Old Testament subject of 'abomination' and see what kind of behavior God will permit in your regular life.

You can be deceived by the attitudes and positions of the philosophers of this world today: "Everything's all right if it doesn't hurt anybody else!" "Anything's all right if it's kept secret and under cover!" Don't you believe that! You had better find out what displeases God! You need to find out what pleases God! You also need to know what displeases God. Whatever maketh a lie, anything false, anything artificial, any false front, that won't be in that kingdom we're talking about! There won't be any eye shadow, because that's a lie! There won't be any plastic surgeons or face lifters over there! Of course, we won't need them. Let's please him and avoid displeasing him.

Someone asks a question.

What's that? "Soap Operas?" That's the biggest lie ever made! There won't be any soap operas over there! I'm not inviting discussion, now.

Comment from someone; not clear.

Well, yes, but I don't want to debate that with you today. I did say that, but that's not a subject for discussion. I realize that; I admit that and I'm not being dogmatic here, but I was just stating my position.

I want to read one more like this over in Revelation 22. He's still talking about that city, talking about entering into the gate, through the gate, into the city. He says that, outside the city, (left out, they don't get in) are dogs, sorcerers, whoremongers, murderers, idolaters.

What is a 'dog'? Scripturally, it's somebody that returns to his vomit. In other words, it's a backslider. Opal Lee was telling us the other night about when she, as a teenager, some of her girlfriends were teasing her. They were trying to scare the hiccups out of her. She had a bad case of the hiccups and one of her girlfriends undertook to scare the hiccups out of her. She said, "I heard Aunt Belle said about you that you was slide backwards." She knew something like that. We talked like that. She didn't know the correct language. She said, "Aunt Belle said you was *slide backwards.*"

Opal Lee braced up and said, "I ain't slid backwards no more than Billy is! A minute later, her girlfriend asked her, "Where did your hiccups go?" It scared them out of her! It shocked her hiccups out of her.

The people that slide backwards don't get into the city...and all those other evil things. Well, that's something you're to shout about! You can be glad that such people will finally be left out! We should be glad for that and be sure that you and I are not among them that are left out! We don't want to be left out!

I don't want to be left out of you brethren! I want to be included; I want to stay a part of this, a part of this move of God! It's the move of God in spite of all its flaws, in spite of whatever weaknesses I have, whatever mistakes I may make! Don't hold the whole movement, or the whole brotherhood, accountable for that! We ought to help each other and correct each other when it's needed.

Chapter 7

Demons; the Devil; the Dragon

April 6, 2002

People like Afshar here are proof that we haven't lifted up Jesus enough in this world. We take so much for granted about our concept of God and his Son here in America we sort of feel like everybody must see it that way, but they don't. It's because they've been taught different ideas. They have different concepts of God. We need to lift up Jesus so that all the world can know him.

God is lifting him up because he humbled himself under the mighty hand of God. God has been exalting him in due season. He exalted him immediately after he humbled himself in this world. God has *"given him a name which is above every name,"* Paul said. That was immediate by the time of the Early Church. Jesus had been given that Name which is above every name. The Early Church was preaching the Name of Jesus as a source of power and authority, or at least, a channel for it. It's a channel for the authority that comes from God.

All power comes from God. Paul said that in Romans 13. Power in the church comes through Jesus. The time is building up when power in this world will come through Jesus. Right now, most power in this world comes from God, all right, but it comes through a different channel, through what some have called the 'left hand' of God. But, Jesus is going to subdue the left hand and accept all the power in heaven and earth. He said, before he died, *"All power in heaven and earth is given unto me."* I think the tense there means *"It is being given unto me."* But, it hasn't all been turned over to him, yet. Not all that authority has been transferred to Jesus, yet.

What the Bible calls 'Satan' still has authority in this world. It's pictured as a great red dragon in the book of Revelation. It's a picture of civil power. Civil power in this world usually doesn't recognize religious authority; they tolerate us. In America, especially, toleration for religious ideas is built into the constitution, but it doesn't give us any authority in the world. It only gives us authority among ourselves and allows us freedom to exercise the power God gives us among ourselves. They don't recognize our authority to exercise power in the world.

You can't go to Congress and tell them what to do. I can stand up here, or any of you can, and tell us what we ought to be doing. They won't let you do that in Congress or the Supreme Court because they're not subject to religious authority. They're part of the world system, the dragon system.

You can't call the police just because you feel the devil around. If we could call the police every time the devil comes to church, things would be simpler, wouldn't they? That would violate the principle Jesus gave us when he said, *"If Satan cast out Satan his kingdom is divided."* You can't call the police to cast out the devil because they are part of the devil's system; they're part of the dragon. They don't approach the devil, they don't see the devil the way you do. You can feel evil but most policemen can't feel evil. On that same level, they may learn a kind of animal instinct for danger. They can sense danger around and learn to observe the signs. There are a lot of signs out there in the underworld.

They're not taught to deal with evil spirits, something that is invisible, some '*thing*' that is supernatural. It's something God has created that this world can't see, so they don't want to recognize it. It is ironic how hard the astronomers and cosmologists are searching for what they call 'hidden matter', that is, matter that can't be seen. It doesn't interact with normal matter. They deduce its presence by its influence in the form of gravity.

That's somewhat like the argument we use about the Holy Ghost. It's something you can't see and it's a power. Jesus compared it to the wind. The wind gets pretty strong sometimes and blows things away. Jesus said that everyone that is born of the Spirit of God is like the wind. *"It blows where it listeth,"* or that is, where it takes a notion. Of course, the wind doesn't have any notion, but something makes it blow in different directions. It blows wherever it is inclined by hidden forces to blow and you can't change that unless you can call on a higher power.

I heard Brother Patton tell, one time, about the Jessup brothers setting up a tent for a meeting, a revival up in Fort Worth. A storm started blowing in and it looked like it would blow their tent away. He said one of the Jessup brothers ran out there and said, *"I rebuke you, wind! You go around this tent!"* There was a thunder storm approaching but it just went around them. He said it blew on both sides but it didn't blow where they were, where that tent was.

Very seldom do you get to do that, isn't that right? You don't often get to do that. They had one of these big preachers on television that has since been disgraced. Years ago, there was a hurricane approaching the east coast. On his television show, he rebuked that hurricane and commanded it to go somewhere else. It did. It turned and went back out to sea. He claimed credit for that. I don't know if he deserved credit for it, or not.

A lot of people would like to command the winds and the waves like Jesus did, but hardly anybody ever succeeds. By and large, the wind blows where it wants to and you can't stop it; you can't change it. It's invisible; you can't see the wind. You only see the effects of it. But, you can feel it. The wind has effects that make the trees wave and wiggle out there. You can tell the wind is blowing just by looking out the window and looking at the trees. You can get out in it and feel it in your face. It exerts a force on you.

What the astronomers are calling dark matter, they only theorize that it is there. They can't prove that it is there, but they see the effects of something in the force of gravity in the universe. While they are looking for invisible matter, they will not consider invisible people, like evil spirits. You couldn't sell them on the idea that there could be people right around you whispering in your ear. I don't want to take the position that we're accused of, that *'the devil sits on my shoulder and whispers in my ear'*. But, it is possible for an evil spirit to plant a suggestion in your mind.

God himself has taken advantage of that capability, a few times. One of the confusing things about the subject of evil spirits, one of the reasons a lot of the brethren in this body don't want to consider evil spirits being what the Bible calls the 'devil' is because the devil is, obviously, presented as an enemy of God. That's one reason for connecting it to the carnal mind. The carnal mind is specified to be an enemy of God. If God only had one enemy, it would have to be that one. God sort of muddies the waters when he commands and directs forces that may, or may not, choose to obey him. When God gives a direct command and enforces it, whoever he's commanding doesn't have the option of disobeying.

There have been people that God used who had no idea that God was using them. That was the case with Pharaoh in Egypt. God said, *"I'll harden his heart; I'll fix him where he won't let Israel go."* He did that about ten times. Pharaoh didn't know it was God that was changing his mind. He didn't know that he was doing the will of God when he was resisting the will of God as expressed through Moses.

That's a little paradox right there, isn't it? It was the will of God for Israel to be let go, but it was the will of God for Pharaoh *NOT* to let them go! Do you see how confusing the Bible can get sometimes? Moses was doing God's will in trying to get Israel released. Pharaoh was doing God's will in refusing to release them. You can't always take stories at face value. You have to dig down for motives and backgrounds and ancient history, not just recent history, but *ancient* history.

Even before the foundation of the world there have been things happening. Do you understand that? Things have happened before the foundation of the world. Everything didn't happen before the foundation of the world. God didn't make every decision before the foundation of the world, but he made some. One of the decisions he made before the foundation of the world was that Jesus would become the head of God's people. I don't know if all of God's people have always been happy with that decision, but it's his decision. It was God's decision before the world was founded.

Now, there were decisions made at the foundation of the world that were caused by conditions at the foundation of the world. I know that is heresy to some people who believe that God can't be influenced by anything, that nothing influences God. But, you really can't accommodate all the scriptures about God if you take that position.

What happened at the foundation of the world was that sin entered into the world. The world we're talking about is the human world. What other worlds there have been, whatever worlds exist out in the universe is none of our business because God hasn't given us any information about them. The scripture says, *"The heavens belong to the Lord our God but the earth hath he given to the children of men."* This earth is our sphere; this is where we operate; this is where we have a right to know some things. I call it a right, whatever right God gives us. When God gives us a responsibility a certain right goes with that. Everything else is just privileges. Things you know that you don't need to know are just privileges. But, the things you have to know to do the will of God, those could be considered rights by some definitions.

"The earth hath he given to the children of men." This world down here is the world foundation that we have to deal with. It's what God has told us about. That world up there where the angels live, we don't know much about that. We're only given hints about it. There were not even any hints given about it in the first chapter of Genesis. There's nothing in the first chapter of Genesis, for example, that mentions the creation of angels. Take a look at that.

It mentions 'heaven', all right, but you have to dig out which heaven it's talking about. We learned, a long time ago, around here, there is more than one heaven. In verse six of Genesis 1, God says, *"Let there be a firmament,* (or an expanse, or separation), *in the midst of the waters. Let it divide the waters from the waters. God made the firmament and divided the waters which were under the firmament from the waters which were above the firmament and it was so."*

Whatever God said came true. *"And God called the firma-*

ment heaven." Now let's see if we can ascertain how far that heaven reached, what kind of heaven that was. That wasn't Third Heaven that stood between the waters and the waters. Draw a line if you want to, if you like to draw lines in your Bible, from that heaven in the eighth verse to the heaven in the twentieth verse. In the twentieth verse, God said, "*Let the waters bring forth abundantly the moving creature that hath life and fowl that may fly above the earth in the open firmament of heaven.*" Connect those two heavens.

The open firmament of heaven is the heaven the fowl fly in; the heaven the birds fly in. That's not Third Heaven, Second Heaven, or even First Heaven, but it's the natural heaven that the birds fly in; in other words, the atmosphere. That's the only heaven we have described in the story of creation. There's nothing mentioned in here about the creation of Third Heaven where God is, or any other heavens that he operates in that we may not know anything about.

There is a heaven surrounding this earth that the birds fly in that we call the atmosphere. God created *this* heaven and *this* earth in the beginning that we're talking about. In the beginning God created the heaven and the earth. But, that's not the heaven the angels live in; there's no mention of that heaven in here. No time is specified for the creation of angels or evil spirits. They are simply introduced later on in the story because they were acting. God was using them at times. Sometimes, they may have been acting on their own, but they impacted upon humanity.

We're finally told something about demons because they do impact humanity; they have an effect on us. We need to know something about them. You could argue that we have a right to know something about devils. By the way, that's another use of the word 'devils' there. It's curious that the King James Version chose the word 'devils' to translate the word demons. I don't know if any other version does that. And, there's no obvious reason why the King James translators did that. Why didn't they just call them 'demons' that Jesus and the apostles cast out instead of calling them devils?

I always think there's some reason behind the peculiarities of this Bible, this King James Bible. I think God was more involved in the production of this Bible than he has been in most versions. I don't say God had nothing to do with other versions. Every language needs its own version. The other languages can't use the King James Version. The Bible has to be translated into every language. God wants every nation, kindred and tongue (that's language) to hear his word.

There's a famous example of the difficulties of translating into other languages. A lot of you heard the story about the translator who was translating the Bible for some South Sea Islands group. It was located in a part of the world where they had never seen snow so they didn't have any word for snow. Snow didn't exist on that island so snow didn't exist in their language.

When they were translating the first chapter of Isaiah where they said, "*Come, let us reason together. Though your sins be as scarlet, they shall be white as snow,*" they couldn't translate that into that particular language because there was no word for snow. If they invented one, they still wouldn't know what it meant because they had never seen snow. They didn't know how white it was. That translator took the liberty to translate that verse as "white as coconut meat" because they had coconuts on that island. "*Come, let us reason together. Though your sins be as scarlet, they will be white as coconut meat.*" Those islanders knew what that meant; they knew how white that was! So, it made good sense.

But, this Book here has been so influential in modern world history that I think God pretty carefully oversaw and dictated the production of it. I think a lot of its peculiarities have meaning. I suspect the meaning for this peculiarity that they translated 'demons' as 'devils'—remember, the translators didn't know what they were doing when they made this choice any more than Pharaoh did. This was God's choice!

You may say something sometime that you don't have any idea why you said it, or you may mean one thing and God means another when he had you say it. That happened in the book of John when the Jewish council was gathered together. I think this was after the resurrection of Lazarus. They wanted to decide what to do about Jesus.

Caiaphas, the high priest, spoke out in that council and said, *"You ignoramuses don't know anything! You've not considered that it's expedient that one man die for the people!"* He meant one thing but the Holy Ghost had him say that to mean another thing! His meaning was that *"We can sacrifice this 'cat' Jesus!"* (To be flippant!) *"We can sacrifice this guy Jesus and spare the people a lot of trouble. Because, if we let him start a revolution like he's threatening to, the Roman armies will be in here and blood will run in the streets!"* That was his idea of one man dying for the people.

John said the Holy Ghost had him say that to signify that Jesus should die, not for that people only, but for all the people of the world, the sins of the whole world. So, Caiaphas never knew what he said. That is, he knew the words he said but he never knew why he said it. He meant one thing, but God meant another.

I think the translators... I'm not sure what they had in mind. Maybe they just went blind and didn't even consider the paradox in the words they used to identify demons in the scriptures. I think God did that to call attention to the fact that demons are identified with the devil in the scriptures, not the flesh. He never did use that as the flesh or the spirit of Adam. There's nothing in there that connects the spirit of Adam with the word 'devil'. The flesh is one subject and the devil is another subject.

Jesus himself tied the devil and evil spirits together, particularly in the twelfth chapter of Matthew when they tried to trap him and the disciples. They were criticizing Jesus' power to cast out demons. They said, *"That guy must be using the power of Beelzebub, the prince of the devils."*

Jesus' responding argument (He used a logical argument; not a scriptural response, but a logical response.) that if Satan is casting out Satan, then his kingdom is divided. It was Jesus who brought up the word 'Satan' right there. The Jews didn't bring up the word 'Satan'. They just brought up 'Beelzebub'.

But Jesus identified evil spirits with Satan and said that if one demon is casting out another demon, that is equivalent to Satan casting out Satan. Each demon is part of Satan.

Just like each member of Christ is part of Christ. Do you see the similarity? There is, maybe, one conflicting or confusing facet of the subject of Satan that has to be tied with that. You have to show how evil spirits are involved in the dragon, the great red dragon over in Revelation. We all identify that with people. That's a collection of people. It's a body of people, but it's a body of people that's controlled, not by Jesus, but by the evil spirit kingdom.

An example is the temptation of Jesus where Satan said, *"I can give the kingdoms of the world because they are committed unto me."* He was in charge of that. This is the most clear-cut case in scripture of Satan being identified and named as the red dragon. Twice in the Book of Revelation (the thirteenth chapter isn't it? or the twelfth chapter and the twentieth chapter) it mentions that *"old serpent called the devil and Satan."*

Let me introduce, here, the subject of the dragon in the Old Testament and show how the Bible treats, identifies and names a dragon. Jeremiah 51:34 says, *"Nebuchadnezzar, the king of Babylon, has devoured me."* By the way, this is God talking. Can anybody devour God? How would you eat up God in that aggressive, antagonistic sense? God was complaining that *"Nebuchadnezzar has devoured me."* Well, he was devouring God's people. By devouring his people, you're devouring God.

We used to have a saying that we may need to resurrect in our meetings: "When you weary God's people, you weary God." Do you remember how we said that? Maybe you never heard that said. It seems like I heard Brother Jolly say that. I've heard that for many years used on people that give long-winded testimonies, dry discourses and long sermons and wear people out. Whatever you're doing to God's people, you're doing to God.

Jesus said, *"Inasmuch as you've done it unto the least of these you've done it unto me."* So God is complaining and criticizing Babylon, this civil power here. *"Nebuchadnezzar, the king of Babylon hath devoured me. He hath crushed me."* Well, because he had crushed Israel. *"He hath made me an empty vessel."* That's what he did to Israel. *"He hath swallowed me up like a dragon."* So, there's the Bible clue to the distinguishing characteristic of a dragon. That's the mark of a dragon.

You know what the mark of a beast is. This is the mark of a dragon: he swallows everything up. When you understand a dragon to be the empire-building side of civil power, that's what civil power always culminates in if it gets a chance. It builds up a big empire and conquers all its neighbors and keeps getting bigger by swallowing up all the neighbors, not allowing any nation to exist independently. That's been the object of every empire. Every great emperor wanted to rule the world. Alexander the Great's ambition was to conquer the whole world. Well, he didn't conquer the whole planet; he didn't have enough transportation; he didn't have access to the whole planet. But, he conquered all of it he could get to, as far as he could reach. Since then, men like Napoleon and Hitler have wanted to rule the world. They wanted to establish their rulership over the whole world. That's the empire spirit, the spirit of the dragon. That's the perfect description of a Biblical dragon.

A few times you see the word 'dragon' used in the prophets when it's just talking about wild animals. It may have meant wild goats, wild dogs, jackals, some people suggest. But when you find it used in a prophetic sense like this, it's talking about the spirit that gets in strong nations and strong rulers to swallow everything up.

Someone comments—not heard.

Yes, I'm going next to Ezekiel 29, but I want to make this comment right here as we're going over there: Observe that God gave a name to this dragon. He named it 'Nebuchadnezzar' when clearly, the body of the dragon was the whole Babylonian empire. It wasn't one man. One man can't be a dragon. It takes a big body of people to be a dragon. Nebuchadnezzar wouldn't have had any power if he hadn't had a big army. It was all those other men with swords on their sides that made Nebuchadnezzar powerful. He was strong and powerful because he had backing. That whole body of people was the dragon but in that day and time it was called 'Nebuchadnezzar' because Nebuchadnezzar was the spokesman. He was the mouthpiece; he was the leader. He was the one in charge, so the dragon bore his name at that time in history.

I see another time in history. In Ezekiel 29 there is a similar example. Verse 2: *"Son of man, set thy face against Pharaoh and prophesy against him and against all Egypt."* When you prophesy against Pharaoh, you're prophesying against all Egypt. *"Speak and say behold I am against thee, Pharaoh, king of Egypt, the great dragon that lieth in the midst of his rivers."* If you can enumerate all the seven heads of the dragon in Revelation, you will remember that Egypt was the first one: Egypt, Assyria, Babylon, Persia, Greece and Rome; then Rome again.

It wasn't just Pharaoh, even though Pharaoh is called the dragon here, but it was Egypt that was the dragon and Pharaoh was the leader of it. He was the ruler; he was the head on that dragon. That dragon didn't have seven heads. He was one of the heads on the Great Dragon. The Bible changes pictures a lot of times and the pictures get tangled up. You see all these dragons back in the Old Testament. Egypt, Assyria, Babylon, and Persia were all heads on the Great Red Dragon in the New Testament.

Again, you see the principle here that God named the dragon by the name of its leader. When we turn to Revelation 12, we see that John did the same thing. But it was the seven-headed dragon this time. He wasn't addressing any one of those seven leaders, but he named it by the leader it had all the way through. Those seven leaders had a leader; not just God.

I remember Brother Don Patton raising a question one time in one of our meetings. We were debating whether there was another head behind the seven heads. I realized then that he, himself, saw another head behind the seven heads, but he saw it as God. He didn't see any other head between God and the seven. It appears here that God put another head between him and the seven. He called it the Devil and Satan. *"The great dragon was cast out, that old serpent who is called the Devil."*

Well, the dragon itself is not the devil, but it's the body of the devil. It's the group that is headed and led by the devil and Satan. It's that old serpent which deceives the whole world. By the way, there is the key word to describe a Bible 'serpent'. It's a 'deceiver' and there are lots of them around! Jesus spoke to a generation of vipers and serpents. They were deceiving and being deceived. There is a generation of them today.

We live in a time when you can still quote David in the Psalms: *"I said in my haste all men are liars."* You can say all women too and you don't have to be too hasty about saying either one. That spirit of the serpent is upon humanity. That's what a serpent is about. When the title 'serpent' is applied, it is describing the deceptive characteristic of that person or that being.

We're looking today at the growth of the dragon. Some are trying today to make this country one of the heads on the dragon. But that is difficult to do with all those seven heads already there. It's hard to get another head on where another head already is. You start having a conflict when you start trying to put a head where a head already is. There are plenty heads on the dragon already.

But significantly, it's in the news now. Not just our preachers, but news commentators and analysts are starting to use the word 'empire' about the United States. You may have seen that in the newspapers and news magazines this last week. It's becoming more and more common for news analysts to point out the growth, the phenomenal growth, of the power of the United States in our time. It is a manifestation of dragon power, but it's not the great red dragon. It may be part of the body, but it's not one of those heads because those heads are already there and occupied. One of the articles I read a few days ago attempted to compare the United States' present position. It's what they were willing to call 'empire', comparing that empire-building activity with what the Caesars did in Rome.

In the nineteenth century, there was the British Empire. It was clearly accepted in the world as being an empire. They were able to brag, in those days, that the sun never set on the

British Empire. The Caesars couldn't say that! Alexander the Great couldn't say that but the British kings and prime ministers could brag that "the sun never sets on the British Empire," because it had spread around the globe. The sun was always shining on British territory somewhere. In those days, that was true. However, the British Empire was not a universal empire in the sense that the Roman Empire was. The British Empire never tried to take in every piece of neighboring territory. They didn't see the necessity for that.

They maintained an empire that was big enough, far-flung enough and powerful enough to look after their interests. But, they didn't try to subdue the whole world. Every one of those seven heads has made an effort to subdue the whole world as far as they could. They did it by defeating their competition. They conquered the competition. Great Britain did not defeat their competitors; they simply stared them down when they needed to and maintained enough power to hold them at bay.

Likewise, that is true of the United States today. We did not defeat the USSR. We did not cause the collapse of the USSR except, perhaps indirectly, by keeping them involved in such a hard economic race, a military race that they finally just got tired of and dropped out of the race. We never fought the battle that conquered them and gave ourselves the right to declare ourselves the winner. So in that respect, we resemble the British Empire today a lot more than we resemble the Roman Empire.

The reason I make that comparison is because none of us is trying to make Britain one of the seven heads on the Beast. The reason we don't is because their day is over. We can see that they did not hold that strategic position in human history. They were powerful in their day, in their time, but they didn't figure in human history the way the Roman Empire did in changing things.

From the Bible standpoint, what makes all those empires important is that they affected the people of God. There may have been equally powerful empires over in China at the same time that some of those empires were in the Western world or the Middle East. But China was not having anything to do with

God's kingdom at that time, so they are not ever recorded in the Bible. The Bible only takes notice of what was important to God's plan.

As powerful as the Moslem empire was in its heyday it could have had a run at being one of the heads, if you're just looking at power. But, they weren't controlling the church. The Jews and the Christians were not living under their power, their rulership. They were still under that seventh head, papal Rome. All the time that the Moslem empire was waxing and waning, the Church, the plan of God, the kingdom of God in this earth was suffering and wavering under that seventh head. That can't be changed. That's a fact of history that we can't change. But, we can watch for God to use the USA as he used Great Britain and many other powers in their time.

I remember another empire during the Middle Ages that tried to become great. It wanted influence. It was called the Holy Roman Empire. I think it was the historian Edward Gibbons who remarked about that one that it was neither holy, nor Roman, nor an empire. It just wanted to be; it had aspirations.

I still say that a democracy is too soft, too sympathetic, too subject to media manipulation and the will of the people to ever make those hard-headed, cold-hearted decisions that it takes to maintain an empire that would qualify to be a head on the dragon, the beast.

But, there is another beast coming forth as described in Revelation 13, "*a beast with two horns like a lamb but he spake as a dragon.*" He wasn't a dragon, but he talked like one. That beast is not one of the seven heads. If it was, it would have been pictured with seven heads and ten horns just like the dragon and the beast that came out of the sea were pictured. Both the dragon and the beast that rose up out of the sea had seven heads and ten horns. They had the *SAME* seven heads and ten horns. The seven heads on the beast are the same as the seven heads that were on the dragon. It's just placing them on that dragon, as heads, in their turn.

The dragon, as it was appearing and the time that it appeared, in the twelfth chapter, was the pagan Roman Empire ruled by the Caesars, the Roman emperors. They were fierce, cruel and strong. No army, no nation could stand against their armies. They enforced their will wherever they went.

That was the sixth head. That was the time, right then, the dragon was functioning under that sixth head. The other five heads had already had their day and passed. They're pictured on the dragon because the dragon is something that lasted from the beginning to the end and the end is not here, yet. The heads had their limited day but the body of the dragon, civil power directed by Satan, has existed from the beginning of civil power in the days of Egypt and will exist on down until the destruction of civil power in Gog and Magog, after the Thousand Years.

Those seven heads, each one has its time and sphere. It's interesting to note that the seventh head is going to come to an end long before the dragon comes to an end. The seventh head is going to be destroyed in the Battle of Armageddon. That head is given power by the ten kings that are yet to appear. Well, the eighth is the seventh. Let's read that in the seventeenth chapter of Revelation and see what the eighth head is.

We've been talking about seven heads and ten horns. In the seventeenth chapter, third verse: *"He carried me away in the Spirit into the wilderness and I saw a woman sit upon a scarlet colored beast* (or a red dragon*) full of names of blasphemy having seven heads and ten horns."* Get that number fixed in your mind. There are seven heads on that beast, no more, no less.

He begins his explanation in the seventh verse: *"The angel said unto me wherefore* (or, why) *didst thou marvel? I will tell thee the mystery of the woman,"* (Thank God for somebody to explain these mysteries!) *"...and of the beast that carrieth her."* It was a mystery; both of them are a mystery. *"The beast which carrieth her...that had the seven heads and ten horns."* Again, it's just seven heads. *"The beast that thou sawest was, and is not and shall ascend."* That means that the time when John was getting this revelation, that beast had existed; that was in John's day. That's the time that was; it's past now. It's past tense to us. And there comes a time when it *"is not"*; that is, it ceases to be strong enough to exercise power. That time came at the end of the Dark Ages.

"...and shall ascend out of the bottomless pit and go into perdition. And they that dwell on the earth shall wonder... when they behold the beast that was, and is not, and yet, is." That means he existed for a time and then he lost his place and either went out of existence or just went out of power. The fact is, he just went out of power. He didn't go out of existence. That's proved in other scriptures. *"And yet is, again."* He comes back to rule again.

That's part of the history of that beast. *"Here is the mind that has wisdom..."* The seven heads... (if you're wise you can understand this) the seven heads are seven mountains. We're talking symbolically, now, reading in the book of Revelation. It's a symbolic book. Don't think of seven literal hills that Rome is built on, but think of seven great powers.

A mountain represents a great power in scriptural symbolic terms. There are seven mountains, seven great powers, seven great heads, seven *governments*. We've already established that heads are governments, heads of groups of people. So, the seven heads are seven governments on which the woman, that false church, sits. In other words, those governments have supported false religion. Every one of those empires has had false religion in it. They are great civil powers, except for the seventh; it was a religious power. It's different from all the rest.

Each head has had both religious power and civil power in it. But, for the first six heads civil power was in charge and religious power was assisting that civil power. But when the seventh head came along, the order was reversed. It's described in the thirteenth chapter as that *"beast that came up out of the sea and the dragon gave that beast his power and seat and great authority."*

So that previous empire, that previous power, transferred its support to that religious power. Instead of religion supporting government, the religion became a government supported by civil power. That is, the armies, the police forces, the generals threw their weight behind that religious leader and made him, in effect, an empire. The Roman pope became, effectively, a Roman emperor because he had the same backing that the emperors had had: armies and policemen who would arrest you and put you in jail if you didn't obey his authority.

For 1,260 years he held that authority; he exercised that kind of power. That was the seventh head. And that is the one, by the way, that was, and is not and yet, is. That didn't apply to those first six heads. They all were and then, were not, and that was it! But this one *"was, and is not, and is,"* again. None of the other six came back again.

Where is it that mentions the eighth? I've missed that verse. Let's read the tenth verse. There are seven heads, seven mountains, seven governments on which the church sitteth and there are seven kings, governments. He's explaining it there. Those seven heads, seven mountains are seven kings. That just means governments, not particularly one man. Most of those governments were headed by one man, and in fact, the seventh one was, too.

The kings are governments and governments are successive. They don't necessarily fall when that one man dies and another man rises to take his place. There are seven governments in the tenth verse. Five of those governments are fallen; they're gone. One is, and the other is not yet come.

The one that 'is', at that time, was civil Rome. Now, that's not to be confused with the previous expression *"the beast that was and is not and yet is."* This is different. Five are gone, historically. One is—right now, John, when you're here writing this! Five are fallen: Egypt, Assyria, Babylon, Persia and Greece; those are all gone. "*One is*": Pagan Rome! That was the government John the Apostle lived under. *"And the other is not yet come"*. Papal Rome! It hadn't got here when John wrote this. But John was a true prophet! It did come! That other one did come!

But it was papal Rome that had that description; that's the one that completed the cycle of *being* and *not being*, and *being again*. That didn't apply to any of the other six. "*When that seventh one comes, he must continue a short space.*" We've had lots of trouble over that 'short space', haven't we? What is a 'short space'? How short is a 'short space'? It depends on what you're talking about, doesn't it?

Our lifetime is a short space. A brief coffee break is a short space. A thousand years is a short space. It just depends on what you're comparing it to. Let me give you some scriptures to help explain that. Look at this one in Isaiah 54:7 about a short space. This is God talking to Israel. Some may think the sixth verse is talking to the church, but I still say it's talking to Israel.

Sixth verse: *"The Lord has called thee as a woman forsaken and grieved in spirit, and a wife of youth, when thou wast refused, saith thy God."*

7: *"For a small moment have I forsaken thee..."* That's been two thousand years now. Two thousand years is a small moment in God's plan. For a small moment he has forsaken the Jews. *".... but with great mercies will I gather thee."*

8: *"In a little wrath I hid my face from thee for a moment..."* (Two thousand years) *"...but with everlasting kindness will I have mercy on thee, saith the Lord thy Redeemer."*

Here's another one in Revelation 12:12: *"...rejoice, ye heavens, and ye that dwell in them. Woe to the inhabiters of the earth and of the sea! For the devil is come down unto you, having great wrath, because he knoweth that he hath but a short time."* Now, how much time did he have when that happened? He's had about two thousand years because his 'coming down' was when he was cast out of heaven back there in that Early Church. It's been a 'short time', nearly two thousand years.

Now, going on to the eleventh verse: *"And the beast that was and is not..."* Now, we're getting back to that expression from the eighth verse: *"was, and is not and yet, is." "The beast that was and is not, even he is the eighth."* But, there weren't eight; there were only seven. Every time he counted them there were only seven heads, so how can one of them be called the 'eighth head'? It's because he is, again. He was, and he is not. He was the seventh, then he is not anything, and he is, again. That makes him the eighth government; the eighth empire. It's a reformation, but it's the seventh one that has come back again. It's the last one that is doing that. It's Roman religious power that is coming back again. Roman civil power is not coming back again to be the eighth head. It is Roman religious power that's coming back to be the eighth head, the eighth government. It's that old seventh head come back again.

He's still around! He never did disappear! He *'was not'* in power! He *was* in power! He *was not* in power! And, he *is again* in power! He's coming back in power, now! It won't be long! There is another power that I mentioned a while ago in the thirteenth chapter that is rising up to give power to that system, that renewed Roman religious power, just like that old civil Roman Empire turned power over to the religious power at the beginning of the Dark Ages.

See, religious power has no power to enforce without civil power to enforce it for them. The papacy, as it appeared in the Dark Ages and the early Middle Ages had civil power. The kings around it carried out its will, carried out its commandments until finally the pope could call for a Crusade to go fight the Saracens and retake Jerusalem. People rose up out of all the European kingdoms to go over there and fight in the Crusades. He had civil power that he could use.

Now, in the return of that head in the form of the eighth government, he's going to need some civil power. It's described to us in 17:12: *"...the ten horns which thou sawest are ten kings,"* (or, ten governments) *"...which have received no kingdom as yet; but receive power as kings one hour* (that's fifteen years.) *with the beast."*

13: *"These* (ten) *have one mind, and shall give their power and strength unto the beast."* But, that same condition is described in the thirteenth chapter as the *"beast that came up out of the earth; and he had two horns like a lamb, and he talked like a dragon."*

14: It says he *"causes them to make an image to the beast which had the wound by a sword, and did live."* He's making an image, in other words, to that Roman religious power.

15: *"And he had power to give life unto the image of the beast,"* So, he's got enough civil power, or influence with civil power, to back up that image of the beast and make it be alive. "*...that the image of the beast should both speak,*" (I wonder what it's going to say!) "*...and cause that as many as would not worship the image of the beast should be killed.*"

He's going to back up the words of the Roman religious power. That's very clear to us, isn't it? Where does the World Council of Churches get its power? They get their power by being part of a democracy. They vote; they can buy votes; they can swing votes. They can influence the government of the United States and sway civil power behind that religious system. Do you see that?

So that may be the mission of the U.S.A, but it's not to be another head. It's to *support that head*! The head's got to have support! It's got to have some support since it's a religious power and has no earthly power of its own.

Well, praise God! We're watching prophecy come to pass! World events are compelling the United States to use its power. We don't like to use power! We don't want to use power as a democracy! We dislike being the world's policeman but we can't help ourselves! World events are driving that! The needs are too great; we cannot ignore them!

So, you keep reading your newspaper and see what God did last night. You come here to church on Saturday night and watch what Jesus does. We get to watch both God and Jesus work. Amen? Praise God! Well, I like to watch Jesus work tonight! This is really more important, in the long run, than what God's doing out there. God's going to acknowledge that when he turns it all over to Jesus and backs up to take a rest! God's going to back up, one of these days, and take a rest. He tried, seven thousand years ago, to take a rest. We wouldn't let Him; Adam and Eve wouldn't let him rest.

But God's going to get his rest when his Son is in charge shouldering the burden! He's got broad shoulders and they're getting bigger! He's being promoted! God is lifting up Jesus, as we said in the beginning. He lifted him up when he set him at his right hand of power in the Heavens and made him the head of the church. He's going to lift him up again, a little higher, by setting him over all the earth! He's the Prince of the kings of the earth! He's going to be in charge of all of them!

Down in the days of the Resurrection, after the Thousand Years, he will promote him again. I think Jesus will count it a promotion when God accepts the rulership back from him, when Jesus has got all the work done and he hands it back to his Father as a gift. *"Here it is, Father. The whole earth is at rest."*

I like that expression. That's back, I think, in *Zechariah 6*, where those four horse trailers went out from between two brass mountains. Some of them went out to walk to and fro through the earth. When they came back, they reported, *"The whole earth is at rest."* That didn't last long, did it? That was a peaceful period in, I suppose, the Grecian Empire. There was peace for a little while after Alexander died and the four generals split up the territory. The whole earth rested for a little while. But, it didn't rest very long! Here came the Romans! Very quickly, the Romans appeared and blood ran in the streets again!

There'll never be any lasting peace until the Prince of Peace, the Prince of the kings of the earth, takes control and brings peace! Then he will deliver a peaceful world back to his Father! I think Jesus will accept his position by the right hand of power again as his final promotion. I think he will feel exalted by then!

LIFT HIM UP! WILL YOU? LET'S LIFT HIM UP TONIGHT! God keeps lifting him up! Let's help him! I thought that was a good sound in the beginning of the service after that good song. There was a roar, like the voice of many waters.

Question: "Would you please explain I Samuel 19:9? There are several references in I Samuel about Saul's evil spirit being from the Lord. How is this possible?"

Well, evil spirits are from the Lord the same way Pharaoh was from the Lord and Nebuchadnezzar was from the Lord. How does that verse go in Proverbs that says, *"The Lord has made all things for himself, yea, even the wicked for the day of evil."*

A lot of our brethren are pushing the idea now that God creates evil spirits all the time, as he needs them. I have a hard time viewing them that way because they are obviously sciential, that is, knowledgeable beings that have a sense of self. They know who they are. They also know that they are under judgment. They know they've got a day of destruction coming.

My concept of God doesn't allow for God creating beings like that, creating them in that condition. But that was Brother Sowders suggestion about them; it was his guess. But, he admitted that it was just a guess. When he was pinned down, Brother Sowders admitted he didn't know the origin of evil spirits.

I'm afraid we still don't know the origin of evil spirits. But, we do know they're here. Brother Sowders knew they were here. He had experiences with them. Many of us are having experiences with them. We see that God uses them, sometimes in strange ways. Let's look at this particular case in I Samuel, just to answer the question.

I Samuel 19:9 says, "*The evil spirit from the Lord was upon Saul as he sat in his house with his javelin in his hand.*" I don't think that was the first time it mentions that evil spirit. It was a spirit that God sent to trouble Saul.

God sent another evil spirit to deceive King Ahab. Whether God sends every evil spirit to do everything that they are doing—that calls for discussion and study. We're not settled on that. There are all degrees of belief on that. Some people feel God controls them perfectly, that they never do anything but what God tells them to do. That was why I threw out that brief example over in the Brownsville meeting, pointing out that God uses a lot of cases like Nebuchadnezzar and Hitler when they don't even know they are being used by God. Other times, God has used people who didn't really want to do what God was telling them to do. Some of us may have fallen into that category, sometimes.

It just doesn't appear that evil spirits are always comfortable with what they're doing. They weren't very friendly with Jesus and they're not very friendly with us. We don't want to get very friendly with them. They don't act like they're happy when we're having experiences with them. God can send one and make him do his will like God can send you and make you do his will, whether you want to or not.

Here's a Note: Number 1: "The scripture does not say anything about darkness being created."

I think I can quickly explain that. It's because darkness is not a 'thing'. Darkness didn't have to be created. Light is what had to be created. Darkness is nothing but absence of light. So obviously, there was nothing but absence of light before light was created.

Number 2: "Why is 'Heaven' capitalized in Genesis 1:8?"

I'll have to tell you that it wasn't in ancient times. That's one of the peculiarities of the King James Bible and other translations. Moses, when he wrote that, did not know about capitals.

Number 3: "Light was mentioned in Genesis 1:3, but the sun was not created until Genesis 1:14, the fourth day."

Well, light can come from a lot of places beside the sun, can't it? You can light a candle; you can smear phosphorous around. You can make light from a lot of different sources, and so can God!

Question: "Is Job 40:15-24 and Job 41, the whole chapter, talking about the power and authority of the devil? I guess that's talking about Leviathan and Behemoth. It seems to me, when I read these verses that the Lord is telling Job that the devil is behind his sufferings. The Lord goes on to elaborate to Job about how much supernatural power the Lord allows the devil to have."

Well, you may have something there. That was the first hint that the devil was behind his sufferings. He knew enough not to blame it on God because God could have prevented it from happening. He may not have known that God gave specific permission for it to happen, but he, obviously, had been conscious of that hedge God had kept around him for a long time.

Suddenly, the hedge was gone. He quite rightly blamed God for that. But Job didn't know, until somebody told him, that Satan had talked God into that. Nobody likes to hear that, that somebody could talk God into being mean to you. There has to be a lot of explaining done over that. We don't have time to explain it tonight.

It does look to me like Leviathan, over there particularly, is a type or symbol of the great dragon, or something of that nature.

There are people that are not here tonight who wish they were; they wish they could be here. Aren't you glad you're able to be here? Let's make it our practice to come when we can because the time is coming when you can't. As Paul said, "*Work while it is day. The night cometh when no man can work.*" You had better come to church while you're able! The day may come when you wish you could come and you're just not able. Nobody is to be criticized or blamed for that; they are to be sympathized with, prayed for and supported, comforted.

Let's stand and thank the Lord for the mysteries he has let us see into, for the health that he's given us and pray for those in failing health.

Chapter 8

THE MINISTRY'S JOB

January 11, 2003

Well, thank God for hunger pangs. There's something wrong with you if you can't have them. God has given us normal reactions and protections. Sometimes, you hear of people who are born with an inability to feel pain. They are subject to all kinds of accidents and physical injuries because they don't know when they are being hurt. And if you could never get hungry, maybe you would never eat; you would just starve to death. God in his wisdom gave us these feelings, desires and protective instincts. If anything interferes with that, it needs to be investigated, doesn't it?

Be careful how you let what is around you affect you. Let the Holy Ghost affect you. It's around! Thank God for the Holy Ghost hanging around! (If that's the right term to use.) The Holy Ghost is always around us. I know we can grieve it away in its activity, but it never actually leaves the scene. The Spirit of God is flowing out from him like sunshine from the sun. You can get in the shade where something is blocking it out and you miss out on it. Step out in the sunshine again! Step out in the Spirit again! Step out into the Holy Ghost and remain free from all evil influences.

There are evil spirits in this world, what the Bible calls devils in the King James Version. I think every other version just calls them demons. For some reason, the King James translators chose to not use that word, so they assigned the word 'devils' to evil spirits. They are not omnipresent, but they are ubiquitous. Do you understand that term? Do you know the difference between those two words?

The Holy Spirit of God is omnipresent because it is everywhere at the same time. It can spread out enough to be everywhere. But, an evil spirit is an invisible evil person. It can't be omnipresent; it can't be everywhere, but there can be a lot of them and be enough of them to be everywhere. That's what I mean by ubiquitous; they're just here, there and everywhere. But, it's just different specimens in different places.

The Bible gives us the precedents we need for dealing with those spirits. Jesus gave the apostles power to deal with devils, demons. I like the one in Mark. It's the one most condensed in the assignment, the job description he gave to the apostles. Mark 3:14 says, "*And he ordained twelve that they should be with him and that he might send them forth to preach.*" The job of the twelve apostles was to (1) preach, (2) to have power to heal sicknesses and (3) to cast out devils. Those three things were the marks of the apostles. Mark, himself, recognized them. Mark wrote down the marks of the apostles. Those three things were what Jesus assigned the apostles to do.

There were other people who did those things. There were other preachers in the church besides the apostles. There were other people in the church that had the gift of healing besides the apostles. In fact, the whole church has that, to some extent, but especially when we all unite as a whole church. When we unite as a whole church we've got great power with God to get sicknesses healed and devils cast out and evil rebuked back and all kinds of circumstances changed. God's people have prayed away many a danger, prayed away many oppressions, prayed away many a problem!

There was a Body gathering in Paducah when Brother Leniger brought a problem before us. The whole meeting there prayed for his little boy and God healed him. He had some kind of brain disfunction that showed up suddenly, about the age of ten years old. A lot of people who saw the manifestations, the symptoms, compared it to demons. Some told him, "Your boy has a devil. You've got to have it cast out."

Brother Leniger didn't want to believe that. He went looking for medical solutions, but the medical solutions fell short. His boy was not getting well with all of the medicines and treatments that the doctors were giving. Finally, he brought the problem to the church and the church prevailed upon God.

They prayed and the boy got well! Isn't that like so many testimonies in the Bible, in the New Testament?

People came and prayed to Jesus. Do you realize that is what they were doing when they said, *"Lord, heal my son; Lord, heal my servant; Lord, heal me."?* They were praying to Jesus! Look at all the prayers he answered! A man whose servant was sick and about to die came to him. He was a man who was benevolent in his attitude; he loved his servant. Not only did he need his servant, his servant was valuable to him, but he had a genuine tenderness in his heart. He loved that servant like a brother or like his own son. He came, out of the sincerity of his heart, and begged Jesus to do something for him. Jesus told him, *"Go your way; your servant is well."* He went home and found his servant well. He inquired around the family, *"When did he turn for the better?"* They named a certain hour yesterday. He realized that was the time of day when he was talking to Jesus and Jesus told him to go home, that his servant was getting well.

Jesus came down from the Mount of Transfiguration experience with Peter, James and John and found the rest of the apostles trying to cast a devil out of a little boy. They were having trouble with it. Some demons are harder to cast out than others. You can just apply reason to that situation and assure yourself that those brethren didn't satisfy themselves by saying once, "Come out!" and then give up when it didn't come out the first time. They were working at it when Jesus got there. There was considerable commotion in the camp; they were still trying to get it done. They couldn't figure out why it wasn't working! It had always worked before! Jesus had given them the power to cast out devils, but here they had run into a case where it wasn't working! What was wrong with the power Jesus gave them? They didn't understand it. They tried another time, kept trying to make it work.

Jesus himself arrived and rebuked the devil and drove it out of the boy. They wanted to know, *"Why couldn't we cast it out?"* They were still puzzled. It had always worked before, why didn't it work this time? Jesus said, *"Some are harder than oth-*

ers; this kind doesn't go out but by fasting and prayer." When Jesus got there, the father of the little boy prayed to Jesus, *"Oh, Lord, help me. If you can do anything, help me."* Jesus said, *"All things are possible if you can believe."* He said, *"Lord, I believe. Help my unbelief."* So, Jesus immediately helped his unbelief. He cast that devil out! That helped his unbelief! He didn't have any unbelief left after Jesus got through healing his son of that demon possession.

That spirit was interfering with that boy's brain chemistry and causing him to roll around on the ground, sometimes roll over into the fire. They had to watch him constantly because he would lose consciousness and lose his self-awareness. He would go out of himself, so to speak, losing control. Something was taking over his brain, causing his body to behave in those strange ways.

Jesus and the apostles went up to a foreign country. They went up there to rest; they didn't go up there to work. They weren't on a missionary journey that day; they were taking a vacation. Jesus and the twelve apostles went on a vacation to a foreign country. People heard about them, heard they were in town. If you can solve people's problems, you won't get much rest. You'll be too busy solving people's problems.

This Gentile woman had a problem. She was a mother; she had a daughter twelve years old that had a devil, possessed with a demon. It was interfering with her brain chemistry. That little girl was being affected, bothered, sickened by an evil spirit. That woman came praying to Jesus, *"Lord, heal my daughter."* At first, Jesus rejected her; he said, *"It's not time for that. It's not right to take the children's bread and cast it to the dogs. I'm not sent but to the lost sheep of the house of Israel."* That woman didn't give up. She hadn't heard the parable, I don't guess, where Jesus taught about the unrighteous judge. *"Keep on knocking! Keep on praying!"* She just knew that principle; she believed if you don't receive the first time, ask again! If at first you don't succeed, try, try again! She knew that principle even if she didn't know the proverb. She kept begging him.

When he made the parable about casting the children's bread to the dogs, she said, *"That's right, Lord; that's a valid principle, but don't forget that even the dogs grab up the crumbs from under the children's table. They get their little portion, whatever they can. They don't get the whole meal, but they get a little bit."* That affected Jesus the same way the centurion affected him when his servant was sick. That was another Gentile, by the way, although he may have been a Jewish convert by then.

When Jesus responded to that centurion he said, *"I have not found so great faith, no not in Israel."* He had found some faith that day outside of Israel when he healed the centurion's servant and he found some more faith outside of Israel in the Syrophonoecian woman when she came to him praying for the healing of her daughter. She touched Jesus' heart. She didn't have to find Mary and get Mary to prevail upon her son, Jesus. Jesus was touched; he had a tender heart. He had feelings; he had emotions; he had sympathy.

He thought, *"This is too much. I can't turn away a prayer like that."* He said, *"Great is your faith. Be it unto you as you will. Go home; your daughter is well. That demon is not interfering with her brain chemistry any longer."* She went home and found her daughter resting on her bed, sound and well.

It's wonderful to be able to turn to God! Jesus was the power of God for them. They prayed to him and got answers. Thank God! We prayed to God and we got answers for that little boy in Paducah, Kentucky a few years ago and got an answer! The answer went over to Oklahoma City! We were in Paducah, Kentucky but the answer went to Oklahoma City! The little boy was healed! Praise God! Wonderful to turn to the Lord and know him, not be afraid. Don't be dismayed; *"in nothing terrified by our adversaries."* There is nothing too hard for God! There is always hope! There is always light at the end of the tunnel, as we say. That is a modern day parable: "Light at the end of the tunnel". They never said that in the Bible. It was hard to find a tunnel. They didn't have as many tunnels as we do nowadays.

They understood the principle: There is hope. Keep on looking down the line, down the road for God to come on the scene! There is hope of better things! Praise the Lord! Whatever your problem, whatever difficulty you find yourself in, there is hope for you! Jesus holds out hope for you! Don't give up your hope! You are saved by hope, Paul said! You must have some faith and confidence in God! *"Cast not away your confidence which hath great recompence of reward!"* It pays off to have confidence in God! You can get the things you need.

I want to thank all of you for praying for us on this trip to the meeting this week. We had a great, profitable meeting in Brother Evon George's church over in Fort Lauderdale, Florida. It's been there twenty years or so. About twenty years he has been preaching there, building that church. He's got a nice church building. We lent him some money a few years ago when he needed some money to finish up the landscaping or something and get into his building. He is in a city where they have strict building codes. I'm afraid we are too, now. We weren't then, but we probably are now. We haven't had much chance to try them out yet.

He had spent all the money he had trying to get the church house ready. I think he said that after they bought the property and spent all their money on the land, they had their first service under the trees. He told a story about having the first service under the trees. They wouldn't let him into the building until he got everything right. He had to get everything right, even to the landscaping. He had to have the parking lot paved and shrubbery placed around the place. It's amazing what they require to let the people get in to worship in their own paid-for church house.

So, we gave him a no-interest loan of a few thousand dollars to finish up his landscaping. He has since paid us back. They have a nice place there. If you're ever down in south Florida, go by and visit the Fort Lauderdale assembly. It probably packs out six hundred people when they fill it up. It's neat, nice, and the grounds are neat and well-kept. You can tell they pay a lot of attention to it. Somebody takes an interest in it. Somebody dedicates themself to doing the work, keeping the grounds looking good.

God needs a lot of people that are willing to work, willing to give their time and their expertise. While they're dropping money out of their billfold into the offering during the services, they're coming during the week and cleaning the church, dressing up the grounds, planting flowers and, at a time of a meeting like this, they are cooking and serving. That is a laboring, active church.

He put me under conviction telling about how they fast and pray in there. They do a lot of fasting and praying in that church. They fasted and prayed quite a bit for this meeting. And, it did seem like God helped us. He helped us over the crisis. I expected us to have some tension, some strain because of Brother Leniger being gone; all the authority he had and all the time he took in all the meetings. I'm not speaking negatively about him, he just did a lot of work. He fed us a lot and directed us a great deal, spiritually speaking, in the meetings. With all that gone, missing, there was bound to be a reshuffling. All us preachers now have to test our new limits and see what our new limits are with Brother Leniger gone. So, there was a certain amount of confusion, especially in the opening service the first night. We were trying to do business that was probably premature; it wasn't time for it, yet. We quickly got that spirit settled down and got down to spiritual business, got down to real business for God.

I thought we had a good meeting. I was struck with a scripture that Brother Mickey Smith used the last day. It is in the last chapter of Zechariah. He wasn't using it the way I'm using it right now. He just used it in passing on another subject. But it called my attention to a couple of phrases in the third verse of Zechariah 8, where it says, *"Thus sayeth the Lord, I am returned unto Zion and will dwell in the midst of Jerusalem and Jerusalem shall be called a city of truth."* A city of truth!

Jerusalem has always been known as the holy city, but I like that phrase, 'a city of truth'. I'm willing to spiritualize all this and apply it to the church today, but first, we place it in its setting back there in the restoration of the natural Israel when they were just coming back out of the Babylonian captivity. The city of Jerusalem and the mountain of Zion had been forsaken for seventy years. They came home, finally, and reestablished themselves there in the holy city. It was still a holy city after it had been neglected for seventy years. It was still holy ground; it was God's chosen location. But, he named it a city of truth; he prophesied a time when Jerusalem would be called a city of truth and God would dwell in the midst of them.

I know that's happening, coming true in the church. I like to apply that thought of 'truth' connected with the next phrase '*the mountain of the Lord of hosts shall be called the holy mountain*', connecting truth and holiness with the people of God, especially with the central framework of the people of God, the capital location, the government seat. Jerusalem, Mount Zion, was the government seat. That is to be a place of truth and holiness. More and more, we must contend for truth and holiness! We can't just settle for truth! We need to add the holiness! We've got to have holiness mingled with our truth. Our truth should promote and produce holiness! Thank God! I want to emphasize that; work on that more and more as we go on into the future, and I mean the near future.

My future here on this earth is short. What I do, I must do quickly. Several of us are in that condition now. We are having to wind up our career. We want to wind it up and cut it short in righteousness. We need to do a quick work and cut it short in righteousness. We are looking for God to do more things among us. I, for one, am holding out for Brother Leniger's prophecy to come true about this very year. He believed that God had showed him this was to be a year of jubilee, measuring back from the move of the Spirit that took place on the campground in 1953. It began there at the campground and spread throughout the whole Body as people took the experience home from there.

It would be wonderful to see something equivalent, something similar or something superior to that happen in our time. We need a move of God now! It was a time when God was… as

Brother Jolly assured us at that time. He evidently knew what he was saying because he had been prophsying that move. God had told him, he said, that he was going to do something spiritual on the campground. He told the people, "Don't wear your best suits when you come to the campground this time; don't wear your nicest clothes when you come up to the hilltop this year. Come prepared for a wave of the Spirit."

Evidently, he knew what he was talking about! It happened! It broke out the first night. People began to fall out under the Spirit, not only inside the tabernacle, but out on the grounds in the gravel pathways and in the roads. All over the hilltop people were rolling around in their suits and their nice dresses and their fancy shoes, kicking and scratching in the gravel, scuffing up their shoes, dirtying their clothes. They were generally slain by the Spirit of God. It was a mighty work! It was a mighty move of God! At the same time, Brother Jolly told us what was going on. He said, "God is forgiving the sins of this body of people."

We need that again, not only individually, but collectively. We've committed lots of mistakes and errors and grievances in the last fifty years. We need another clearance, letting every man return to his own possession, going home free. Wouldn't you like to go home free from all guilt, not owing God or your neighbor anything? Wouldn't it be wonderful if we could have a service here and go home with all debts cancelled. Every debt cancelled! What a wonderful thought! What a hope! Something to pray about! Why don't we seek God and prevail upon him; try to help that vision come true?

That was the vision Brother Leniger had before he passed away. I hope he was correct! I hope he got it from God! I'm praying that comes true at the campground or somewhere during this year! That we have a move of the Spirit that nobody can deny, nobody can ignore! I wish we could have one that nobody could miss out on, but that isn't possible. Somebody mentioned at this meeting that there are still people around that would testify that they didn't get anything on the hilltop in June of 1953. They were there and saw it but didn't participate in it; they didn't get the experience.

Don't let that happen to you. When God moves, don't let it pass you by. Don't be so unprepared and skeptical and not expecting anything that when something unexpected comes, you can't grapple with it; you can't grasp it. When God pours out his blessing, jump in immediately! Be like the people waiting at the pool of Bethesda when the angel troubled the water. Everybody made a mad rush for the pool as soon as they saw that water being troubled. Bless his heart, there was a lame man there that just wasn't fast. He couldn't help it; it wasn't his fault he couldn't get to the pool. He was crippled and couldn't move that fast. Somebody always beat him. The first one in the pool got healed.

Here came a preacher walking by one day. He looked at him and asked, "*Would you like to be healed?*"

"*Oh, yeah, I would love to get healed, but every time the angel troubles the water, I'm too slow; I'm too crippled. I can't get there first.*"

Jesus told him, "*Take up your bed and leave here.*"

He grabbed up his bed, grabbed up himself and left. He ran away from there; went through the city carrying his bed on the sabbath day. Somebody stopped him and said, "*What's wrong with you man? Don't you know it's the sabbath day? Don't you know not to carry your bed, your burden on the sabbath day?*"

"*Well, I apologize, but the man that made me well told me to carry my bed.*"

That made those Bible teachers mad. But, it made the lame man glad. He was healed; he was well! Praise God! You may be emotionally slow, or something. I'm a little bit that way, myself; slow to decide, slow to make a decision.

Comment or question—not clear.

Yeah, that goes along with the thought you need to be active. It fits with the parable of the woman who wouldn't give up. She kept pursuing the judge until he answered her prayer. The other cases we've described here tonight were other people who prevailed upon Jesus to do something.

Jacob, when he was endangered... When you read that story of Jacob wrestling with the angel, try to put yourself in Jacob's shoes and realize what he was feeling. Jacob was scared that night; he was terrified. He felt led of God to go back to the old home place but big, bad brother Esau was down there close to the homeplace. Big, bad brother Esau was still mad at him. When Jacob left there twenty years before, big, bad brother Esau said, *"Just wait till Dad dies; I'll take care of Jacob."*

Now, Jacob is going home. He sent a messenger, sent word ahead of him to brother Esau, *"I'm coming home, brother Esau. I will see you in a few days."* The messenger came back and said, *"Esau has four hundred soldiers and is coming to meet you."* Jacob was scared. He had a right to be. He had defrauded his brother; he made his brother mad. If it's ever right to get mad and want vengence, Esau was justified. He had been cheated. Just speaking from the natural and the carnal mind, you wouldn't blame Esau for being mad, would you?

Thank God, we've learned to look at things differently today. If you were Esau now, you wouldn't still be mad at Jacob, would you? We don't know. Esau must have still been mad, or else why was he coming with four hundred soldiers? Jacob heard that. He was in an extremity; his life was at a crisis. He was liable to lose his own life, the lives of his wives and children and everything he had. So, he made the best plans he could. He divided his crowd into little groups so that if Esau swallowed one group, the other groups might escape. Maybe somebody would get away.

Can you imagine yourself now in Jacob's shoes? He sent the rest of them on ahead to cross over the river that night while he stayed back with the campfire one more night to pray. He lingered behind to pray. It's a good thing he did. Don't ever forget to pray, no matter how bad it looks; no matter how many enemies you've got lined up against you; no matter how insoluble the problem is, don't forget to pray. Jacob lingered behind to pray. While he was praying, somebody came to him.

I can't imagine how they greeted each other and how they got started in that wrestling match. I've heard that occasion described like this: They were wrestling in words; they were having an argument. The angel was trying to show Jacob what kind of man he was. "Look here how you've treated your brother. No wonder he's mad at you. Look how you treated your father-in-law. How can you live with yourself? You crook, you! God called you to be a preacher and you're as crooked as a snake! You're as crooked as...," I had better not say 'lawyer'; we might have some Christian lawyers around. Maybe that was going on, but it's hard to get around the physical aspect of the wrestling match because when the angel saw that he couldn't pin Jacob to the ground, couldn't hold his shoulders to the ground, he touched him miraculously in his thigh and gave him a hitch in his thigh; he gave him a charley horse. As hard as Jacob was, the angel couldn't wrestle him, so he crippled him. As far as I know, it sounds like Jacob was crippled the rest of his life. He went on the next day limping on his thigh. He was walking with a limp after he got through wrestling with that angel. Just arguing over being a thief and a crook wouldn't do that to your thigh, would it? The angel did do some talking to him and Jacob, no doubt, had done some talking.

There's something special about this wrestler. Jacob knew the angel could help him. He started praying. When the day began to break and the sun was coming up, the angel said, "*Let me go. It's time for me to go; I've been here long enough.*" Jacob just held onto him. I don't know if he had the angel's shoulders pinned to the ground, but he held onto him and wouldn't let him go. He said, *"I won't let you go till you bless me."* Somehow, he sensed that the man he was wrestling with had pull with God. Amen! When you find somebody that's got pull with God, hold onto him! Keep him around as long as you can! Then, when he's got to go, ask him for a blessing.

If he just says, "God's speed or God be with you, it may mean something coming from him." All kinds of other people say that and it doesn't mean anything, but coming from him it might mean something. So, that angel began to bless him. He said, *"You've had the name of a crook. Your name is Jacob, supplanter, deceiver, cheater, swindler."* (That's what the word 'Jacob' meant.) But, he said, *"From now on, your name is go-*

ing to be Israel, (which means something like 'prince of God') *because you've got power with God."* Jacob had a calling of God on his life. When he prayed he had power with God. God sent that angel because Jacob was praying.

Some day when you're praying, God may send an angel to your rescue. God may meet you in the person of an angel from the throne of God. Gabriel might stand by your side and say, *"I'm Gabriel that stands in the presence of God."* I can just see Gabriel sticking his chest out a little bit when he says that. *"I'm Gabriel that stands in the presence of God!"* I'm no ordinary angel, that's what that means! Amen!

Not only did something happen to Jacob. He had a different spirit from that night, but something happened to his enemy, big, bad Esau. Esau had an entirely different spirit when Jacob finally met him the next day. When Jacob met Esau and his four hundred soldiers, Esau was ready to throw his arms around him and welcome his long-lost brother, Jacob. "*Bless your heart! Good to see you, boy! Where you been so long? What's all these gift-wrapped sheep and cattle I saw coming down the road? Keep that for yourself; I don't need it."*

"No, you go ahead and take it," Jacob said, *"I've got plenty. Just to see your face and have your approval and your forgiveness..."* It didn't say those words there in the Bible, but they may have said them, actually, to each other. *"Just to have your forgiveness is worth it all."* Jacob had needed that forgivenss for at least twenty years. A weight of guilt rolled off his shoulders. He had peace with his brother from then on. When old Daddy Isaac died, the two brothers got together and carried him to his grave; laid him beside Abraham and Sarah. They had peace; they were never enemies again.

That's what prayer can do! You may think, "I'll never get along with so-and-so!" You don't want to, read bad! About ninety percent of the trouble, most of the problem is *not wanting* to get along with so-and-so. "After what they said about me! After the way they treated me?" But if you really want to get along with so-and-so, pray about it! When you pray, God will change their spirit and yours, too! Don't forget to pray! Praise God! Where was I? How did I get on that anyway? Thinking about trying to give a brief report on the meeting.

Good things happened at the meeting; we had good thoughts and good experiences. Here's something that sort of goes along with problems and difficulties. Brother Rader had a brother there, a young brother from his church that had been charged with sexual harassment on the job. That's a serious charge if you are in a high position in a company. If some woman charges you with sexual harassment you can lose your job; you can be fined; you can be sent to jail.

Because of that man's position in the city, it was broadcast on television, on the news; his name was smeared in the paper. It was told that so-and-so of this company was charged with sexual harassment and was being prosecuted in the court. The case dragged on for years, a couple of years. He was finally cleared of all charges. That's what Brother Rader was announcing. He was letting everybody at the meeting know that the brother had been cleared of all charges. His name is clear; there is nothing against him. The case was dismissed. He's not guilty of those things he was accused of.

Some women just got together and saw him as a target and made up a case against him. His name is cleared. The brother was there. You could tell that, even though his name is cleared, he is still wounded. This is something I want everybody to become aware of. You can do psychological damage to somebody and it may not be easy to get over. It may take a miracle of God to get over that psychological damage. I was a little disappointed in Brother Rader later on in the meeting, but yet I did see his point. I reacted to him at the time, but he was talking to us later about not getting carried away with psychiatry's ideas and methods and solutions to people's problems.

Brother John Peach is having his ministers' meeting in March; he's going to have a counselor, a specialist in sexual abuse cases, especially pedophilia. He will speak to the brethren and their wives, all that want to come early for the meeting and get in on that seminar. I urge everybody to come. I think it will be profitable; I think we need the education. We need to know, for one thing, how much damage abusers are doing to somebody when they are not breaking their leg, when they're not leaving them black and blue. They're not causing physical injury. Sexual abuse causes psychological injuries.

A lot of people don't realize how serious those injuries can be and how hard they can be to heal. Brother Rader's advice to us was good; it was correct that you've got to help people keep a positive attitude; keep an upbeat outlook and believe, "I can conquer this by the grace of Jesus Christ!" God can help you; God can heal you. That's what we, as preachers, have to tell people when they come to us with their problems. He didn't want us to pet people too much and sympathize too much with them because that allows people to sometimes sink into self-pity. Self-pity never does any good; it doesn't heal anything.

What I want the brethren to get out of that seminar is an understanding of how much damage abusers are doing. You can't judge the abuser until you understand that. If you think the damage he did is easily repaired, then it doesn't call for very much punishment or it doesn't incur very much guilt. But when you see the damage that is actually done, how long it can take, how long some people suffer with it because God doesn't heal it instantly.

God heals some sicknesses instantly, but a lot of them he lets us suffer with a long time while we are learning lessons from it. Not only is the person suffering learning lessons, but the people who are living with them and praying with them, praying for them may be learning lessons. A lot of people that have been abused, mistreated, suffering psychological injuries, are not getting well, partly because God wants to teach us preachers a lesson. He wants us to understand more about mental problems; mental and spiritual pain and suffering. God wants to make us aware of that

I remind you again: I've ordered a set of tapes on the subject from The Church and Tax Laws business, run by some legal accountants who put the program together for the use of churches to educate their people about these things. The other consideration is that we need to be able to recognize things that might be going wrong in our midst; people that might be contributing to injuries like that, causing damage to people right under our noses and we don't even see it, don't even know it. We would do well to know how to look for it.

So, the counselor in the field of pedophilia is going to be there at the Mount Carmel meeting. If you're interested, that is the correct pronunciation of the word: pē-do-philia. Most everybody at the meeting called it pĕ-do-philia. There is a lot of confusion and disagreement about how to pronouce it. I heard it explained on the radio not long ago on the derivation of the word. It comes from the same root source as the word 'pediatrician'. 'Pē-do' pertains to children. A pediatrician is a children's doctor. A 'pēdophile' is a person who is sexually attracted to small children. 'Pĕ-do' pertains to the foot. That is an entirely different root word. We're dealing with pēdophilia.

It's one of those words like some of those long words in the Bible that you might not be familiar with but need to get familiar with: concupiscence, lasciviousness. Those are Bible terms. We are adding pedophilia to the list. Maybe, if Paul were here listing the works of the flesh nowadays, he might add that one to the list. He had lasciviousness in there, didn't he? It was somewhere in his writings. So, you can add that to the list of the works of the flesh. When Paul finished his list, he said, "*...and such like.*" And other things like that; everything that is wicked, evil, unclean and damaging and hurtful is a work of the flesh. It's not a work of the Spirit, it's a work of the flesh!

Note though; take notice. Read the Bible attentively, as I told the brethren in the airport yesterday. Notice that he did not include marriage in that list. It wasn't just sexuality he was speaking against, but it was the wrong use of sexuality: adultery, fornication, lasciviousness, lust, what we call the 'lust of the flesh'. Even that term can be softened by calling it the desires of the flesh. Sometimes, it will help you understand the use of the word 'lust' in the scriptures. Most of the time, when the word 'lust' is used, it is talking about an inordinate desire, an extreme desire, an uncontrollable desire.

It's what Brother Rader was describing as lack of self-control. He had a good point there; he said a lot of good things. I like what he said, but I don't want to minimize the actual suffering and discomfort of people who have been wounded in any way, by any means, not just these we are talking about.

Question: "If you know that somebody in the church has abused children, is it our duty to warn others to not leave their children alone with the man?"

Well, yes it is! If we know somebody has that tendency and is a genuine threat and danger to little children, it is our duty to protect those children. Keep them away. This is the trouble a lot of preachers, priests and religious leaders have fallen into in our generation, letting those things go on without providing proper protection for the children. Finally, the legal climate has caught up with that. They've established laws and legal structures whereby everybody is held accountable for the welfare of the children.

There is really nothing wrong with that. We need to all consider ourselves accountable for the children's welfare. Everybody should feel responsible for the safety of the kids—pardon the term. Everybody should feel responsible and accountable. If you can stop somebody from being hurt, it's your job to do it. Help me find that Proverb that goes something like this: "If you know that somebody is being hurt..." I can't quote it. "... *and you do nothing about it.*" It says that God sees that. Does anybody recognize what I'm talking about? I don't even know what word to suggest to look it up by right now. There is a proverb that warns you that God notices when you turn your back on somebody who is being mistreated and you don't come to their rescue. God will judge that neglect, that callous disregard for other people's suffering.

That is a spirit of apathy, Brother Wright says. We cannot be apathetic to other people being mistreated, especially to child abuse of defenseless children. God takes special notice of the widow and the orphan. Those are people who don't have much help; they are relatively helpless. They don't have many resources. Especially in Bible times, there was nowhere a widow could turn except to the works of her own hands and the charity of neighbors, the kindness of people around her. God took a special responsibility for the widows and the orphans. He didn't want us to leave them up to God, just turn our backs and go the other way and say, "Well, God is taking care of them." He expected us to see those needs. God would choose to meet their needs through us. God would like to meet poor people's needs through us.

This is one reason we feel burdened and responsible about the needs down in the poor island of Haiti. There are so many poor people there that can't make a living. They don't have any help. They have nowhere to turn; they can't get a job. Every person that gets a job on that island is supporting at least a half dozen other people around them, the rest of their family, nieces, nephews, uncles, grandparents. They have a lot of people dependent on their paycheck. That's the reason for so much begging. A lot of the preachers' saints come to them after the service, asking for a nickel or a dime to get something to eat. They're hungry; they may not have had anything to eat all day. That goes on right down here seven hundred miles from Miami, not very far away from us. And yet, we've got nearly everybody up here who never thinks about that; they never care enough to send an offering once a month to the mission fund to help the poor people over there.

We can't help nearly all of them; we can't make a drop in the bucket. One thing they warn you about if you go visit Haiti is, don't let your sympathy run away with you; don't feel like you have to meet every need that you see. You are going to see a lot more needs than you can meet. But, it's wrong to do nothing. It's wrong to do nothing! We ought to be doing something.

We don't have any precedent and this holds some of our preachers back from contributing like they should. We don't have a precedent in the New Testament for setting up a general fund like that for the whole Body. But, they did set the precedent in the city of Jerusalem which was the whole Body for awhile. When the church was getting started, the whole Body had a general fund there in the city of Jerusalem to meet the needs of the poor. Later on, at least twice in Paul's career, he helped raise offerings to take to the church at Jerusalem. I don't know how well they had it organized but I'm sure they just didn't send Paul and Barnabas down there with the offering to walk the streets and pull it out of their pockets and give it to whomever they met.

I think they did it like the people did there early in the game in Jerusalem when people were selling what they had and brought the money and laid it at the apostles' feet. The leaders of the church were responsible for the handling of the finances, meeting the financial needs of the church. Later on, when Paul took offerings down there, you just know he took it to the ministry and turned it over to them. They were accountable then for knowing who needed help and getting the help to them.

Our churches here in the Houston area have contributed for a long time on a monthly basis to the fund that is dispensed among the poor, mainly the preachers and some orphanages down in Haiti. Brother Leniger used to manage that. He was responsible for dispensing the funds, but he's gone. We're having to discuss and try to discern the will of God about how to do it and who to involve in it from here on. Y'all pray for us! That's where a lot of the confusion arose in this meeting! Trying to answer that question! We never did get it answered. Like I said, it was probably too early, too premature. Eventually, it will have to be answered.

Proverbs 16:1. Let's try that one. *"The preparations of the heart in man and the answer of the tongue is from the Lord."* That's good, as far as it goes. Try the next one. Proverbs 21:2: *"Every way of a man is right in his own eyes but the Lord pondereth the heart." That's a good one, isn't it?* Verse 13: *"Whoso stoppeth his ears at the cry of the poor, he also shall cry himself, but shall not be heard."* That's close to the one I was looking for; it conveys some of the thoughts. There is still another one in there that is more pointed as a rebuke to the person that hides his eyes from the plight of the poor.

Proverbs 24:11: Yes, this is it! *"If thou forbear to deliver them that are drawn unto death and those that are ready to be slain* (Somebody's being taken advantage of. Somebody's being unjustly persecuted and you forbear to deliver them when you know that they don't deserve that treatment.) *if thou sayest, behold we knew it not."* "Well, I didn't know anything about it; nobody mentioned it to me!"

Well, you better be telling the truth! If you did know it, if you heard it, if you saw it and you were somehow aware of it, even though you didn't feel like you were involved personally, here is what God says in verse 12: *"Doth not he that pondereth the heart consider it?"* Doesn't God consider what you really knew? You may be able to deny it in a court of law and say, "Well, I didn't know it; that case wasn't brought to me." But there is a court of law in the sky that knows whether you knew that or not! *"And he that keepeth thy soul, doth not he know it? And shall not he render to every man according to his works?"* (Or, his lack of works) That sounds like a good stopping place. Let that soak in. We ought to pray.

Question: "Should we tell you who the abuser is?"

That's a loaded question. The obvious answer is yes. The leadership needs to know who is dangerous. But there will be other scriptures we have to abide by when an accusation is brought to us, especially depending on who the abuser is. One scripture tells us to not receive an accustion against an elder except before two or three witnesses. It just means you have got to have plenty of evidence. One case is not enough evidence. Just like the case of the brother from Louisville, it could be a false accusation. We always have to bear in mind that the accusation could be false, no matter how credible you are, how honest you are and how much you expect to be believed. We cannot take judicial action on the testimony of one person.

Here is a question that was discussed at the meeting: "If a minister is guilty of something like that, will God forgive them and can they still work in, or with, the ministry? Well, there are two answers to that. God will forgive them but they may not any longer be able to work in the ministry. A person may find himself disqualified from working in the ministry and need to back up, sit back and get saved. He needs to get his own soul saved without trying to save other souls by working in the Gospel. These are painful thoughts, painful facts. The facts are sometimes brutal, as Brother Watson calls them.

Question: "What scriptures are there backing the speaking in tongues as a requirement to make the Bride?"

Well, that's for tomorrow; we'll save that one. It's off the subject here tonight.

Question: "Could you please explain Genesis 30:31-42? It's not clear to me how the rods increased Jacob's cattle."

Well, I would save that one for tomorrow, too, but it's easy to give a quick answer to that. The answer is, they didn't. But, Jacob thought they did; he thought it would work. Actually, what was happening was God was making Jacob's cattle bear fruit. God was making Jacob prosper all his life, but Jacob thought he was doing that himself by tricking his father-in-law out of them by setting those striped rods out. Jacob wasn't a scientist; he was an ancient shepherd, a relatively primitive shepherd. He thought it would work and he was willing to use that trick against his father-in-law. I'm sure that's one of the things the angel wrestled with him about.

Chapter 9

The Apostleship

September 1, 2003, Gospel of the Kingdom Campground

All the other preachers that I've sat under are dead and gone. Brother Whittle—live forever! I miss the covering that those men provided. The burden, the responsibility has passed on down from that generation. Another thing that does my heart good is to see God raising up new men, younger men. I see that this is not going to run out, but there will continue to be a leadership for God's people.

I'm pleased with this meeting. I've enjoyed everything that's been said. It's been so good. The Lord is still meeting with us. I don't want to start coming to meetings where the Lord doesn't meet. But, the Lord Jesus is in the meetings! He's providing the missing ingredients that we need.

I thank God for Brother Clarence Rader. We repent, Brother Rader; we needed the rebuke. We have put off too much, too long. I appreciate men that can call to our memory the things we've forgotten. We forget too much! Every once in awhile we need to be reminded of our past, our history, the ways that God met with us.

The last year that we spent under Brother Jolly, back in 1965, he spent several meetings that year reminiscing and telling us the old stories about Brother Sowders. We needed that. We need those things. We've needed them ever since. I'm glad we still have Brother Rader here as a direct connection with that time period. Brother Rader—live forever! Everybody pray for Brother Rader! Give him another miracle! Amen! Surely those testimonies today will impact the prayer line tonight. Our faith can stand some increasing.

Even the disciples said that to Jesus, one time. He had said something hard to understand and they said, "*Increase our faith.*" They were having trouble believing everything he said.

We may still be having trouble believing some of the things that get said. The Lord says to us, or has said to us--I mean he has people saying to us, and we may wrestle with some things until the Lord increases our faith and helps us believe all the things we need to believe. Praise God!

I enjoyed Brother Allen's talk yesterday, especially as he was drawing to a close. He began to speak to the ministry, saying things to and about the ministry. That's what I feel like speaking on today. I feel like speaking to the ministers. I may be opening a different channel, but there is more than one thing that needs to be worked on. I think the whole crowd can enjoy it, because most everybody is conscious of at least some of the problems existing among the ministry. If you're not—enjoy your ignorance while it lasts! (Congregation laughs)

That's not an insult, by the way, just recognition of the fact, as Solomon said, *"He that increaseth knowledge increaseth sorrow."* The more you learn about the problems of the ministry, the more things you will have to worry about. Would you rather use the term 'be concerned about'? There are things to be concerned about. When Brother Clyde Patton first came up to this hilltop he was new and impressed by everything he was seeing and hearing. It was so exciting and wonderful and encouraging! He was just happy and rejoicing! But he overheard Brother William Sowders who was standing outside somewhere on the grounds, looking out over the scene, make a remark to himself (I guess), "I'm so discouraged. I don't know what to do."

Brother Patton couldn't figure out how he could be discouraged with all of this in operation, all the success his ministry had had and everything that was going on was wonderful. It was so wonderful! But, Brother Sowders was aware of problems in the ministry, problems among the ministry, foreseeing trouble, a lot of which did come. But, we're still here today after surviving all the troubles. And, we continue to survive them. We continue to have trouble. We continue to have problems. That will continue as long as we're in this world. But with the Lord leading us, we will continue to survive all the problems and difficulties.

Somebody spoke earlier in this meeting about the needs. Brother D.L. Jones reminded us of the twelve oxen under the laver, holding up the molten sea on their backs. They had their hinder parts together, showing that they trusted each other. I feel like, in this ministry, we pretty well trust each other as far as integrity goes. I'm not afraid to turn my back on you brethren. I don't think any of you would hurt me intentionally. I trust your integrity. What we don't trust fully is each other's wisdom and judgment. That is a fact of life, isn't it? Any of us can make a mistake. That's why we need a multitude of counselors; that's why we need a *ministry* and not a *minister*. We need a ministry leading us. The Lord has provided us with that.

Every one of us needs to remember, as ministers—by the way, I'm Billy Brown from Houston. I'm glad I've obtained a part of this ministry. I say I'm glad inspite of the fact I never wanted to be a minister. After the Lord made me a minister, I wanted to be a good one. I've prayed many times, "Lord, make me an able minister of the New Testament." As somebody said, he's still working on us. Brother Rader said, "God's a good sculptor." So, he's still trying to answer my prayer. I don't guess you need to pray for God, but you need to pray for me, that God can answer my prayer.

We all want to be able ministers, don't we? That sometimes drives us to want something the Lord didn't give to us or doesn't want for us. What I want to speak on is accepting our place in the ministry. I'm going to have to deal with the apostleship a little while here. Y'all try to follow me and I may say something you haven't heard before about apostles.

The first thing I would like to show is the uniqueness of those first twelve apostles. There has never been a group of men like them and never will be! They were unique; they were called for a special purpose. It wasn't so much the greatness of their gift as it was the uniqueness of their qualifications that made them what they were. Those men were called of the Lord Jesus; they were chosen of him. There wasn't that much, or didn't seem to be that much, special about them; their personalities, their talents didn't seem that special. In fact, in Luke 6 where it names the twelve apostles, it says Jesus chose twelve men whom he *named* apostles. If he hadn't *named* them apostles, nobody would have known they were apostles. But, he pointed them out; he singled them out and appointed them to be apostles. He told everybody who they were. You can assume, I think, that Jesus made an announcement to the multitudes at some time or other, made it clear who his apostles were. They were called to be with him.

I want to note how Mark worded it in Mark 3:14. It says, *"He ordained twelve that they could be with him and that he might send them forth to preach and to have power to heal sicknesses and to cast out devils."* That is the most succinct and brief description of their calling in all of the Gospels. Mark boiled it down to three things: to preach, heal sicknesses and cast out devils. Presumably, that is the example for all apostles of all times.

That first qualification that they should be with him, no other apostles could ever match. That was what made those twelve unique. They were chosen to be with Jesus from that time on. At the time he chose them, they had already been with him from the baptism of John. When we come to the choice of Matthias in the first chapter of Acts, that was the qualification in that chapter. Peter said, *"One must be chosen from among those, that few who had been with us from the baptism of John until the time he was taken up from us."* There were some people that stayed with Jesus that whole time period, three and one-half years of his ministry. From the time he was baptized and anointed to his ministry until the time he ascended up into heaven, there were some people who were around that saw all of that. There were a few.

The twelve were chosen out of that group. They had that qualification. They needed that because their job was to witness to the fact of Jesus Christ, the fact that he was not just a made-up story. He was not just a myth; he was not just a phantom, what they would call today a holograph that appeared to be there but wasn't. How many of you have actually seen a hologram? Brother Mark Pierre carried a group of us to the

Federal Reserve Building in New York City, a place where they have gold bricks stored in vaults down in the basement. But up in the lobby where you go in, there is one on display. One gold brick is on display mounted up on a stem. A sign says you are free to take that if you want to. You can grab it and walk off with it. But when you try to grab it, your hand just goes through it; it's not there. It looks like it's there. You would swear it was there. You can look at it from all sides. You can get around it and it's all there. As far as your eyes go, it's real. But, it's just a phantom. There's nothing there. You reach out to touch it and there is nothing substantial there.

This was a charge that some people in the latter part of the early church period began to make about the activity of Christ because their doctrine led them to believe that the real son of God would never come down here and live in human flesh; he would not pollute himself with that. So they thought that Jesus was a phantom, that he was a vision people saw and heard. This is what the apostles were prepared for, as much as possible, to forestall and prevent that kind of mistake. That was a deadly mistake! That kind of doctrine led people to believe you could not possibly be like Jesus. It was idle to teach those people that Jesus is your example. Christ is our example and we are supposed to imitate him. We're to live like him; he showed us how to live. They didn't believe that because they didn't believe he suffered, being tempted in all points like as we're tempted. They didn't believe he was in this kind of flesh.

So, the twelve apostles were the witnesses of the corporeality of Jesus. They could say, as John said in the first chapter of I John, "*That which we have seen and heard declare we unto you. That which our hands have handled of the Word of Life.*" He was emphasizing that. Peter would say, "*This voice we heard when we were with him in the holy mount...*" They had experiences they could appeal to.

Old Brother L.C. Anderson used to tell us down in Cisco, Texas that, "a man with an experience is never at the mercy of a man with an argument". They could meet all those arguments, doctrines and religious inventions. They could meet it with their testimony. That's what they were supposed to do. There never was another apostle with those qualifications; not even Paul had that qualification. Paul wasn't with Jesus from the time he was baptized until the time he was taken up. He was a witness of the resurrection of Christ. It's stated that way somewhere in there. They were to be witnesses of his resurrection. Paul was made a witness of his resurrection just by the fact of seeing Jesus sometime several years after his resurrection. Paul saw Jesus alive. He would testify to that, but he couldn't tell all those stories like Brother Rader could tell here today about things he saw. Brother Rader saw things happen back there.

Paul had to tell, like we do today, the things those original twelve apostles told. So when Paul said, "*We're built on the foundation of the apostles,*" he was talking about those twelve apostles. "*Other foundation can no man lay but that which is laid which is Jesus Christ,*" that Jesus Christ the twelve apostles described. He laid the same foundation that we lay today. That's the only foundation any apostle can lay today, the foundation of Jesus Christ as those twelve apostles described and presented him in their ministry. They were so great, so powerful; their words, deeds and actions were so powerful that then, just like it is now, it made a lot of men desire to be apostles.

Time was, in this body of people, when everybody wanted to be a teacher. Men would stand in the pulpit and teach for four or five hours just to prove they were teachers because they had seen Brother Sowders and Brother Jolly do that. Certain men back there were gifted enough to do that and hold your attention. Every man wanted to be a teacher because that was what was being magnified. But even then, even at the time I came in, in the early fifties, the subject of apostles was coming to the front. One time, Brother Patton took Brother Kenneth Dreymala, one of the young single men in the Houston church at that time, a young man called to the ministry and showing signs of a gift in his life. Brother Patton took him on a trip up to Cisco, Brother Anderson's church.

Brother Patton told when he came back, reporting on the trip, bragging about how Brother Kenneth Dreymala got up in that church. He said, "I saw the spirit of a teacher come on him." For some reason, Brother Kenneth wasn't present when Brother Patton gave that report, so I was telling him about it. Kenneth was my best friend in those days. He questioned me. He wanted to know just how he said it. I could tell he was a little disappointed that Brother Patton didn't say the spirit of an apostle came on him. That was already working in us in those days.

Years later, it developed to where Brother Patton almost stopped any of us from wanting to be called teachers. When he got to describing how teachers can be blind to the needs and conditions of the crowd; all they are thinking about is their subject, their sermon. They just want to give what they have studied out. He stopped us from wanting to be teachers. By that time everybody was wanting to be apostles.

After Brother Patton died and the burden of his work, at least locally, passed on to me along with the assistance of Brother George Wright and other brethren that have stood with me. Since then, people began to provoke me to declare myself an apostle.

Where is Brother Johnny Miller today? He would enjoy this! (Congregation laughs.) He didn't get to come, did he? Is he here? Where are you, Johnny? All right, stand up! Brother Miller has been voting for me to be an apostle! (Laughter) Some have been voting for me and some voting against me! (Laughter)

In the midst of all that I began to consider whether the Lord might be adding that to my gift. But what the Lord finally showed me is that I don't need that. You don't have to be an apostle to have some authority. This is one of the corrections I see that we need to make correcting that mistake in assigning supreme authority to the apostles. Supreme authority did rest, at first, on those twelve apostles. In the Jerusalem church, supreme authority rested on them. And wherever an apostle like Paul went and opened churches, he held supreme authority in those locations and conditions. But when Paul got among the rest of the apostles he did not have supreme authority.

What I want to try to show you here today is that the apostles as a group didn't continue to have supreme authority in questions that came up. Their authority may have been greater than all the other gifts but it was still not enough for them to ignore the other gifts. Let's see if we can pick out some scriptures in here about the activities of the apostles.

In the second chapter of Acts, after that great event, after Peter's great sermon... there are several things I want to point out here in Peter's ministry. Verse 42 says, *"They continued steadfastly in the apostles doctrine and fellowship and in breaking of bread and in prayers."* That right there, I think, is the scripture that became the basis for this feeling that the apostles ruled supreme in the area of doctrine. "*They continued steadfastly in the apostles doctrine...*" The only time I ever, to any degree, openly claimed apostleship was when that came up among us. Somebody was teaching that the apostles make the decisions; they decide doctrine.

I said, "If you're defining it that way, then you are putting me in because doctrine is my specialty. That's what I do."

But, let us pursue this thought through the book of Acts here. I think there is a place in the fourth chapter. Y'all help me find it where it's reiterated somewhat like that. I don't know if I can find.... Well, here's one I want to point out about the job of the apostle in Acts 4:33. It says, "*With great power gave the apostles witness of the resurrection of the Lord Jesus.*" That emphasizes what I said a while ago that their job was to testify to the reality of Jesus. Not only did he live and preach and heal and work miracles and die and get buried, but most important of all, he came alive again! His Resurrection! They gave witness to his resurrection! The whole Christian faith is founded on that. Paul said in I Corinthians 15, *"If Christ be not raised you are yet in your sins."* You haven't got any benefit out of the Gospel if Jesus did not come alive and come out of the grave! *"With great power gave they witness of the resurrection of the Lord Jesus and great grace was upon them all."*

Now, let's look at some of the things Peter said in Acts 10, speaking at the house of Cornelius. In verse 38, he spoke of "*How God anointed Jesus of Nazareth with the Holy Ghost and with power, who went about doing good and healing all that were oppressed of the devil, for God was with him.*(39) *And we,"* Peter said, *"we apostles are witnesses of all things which he did, both in the land of the Jews and in Jerusalem, whom they slew and hanged on a tree."* No other apostles can ever make that claim. (40) *"Him God raised up the third day and showed him openly,* (41) *not to all the people, but unto witnesses chosen before of God."* That's the apostles, the twelve apostles chosen before of God to be witnesses of the things Jesus did. *"...even to us, who did eat and drink with him...,"*

He's trying to make it real, concrete. There's no mistake. It wasn't just an imagination. They really had constant interaction with him. They had daily social interaction with Jesus; they were with him. They were qualified to tell that he was real, that he lived in a fleshly body; he lived in a human body. That's one of the central facts of the New Testament. The New Testament lays great emphasis on that. Jesus lived in a human body.

This new thought that has cropped up with semi-scientific background in recent years, the seed of the woman, the idea that Jesus' birth of a virgin preserved him from the problems that are inherent in human flesh is an attempt to get around the fact that Jesus was tempted in all points like as we are tempted. It was necessary; that early church understood that it was necessary for people to understand that Jesus could be tempted, that he could feel carnal temptations. It's still necessary to believe that. If you don't believe that, you won't overcome. You will never overcome the flesh if you don't believe that. Lack of that support in your mind will undermine your zeal to overcome. As long as you feel like Jesus had an advantage you can't have, then you won't pay the price that Jesus paid.

So, they *"...did eat and drink with him after he rose from the dead.* (42) *And he commanded us to preach unto the people and to testify that it is he which was ordained of God to be the Judge of quick and dead.* (43) *To him give all the prophets witness, that through his name whosoever believeth in him shall receive remission of sins."*

Now, there is the apostles' doctrine! We are reading here the apostles' doctrine. Jesus *"was ordained of God to be the Judge of quick and dead and whosoever believeth in him shall receive remission of sins."* That was the twelve apostles' doctrine. Nobody can mess with that foundation! Nobody can change that doctrine! Nobody can improve on that! But that, of course, that amount of doctrine does not answer all questions that come up. The minds of people are so fruitful and productive, probing at details, implications and ramifications we can always bring up some questions.

Questions like that came up in the early church. By the fifteenth chapter of Acts, they were having arguments over doctrinal questions. The apostles and elders, certain men who came down from Judea taught the brethren a doctrine. *"Except you be circumcised after the manner of Moses you cannot be saved."* That was a very provocative doctrine. It got lots of attention; it made people think. All those Gentiles were saying, "I haven't been circumcised; I'm not keeping the Law of Moses." They began to question the basis of their salvation.

"When therefore Paul and Barnabas had no small dissension and disputation with them...," Just observe from that fact that the word of the apostles was not sufficient to carry the day. It did not stop other preachers from arguing about it. *"...they determined that Paul and Barnabas and certain other of them should go up to Jerusalem unto the apostles and elders about this question."* That is, the apostles and *other* elders, because the apostles themselves are elders. Peter called himself one. But, it's the apostles and rest of the elders.

What I'm trying to do today, I'm trying to help the apostles help the rest of us elders understand the part that all of us have to play. We've got to cooperate with one another. *"Being brought on their way...,"* and so on. In verse 4, *"And when they were come to Jerusalem, they were received of the church, and of the apostles and elders and they declared all things that God had done with them.* (5) *But there rose up certain of the sect of the Pharisees which believed, saying That it was needful to circumcise them and to command them to keep the law of Moses."*

Observe that the original apostles' doctrine did not answer, did not settle that question. There was nothing in their testimony of the life and ministry, death and resurrection of Jesus that answered that question. There may be implication you can find in there, which they did, but it wasn't clear enough to settle the question without a conference. There had to be some discussion of it. Verse 6: *"And the apostles and elders came together for to consider of this matter."* It did turn out to be a couple of the apostles that finally spoke the correct solution, the correct answer. And it was convincing enough, the arguments they made, not their positions as apostles, but the arguments and wisdom that they had was able to convince and silence the crowd. It did not fully convince everybody, but it carried enough weight to conclude the meeting and arrive at a more-or-less official decision for that meeting.

You can tell it didn't change everybody because, years later, Paul was still complaining about Judaizing preachers deceiving his churches. At least, by that time, he had an official proclamation that came out of this meeting in Jerusalem to appeal to when he had to deal with those questions and answer questions about his doctrine. So, that was the way this chapter wound up down in verse 22: *"Then it pleased the apostles and elders, with the whole church...,"* The whole church. The whole church was pleased with that. So, that was a decision made by the whole church there in Jerusalem, *"to send chosen men...,"* with a letter. (23) *"And they wrote letters by them after this manner: The apostles and elders and brethren...,"* to the brethren which are the Gentiles, *"...send greeting unto the brethren which are of the Gentiles in Antioch and Syria and Cilicia."* Etc.

I think, even over somewhere in the next chapter, 16:4, it says, *"...they went through the cities, they delivered them the decrees for to keep, that were ordained of the apostles and elders which were at Jerusalem."* So, from then until now, that is what it has taken to ordain decrees and make decisions for the church. It takes a meeting like this; it takes these threshing-floor meetings, general conventions of the Body of Christ. It takes a brotherhood. That's what I'm telling you. This burden is spread upon all of our shoulders.

I will point out again that the authority of the apostles is not all equal. I said you don't have to be an apostle to have some authority. You only have the authority—whatever your gift—you only have the authority that God gives you. The apostles didn't all have the same authority. Some were greater than others. Paul said in Galatians; he mentioned three apostles in Jerusalem that seemed to be pillars. Evidently they stood out among the rest. Then, one time he said, *"I was not behind the very chiefest of the apostles."* So, there must have been chief men among the apostles. Consequently, we see that the authority doesn't come with the gift. Authority is a separate gift; it's something God gives you.

Your gift will make room for you if you use your gift. But it will only make room for you to use that gift. Your gift may never make as much room as you would like to have. If you're bothered with ambition or comparison with others, then that will always be a problem. Your gift will only make the room that you need to have and God will give you the authority that goes with the job he hands to you.

From the beginning, nine years ago, I've been saying that I dwell in an apostle's room. God has given me the authority I need to deal with that condition locally. Whatever other prominance a man comes to, it doesn't all depend on gifts. A lot of the prominance of a particular minister comes from other things. There are several things that contribute to prestige and influence. Integrity is one thing. Skills and natural abilities can help that; even perhaps, the accident of circumstance.

Maybe you think God has planned all that out from the beginning, and of course he could. He certainly has the power to do that. But it does appear that God refrains from doing everything he could do to see what we will do. God will let you be tested and tried. He will set opportunities before you that you may or may not live up to.

Brother Whittle pointed out, a while ago, a little comment in there about how God could call us and we could still fail. God could put his hand on us, any one of us, God could have his hand on us. That may have happened to some apostles in the

New Testament. It's hard to find an exact example, but I'd like to read a few verses in II Corinthians 11. Throughout the book of II Corinthians, especially in the tenth and eleventh chapters, Paul was defending himself against other preachers who were trying to undermine his position, his influence in Paul's churches, the churches Paul had planted.

He wasn't able to stay with them very long at a time and other preachers would come and preach in his churches and present their doctrines, their positions, their persons, themselves as being great in God. They would seek to win the loyalty of the people away from Paul. He said, "*I'm jealous over you with a godly jealousy.*" I'm struck with the similarity of that word 'jealous' to the word 'zealous' in the English language.

Many people are zealous for certain things. Paul was zealous for his ministry; he was zealous for the welfare of his people. He was jealous over them because he was zealous for them. Other men were coming by who were zealous for their ideas, zealous for their doctrine. They were taking advantage of their natural advantages. Paul had to defend himself against that in verse 12. In verse 9, he reminds these churches, "*When I was present with you and wanted* (or lacked*) I was chargeable to no man, for that which was lacking to me the brethren which came from Macdonia supplied; and in all things I have kept myself from being burdensome unto you, and so will I keep myself.* (10) *As the truth of Christ is in me, no man shall stop me of this boasting in the regions of Achaia.* (11) *Wherefore?* (Why?) *because I love you not? God knoweth.* (That's not it!) (12) *But what I do, that I will do, that I may cut off occasion from them which desire occasion;* (That is, people looking for an excuse to criticize Paul.)

They were looking for weaknesses, looking for things people might resent. If he took too much money from the churches, they would have used that against him. They would have used that to undermine people's confidence in him: "All he wants is money! He just wants your money!" So, Paul wouldn't take any money from those churches in Achaia. He took it from other places, but there was a spirit working in that region of the country. He had to show himself not desiring filthy lucre, not interested in money, so he refused to take any support from the churches in that part of the country. "*...that I may cut off occasion from them which desire occasion; that wherein they glory* (whatever it is they've got to brag about) *they may be found even as we.* (They're no better than we are, in other words. They may be wealthy enough to travel at their own expense,) but, "*So have I,*" he said. "*I worked and supported myself and those that were with me.*"

Those were the kinds of arguments he had to make to defend himself against people he called 'false apostles'. (13) "*For such are false apostles, deceitful workers, transforming themselves into the apostles of Christ.*" I wish I knew more about these particular false apostles. There are two kinds of false apostles in the Bible: There is the kind that simply never were apostles; they just tried to be; they claimed to be. That early church developed a way of trying them that said they were apostles and were not. But, it's harder to deal with people that really were apostles; they used to be apostles. Maybe they still are; maybe you could still call them apostles. They still have that gift and power and skill, but they've apostatized; they've gone astray. They have fallen into heresy, so they have made themselves false apostles.

Another attribute I mentioned a while ago, I wanted to help the apostles help the rest of us because that is one of the marks of a true apostle. He strengthens the brethren. That is what Jesus told Peter to do, "*When you get converted, strengthen the brethren.*" That's what he did. He went throughout all the churches, confirming the churches. He supported, gave advice and leadership even to the rest of the apostles. That's what an apostle is supposed to do: strengthen the brethren. If he weakens the brethren, he makes himself a false apostle. He may be a very great apostle; he may have all the power and that gift working in him. He may have a lot of natural ability.

More than any of the other gifts, the temptation of the apostle is to lead away disciples after himself, partly because that is so easy for him to do. The apostle has a way with people. He can sway a crowd; he can have you up on the edge of your seat one minute and then sitting back relaxed. He can have you in tears and a few seconds later, in peals of laughter. We used to watch Brother Patton do that in the local church. He had a gift; he had a skill. In his preaching he could tell some sad story in a way that would get you to cry. The whole crowd would be sitting there just about to break into tears. A few sentences later, he was off in something light-hearted and comical and have us all laughing, pulling things out of the word of God as well as experience.

But, that gives an apostle the opportunity, the power to sway people and lead people astray if he himself goes astray. That's just another sign and example of how the apostle, as well as all the other gifts, need the rest of the ministry. We all need a multitude of counselors. Not a one of us is sufficient unto himself. Not a one of us is safe if we ignore the rest of us. We all belong to each other and we all need each other. We have got to remember our place in God and what its limitations are.

I think it is significant that he gave an order of priority. There is an order of priority among the gifts. Verse 31 shows that some gifts are greater than others. He called it 'better'. He said, *"Covet earnestly the best gifts."* So it's no sin to desire to be an apostle, if that appeals to you. It's no sin to desire to be in the ministry. I never did until I got in the ministry, but it wouldn't have been a sin. I've observed a lot of young men that did desire it. *"He that desires the office of a bishop desires a good work."* You are not to be condemned for that, but you do need to be careful and be willing, finally, to settle for what God gives you. If you covet the best gift and you get the second best gift, are you going to be unhappy? Here, you've got a great gift, the second best gift in the kingdom; thousands of people envying you for what you've got in God. But, you're envying somebody else, so you can't be happy; you can't enjoy your gift and you can't use it much to bless the rest of God's people because of your dissatisfaction with your gift. That's one of the things I'm working on today.

After God has showed you what your gift is, don't desire a different one; don't wish for somebody else's gift. Don't covet what other people have, but use what you've got! And, you may become greater! You may become more prominent and stand up higher in this local crowd at this present time than greater gifts are doing! As I said, that depends a lot on your integrity, your dedication, your activity and how productive you are. So use your gift! Covet earnestly the best gifts, but there is something better than the best gifts. *"Yet show I unto you a more excellent way."*

I'm not sure we should even present it as a pattern to follow or to expect. There are just a few scriptures that might leave a door open for that to happen if a person's position changes, and of course his responsibilities change, and God gives him the qualifications for fulfilling the job he puts him in. I heard the same thing you heard and had the same questions about it. But, there are these men the apostle Paul left behind. Some people feel like some of them may have stepped into apostleship after he disappeared. That's tenuous; there is no way to pin it down and prove it. You can take the apostles themselves after the twelve, particularly Paul and Barnabas. They didn't seem to begin their ministry as apostles; they're not doing the work of an apostle. They were among the prophets and teachers in Antioch. They had been called to become apostles. They were not apostles when they started.

I've been saying it many times, that we've got all five gifts pastoring churches. Maybe they've all got the gift of pastor, but some of them have got other gifts beside that. Or maybe there are gifts pastoring but they are not even gifted pastors, they're just able to do the job as Paul said to Timothy, *"Do the work of an evangelist,"* just because it needed to be done. He needed to take care of that side of the church.

One of the points I've been wanting to get to is that when it says "*the spirits of the prophets are subject to the prophets*", it includes the apostles among the prophets. Even the apostle is subject to the brotherhood. You can't work independently and work in order. Order involves others. You've got to work in a community, in common with others.

In response to this discussion, I would like to make a tentative suggestion and see what y'all think about it. Can an apostle plant a church without ever being present in that church and that church be said to be planted under his ministry. One of the examples I'm thinking about is Colossae; the church of the Colossians. That church evidently got started by somebody going out from Ephesus and starting a prayer meeting, starting a street meeting or something. Churches spring up sometimes that way without a preacher going with the intent of starting a church. Churches sometimes just happen. You have to figure out how to set them in order then. Colossae may have started like that, just somebody that had been under Paul's ministry and had at least seen what he had planted in Ephesus and carried it to Colossae.

Paul wrote them a letter. At least he had that much input to that church. They certainly must have recognized him as their apostle. He may never have showed his face in that church.

Here's another example that may not be helpful to us in this present distress, but just to add facts to facts, a lot of the churches in Judea in the early part of the book of Acts just happened. Nobody intentionally started those churches. When the persecution broke out after the stoning of Stephen a lot of the people were scattered abroad and they just went everywhere preaching the word by telling what they knew. They weren't all preachers; they were more of the saints that scattered. The apostles particularly stayed behind in Jerusalem in spite of the persecution. But saints and student ministers, all kinds of people fled the dangers and went into other small towns round about and told what they had been hearing and doing. And automatically, under the influence, the inspiration of those testimonies, churches gathered together. People got interested.

A church got started down in Mexico about like that. Sister Ramirez went down there just to visit home folks and got to telling Bible stories to the neighborhood kids. They gathered their friends and before long they had nearly a hundred kids coming out every day to hear her tell Bible stories. The parents heard what the kids were hearing and they showed up on the doorstep wanting to hear those Bible stories. Before she knew it, she had a church started a week before her husband got there.

They began to ask Bible questions. She was telling these Bible stories and that provoked questions. She would say, "Well, my husband will be here next week. He'll answer that question." And, the church started. I don't know if we even know how the church in Rome got started. There were believers there.

After having said all this today, I'm whatever I've been for the past nine years. If you've been looking to me for leadership, you're still safe. I'm a man that will keep you within the perimeters of the Body of Christ. You don't need to apologize for not being under a specific apostle. The spirit and the influence of the apostles pervade this body. If you feel a need to be under a specific apostle, you can surely find one who will be willing to be over you! (Laughter)

If you are an apostle, don't deny your calling. You may have to back up from some of the mistakes you make when you make them, but magnify your office, not by bragging on it, but by laboring in it. And so with all of the gifts, let's magnify our office by laboring in our gift, pursuing our calling, letting the Lord use us. If all the prophets will prophesy, if all the teachers will teach, if all the pastors will provide shepherding for the flock and all the evangelists will evangelize and even if all the apostles apostle-ize, God will raise up another crop to have a complete ministry. Jesus Christ is going to have a complete ministry that will not divide, separate and scatter themselves or God's people. We're standing together today!

Chapter 10

Charity; Spirit, Soul & Body; Death

March 27, 2004

"Ye shall know the truth and the truth shall make you free." That's his gift to us. He was himself the truth. He was the truth. He was the one that makes free. "*Whom the son makes free is free indeed.*" And he was the gift of love, wasn't he? The band got us thinking on love a while ago. So it called my attention to how many kinds of love there are in the Bible; how many kinds of love we are capable of.

The greatest love, of course, is the kind of love that God has. Most commonly, that's the word agape in the Greek testament, frequently translated as charity in the King James Version. Charity is a very popular word and subject among us. Our greatest preachers have taught us about New Testament charity. I Corinthians 13: "*The love of God—charity.*" That's really the word that was used in John 3:16, "*God so loved the world,*" and it was that kind of love, that benevolent love. John said in another place that "*We loved him because he first loved us.*" Well that gave us a reason.

But, why did he love us? Why did he first love us? Well, it was because we needed love. That's the only reason he had to love us, because we needed love so badly. If it had not been for that, if God hadn't met our need, we would all have ended up in oblivion; we would have perished. "*God so loved the world that he gave his only begotten son that whosoever believeth in him should not perish,*" should not disappear into oblivion.

But that was a great love and we're capable of that. We're supposed to have charity too. We're supposed to have the kind of love that God had for others, when you love people for no reason at all. Now we've already said we love God because... Of course, we have many reasons, but because of that one, first of all, that he first loved us. But if you become like God, then you'll love people that you don't have any reason to love except just the fact that they need love. They need to be loved. And you will be able to view them, empathize with them like God does. God has compassion for people that need love. They may not deserve it, and usually don't.

We didn't deserve love; the world didn't deserve the love of God. The world didn't deserve the gift of his Son, Jesus, but they sure did need it. We sure did need it. God loved us enough to meet those needs. I sense then, God has found other reasons to love at least some of us, some of us out of the world, us that came out of the world and have followed Jesus. Jesus said, in the sixteenth chapter of John, "*The Father loveth you because you have loved me.*" The word was not agape or charity there, but it's a word that means friendship, the kind of love you have for your friends.

Jesus had already, in that discourse, accepted his apostles, at least his close disciples, as his friends, which was a promotion he had just given them. They hadn't always been his friends; they had been his disciples before they were his friends. But he said, "*Now I'm starting to call you friends.*" That's an expression of a different kind of love. You love your friends in a different way from the way you love your disciples. Some of your disciples may not be loveable; it may be hard to find reasons to love them, but friends you love for different reasons. You have what we'd call in modern times, a liking for them. You have a liking for your friends.

But God took a liking to those twelve apostles because they had taken a liking to Jesus. They had shown favor to Jesus and so God showed favor to them. And in there is what is called 'brotherly love' elsewhere in the scriptures, the kind of love that brothers in a family have for each other and spiritual brothers in this spiritual family are supposed to have for each other. And all those forms of love, except the agape or charity love are subject to failure.

This is why Paul emphasized in I Corinthians 13 that "*charity never fails.*" What he meant by that is, it never runs dry; it never is used up, never runs out. You can always have it because it's an attitude that you decide to take toward people. You decide to hope for their welfare. You decide to do them favors. You decide to be benevolent toward them. It's a decision you make. You can do that for anybody. So that never fails. Brotherly love is liable to fail. Brothers get into fist fights sometimes. They get mad at each other. Their brotherly love comes to an end or it gets interrupted and friends sometimes turn against each other. They have fallings out, but your charity never fails. You can always have charity.

Significantly though, we more enjoy those other forms of love. It's not always fun to have charity. You may have to force yourself to have charity. You may have to remind yourself, "I need to have charity for these people like God had for me."

But charity is not just a good feeling although you can feel good about being benevolent. That's why a lot of wealthy people give large bequests to public charities. Many times they get a good feeling out of it. There are other reasons to do it. There are real true reasons to do it but many people give because it makes them feel good. But the other forms of love are good feelings. Love you have for your friends, that's a good feeling. You feel good towards your friends.

Brotherly love, that's a good feeling. You really enjoy being around your brothers and sisters. That's an enjoyable love and that's the kind of love we all want. We enjoy giving it and enjoy receiving it. We may enjoy receiving charity until we find out what it is. When I found out y'all were putting on charity with me that took a lot of the fun out of it. It took a lot of the joy out of receiving all that love. I found out it wasn't because you thought I was loveable, but you thought I needed love real bad. So you gave me love from a standpoint of charity. Well I'm glad you did that, but I hope you're not still having to do that. I hope you feel brotherly love for me now, and friendly love.

I hope we've got that far along to where we can all feel good toward each other. The Lord promises that, but everything starts with real godly love, love that caused Jesus to lay down his life for the brethren. It wasn't friendship or brotherly love that made him do that, but it was charity. It was a real sincere desire for their welfare that he had before he came to this world. Before he ever became friends with any of them, he had that intention. He made up his mind to do that.

This is one of the wonderful things about love, real true godly love, and it's the thing that makes it possible for us to recover what Adam lost in the Garden of Eden. It culminates into everlasting life. Adam lost his life, didn't he? He lost ours too. He lost our lives in the garden. But one scripture, somewhere in the Psalms, said about Jesus, *"I restored that which I took not away."* That's what Jesus came to do. He came to restore what Adam took away. He restored to us everlasting life. What a gift! The gift of life! That's what we're working on, what we're experiencing already as our reward. We already have life if we don't do what Adam did and lose it. Adam had life and he lost it. Now you have life when the Lord gives it to you. When you get the gift of the Holy Ghost, you get the spirit of an endless life. Don't squander it this time. Don't waste it.

Before we leave tonight, we might consider some Bible questions that have been handed in. This is from somebody who is really studying the Bible. It really adds up to about 24 or 25 questions. We can't cover that many tonight, so we may end up raising more questions than we answer. Many times you do that when you're dealing with involved subjects. If you don't have a lot of time to make it clear you may stimulate more questions than what you answer. But sometimes, that's good to help us study. It shows us the lines to study in, gives us some guidelines for pursuing Bible questions.

This note begins with the question: Is there is a spirit of death? It assumes that question: Is there a spirit of death? Actually the Bible doesn't designate a spirit of death and it would be unnecessary for there to be a spirit of death or an angel of death. We sometimes hear about the angel of death. God can send an angel to destroy somebody, true, if he wants to destroy them out of time or ahead of time. But there is already a curse of death upon every one of us until the Lord lifts it. And even now it's still upon our bodies. And so all God has to do is leave us alone and we'll die. He has to come to our rescue and get involved and intervene to keep us from dying.

The example that's frequently used is his sending the death angel throughout the land of Egypt on the night of the first Passover to destroy the first born in every house. Actually when he was describing it there in Exodus, the Lord said he was going to do that himself. He didn't say he would send an angel. Now, I think we can assume that he did. I don't suppose that he himself personally visited every household that night with a plague. He did use the term "plague."

That was a peculiar plague, wasn't it? It was contagious to every first born. Only the first-born caught it. Nobody else caught that disease. But they all caught it and died all at the same time that night. But there are many ways to die, many possible ways to die. You could be your own death angel. Some people commit suicide, destroy themselves. And so they die before God would have chosen for them to die. But, we don't need a spirit of death to die.

There's a string of questions here including questions about devils and demons and spirits and evil spirits and angels, which would take too much time to delve into tonight.

Question: "How could good angels and bad angels fight?"

Well there has probably been more than one war in heaven. The one you read about in the twelfth chapter of Revelation was the war between the church and the world that broke out on the day of Pentecost. It was particularly between the church and the civil world.

As Paul said one time, the weapons of our warfare are not carnal, there're spiritual. We have spiritual weapons. This is a spiritual war. And we're in a constant battle against evil in many forms. "*We wrestle not against flesh and blood, but against principalities and powers and spiritual wickedness in high places.*" So there is a constant battle against truth and error, against good and evil in the church. And the church has to fight to keep the world out.

The church in that day had to fight to keep civil power from taking control of them. Civil power at that time was used to being in control of religious power. And the church appeared on the scene on the day of Pentecost without any authorization from civil powers. They never said, "We have no king but Caesar." It was the Jewish church, the Judaist church that said that. "*We have no king but Caesar.*" They recognized that civil power. But it was Peter and John who were themselves subject to that civil power. Those apostles said to those religious leaders, "*Whether it be right to obey God or men, you be the judges yourselves.*"

Who could answer that but one way when the question was phrased that way? It's like stating a legal given. It's a given that we're supposed to obey God so nobody could answer that question any other way. He just put the adversaries in a trap. But there's constant war between the world and the church.

Perceptively, this questioner commented here: "If an important question was not asked; please feel free to explain anything you feel that is important." Obviously, we could ask a lot of questions. The questions would be unending if we went deep enough into all these subjects. But then he organized a set of questions here about death: "What happens at the time of death? What exactly are we?"

Well, to give a Bible answer to that, we are persons consisting of body, soul and spirit; or as Paul ordered it, spirit, soul and body. We have those three parts. What occurs at the moment of our death? Well what occurs at the moment of our death is that the soul ceases to be alive. Commonly, that happens because the body that was supporting the soul and keeping it alive dies.

At this time, and in the scheme of things where we have lost that eternal life that God gave to Adam, we are completely dependent upon the life of the body. When the body dies, the soul dies. Now there are some people that get out of that category; they can live on without the support of the body. Jesus illustrated that in Matthew 10:28: "*Fear not them that kill the body and after that have no more that they can do,*" They can't hurt you anymore after that. "*...but rather fear him that hath power to destroy both soul and body in hell.*" That's God. That's a special class of people that can live on after the body is destroyed.

Commonly, when the body dies, as Solomon worded it somewhere in Ecclesiastes, the body returns to the dust from whence it was taken. The spirit returns to God who gave it. He didn't even mention the soul there because the soul cannot exist without those two elements being together. If the soul loses the spirit and body, the soul cannot even exist.

So where does the soul go when it dies? It doesn't go anywhere. It goes out of existence. It has to be brought back in a resurrection, has to be re-created in a resurrection, if it ever comes back. That's a reward that God gives to some people. He promised a resurrection to the people that fear him.

What is our spirit? Well it's that part of us that God gives to keep the body alive. It keeps the soul alive. The soul influences the spirit and you can feel it. Everybody has a spiritual component. It's not made out of matter. It's a spirit substance. But it's a substance that can't be investigated by material instruments and that's why scientists have yet to discover it. It may be something like what the astronomers are calling dark matter or dark energy. Who knows about that? We only know what God tells us, informs us, until the astronomers discover something else about it.

This has been hidden from the investigative mind of man from the beginning. We cannot investigate the spirit, but you can do your own investigation up to a point. You can have experience with the spirit. Jesus compared it to wind which is something else that's invisible. But, the wind is made out of matter and the spirit is not. So the scientists can investigate wind but they cannot investigate the spirit.

You can feel both of them. You know you can feel the wind. You go out here and feel it in your face and it blows the trees down sometimes. And we can feel the Spirit. We can feel God's Spirit sweep through here. Our spirit contacts his Spirit or, if you want to word it the other way, his Spirit contacts our spirit and we feel it just as clearly as we feel the wind on our face. We feel God's Spirit on our spirits. Hallelujah! It's a good feeling if you're acquainted with it! It scares people that are unacquainted with it. We've had people jump up and run out of church when they felt the Spirit of God sweeping through here.

By the way, when I say everybody has a spirit—that includes God. God has a spirit. His spirit is called the Holy Spirit. That's not another person in the Godhead, but it's a spirit of that person, God the Father; it's his spirit. But he's given you a spirit and your spirit can be felt too. It's not as powerful as his and can't be felt as far away. How far away it can be felt depends on how mad you get, usually. Of course, you can generate a good spirit too. It doesn't always have to be a bad spirit coming from you.

What is our spirit? What is our soul? Our soul is the conscience, the conscious part, the thinking part of the person. It's the self-aware part of you. Superficially, you could define it as the mind; the entire mental processes, conscious and unconscious. But like spirit, it's not a substance, it's a process. It's the process of living. When the body stops living, the soul stops living because that process ceases and the consciousness ceases and there's no soul without the ongoing process. The body can be lying there dead. The soul can't be lying there dead any more than a fire can lie there dead. I sometimes compare body, soul and spirit to the matchstick, the fuel for the fire. The spirit corresponds to the oxygen in the air that gives life to the fire. The fire itself is an allegory of the soul. The soul is started up when that process starts up.

Now this is what God did for Adam: He created Adam out of the dust of the ground but he was only a dead, or non-living, body. He was a non-living body until God breathed into it the breath of life. He breathed into him his spirit and man became, Adam became, a living soul at that time. The body was not really Adam; that was just Adam's body. That was his house. His house was prepared for him. God built his house before he put him in it to live in. But when he lit him up, when he struck the match, when he lit him up that fire came alive. That was Adam's soul.

And since then Adam went to lighting other matches. He lit other people up. You know you can light another match. You strike the first match, and then you can stick that match to another match and light it. You don't have to strike every match. You can keep lighting them with each other, because the fire transfers itself. It starts the process. You can blow one of them out and the other matches will still be burning. That's what finally happened to Adam. He went out but all those other matches he lit up were still burning. And they lit others matches until you and I got here and our fire is still blazing.

Let's pray for Bro. Zinn. He's an example of the scripture. God promised that when he blesses a city, even a spiritual city, he said there would be "*old men and old women in the streets, every man with his staff in his hand for very age.*" We finally get there, every one of us. But that's a blessing to live that long. It's a blessing to a country or a city to have old people in it. It's a blessing to a church to have old people in it. We hate to lose them when we lay them down in death, but that is the final result of growing older. It's the destiny of all of our bodies.

That scripture went on to say also there would be little children, boys and girls playing in the streets of the city that God is blessing. All of that signifies the future of that city. It's going to last a while. It's a fact that we've got old people leaning on our staffs; we carry our walking canes. I've got one that I carry sometimes when I get to feeling lame. That's a sign that we've been here a while.

This church has been here a while. It's not something just invented last night. We've been here a while, long enough to have people grow old from childhood. Some of us have been in this from childhood almost. I was still a teenager when I came into this church. Now I'm fixing to turn seventy next month. And I've got two or three walking canes over at the house that people have given me over the years, getting ready for this day. But I know my flame is burning low. It's going to go out one of these days. This body won't live on. And if my soul is not hooked up with God, kept alive by the Holy Ghost, it won't live on. When the body dies, the soul will die.

People are always asking, "Where are the dead?" I can still remember Brother Patton talking on this one time. He said,

"Silly, they're dead!" It's just as simple as that, but people don't want to accept that. Preachers post that sermon announcement on their marquees for Sunday morning: Come and hear Brother So-and-so, Dr. So-and-so, preach on, "Where are the dead?"

Well if they're dead, they're dead. They ***are not anywhere***! The bodies may be in the grave, but the soul is not even in the grave. The soul is only symbolically in the grave. The soul disappears; it goes out of existence. The Bible puts it this way. It says, "They ***are not.***" They ***are not*** any longer. They ***are not*** any more. They ***are not*** anywhere. They ***are not*** anything. They just **are not**. That's talking about the soul. The soul is the person; the soul is that capital letter 'I'. ***I*** am a soul living in a body, having a spirit, manifesting a spirit many times.

And that brings up then, "What happens to the spirit?" the outstanding example being Jesus, and also Stephen. I think it says about him that he gave up the spirit or gave up the ghost, which is another term for spirit. When people give up the ghost they're giving up that spirit of life that they had. So they don't have it any more. Solomon said the spirit returns to God who gave it, but that doesn't help the person that had it. It's God taking it away from him and he doesn't have it any more.

When Jesus gave up the ghost, he just gave up his life. He gave up his spirit. The spirit itself being indestructible, it went back to God who gave it. But, that wasn't Jesus going back to God. Jesus' soul died because his body died. God had withdrawn the spirit from it that would have kept him alive and so Jesus' body went to the grave. But in reality, his soul went out of existence. Symbolically, it was called 'in hell' or 'in the grave' when he said, "*Thou will not leave my soul in hell or suffer thy holy one to see corruption.*"

But these myths and theories about Jesus going down to hell and preaching a revival down in hell for three days and nights, are mythological. Jesus wasn't doing anything while he was dead. He "*poured out his soul unto death.*" Jesus' soul died and that was the supreme price that he paid. He died that you might live.

After he spent those three days in the grave, God raised him up again, raised him back to life. He came alive again. That flame blew up again. It flickered into life again. They've got these birthday candles now that you blow out and when you turn your back, they light up again. They flame up again; they won't stay dead. Well Jesus stayed dead for three days and nights and then God lit him up again. He came alive forever more! Amen! Never to die again! He was dead and now he's alive forever more! That spirit returned to him and he's alive forever now.

I just want you to know that when you give up the ghost or you yield up the spirit and say, "Lord Jesus, receive my spirit," you're not going with it unless you're ready and qualified, your work is finished and your growth and spiritual development are complete. That's the only way you can go with your spirit to the Lord.

Now there have been people that did that. Paul said, "*It's better for me to die and be with the Lord, but it's better for you if I remain here.*" There were people… and I've already quoted Matthew 10:28 "*Fear not them that kill the body and have no more that they can do.*" That's what they did to those martyrs of that early church. They killed their bodies, but they couldn't kill their souls. Their souls had quit living on, or depending on, the life of those bodies and were living on the Spirit of God. They were hooked up to an eternal life source already.

That happens when you get the baptism of the Holy Ghost, or what's called in other scriptures, 'spiritual birth'. You get hooked up with that Spirit of life and if you let that life do for you what it's capable of doing for you, it'll transform you into the image of Christ and you can go where Christ is. But as long as there's something in you that's different from Christ, if something about your character is different from Christ's, then that will hold you back. It'll bind you to the flesh; you'll still remain trapped in the body. When it dies, you'll die with it and wait for a resurrection.

See, there's more than one resurrection in the Bible. In Hebrews 6, it puts that in the plural: doctrine of resurrections, and baptisms and eternal judgment. Maybe it's baptisms I'm thinking of that's in the plural there, but there is more than one resurrection. We see that, in Revelation 20, he said, "*Blessed and holy is he that hath part in the first resurrection.*" Well, the first resurrection is not the last resurrection. And before he finishes that chapter, he describes another resurrection for some other people that might have to contend with second death. "*Blessed and holy is he that hath part in the first resurrection; on such the second death hath no power.*"

They have already overcome death completely. They don't have to worry about second death, but people who have slept in the grave and have been brought up again in the final resurrection will still have to worry about death until they complete their soul's development and their spirit's development. They have to be completely developed into complete Christians; completely into the image of Christ before they are free from death. And while that process is going on, that lake is still out there.

There's a lake in that twentieth chapter, the lake of fire. It's called 'second death', isn't it? Revelation 20:24 says, "*Death and hell were cast into the lake of fire. This is,*" (He said this lake of fire is) "*the second death*". And that's the death that the people in the first resurrection don't have to fear. Verse six says, "*Blessed and holy is he that hath part in the first resurrection; on such the second death hath no power.*" "*But they shall be priests of God and Christ and shall reign with him a thousand years.*"

But during the thousand years that they are reigning, the people who are waiting for that other resurrection are still dead and when they come up finally, later in the chapter, they still have to worry about second death. It has power over them for the same reason that first death had power over them because they were not fully developed yet. The Holy Ghost had not finished its work on them, so that process must be completed in that final resurrection. And finally, when that's done, there's nobody left that can die.

See, when you get in that condition, you can't die anymore. You can get into a condition where you can't die. Wouldn't you like that? Nothing could kill you because you can't die. When it's that way, when nobody can die anymore, there's no more death, first or second or any number. There's no more second death. There's no more lake of fire, because there's nobody to die, nobody to cast into it. Solomon said, "*Where no wood is, the fire goes out.*" So when there are no more souls to go into death, then death ceases to exist.

I Corinthians 15 where Paul said, "*Jesus must reign till the last enemy be de*stroyed," isn't that what he said? Let's look back at that. First Corinthians 15:25: "*He must reign till he hath put all enemies under his feet.*" The last enemy that shall be destroyed, so it says it both ways, the last enemy that shall be destroyed is death. Death is going to be destroyed, thank God.

That doesn't mean that some people won't still be dead. But a dead soul, I've already told you, is no soul at all. There are no dead people to be literal about. There's no such thing as a dead person. A dead person is no person at all; he's out of existence. He is not. He's one of those that "*are not*". So, there's nobody to keep the lake of fire going. The lake of fire "is not" after that. The lake of fire is destruction. When there is nothing left to destroy, there's no more destruction. That's simple, but it's hard to believe.

I've touched on a lot of these questions without officially recognizing them. He mentions here about the death of Jesus: "Please notice that Jesus said, 'spirit' not 'soul' when he said, "*Into your hands I commit my spirit.*" Where did Jesus go?" Well he went into death; spirit, not soul.

Comment: "These terms are often used interchangeably."

Yes, but they should not be. They are not interchangeable. Spirit and soul are different things and this is what's caused a lot of the confusion. It's what caused a lot of preachers to stand by a graveside, saying those last few words before they lower the body into the ground, and say, "This person is not here, weep not for them. They're already shouting the streets of glory. Uncle John's already met Aunt Suzy, and they're happy with Jesus right now. Don't cry for Uncle John." It's partly because of that scripture that said. "The spirit returns to God". But that spirit's not Uncle John. Uncle John's spirit is not Uncle John.

Comment—not heard clearly.

That's true, it is a question. However the question does presume a condition, but as I said, the condition being misunderstood because of the way it's worded. What chapter is that? Third chapter? Verse 21 then says, "*Who knoweth the spirit of man that goeth upward...*" but that's still not the one that I'm referring to. There's another one in here later in the book. It's chapter 12, verse 7, "*Then shall the dust return to the earth as it was.*" The dust is the body. The body is made out of the dust. The spirit is not made out of dust. The soul is only symbolically made out of dust because it's tied to the body, but the dust literally is the body, returned to the earth, as it was, where it came from.

"*And the spirit shall return unto God who gave it.*" That's the breath of life because there's more to it than just oxygen. There's a spirit of life that God gives and withdraws. But as I pointed out, when that spirit returns to God, the person that had it has lost it. It's not keeping him alive anymore, so it allows him to die. Uncle John, unless he was an overcomer (what the Bible calls an overcomer) and his spirit has been perfected, if he's one of those just men made perfect, then he has gone on somewhere.

The Bible describes it as being under the altar, because there's no place made for him even yet in heaven. Jesus said, "*I go to prepare a place for you.*" But some years after Jesus said that, John, who reported that he said that, made this observation, "*No man has entered into heaven, but he that came down from heaven.*" When John wrote that, Stephen had already been martyred. Probably many others were also, by that time, because heaven wasn't ready for them. They were ready for heaven, but heaven wasn't ready for them and they're called '*under the altar*'.

There's a place reserved for them while they wait for us. It's not so much that heaven's not ready for them, but ***we're*** not there yet. And we're all going in together. They won't go in until we can all go in together. Let's read that in the sixth chapter of Revelation--very enlightening scriptures about where that peculiar class of dead are, because they are not dead, not literally. They're called '*dead in Christ*'. They are among that group that Solomon said, "*I sleep but my heart waketh*".

Your soul can be awake; the new man can be awake and the old man can be asleep or dead, or vice versa. The old man can be alive and the new man can be dead in there. We had better wake up that new man. Paul said, "*Awake thou that sleepeth and arise from the dead and Christ shall give thee life.*" That's one scripture that implies that a dead man can assist in his own resurrection.

It's because these things are not literal. It's because we're not literally dead that we can assist at our spiritual resurrection. We are spiritually dead, but there's something about us that's still alive and can make decisions, and you need to make that decision to accept the Lord, accept God's way. You can make that decision.

Where were we? Revelation 6:9 "*When he had opened the fifth seal...*" This is visionary, symbolic, all of it. It's not a literal place, but it's a spiritual condition. As far as what literal place those people are at, we're not told, but they're in a spiritual condition which is described here as being '*under the altar*'. "*I saw under the altar the souls of them that were slain for the word of God*".

Their lives had been offered for the glory of God. They were slain for the word of God and for the testimony which they held. The testimony which they held was what they believed and preached. That was their testimony; it was the things they said about Jesus or the things they said about the word of God. They were slain for what they preached and when they were martyred their bodies were killed, but they didn't die. They had been granted eternal life. They were already in the first resurrection. They had part in the first resurrection.

When did they get resurrected? When they got the Holy Ghost! That's all the resurrection they ever needed. They remained alive, never died again, never needed another resurrection. They needed a new body to live in and that's prepared for them. That new body was ready for them when they died. And they're not floating around out there in empty space waiting to get that new body.

That would be an uncomfortable condition as Paul made clear in II Corinthians 5 where he said, "*In this tabernacle we groan, not that we would be unclothed, but to be clothed upon with our house which is from Heaven.*" I'm not wanting to be just outside a body; I'm wanting to be inside a better body. The Lord has a better body prepared for me. You all pray that I can get to it. Pray that I can qualify for it and let the Holy Ghost make me that kind of person, and let the truth make me that kind of person. It takes knowledge of the truth to get to that place in God.

Let's read some more here in Revelation. "*I saw under the altar the souls of them that were slain for the word of God and for the testimony which they held and they cried with a loud voice saying how long, oh Lord, holy and true, dost thou not judge and avenge our blood on them that dwell on the earth*". I told you this is all symbolic. Those people are not there hollering things like that, but the condition that they died in just makes that kind of statement. Justice calls for that.

It's like Abel's blood that cried to God out of the ground. What did it cry? It just demanded justice. When an innocent person is killed, justice demands something. It calls for justice; that innocent blood demands justice. That's a law of God. So these souls under the altar, they were martyred for the testimony they held. That calls for justice. "A*nd white robes were given unto every one of them and it was said unto them that they should rest yet for a little season*".

So, those souls are resting. They don't have a job to do. They are not ruling, they are resting. Their job is going to be to rule. The overcomers are going to rule the nations with a rod of iron, but they're not doing it yet. They are alive but they're not ruling yet. They are resting until their fellow servants also and their brethren that should be killed as they were should be fulfilled. So evidently that hasn't been fulfilled yet. Their fellow servants haven't been killed as they were yet.

Now you know there have been lots of martyrs down through the dark ages. But down through the dark ages, there were no martyrs like Stephen, like Peter, James and John. There were no martyrs like the martyrs of that early church. They were honest people, sincere people, that gave their lives for their testimony, but they were just not that kind of people. There were not many of them, maybe a few scattered through there, but not enough to finish the number yet.

They are still waiting for the rest of us. Let's include us in there. They're still waiting for the rest of us to get there and join them and that's the group that Paul referred to in I Thessalonians 4 by saying, "*Them that sleep in Jesus... the dead in Christ*," he said, "*shall rise first*". We'll start with verse 14 "*If we believe that Jesus died and rose again*," which we do believe, "*even so them also which sleep in Jesus will God bring with him*". God's going to bring Jesus back to this earth and bring them with him.

"*For this we say unto you by the word of the Lord that we which are alive and remain unto the coming of the Lord,*" I wonder who '*we*' are in that verse? It's going to be somebody. Somebody will still be alive when that takes place, "*shall not prevent them*" though, or precede them, "*which are asleep*," asleep in Jesus; not asleep in the graves, but asleep in Jesus. They put the old man to sleep, or to death. They made the old man sleep the sleep of death. "*They that are Christ's have crucified the flesh with the affections and lusts*". That's what it takes to sleep in Jesus.

Those people will come with the Lord "*for the Lord himself shall descend from heaven with a shout with the voice of the archangel.*" This is not symbolic. This is not a vision. This is the plain teaching of the apostle of Christ, "*the voice of the archangel with the trump of God and the dead in Christ shall rise first.*" They're going to rise from wherever they are to come with Jesus; from wherever they've been all these thousands of years, now to come with Jesus.

"*Then we which are alive and remain shall be caught up.*" That's what the word "rapture" means, to be caught up, raptured together with him in the clouds. And that's a literal cloud. It's the kind of clouds that Jesus disappeared into when the apostles were looking at him floating up into the sky, literally, not symbolic. Those are not symbolic clouds. We shall be caught up together with them in the clouds.

If you're talking symbolic clouds, those that sleep in Jesus and we that merge with them, are the clouds. "*Behold he cometh with clouds*,"—clouds of witnesses. But here, he's talking about those witnesses being together in the clouds. That shows that we are no longer bound by gravity. We are not going to get together down here on the ground. We're going to get together up there somewhere off the ground. So if you're scared to fly, buy an airplane ticket and conquer that right now before the rapture gets here!

Question: "Are you making a difference between Jesus and Christ? That's the same thing, isn't it?"

He's talking about what it means to be in Christ, or in Jesus. You can't be asleep in Jesus if you're not in Jesus to begin with. "*They that are in the flesh cannot please God.*" So there's a difference in being in the flesh and being in Jesus. In fact, that's opposite to each other. Those are the contrasts.

As long as you are in the flesh—and we are not talking about being in the body, in the physical body—that's not what the Bible means by being in the flesh. It means being in the spirit, or personality, or character of the flesh. The nature of the flesh is what he's calling the flesh. If you are living according to the nature of the flesh, indulging the lusts and desires of the flesh, then you're in the flesh and you're not in Christ.

You may talk in tongues; you may get in the Spirit from time to time, but you're not really living in Christ. You're getting blessed in Christ occasionally, but you're not living there. To live there is to move in there and stay there and not live according to the flesh, not indulge the lust of the flesh. That's what it means to be in Christ, and if you're living in that condition in Christ, when your body dies you're called 'asleep in Christ'. You just stay in Christ.

Revelation 12:5: The woman in that chapter "*brought forth a man child who was to rule all nations with a rod of iron.*" That's what I said a while ago about the overcomers, those people under the altar. They're destined to rule the nations with a rod of iron, which represents the word of God. Everything in Revelation, by the way, is symbolic. It's spiritual language because it was a vision similar to a dream.

One thing we want to point out here about the woman and the child. The woman is not the child and the child is not the woman. But the woman produced the child. The woman is symbolic of the Church and the Church is not made just out of overcomers. It produces some overcomers and those overcomers enter into a special category that's different from the people that produced them. In fact, it's wrong, I guess, to say that the people produced them, but the people make up the Church. The Church, with all the operations of the Holy Ghost in it and the preaching of the word of God, can produce that kind of people.

And you can be one of those people. You can sit here and just remain part of the woman and never take on the nature of the man child, or you can grow and be part of that birth that's taking place. That birth is taking place here all the time. The Church is in travail. The woman was in pain, "*pained to be delivered.*" It's the business, the job of the Church. The job of the Church is not so much the evangelization of the world as it is the producing of those perfect Christians. That's the real job of the Church. It's easier to evangelize the world than it is to produce those perfect Christians, but the Church is not going to be finished with its travail until it has done that.

And the Church continues on as in the form of the body of Christ on down through the thousand years, but that man child takes a separate position. It's pictured here as a man child because ruling is a masculine characteristic, but it's described in other verses as the bride of Christ because submission to a lord or a head is a feminine characteristic. That group of people operates in both of those relationships. The relationship to the world is the relationship of rulers. Their relationship to Christ is the relationship of servants, or a wife.

Somebody had a question? Isaiah 57 — The spirit going back to God, and what else?

Bro. Paul Davis: "In the fifteenth verse, he speaks of a contrite, humble spirit being revived but then he speaks of these that he will not contend with forever. He says the spirit and the soul both fail which he has made, so is there some symbolism in that spirit failing there?"

Bro. Brown: That's an involved chapter there. He's talking about, basically, the same group at different levels of development. That subject really starts back in the first part of the chapter. We're in Isaiah 57. "*The righteous perisheth, and no man layeth it to heart: and merciful men are taken away, none considering that the righteous is taken away from the evil to come.*" And he goes on talking about those righteous, merciful people. "*He shall enter into peace,*" talking about when he dies, when he perishes in that sense. This particular righteous person perishes, dies, but he enters into peace.

"*They shall rest in their beds,*" (or in their graves, their caskets) "*each one walking in his uprightness.*" Those are live souls. His old body may be in that casket, but he's already got a new body and he's walking in his uprightness. Then he goes into a diatribe against the false church system that persecuted such people. Then, proceeding way on down into the chapter, he starts winding that diatribe up in the tenth verse, saying, "*Thou are wearied in the greatness of thy way.*"

He's still speaking against what he calls the whore up there in the third verse, what he called, in Revelation, the great whore, "*Yet saidst thou not, there is no hope: thou hast found the life of thine hand; therefore thou wast not grieved.*" He seems to be describing self-sufficiency and self-righteousness there. It's people that won't give up and submit to the righteousness of God. They're persisting in their own way. "*And of whom hast thou been afraid or feared, that thou hast lied, and hast not remembered me, nor laid it to thy heart? Have not I held my peace even of old, and thou fearest me not? I will declare thy righteousness*" (in other words thy self-righteousness as filthy rags) "*and thy works, for they shall not profit thee.*"

You can't save yourself by your own works. "*When thou criest, let thy companies deliver thee; but the wind shall carry them all away, vanity shall take them but,"* (he switches back to those other people now) "*he that putteth his trust in me shall possess the land, and shall inherit my holy mountain, and shall say, 'Cast ye up,"* (or build up) "*prepare the way, take up the stumbling block out of the way of my people."*

That's what we're saying tonight: *build up*. Let's build the house of God. Let's restore the Church. "*For thus saith the high and lofty One that inhabiteth eternity, whose name is Holy."* Here's what he says, "*I dwell in the high and holy place, with him also that is of a contrite and humble spirit."* You can dwell in the high and holy place too. God dwells there with that kind of people. It's the contrite and humble spirit that finally gets enough of God to become that complete Christian, a complete overcomer.

"*To revive the spirit of the humble and revive the heart of the contrite ones. For I will not contend forever,"* meaning I will not always be against you. You may feel like, "God's always against me. Things don't work out right for me. It looks like even God's against me." Be patient. God's working on your case. He's working out your salvation. "*Neither will I be always wroth.*" You know God may have been angry with you in a measure in the past. God may have held something against us from the past, but that won't last forever.

God will judge us right here and he will give us a chance to repent, clear things up and go on with him. "*For the spirit should fail before me and the souls which I have made,"* would simply fail if I stayed angry, in other words; "*if I didn't lighten up and forgive and give people another chance."* And he's still talking about those people when he says this, (this is peculiar here in the seventeenth verse) "*For the iniquity of his covetousness was I wroth."* He's talking about what God was angry with in the first place.

God gave Brother Gary Wright something recently, around the turn of the year, about covetousness, about God being against covetousness. The spirit of covetousness gets hold of people; it gets hold of God's people, and God has been wroth against that. He's trying to work that out of us. He's trying to cut that nature out of us. *"I was wroth and I smote him."* He's talking about these people now that he said dwell with him in the high holy place. *"I hid me and was wroth and he went on forwardly in the way of his heart."* You know we've all done it. We've all done it.

But he said, *"I have seen his ways and will heal him."* He saw something about us, some sincerity, some repentant spirit. That contrite spirit--when he sees that, he makes up his mind to heal you. Praise God! Not just a physical healing either, Brother Fritz, but a spiritual healing along with it! Praise God! Glad to see Brother Fritz able to be out here tonight. God has touched him. It looked bad for him for a while. We were worried when he went to the hospital, but he's back in church tonight, whole and sound and well, able to understand these things.

"I will heal him. I will lead him also and restore comforts unto him and to his mourners." That's after he's dead. God restores comforts to him after he's dead. While people are mourning for him, while we're crying around that person's graveside, God's already comforting him somewhere else. Glory! I love that! Thank you for that verse.

Praise God, well I know we've left a lot of things hanging here, but I don't suppose we could clear it all up tonight.

Question: "Samson's death: Was that suicide?"

Well we shouldn't define it that way, because Samson wasn't really wanting to die. He was just wanting to take vengeance on the Philistines.

Question: "Was he forgiven?"

Samson's a study, isn't he? He was a man chosen of God from his mother's womb and yet he was of such flawed character. Samson is a Shakespearean tragedy. We'll just have to leave his judgment in the hands of God. I hope we see him in that final resurrection down there while the Lake of Fire is still burning. We're going to deal with him and preach to him and baptize him and pray him through to the Holy Ghost and get him to talk in tongues and help him escape that Lake of Fire.

Comment—not heard clearly

Yes, he is included in Hebrews 11. That's a good sign. I take that as a good sign.

"*Woman clothed with the sun, the moon under her feet.*" Oh yes, that is an outstanding case of symbolism in Revelation 12, but let's quickly explain it without proving it all. Look at it this way: the woman is the church. It's that church that began in Acts 2 on the day of Pentecost, clothed with the sun, the sun being the word of God. It's the New Testament, a new covenant.

And the moon under her feet; the moon represented the Law of Moses, that old covenant, the Old Testament. That was their foundation. All those people that were in that church in Acts 2 were people that had been trained in Judaism. They had all learned and tried to live the Law of Moses. That was under their feet and they were clothed with the sun. That was a special church that went forth from the upper room on the day of Pentecost. There has never been another church like it. We want to see a reproduction of it. That's what they preached from. When they quoted the scriptures, they quoted the Psalms and the prophets and the laws. That was their background and their foundation.

Question: "Where will we be when we are resurrected?"

You'll be in a church. If you're not in church, find one right quick when you wake up. Find the church and get in it; go on with God. Find ***the*** Church. Well let's thank God. These are interesting thoughts, aren't they? Interesting subjects, deep subjects! We could preach for hours, teach for hours on these things. Whoever you are that wrote this, thank you for this thoughtful, well-thought-out question.

Chapter 11

The Salvation Process

July 31, 2004

Brother Brown begins with prayer:

Thank you, Lord, thank you for the faith that you've stirred within us. Praise God for the commandment you've given us for us to help one another. Thank you for the charity you've created in our hearts. Praise the Lord for making us members of one body. AMEN!

We need one another, Lord! We belong to each other and to you. We need each other. We miss each other when we're not able to be in the meetings. We're trying to do our part and we know you will do your part. You'll add the power, the strength, the spiritual force to accomplish miracles, to change our hearts on the inside. Give us the changes we need to make! Transform us into the image of Christ! Let us be renewed, transformed by the renewing of our minds.

Yes, Lord, we ask for these things. We admit that we can't do it ourselves. We cannot, ourselves, crucify the flesh. Help us, Lord, to overcome! Give us permanent victory; perfect, final victory in Jesus' Name! Praise the Lord God! Glory be to Jesus! Praise His Great Name. Bless the Lord.

All right! It's good for us to be together tonight. I'll say what Peter said on the Mount of Transfiguration, "*It's good for us to be here.*" Lord, it's good for us to be here! We thank you that you've allowed us to be here! Thank you that you allow us to fit together and pull together and work together! Amen!

I appreciate these words from the Bible. They had a long list of scriptures up there on that overhead a while ago. Brother

Lockler was using scriptures, going through the Word of God. The Word of God is quick and powerful, sharper than a two-edged sword, sharper than a surgeon's scalpel! It'll do the job! It'll pierce to the dividing asunder of soul and spirit. It can do surgery on the people of God. I'm glad I learned to believe that while I was still a young man many years ago. I was troubled a little bit about my hope, about what my hope was.

Thank God for a sure hope that anchors within the veil. But, I didn't always have that. I didn't always have my hope anchored tight in there. I went through periods in my younger days when I was filled with doubts and personal weaknesses, wondering whether the Lord would actually include me even though I loved this message. I don't know where I picked those doubts up. Where did they come from, anyway? Is the air full of them? Is the Devil going around planting seeds like that in people's minds?

I just didn't have the faith for myself. I had lots of faith for you folks; I believed you were going to make it. Thank God for all of us that are still here. Thank God for those that have made it in God, to whatever degree that they did, and are gone on now to their reward. We thank God for their faithfulness, their staying on the job.

Brother Patton used to teach us a lot on that, how if you'll stay around where God has access to you.... Well, you think, "God can find me anywhere I go. "*If I make my bed in hell, he's there. If I take the wings of the morning and go to the uttermost parts of the earth, I can't get away from him.*"

What do you mean, "Where he has access to me"? Well, here is where God keeps his tools. God's tools for working on people are around the church and if you leave the church, you leave where God's working. He can catch up with you, all right, but his tools to work on you, perfect your life and put you in the Bride are here around the church, among his people.

He's got some tools out there. The wicked is the left hand of God, but he's not going to turn them loose on you until you've been worked on in here and shown that you can stand that kind of process. People that have become great testimonies in God, like Daniel and the three Hebrew children were, had already proved themselves faithful to the Lord before they were put in those positions where their faith was tested before the whole world. They had proved their faith privately and close at hand. God had confidence that they could stand those tests. Thank God, they did! Thank God they stood the tests!

He was working on them with a lot of things before he worked on them with the fiery furnace and the lion's den. He worked on their mingling with people, learning to get along with people, learning how to influence people the right way. You observe the wisdom that Daniel showed when he and his friends were about to be fed things which were against the Law. They were under dietary restrictions in the dispensation they lived in and they made up their minds they were not going to defile themselves with defiled food, the king's food.

They risked their lives by making a decision like that. The man that was in charge of them, the government official who had them under his care, was frightened for his safety and theirs, too. He said, "*You're going to make me endanger my head to the king.*" He had to be prevailed upon. Daniel had to appeal to him in a way that he could consider and accept, "*Just give us a chance; give us a ten-day trial. If it doesn't work, then we'll try something else.*" He had confidence that God would make it work. He was already standing on his faith at that point in his career. Daniel went on to become a great man of God for a long lifetime because he stayed around.

What I was starting to say was about how the Lord finally changed my mind through a few words that Brother Patton said. One day in a teaching service, he said, "If you'll stay on the job and stay around the church and be faithful, God will finally save you, somehow." Regardless of how hard to save you are, that was the implication. He wasn't saying that, but if you think you're hard to save, if you think, "I'm a hard case. I don't even know if God can change me," well, you just give him time. If you want God to change you, give him time! He can do it!

He can do it, but you have to want it enough to stay on the job and endure the process. You've got to stay on the operating table when he's using that surgeon's knife. And, you've got to stay around his people when his people are misunderstanding you. They may be hard to bear. God's people can be hard to put up with at times. You've got to keep putting up with them to stay around. God's using them to work on you. "*The spirit of a man*," Solomon said, "*is the candle of the Lord, searching the innermost parts of the belly*," or the inside of you. That's what the belly is, the inside of you. It searches what's inside of you.

What's inside you? Well, Jesus said that out of the heart come adulteries, fornications, murders, and a lot of things like that because that's what's inside of most people. If God doesn't get that out of us and put something else in there, that's what will be in us! You can find those things in Holy Ghost people. It's strange to me that some people have a hard time believing that a Holy Ghost person, or any kind of a Christian, could be bothered by an evil spirit, a demon. You can see how bad they're bothered just by the nature of the flesh. That's about as rotten and corrupt as anything that exists.

The fallen nature of Adam is just as low-down and mean and corrupt as most of the evil spirits we've run into. I appreciate the fact that we can deal with demons. God has shown us; he's given us that power. That power is available to a lot of people if they are willing to believe. It's hard for some people to believe it. But, look what Jesus said in Mark 16. This is a passage of scripture that the devil has tried to get taken out of the Bible. Some scholars argue that some of this is not even in there, that Jesus didn't say all this.

We believe this is the Word of Jesus Christ and it's in accord with other things he's said that nobody can challenge or argue about. It fits; it harmonizes with the rest of the New Testament. In Mark 15:16 he said unto them, "*Go ye into all the world and preach the Gospel to every creature*." '*To every creature*' means to every kind of human being, every kind of person, all races, all groups, nationalities and languages in order to save and change them, if they cooperate with it. "*Preach the Gospel to every creature and he that is baptized...*," Notice how important 'baptism' is there. Thank God, we've got a baptistery in here and we can include that experience. Water baptism is important.

It's important that people receive all three baptisms: water baptism, Spirit baptism, and fire baptism. "*He that believeth and is baptized shall be saved, but he that believeth not shall be damned.*" The word *'damned'* just means condemned to whatever their case justifies. Justice will be executed.

"*And these signs shall follow them that believe.*" I want you to focus on that word *'believe'*. We're talking about believers tonight. Right there, Jesus did not make it a prerequisite that you have to have the Holy Ghost and talk in tongues. *"It's to the believer,"* he said. If you look around, you can find believers outside the ranks of the Holy Ghost people. They are few and far between, but they are out there. They have these experiences. There are Baptist preachers and Catholic priests that cast out demons. Some of them end up speaking with new tongues. That's available to them; that's for them. The reason most of them don't speak with new tongues is because they don't believe in it anymore.

The reason most of them outside this group, and some inside this group, don't cast out devils is because they don't believe in it. They don't believe it's real or they don't believe it means what it says. They don't believe it's time for it or they don't believe that we're the ones to do it. There's some lack of belief there. They're not a believer in it. They believe in Jesus Christ and, if they believed in casting out devils, they could have those signs following them. It's not all confined to the Body of Christ

There are lots of signs and works being done out in the religious world. Still, it's going to fade away. There's going to come a fulfillment of Revelation 18 where a voice says, "*Come out of her, my people.*" It proclaims that "*the voice of the Bridegroom and the voice of the Bride shall no more be heard in her at all.*" That hasn't happened yet; or at least, hasn't been completed.

You can find people out there that are able to get hold of God and get in the Spirit enough to have these experiences, especially out on the missionary field. Occasionally, you hear of someone having these experiences. In the eighteenth verse, *"they shall take up serpents,'"* well, we've had people misunderstand and misuse that scripture, even among the Holy Ghost people. They think that it is justification for testing your faith by handling snakes and drinking strychnine. But, that's a case of tempting God when somebody does something like that.

It's like when Jesus was tempted. It was suggested he jump off the top of the temple. A scripture was quoted to justify it: "*You'll be safe. It's written about you in the scriptures that angels will bear you up, lest at any time you dash your foot against a stone.*" Now when we read that, we need to remember that was written about Jesus; it doesn't apply to every one of us. But, Jesus wouldn't even apply it to himself in a forward way, in a presumptuous way. He knew that was in there to protect him against accidents. That's what Mark 16:18 is; it's to protect you against accidents.

If you get snake bit literally—you can use it literally, if you want to, but we've got some good spiritual explanations of these things, too. These things happen literally and the scriptures work. The power is there. When somebody is fed poison by an enemy who is trying to be a preacher of the Gospel, we get testimonies about when that poison fails to work. We have the record of the apostle Paul being bitten by a serpent while he was in his travels for the Lord. He just shook the snake off into the fire and wasn't affected by it. He went on unaffected while the populace, who assuredly knew it was a poisonous snake, stood around watching for him to swell up, fall down and die.

He went on without any effects. He was literally fulfilling this scripture. He had been spiritually taking up serpents for all his ministry, for all his career, but he had a chance to do it literally, in the natural, one time before he died. These things will work where people believe and have faith for it. God has given us virtues, powers that we're not fully aware of.

Brother Gothard calls our attention to the Bible definition of that word *'virtue'*. You hear about virtue contrasted with the seven cardinal sins. We talk about 'virtuous' people just because they're good people. Nowadays, we use 'virtue' as just being goodness; that's the modern definition of it, but the word translated as 'virtue' in the New Testament is most often translated as 'power'. Peter said, "*Add to your faith virtue, and to virtue, knowledge."* There's a long string of things that you are to add to your experience. He's listing things that only God can give you. You can't add the faith that you are to start with, completely. You can have a little bit of faith when you come to God, but experience quickens and strengthens your faith. You're to let your faith grow and then add to that. Let your faith grow by experience and observation and by teaching.

Everything that happens in the church is to strengthen your faith. You're to add to that, virtue. Translate that as power. How do you add power? Well, you let God do it. You cooperate with God. There's a response that God makes to people obeying him. One of those commandments that Brother Lockler was talking about a while ago has a promise attached to it. "*Honor your father and your mother that your days may be long on the land that the Lord gives to you.*" There's a promise attached to that. Paul observed that in the New Testament. "*It was the first commandment*," he said, "*with promise.*" There's a response that God makes to our obedience to all of his commandments and admonitions.

It's God that gives us the power. Paul said in Philippians 2:13, I believe, "*It is God that worketh in you, both to will and to do of his good pleasure.*" So, he gives you the desire which is closely connected with faith. And then he gives you the will, which is closely connected with power, or virtue. And then, all the rest of those things: add to your virtue, knowledge. You cannot just make up knowledge. It's not up to you to create knowledge and add it, but you add the knowledge that God gives to you. God will let you acquire knowledge. He'll show you things if you will show yourself a good steward of knowledge. We're to be stewards of all the gifts of God.

I heard this taught for many years: If you can use knowledge properly, God will let you see and observe things and maybe discern some of the things that are wrong in your local church if you don't get out of your place and try to fix those things that it's not your job to fix. You may see things that are wrong and wonder why the preacher is not taking care of it. Well, there are usually reasons why he's not taking care of it. He may be taking care of it and you just don't know it. He may be being led by the Spirit in how he takes care of it and in how long he bears with it.

We bear a lot of things around here that people get tired of bearing. I know we get tired of bearing and forbearing, but that's part of charity. Sometimes, we get tired of bearing with obnoxious cases and would like to do something about it. Like Brother Sowders and Brother Shelton, way back there in the beginning of their ministry, when they had a certain case in their church that they felt was out of order. It was a woman that would behave and manifest a certain way in the church and disrupt the service.

You know those men were not against manifestations. If someone moves in the Spirit and demonstrates, we approve of that; but there are limits and there is order. When a person becomes disruptive to the service, then that's when we feel like we've borne with them long enough. We've had preachers come around, get up and just grind on us. Every time they showed up you could count on them to get up and grind. They didn't have any vision; they didn't see where they were, didn't know what was going on here, didn't recognize anything different. They would just get up and bore the crowd. You could count on them to do it.

That was, basically, what that woman was doing. Brother Sowders had made up his mind to call her down, stop her. The very service where he intended to do it, he looked out and she got up to do her manifestation and another woman was following her, copying her. The Lord spoke to him and said, "*If one is not enough, I'll give you two.*" They were having their spirits worked on. The ministry, the leadership there, the whole church were having their spirits worked on.

Well, do you want your spirit worked on? You have to want it. If you don't want it, you won't get enough of it to do the job. You'll get up and leave the operating table. One of the points we discussed last night at the Women's Support Group was the question of "How bad do you want to get well?" We were talking about getting well of our emotional wounds and abuses that we've suffered in the past that have marked us. Many of us have been marked by things in our background. We can get well of those things or we can just harbor and treasure our bitterness and resentment of the way we've been treated.

The author I was quoting used this scripture in John 5 where Jesus found the crippled man lying by the Pool of Bethesda waiting for the angel to trouble the waters so he could try to get in and get healed. He had been there trying to do that for long time, but since he was crippled, he was slow and somebody always beat him in there. The first person that would jump in the water after the angel troubled it would get healed. The rest of the crowd then was left out. Jesus walked by and observed this poor crippled man lying there in that condition and he asked him what almost sounds like a foolish question, "*Do you want to be healed*?" He said, "*Do you want to be made whole?*"

Well, what's he doing there?! That's what he's there for, trying to be made whole! Obviously, he wants to be healed! But Jesus always called for an expression, a declaration of faith, like when the little boy that had the spirit that would throw him into fits, throw him in the fire, throw him in the water, sometimes. That's one of our outstanding cases on casting out demons. It said he *'wallowed, foaming'*.

Many people resent our results here when we cast out demons. Usually, some fluid comes out of the victim's mouth. There was one testimony, at least, from the New Testament where that happened. Some fluid was coming out. But, the demon wasn't coming out until Jesus came along. The boy's father was begging for help. Jesus carried on a conversation with this father, "*How long has he been this way*?" The father described his history and said, "*Please, if you can do anything, help us. We need help.*" Jesus said to that father, "*All things are possible if you can believe.*" That's when the man cried, "*Lord, I believe; help my unbelief*!"

I know I don't believe like I should; I know I don't believe enough, but I've got some belief! I've got faith to start with! I'll add to my faith virtue, (or power) later on! Help me right now and that will strengthen my faith! Some virtue will come after that and I will go on and add knowledge and everything.

The point we were developing out of that was that we need to have a determination, a drive to go all the way with God. If you ask people who are in trouble with drunkenness, drug addiction or any kind of sickness, "Do you want to be well; would you like to get well?" why, they would all say yes. But when it comes to suffering the curative process, going through the treatment it takes to get well, that's where many people back out. Some of us, even going to the doctor, are not sure whether or not we want to go through all that suffering.

You get cancer and you know they're going to give you chemotherapy. Your hair's going to fall out and the lining of your mouth and your stomach are going to get sore. You can hardly eat; you throw up and almost die from the treatment. You may decide you don't want to go through all that. Some people make that decision: "I'll just live as long as I can. I know I'm going to die someday, anyway. Let the cancer take me out rather than go through all that treatment."

Some people are like that about the Gospel. They will not accept the sacrifices that the Gospel of Jesus Christ calls for in order to be transformed on the inside! They don't want to be made over on the inside; they don't want it bad enough to crucify the old man, leave him on the cross while he's suffering and complaining, murmuring, saying, "Get me out of here! Get me some relief!" The old man will struggle! He'll cry out! He'll argue; he'll ask for water on the sacrifice. That was one of the features of the Law of Moses. On their sacrifices, when they were offering a whole burnt offering, you couldn't pour any water on it.

You're not allowed to cool the sacrifice down; you're not allowed to cool the heat that God's putting on you. You're to offer yourself a whole burnt offering. "*Offer your bodies a living sacrifice*," Paul said, "*which is your reasonable service, a living sacrifice, holy and acceptable unto God.*" That is your reasonable service. That's not too much! God's not asking too much! He doesn't ask anything of us that we can't supply and he makes up the difference! He enables us to do things we would never be able to do on our own. He enables us to do those things. He's got a way of supplying our needs for virtue or power, the ability to do things.

We're to add to our faith a power that faith produces. Faith is power, and we're to let that work in our lives, let all these things that Peter mentioned in II Peter 1 work in your life! "*Giving all diligence*", he said. Let's back up to the third verse: "*... according as his divine power hath given unto us all things that pertain unto life and godliness...,*" His divine power has given to us everything it takes to measure up to life and godliness. All that we need to live forever and live right (Godliness is living right) all that we need to live forever and live right forever is given unto us by his divine power. "*...through the knowledge of Him that has called us to glory and virtue.*" That's Jesus.

As I said, that word 'virtue' is more commonly translated as 'power'. It's a certain kind of power; it's the power to be good. If you want to translate 'virtue' as goodness, good qualities, it's the power to have those qualities, the power to be good. "*Whereby are given unto us exceeding great and precious promises, that by these promises you might be partaker of the divine nature.*" Divine nature, what is natural to God, what is natural in Heaven, what is natural to the spirit world, you can have that. We've participated in what's natural to this world. And what's natural to the 'old man', we've lived with that long enough. We know it fully, know all that it's capable of but we don't fully know what the 'new man' is capable of.

Let's get full of the Divine nature, get acquainted with it, express it, let it work, do what comes natural in the Spirit. Does that make sense? "*Having escaped the corruption that is in the world through lust,*" *w*e have escaped that. Did you know that? Is that news to you? Did you know that you've escaped the corruption that's in the world through lust? Wake up! If you didn't know that, I want to tell you tonight we've escaped that! Don't go back to it! Stay out of it now! You've got rid of that; stay out of it! Then he says, "A*nd besides this giving all diligence... Seest thou a man diligent in his business? He shall stand before kings,*" great men, not mean, ordinary men.

Giving all diligence, add to your faith virtue, or power to be good. Add to virtue, knowledge, the knowledge of God, the knowledge of the Word of God. You can study; you can have something to do with all of these things. You put your part of effort into it but God makes your effort bear fruit. You know, God can stand in your way and make everything you do fail or he can give you a shove and make everything that you try to do work out and come to pass. He can give you faith and virtue and knowledge and temperance. "*To knowledge, temperance.*" Thank God for temperance, moderation, the ability to know when to stop. Some of us don't know when to stop. We don't know when to leave the table; we don't know when to quit talking; we don't know when to stop arguing. We just don't have moderation. We overdo everything we do.

One of the fruits of the Spirit is temperance. Add to temperance, patience. You've got to have patience to bear these things, bear with people that may be out of the channel. I really don't want to make the congregation nervous. I don't want you to be afraid of missing God. I don't want you to be afraid to experiment and try things. That's not the kind of people we're talking about. When we talk about people that are habitual bores, we're talking about people who are never in the Spirit and they don't know it. Most of us, when we get up and miss God, we sit down and burn. We know it; we know we missed it. And in fact, we may not even have missed it. We may have done pretty good, but we didn't hit a home run. We're not satisfied with just a base hit. We want to hit a home run, so we sit down and burn over that, when actually, we did what the Lord was trying to get us to do.

Most of us are super sensitive along those lines. It's just people that are blind, don't have their eyes open. They don't know where they are. They are, as somebody said, 'like a blind dog in a meat house'. They sense there's something good here, but they can't see it, can't figure it out. They never figure out how to fit in with it. They're just clouds without water, winds without rain. They're never in the Spirit and never miss it—I mean they never miss the Spirit. They never miss what they're missing out on. They don't know there's anything better than what they've had all their lives. People like that come, stay awhile, and move on. God sends somebody else like them after they leave.

We'll never be rid of people like that. Don't think we can run off the people that are boring us and get rid of them. There'll be another one come along pretty soon anyway. Let's exercise patience and sit here and put on charity and bear with things as long as God does. Look at the patience God has. James used that when he was talking about Elijah being '*a man of like passions as we are*'. He prayed earnestly that it might not rain. Then he talked in there about the husbandman, God, who has long patience waiting for the precious fruit of the earth.

I remember a time, about thirty years ago, when we were having major dissension in the ministers' meetings over that scripture in this Body. Somebody was trying to tell us we were using that scripture wrong, trying to apply it to God, that that's just a scripture about patience and about the farmers out here. They plant seed in the soil and then they have to sit and wait, or work and wait, but they have to wait until the seasons come and go and give the grain time to ripen. Finally, they receive the precious fruit of the earth.

Brother Patton got up in one of the ministers' meetings and talked about that scripture. He said, "I listen to these brethren and I try to consider what they say. I try to see if I can believe that scripture that way. I read 'precious fruit' and try to make that beans and potatoes." You can't make that mean beans and potatoes after you've been taught to make it mean the children of God. You've been taught to make that 'precious jewels in the House of God'. You can't look at beans and potatoes and make that percussive sound with the 'p', *p*recious fruit, anymore, because we got a greater lesson out of that just like we got a greater lesson out of Jesus' words in Mark 16, about taking up serpents and drinking deadly things.

We got a greater lesson out of that and we don't even think about snakes and strychnine anymore when we read that verse. We think about handling the spirits of people that Jesus called serpents and scorpions. In Luke 10, the seventy came back with joy because they found out they could cast out devils. Well, that ought to make anybody happy! That ought to make you happy when you find out you can cast out devils!

Jesus said, "*Behold, I'm going to give you power over all the power of the enemy and you will tread on serpents and scorpions.*" He didn't mean that literally, right there. He wasn't talking about literal snakes and scorpions, but he was talking about people and spirits. That includes evil spirits because that's what they were talking about; he was responding to them. *"I'm giving you power to do that,"* he said. They were talking about casting out demons, and he called them, right there, 'serpents and scorpions'. But, it's not limited to evil spirits; it includes spirits of deception and torment.

Those are the identifying features of serpents and scorpions in the Bible. A serpent, in the Bible, is always used as a deceiver. The original serpent in Genesis 3 was a deceiver. He deceived the woman. Adam was not deceived, but the woman, being deceived, was in the transgression. So that serpent was a deceiver. How did he deceive her? By telling a lie; by arguing her out of her faith. He was one of those fowls of the air that came by and plucked the seed of the truth out of her heart. So, the serpent is a deceiver. We have to handle a lot of deceivers and tread on them. We can walk right over them. We've got enough truth in here; we've got enough scriptures in this Bible to allow us to walk right over the deceivers and not look back.

And then, the scorpions: scorpions are tormentors. In Revelation it mentions the torment of the scorpion when he strikes a man. That's talking about something symbolic right there. These demons and wicked spirits and wicked people, wicked human beings are just as bad. They can be tormentors and torment God's people. But there's a liberating power. Thank God for the Royal Law of Liberty here! Praise God for the liberty wherewith Christ has made us free! It can overcome all that torment of the scorpions that have wounded us! A lot of us have been wounded and tormented by scorpion spirits, both human and demon spirits. But, we've been given victory over both kinds, all of them.

You keep coming around here! Stay on this hospital bed; stay in the operating room! This is a surgical suite here and we've got skilled surgeons. They know how to handle the Word of God and they can pierce to divide those evil things out of your spirit that are working on you, hindering you from going on with God. Praise God!

I'm happy tonight! I'm lifted up and encouraged with what God's doing and what he's letting us help him do; letting us share with him. God's letting us help him do things. God needs somebody. I hesitate to say he needs us, but he needs somebody and we can be those. We can offer him ourselves. God doesn't always need you, need me, but he needs somebody, so thank God for a crowd of people around that will offer themselves to the Lord. I love those services when I get to sit and not say anything, but somebody else gets up and says something. And, testimonies and prophets and prophetesses crop up all over the house. I love those services.

I don't have to feel needed and have to be used of God every night, every service, but there needs to be somebody that can get in the Spirit. The Holy Ghost wants to use somebody every time and we go home with something in our bag. We take something home from the service when people will yield to God, let God have tools to work with. Amen! Here's a houseful of tools that He can work with. Everyone is a tool in the hand of God. We're willing to be used of him. If we've got any backwardness or timidity right now that's holding us back, we're trying to get over that; we're working on it. And I—can I say take pride? Is that a legitimate term? I'm thankful that God enabled me to hold on as long as I did when I was wrestling with my doubts and fears and bashfulness. I held on; I stayed in the surgical suite; I stayed in the hospital and went through experiences until I overcame that backwardness and timidity. God helped me do that. I know I could have never done it, but God helped me. He came to the rescue; he caused it to happen.

He'll do the same for you. He'll help you overcome whatever binding influence that has hold of you. He's come to heal the broken-hearted and to give us beauty for ashes, the ashes of a ruined, burned-up life. When God sends a fire and it consumes everything we had, then things turn to ashes. Everything we did in the flesh will turn to ashes someday but God gives us the beauty of the Holy Ghost, the beauty of the Spirit, its accomplishing powers and abilities in place of that.

So, let's go on with this and add to our patience godliness and brotherly kindness and charity. "*If these things be in you and abound they make you that you shall neither be barren nor unfruitful in the knowledge of our Lord Jesus Christ.*" Amen! It's useful, though, to know that just because people have signs following them in their ministry, in their lives, that's not a sure sign that God's in what they're doing. "*These signs shall follow them that believe.*" But, signs of faith are not always signs of God's approval. Are you aware of that?

Brother Sowders gave some very clear teaching one time along that line, showing how people get blessed and get the Spirit to operate in their lives just because the Spirit is there. God's Spirit is everywhere and a lot of people who are not really in the will of God still get in the Spirit. This explains why you can go into any church and see people getting in the Spirit, getting blessed. You see good, honest-hearted, faithful people there and see God blessing them in many ways. As I pointed out a while ago, you can find people out there who cast out devils and have miracles follow their ministry. But, you have to apply Jesus' words in Matthew 7. He said, "*Not everyone who says to me, Lord, Lord, shall enter into the Kingdom of Heaven. Many will say to me in that day, Lord, Lord, didn't we cast out devils in your name? Didn't we preach the Gospel in your name? Haven't we done many wonderful works?*"

Haven't we seen multiplied thousands of people walk down the aisles in our meetings and make a decision for Christ? I read something about that. Statistically, I don't remember the exact figures, but somebody calculated by making polls and following up on things after a few years, that less than ten percent, maybe four or five percent of the people who walk down the aisles and make decisions for Christ in those big campaigns in the big stadiums and the big public meetings, less than five percent of them go on with God after five years. You can't find them in the churches anymore. Only a handful of them really made a firm decision to really go on beyond that with God. So, a lot of that is lost, is wasted.

When the people said, "*Didn't we do many wonderful works in your Name*," Jesus said, "*I will say to them, 'Depart from me you that work iniquity. I never knew you'*." In other words, "*I never had that intimate relationship in the Spirit with you.*" That's what he means by 'knew': an intimate spiritual relationship that he wants to have with a person. They think they are having that just because they get in the Spirit. They may talk in tongues, feel the Holy Ghost and have miracles happen as a result of moving in the Spirit that way. But, God is not using them in what they're doing because they're not coming around where God has his focus, where he's working.

The Spirit of God is everywhere. Like I said a while ago, if you make your bed in hell, God is there, not personally, but by his Spirit. If you wake up in hell, if you're in enough torment, remember God can deliver you from that. Jesus Christ has the keys of hell and of death. You can, through that Spirit, contact God and get out of that hell you're in. You can get delivered from that. But just because you feel the Spirit doesn't prove that you're in the will of God, wherever you are, in here or anywhere else. It requires more than that. It requires that personal relationship.

That's what we, as a ministry, are trying to promote here. We're trying to have a personal relationship with Jesus Christ. You want him to know you; you want him to get close to you. Invite him to get close to you. Don't hold him out there at arms' length and forbid him to interfere with certain areas of your life. Turn it all over to him! Let him take anything away from you that he wants to take away! Let him give anything to you that you need.

We'll wind up with a song here, settle this down and prepare to meet the young people in the morning.

Thank you, Jesus.

Chapter 12

Three Phases of Salvation

October 9, 2004

Some things take God to fix up. There isn't anything he can't fix up. We need to call on him. Jesus always responded to people who came to him for healing. I don't remember him turning anybody away except the Gentile woman, and she prevailed on him. With a little effort, a little persuasion, she persuaded him to heal her daughter who wasn't even there. He can heal those who are not here but are far away, because we pray and ask for them. So, we've got several prayer requests tonight that we'll put with this and we'll go to prayer.

"Lord, there's nothing too hard for you; there's no disease or sickness or failing that falls outside of your sphere of covering and influence. Lord, you see all of your people and you hear every prayer. You're conscious of all our needs; no sparrow falls without your knowledge. We turn to you tonight and know that you're real. We know that you're there; we know that you're imminent, you're present. You're nearby; you're close enough for us to cry to you! Amen!

You've invited us to come boldly before the throne of grace. Here we are tonight, Lord, your children, your family calling on you! Praise the Lord! We're agreed to call upon your name. We trust you, Lord, for these special needs. Bless this little child; bless all of these whose requests have been presented. They're all important to you, Lord, and they're all important to us. Amen! We feel the responsibility; we feel the burden of each other. Praise God!

What a good thing it is to be in the family of God, to be in the Body of Christ, to be in the Church of the Living God! What a blessing you've given us! Praise the name of the Lord!"

We have a wonderful friend in the heavens, Jesus Christ the righteous. He's the propitiation for our sins and not for ours only, but for the sins of the whole world, if the whole world would only avail themselves of that propitiation. Jesus' blood is valuable enough to cover the sins of six billion people today, if they would turn to him. Jesus' blood avails for every sinner that comes to him, every sin that's confessed to him. His salvation is rich and free. What a blessing it is.

Jesus is presented as our advocate. That's how he is described in I John, "*We have an advocate with the Father, Jesus Christ, the righteous.*" An advocate is a defense counsel, somebody that takes up for you in the courthouse. So when we come to God's courtroom with God, the supreme judge, sitting on his throne, Jesus our Savior is there to represent us. Don't try to represent yourself. Every judge in town will warn you against that. I was reading the other day in the news about a preacher that got arrested for resisting an officer, something that seemed fairly trivial. You don't expect preachers, pastors to resist the officers, do you? The Bible teaches against that.

Maybe he was falsely accused; that's what we hope. "*Charity hopeth all things.*" Anyhow, he went to the courtroom without a lawyer and attempted to represent himself. The judge warned him, "That's dangerous. You don't know what you're doing; you don't know the laws. You don't know how the courtroom works. You can end up in trouble."

That's what happened. His self-representation was inadequate and he was convicted. The judge had no recourse; he said he left him under the laws because he wasn't properly represented by experienced counsel. The judge had no option but to sentence him. The judge did have some mercy and called his case back later for consideration of early parole, things like that, trying to make it easy on him.

I'm just showing how dangerous it is to try to represent yourself. Don't take up for yourself against God, the judge; let Jesus do that for you. Let Jesus take up for you! He knows the rules; he knows the laws. He has the Judge's ear. He knows you. He's our mediator between God and man! He's a good one! He does a great job! Don't try to undermine him; don't try to cut him out. Don't cut out this middle man. He needs to be in there. Let's let him do his job. He can deliver us.

There are so many extremes that people go to in religion. They get in trouble that way. There are doctrinal extremes, extremes of belief about God that cause people to miss God. Like one of these songs we were singing here a while ago about Jesus paying a debt he did not owe. We all agree we owed a debt we couldn't pay; everybody within the Christian faith believes that.

A preacher came by and visited us one time and we were singing that song. He left and criticized us for that song because he's a member of a group that believes Jesus was born in sin and had to suffer for his own sins as well as ours. That sort of nullifies his capacity and his position as a mediator. He had to be above sin to qualify to meet with the Father, but he had to be tempted to qualify to represent us through understanding us. He understands both sides. Jesus knows how to live above sin, but he knows what it feels like to be tempted to sin. Praise his name! He's able to identify with us and feel for us. How did Paul put that in Hebrews? "*We have not an high priest that cannot be touched with the feeling of our infirmities.*" Jesus is touched with the feeling of our weaknesses. He knows every feeling that we have, from sickness to sin. He's been tempted by all of it; he's faced all of it, loneliness and rejection, the threats of discouragement.

He wouldn't let himself be discouraged, but he felt discouraged. He knew the feeling of that infirmity. By the way, that is an infirmity; that's a weakness. If you let yourself be discouraged, if you get weary in well-doing, if you get tired of serving God and paying the price, that's an infirmity. Well, Jesus is touched with the feeling of that infirmity. He knows what it's like and knows how to help us get above it. You can rise above all those weaknesses; you can live above the flesh and God will help you in doing that.

Praise God! He even gives us the chastisement we need when that's the answer. He knows what we need and he'll do it for us. Did I understand you, Brother Johnny, to say that Brother Patton gave you a whipping one time? There are people in here who would brag about that if they could say that Brother Patton gave them a whipping when they were kids. Can't you imagine that Jesus himself may have whipped some kid brother of his, if his father was dead as is supposed? Before he went into his ministry, he was having to help his mother Mary raise the family. Do you reckon Jesus ever gave anybody a thrashing? You never thought of Jesus that way, did you?

He believed in the Bible; he understood the principles that Solomon laid down in the Proverbs. Jesus knew the need for chastisement, as Paul did later on in describing God the Father, himself, who chastises us when we need it. I wouldn't be surprised if Jesus didn't whip some little kid in the community or in the family while he was growing up and coming into maturity, becoming a grown man, waiting on his thirtieth birthday so he could enter the ministry.

We do read about him making a whip and driving the animals out of the temple one time, kicking over the bird cages and letting the doves fly away. That cost somebody some money. He kicked over the money changers' tables like kicking over the counter at the bank, scattering the money. Some people even suspect that he may have used that whip, may have slung it or popped it a few times at some of the men in there. It doesn't actually say that he used the whip on the men, but the threat was there. They understood the threat was there. I'm sure they stayed out of the way.

Jesus was practical; he was a practical person. He lived on the natural plane as well as the spiritual. He knew how to mingle and unite the two. That's what you and I have to learn. We've got the divine nature on the inside of us, as well as the carnal nature. We've had a change take place in us that gave us the new nature, but it did not immediately take away the old nature. You have to work some on that process.

We had a change in a moment, in a twinkling of an eye when we got the Holy Ghost. That's not the one Paul was talking about in First Corinthians 15, but it's similar to that. There was a spiritual change, a spiritual connection with the Spirit of God. Our spirit made connection with his Spirit, or his Spirit made connection with ours. That was where the initiative was; God's Spirit came to us and connected us with God. By that connection, you have access to the mind of God. His thoughts can flow into your mind through the Spirit, from his Spirit into your spirit.

Your spirit is a means of conveying information to your soul just as your body is a means of conveying information to your soul. The fact that we are more conscious of the body, usually, than we are of the spirit keeps us in this world, afflicted with the habit of acquiring more information through the body than we do through the spirit. Holy Ghost people are trying to change on that and get more information through the Spirit. Did you know there is a spirit of discernment, a spirit of knowledge, a spirit of wisdom? All those are mental activities and the Spirit of God can help you with those things.

We have had a glorious experience; we came through an outstanding change when we got saved. But we're still having to go through some changes, and we still have some changes to come. That other change in I Corinthians15, *"in a moment, in a twinkling of an eye"* is a change from a natural body to a spiritual body. It's a body; there's a spiritual body. The soul is not to be left floating around without a body to live in. That change we're to experience in that moment when Christ returns to catch his Bride away is a change from this natural body into a spiritual body, a glorified body like his glorious body. All these are different phases of the term 'salvation'.

We're always asking people, "Are you saved? Have you been saved?" This was common back when I was a kid, a Pentecostal boy living among Baptist people. All of my mother's people that we lived among were Baptist. She was a Baptist until she prayed through to the Holy Ghost all by herself. Taking the Bible literally and entering into her closet and shutting the door, she prayed there in the dark until she prayed down what she called the 'fire from Heaven'. She had a vision of flames from Heaven falling on her there in the closet. She talked in tongues; she got a new birth.

And like all of us, she wanted to give it to everybody else. When you get it, you like to share it. It's too good to keep, too good to keep to yourself. You can hardly keep from sharing it. Mother succeeded in stirring up all the aunts, uncles and cousins in our community because they didn't have the same desire she had. They had never had a desire to enter into the closet, shut the door and pray in the dark. That never occurred to them. They didn't even want an experience like she was getting. It caused some distraction, some dissension and argument among our families.

I remember those days, the arguments that were being made; how hard it was to find fellowship, somebody that agreed with you after you got this new experience. This was back in the late 1930s and early 1940s when Pentecostal people were in short supply. We were still a minority here in this country. If we did hear a rumor about some Holy Ghost people moving into the county, we'd talk about it. It would be a topic for conversation. "We heard there are some more `postolics moved in up the creek there, across the creek." We would want to find a way to meet them, get acquainted with them. We had one other cousin across the creek that had the Holy Ghost. We would sometimes walk or ride a donkey, a mule, to meet down on the creek and have a prayer meeting.

We didn't have enough people like us to have church together anymore. We quit going to the little schoolhouse Baptist meetings because it caused too much trouble when we went there. We quit going there and causing trouble, so we were left without any place to go to church for a long time. We were interested; we were hungry. We were looking for other children of God. We had had a sudden change and couldn't keep from advertising it.

You can have this change, too. You can have a new birth; you can be born again! Those were the days when you would ask people, "Are you saved? Do you know you're saved?" This was a trick of the Pentecostal people in those days, "Do you *know* you're saved?" More likely than not, the person you were asking would say, "Well, I hope I am." You could hardly get him to say, "I *know* I'm saved." If you asked a Pentecostal person that, he would say, "Yes sir! I *know* I'm saved! I had an experience! I can tell you the time; I can take you to the place!"

All those other Christians would say, "Well, I hope I am," because they were living in doubt. You don't have to live in doubt. You can have an experience. What we didn't know at that time was, that was just the beginning and not the end of our experience. There are different phases of salvation described in the Word of God.

Let's look at a scripture in Romans, the fourth or fifth chapter. It says we are saved from sins that are past. Help me find that one. Which? Romans 3:25. This is talking about Jesus, what he did for us. This is one of the extremes I was referring to a while ago that people fall into, thinking that you can get all of God with one experience. You can't get all of God in one experience. You can't get all the Lord has for you in one experience. You can't get all the benefit of the Holy Ghost in one experience. You need to keep praying through. You can't get enough tongue-talking in one night. You need to do it again; you need to renew your experience.

A lot of us went through the experience, after we got the Holy Ghost Baptism, of being tempted with doubt. That's very common among Holy Ghost people after you get away and cool off, quit feeling so good. At first you think this feeling will last forever. "I'll feel this way for the rest of eternity." You don't anticipate falling back down into the flesh, coming back down to the ground, coming back off cloud nine down onto the muddy earth.

It happens to you. You wake up one day with mundane surroundings. You've got a job to go to, a living to make, a house to clean or kids to raise, a boss to relate to, a husband or a wife and kids to get along with. You might even find somebody in the church that irritates you or somebody that you irritate and you didn't know you irritated them. When you find it out, it makes you feel let down. Then is when you'll doubt because you don't feel spiritual anymore. You don't always feel spiritual.

This is why we keep telling you that you can't trust your feelings; you can't live by feelings. You need some feelings, but you can't depend on them. You've got to live by faith. You will doubt your experience; you will wonder, "Was that real? Was what happened to me real or did I make that up? Did I do that in the flesh?"

Then, to settle the situation, you need to pray through again. You'll convince yourself if you will pray through to that feeling again, have that experience again. You can't leave it all to one thing that happened to you. Those are the extremes that religious minded people get into: pinning it all on one experience, saying, "I was saved forty years ago and that's sufficient. The experience I had then is sufficient. I'm guaranteed everlasting life. Once saved, always saved; I can't fall." People, by that means, deny themselves further blessings that God has for them.

We need to pay attention to the key scriptures in the Bible. You know there are key thoughts, key scriptures, key words. There is a 'key of knowledge' that Jesus mentioned while talking to the Pharisees. He said, "*You Pharisees have taken away the key of knowledge.*" That lets you know that preachers are expected to have the key of knowledge.

Jesus promised the keys of the Kingdom to Peter and all the apostles, although he was talking directly to Peter, because Peter had just answered the test question that day. But all of them were in on the test; they were all taking the test. Peter is just the one that raised his hand and spoke up for the pop quiz. So Jesus, carrying on a conversation with him, said, "I'm going to give you the keys to the Kingdom," but he was giving them to all the disciples.

We're to look for key thoughts. The key to the Kingdom is the Word of God, the key of knowledge. There's another key, the key of authority, which is something else; another subject, the Key of the House of David.

Let's read this here in Romans 3. We'll start with verse twenty-two. "*The righteousness of God which is by faith of Jesus Christ unto all and upon all them that believe, for there is no difference.*" What he means there is that there is no difference between Jew and Gentile, or between any other classes of people. There's no difference between the classes or races or nationalities or languages of people when they come to Christ.

"*All have sinned and come short of the glory of God.*" Regardless of your color, your height, your weight, your education, your family tree, whatever, you've sinned and come short of the glory of God. Every one of you; every one of us! Let's make that '*us*'; all of *US* needed salvation.

So, we are justified freely by his grace. Verse 24: "*Through the redemption that is in Christ Jesus whom God has set forth to be a propitiation through faith in his blood.*" Propitiation is a word that means something like 'compensation' or 'payment'. He's a compensation through faith in his blood to declare his righteousness, Jesus' righteousness, his blood, for the remission of sins that are past. That is seldom emphasized in the Christian churches. I want you to get that.

When you come to Jesus and are justified by his blood, what you get is forgiveness of sins that are past, remission of sins that are past. That's what you repent of when you go to the altar. If you're coming to the altar for the first time, seeking to get saved, people will tell you to repent. Maybe you've already heard the preacher say it, "Come down here and repent of your sins and pray through and touch God. God will save you."

What are you repenting of? Well, the sins that are past. You can't repent for things you've never done. You can't repent there at the altar for sins you may commit in the future. Neither can you receive judgment ahead of time for those sins. We can't judge anybody for what we suspect he might do. They don't do that even in the unjust courthouses down here. They won't put a man in jail because he *may* kill somebody someday. You have to wait until he does it. Only then can you judge him.

So, God isn't judging sin that you may do someday when you come to the altar and repent; it's those past sins. That's what we call one of the three phases of salvation: Forgiveness of sins that are past. I have been saved from my past sins. That's what I got when I repented. That was sealed by the blood of Christ when I received the Holy Ghost. That was just dealing with sins that are past. Yet, there's more in the Holy Ghost than that. The Holy Ghost is about more than just sins that are past. It's a means of dealing with those sins that are future.

Let's look ahead here in another chapter. In Romans 8 he told the difference between being in the flesh and in the Spirit. Verse 13: "*If you live after the flesh, you shall die.*" He's talking to all of us, saints and sinners, godly and ungodly, believers and unbelievers, saved and unsaved. If you live after the flesh, you'll die. The wages of sin is still death, just like it was in the Garden.

If you live after the flesh, you'll die. But, here's what the Holy Ghost is for: "*If you through the Spirit do mortify*" (or kill out) "*the deeds of the body, you shall live.*" That's what you're doing right now. You're killing out the deeds of the body using the Holy Ghost. You don't get it done in one night. You don't get it done the first time at the altar. I know you get up from the altar talking in tongues and you feel like "I'll never be tempted again. Nothing will ever tempt me again. Sin is no longer a problem." But it's later on down there, after you come down off cloud nine back down to the mud again. You have to become practical and deal with everyday affairs. You have to continue living in the flesh but learn to not live according to the flesh.

We have to continue working in the flesh without doing the works of the flesh, killing out the deeds of the body. It takes the Holy Ghost to do that. The Word of God won't do that for you. The Word of God will bring it to your attention. It'll teach you what you'll have to overcome. It will describe to you the kind of person you need to become in Christ Jesus, but you'll have to have the Holy Ghost to accomplish it.

That's what Jesus said back in Acts 1: "*You shall receive power after that the Holy Ghost is come upon you.*" Well, the kind of power he was talking about was power to kill the flesh, to live above sin. Anything else, those men already had. He had already given those men, the apostles, power to heal the sick, raise the dead, open blinded eyes, cast out devils. Powerful men he was talking to. But he said, "*You'll receive power after that the Holy Ghost is come upon you.*" The power they were going to receive through the Holy Ghost was power to live above sin, power to mortify the deeds of the flesh.

Put that then with this one over in the last or next to last chapter of Romans where he said, "*Now is your salvation nearer...*" Isn't that in the end of Romans, chapter 13? "*Now is our salvation nearer than when we first believed.*" Somebody find that one for me.

Romans 13:11: "*Knowing the time...*" do you know what time it is? Here's what time it is: "*It's high time to awake out of sleep,*" That's what time it is. "*...for our salvation is nearer than when we believed.*" That means we're closer to being saved now than we were when we started. That means we were not fully, completely, eternally saved when we were forgiven of our past sins. We were partly saved. We were saved from those past sins.

Brother James Sowders used to tell about a little child, a little girl, who came to him to be baptized one time when he was in the baptistery. She was so small, he wondered if she was old enough to qualify for baptism. He asked her, "Honey, are you saved?" She looked up at him and said, "I'm a little bit saved." He said, "I couldn't say it any better than that, myself." She qualified; she was a little bit saved. He ducked her under the water. She was going on to become completely saved.

This is the Second Phase of salvation: I am now being saved from the process of sin. Jesus saved me from my past sins, but now he's busy saving me from the tendency to commit sin. That's got to be dealt with. Everybody knows that's got to be dealt with. Everybody that doesn't believe you can live above sin believes it has got to be lived above if you ever make it to Heaven. They just think you're going to get up there and start living above sin. How do you expect to overcome when you get to Heaven if you don't overcome here?

The promises are given to the overcomers down here. The overcomer does his overcoming down here. When you get to Heaven, you don't have to overcome anything. You don't do any overcoming up there except to help overcome the sins of other people, overcome the sins in the world. You may come out riding one of those white horses. According to Revelation 19, there's an army of white horses following Jesus who is riding his white horse. What are they riding forth for? They're going forth to battle; going out to defeat the Beast, the Dragon and the False Prophet. That's because they have already defeated themselves; they have already crucified the old man. They're not having to overcome anything in themselves; they've already done that.

That's the point you finally come to where you have got it done, where you can say like the Apostle Paul, *"I have fought a good fight."* Let's take it a phrase at a time: That signifies that he wasn't still fighting, doesn't it? It sounds like he's won the fight. He's finished the fight. He didn't have to fight anymore.

"I have kept the faith." He had done his part of defending the faith. He was the defender of the faith in his day. What else did he say? *"I have finished my course."* He didn't have anything else to do. There's just a reward waiting for him now. He had already finished his course when he said that. He wasn't waiting until he got to Heaven and finish up there, overcome up there, get the victory up there. He got the victory down here. That's what an overcomer does.

I used to hear Brother Patton describe it this way back out in Port Houston. He said, "An overcomer is a guy that knocks the other fellow out and looks around. He's more than a conqueror. He conquers this adversary and looks around for another one. 'Anybody else want a piece of this?' (laughter) 'Anybody else want some of this?'" He's more than a conqueror; he can conquer and conquer again. So, he gets his job done. You've got to get the job done. You've got to keep the faith. You've got to finish your course.

"Henceforth, there is laid up for me a crown of righteousness which the Lord, the righteous judge, will give me at that day." There's this theological dispute about eternal security. People tell you, "I would hate to be worrying about my salvation; I'd hate to think I could be lost again after I've been saved." They believe they are eternally secure. Well, you can become eternally secure.

Paul reached that point. He was eternally secure. That is the Third Phase of salvation: saved completely from sin. That means saved from death because death is the wages of sin. When you are saved from all sin you have become a just person made perfect. That is in Hebrews 12:22 where he said, "*You are come unto Mount Zion...,*" spiritual Mount Zion. He's already previously explained that it's not the natural mountain he's talking about, the Mount Sinai that Moses came to, but he says, "*... we've come to Mount Zion, unto the city of the living God.*" Well, the Mount Zion we've come to is the church. That's a high place. "*Wisdom cries in the high places of the city.*" The pulpits of the churches are the highest places in town. They preach the highest standards; they preach high morality.

All the churches, all the pulpits, have good standards of morals unless they're being corrupted by the morals of the day. You can let that happen to you. You can let your conscience become seared. Even the conscience of a preacher can become seared as with a hot iron. Somebody needs to find me that poem. I want to copy it down and learn it or at least have it available. It talks about sin, how it looks when you first see it, how horrible it is. Then how, as you keep looking at it you get better acquainted with it, get used to it. Some of you remember that little ditty, don't you? Find it for me. I've probably got it hid in my notes somewhere.

It's a principle with us that we can learn to accept wickedness and evil. We can let down. The things that we used to automatically turn away from, turn our back on, we can weaken and accept and become corrupt. But we've come to The Mount Zion where wisdom is to be preached. If wisdom isn't crying in this pulpit, we need to invite it in, get more of Jesus in here. I Corinthians 1 says, "*Jesus is made unto us wisdom, righteousness, sanctification and redemption.*" Jesus is a fountain of wisdom. If we keep him in here, we'll have lots of wisdom.

I feel like we have a lot of the Lord Jesus in this church. We may not have all of him, and I don't even mean the idea that we could get him exclusively and nobody else could have him. All the churches need to have all of Christ. Do you see what I mean? We can't get by with just part of Christ. We need all of Christ, all the attributes, all the aspects of Christ in this church and in every other church in the Body of Christ. We need the five gifts of the ministry, the various gifts of the Spirit, the fruits of the Spirit. We need all of them. We'll have plenty of wisdom when we get that.

I'm generating questions here and can't get around to them. Let me finish this passage and I will turn to some of the questions.

The Heavenly Jerusalem, the Mount Zion, the City of the Living God is the heavenly Jerusalem. It includes an innumerable company of angels. I think that's real angels. I don't think that's talking about you and me being angels. I think that's talking about generally invisible angels. I believe in angels, don't you? I believe in old-fashioned angels. I know that the ministers are the messengers of God. I know that the church, the Body of Christ is an angel, in a sense.

But I still believe in Third Heaven angels, God's angels. These angels down here are Jesus' angels. God has angels that come down here; He sends them. Those are the angels you read about throughout the Old Testament. We've come to an innumerable company of them. They're associated with the church. God is using them more to help the church than anything else.

He said, "*These things the angels desire to look into.*" They're interested in the church more than anything else. I don't blame them. If I were an angel, I would be, too. I wouldn't want to be stuck over in Iraq or in China helping keep the peace over there, or struggling with all the things that go on in politics. I wouldn't want to be too involved in politics if I were a Third Heaven angel. I would want to know what was going on down at 548 South Houston Avenue in Humble. "*...to the general assembly and church of the Firstborn.*" That's what this, the Body of Christ, is supposed to be: the general assembly and church of the firstborn; Christ himself being the firstborn. "*... which are written in heaven.*" These people in this assembly are written in Heaven and not in the earth. Do you know the difference?

Do you know how to get your name written in the earth? Join a church somewhere where they write your name down in a book. Then, if you want to change churches, they will send the new church a letter with your name on it. You can move your name from this church to that church down here in the earth. Somewhere in the Old Testament it says, "*They that forsake me shall be written in the earth.*"

Do you know how to get your name written in Heaven? You have to be born into the family of God. God has the books on all his children. He doesn't keep books on everybody. God's not listing the names of the ungodly, but he lists the names of his children. When a new person is born into his family that name goes into God's book up in Heaven. You can have your name written in Heaven. You can sing joyfully the old choir song "There's a new name written down in Glory, and it's mine, oh yes, it's mine!"

I still like that. Somebody ought to learn that and sing it again. Somebody tried to take that revelation away from us, telling us that if our name was written in glory, it's been there for thousands of years already. I don't believe that, but I believe I did get my name written down in Glory when I turned to the Lord and became a child of the Living God. Amen!

He didn't need my name from the foundation of the earth. He needed it when I came to him, because he wanted to know me from then on. And we've come to God. He's part of the church. In a sense, He's connected to it. We don't call him the head of it, because he turned that headship over to his son. I've heard God described as the heart of the body, pumping the blood throughout the body; that blood being the Holy Ghost. That's the blood of Jesus. The Holy Ghost is God's blood and he furnishes it to the whole body. We live by it.

That's the only way you can live forever. That's why it's necessary to get the Holy Ghost. Sooner or later, you're going to have to get the Holy Ghost because that's the Spirit of everlasting life. God, the judge of all—and this is what I was trying to get to, "*and to the spirits of just men made perfect.*"

That's part of the Third Phase of salvation. You become just after you've been justified. There's a theological doctrine, justification by faith, but the way it's generally presented is as one of those extremes. Just faith in the blood of Christ takes care of your justification and makes you just, even though you know you're not just. That doesn't make sense. It's not logical. What justification by faith does is justify you from the guilt of those past sins and let you turn over a new leaf, let you make a new start, start with a clean slate and go on from there. Every time after that, if you sin, bring that sin under the blood immediately; get it justified.

The process ends with you becoming a just person, not needing any more justification. When you get to where you don't need to be justified anymore because you're a just person, then you're approaching that point where you can be made perfect. You can go on to perfection and be made part of that Mount Zion. You've fought a good fight when you get there.

Question—not clearly heard

Yes, the same way as imputed righteousness. Imputed righteousness gives you a start. You can't live on that forever; you've got to become *intrinsically* righteous. That's a term I use to explain it; that's not a Bible word. You've got to become righteous. God wants to make you righteous. To do that, he first imputes Christ's righteousness to you and gives you that standard to live up to. He gives you the power to live up to it through the Holy Ghost.

The time will come you won't need Christ's righteousness imputed to you. You've already got it and it is part of you. You're as righteous as Christ at that part. That sounds blasphemous, almost, doesn't it? But, that's the height that Christ wants to lift us to. Somebody said that God loves us like we are, but he loves us too much to leave us like we are. He's transforming us into the image of Christ. When we become the image of Christ, we'll look just like him, behave just like him.

Note: "Please explain Hebrews 10:26 in reference to us receiving the truth."

Back up a few chapters here. *"For, if we sin willfully after that we have received the knowledge of the truth there remaineth no more sacrifice for sins."* That explains what would be the condition of a person who has gone to that Third Stage of salvation and has received a full knowledge of the truth. Of course, a person that has gone all the way to that Third Stage and has fought the good fight and become perfectly just and justly perfect would never fall away or sin willfully. He has reached that stage of eternal security.

But there's a gap right in there, just before you get to that point where you would still be in danger. We cannot afford to let down. The more knowledge you get, the more is required of you and the more dangerous it is to let down and fall into sin. There's where sin might become willful sin instead of accidental sin or overpowered sin. Things like that God uses to excuse people and give them another chance while they're in this development stage. Once we've crossed that stage God is expecting perfection of us. Then if we sin, it's willful sin. What He says about it. "*There remaineth no more sacrifice for sins,*" after that.

Christ's sacrifice on the cross cured your sins that are past. If you've sinned since then you need to come to the altar and repent again of that sin. You can still appeal to Christ's sacrifice on the cross. But when you have progressed to the point where you have received the full knowledge and the full power of the Holy Ghost to live above sin, then you can no longer appeal to the sacrifice of Christ on the cross because it has already done its complete work for you. It's done what it's supposed to.

Jesus said that the Spirit of Truth would guide us into all truth. When it finally does that, that's all it can do. That's all the truth it can give us. It is the power to "*...mortify the deeds of the body.*" Romans 8. When we learn all about the deeds of the body and have that power to mortify them, then if we fail to do that, it's charged to us; it's our fault and there's no sacrifice for that because Jesus is not going to die on the cross again.

"*By one sacrifice he perfected forever them that are saved.*" There won't be another sacrifice for any of them that are saved and fall away, who let down from that position. "*There remaineth no more sacrifice for sins but a certain fearful looking for of judgment and fiery indignation which shall devour the adversaries.*"

Note: "What is our teaching on suing a business?"

Well, that's not something we can give a general answer to. You need to consult about the particular case.

Question—not understood

A similar passage, Hebrews 6:4 says, "*It is impossible for those who were once enlightened ...*" That's the same language, almost, as in 10:26: "*... and have tasted of the Heavenly gift and were made partakers of the Holy Ghost.*" That goes with it. He didn't mention that in 10:26, but that's part of the enlightenment. Part of the enlightenment you get through the truth is about the baptism of the Holy Ghost. There's a whole doctrine back there in the second verse about the doctrine of baptism*s* (with an 's' on it). The Holy Ghost is one of them. "*....and have tasted the good word of God and the powers of the world to come.*" 'Powers' is an ambiguous word there. The Holy Ghost is a power. But the people who have the Holy Ghost, especially the people who have a calling and responsibilities and gifts from God are powers. Yes, Bride members and the ministry, especially the leadership.

In Romans 13 he used that expression about powers: "*Let every soul be subject to the higher powers.*" He's not talking about forces like the Holy Ghost, but he's talking about people that have authority. Be subject to people that have authority. If you've been tasting the good word of God and tasting the powers of the world to come, "*it's impossible,*" it said, "*if they shall fall away* (or turn away) *to renew them again unto repentance.*" It's the same reason as 10:26: "*Seeing they crucify to themselves the son of God afresh.*" You can't do that.

You don't get away with that. You can't really crucify the son of God again, but that's what you're calling for. That's what your sin requires when you've sinned after reaching that height in God. We use a type on that of Moses' experience in the wilderness, talking to the rock one time and smiting the rock another time. The rock typifies Christ; he's the rock that was cleft for you. The first time Israel got thirsty and God brought water out of the rock, he told Moses to take his rod and smite it. Waters gushed out of the rock.

That's a type of Jesus, the Rock of ages, being smitten; and living waters came out of him. In John 7, the last day of the feast, Jesus stood and cried, *"If any man thirst let him come to me and drink. Out of his belly shall flow rivers of living water. This spake he of the Holy Ghost, which they that believe on him should receive when the time came."* Jesus is the rock that was smitten to give us the Holy Ghost. That also gave us cleansing from sin, forgiveness from sin.

Years later, another time Israel got thirsty and there was a rock. God told Moses that time, *"Speak to the rock."* Like prayer, you can speak to Jesus; you can pray. You don't need to smite him again. We can't put him on the cross again. All you have to do is talk to him, now. If you need another blessing, ask him for it. Pray through. Talk to the Lord! You can just speak to him and get what you need. Come in his name to the Father because he authorizes you. He gives you the authority of his name to go straight to God and make requests to him.

Moses made the same mistake that Paul is threatening people with here in Hebrews: "*If they shall fall away again, it is impossible to renew them again to repentance.*" Moses made the mistake of smiting the rock again. You can't get by with that. If you try to smite the rock again, you pay the penalty for it. Moses' penalty was death, literal death before he could enter the Promised Land. He paid the price. Moses was a man who could occasionally change God's mind. He changed God's mind a time or two in the wilderness.

But, he couldn't change him on that. He tried to change him on that point. God said to him, *"Because you disobeyed me, you will die on this side of Jordan. You won't get to go into that good land."* Just before he died, Moses brought it up again: "I'd like to go over and see that good land." God cut him off curtly, *"Don't ask me again; don't bring it up again."*

Moses had to die on the other side of Jordan because he had smitten the rock when he was supposed to speak to it. That typifies something to us. If we sin again and do something that would call for another sacrifice of Christ on the cross to save us, we just won't get saved. We'll never make that Third Stage of salvation; we'll be cut off.

Note: "I read this in a church program: The ultimate aim of the human mind in all its efforts is to become acquainted with the truth. Is this Biblical?"

I guess that's right. Is it Biblical? Well, it's just a fact isn't it? The ultimate aim of the human mind is to become acquainted with the truth. That's what a mind is for, to comprehend the truth.

All right, have I answered the questions? I guess I have. I wanted to answer some questions tonight about the phases of salvation and what it means to be completely saved. To be completely saved is not just to accept Jesus as your propitiation; it's not just to accept the Holy Ghost by faith and trust that you've got it. It's not just to have your name written on a church book.

To be completely saved is to be, how shall I describe it? Beyond and above temptation. Praise God for that much truth!

Chapter 13

The Light of the Glorious Gospel

March 12, 2005

There's a lot of repetition in the things we're saying and doing right now, but they are things the Lord is emphasizing. And, I'm so happy and thrilled to see the will of God being done. I'm doing my best to get my mind and my will in line with the Lord's will. That was really what I felt in that car wreck my wife and I had a couple of years ago. It was a reminder from the Lord to not go beyond his commandment, nor to fall behind either, but to do exactly what he says. We're embarked upon a technical enterprise and it's easy to do damage to the work of the Lord by misunderstanding and pursuing our own will in matters.

The Lord wants things to work out right. Things have to be done right; they have to be done certain ways to work out right. I know that none of us on the different sides of the divisions that we've had, none of us understands perfectly everything right. We've got our own viewpoint. The Lord is bringing us together to affect each other's viewpoint.

The brethren that are coming here may have their own motivation, but God has something in mind at the same time. He wants them to come here and see how things work under the order that we have. And he wants us to go there and see how things work under the order that they have. There will be a blending of ways and methods so that everything works better for everybody. That's how it's going to come out.

I know that we've been talking constantly about this now for over a year here in this church. And it seems like we're riding a hobby horse, but it's what the Lord is concentrating on; it's what he's pushing right now. This is what the Spirit is saying to the churches this year, at this hour, at this time. We're to cooperate with God. We must work with him while he's working on this project. He'll get this project done and do something else. At about the time he switches over to do something else, some of us will wake up and want to jump on this bandwagon when this bandwagon's already got to its destination. Don't miss out! Get on board! Climb on the wagon and let's work together and do what the Lord is doing right now!

There's so much good in this. Like Brother Watson said, I can see problems in the future. I can see where strains and tensions will develop and we'll have disagreements. That's natural as long as you're dealing with people that are, in some degree, still in the fallen condition. You see us there, don't you? You see yourself there; you see me there. We're still, to some degree, in a fallen condition. God's lifting us out of it, but he hasn't got us all the way out yet, so we're bound to have some troubles. One of the Christian poets said, "To live among saints in heaven, that's all bliss and glory, but living among saints on earth, that's another story." Until we learn how to be saints on earth, we'll never get to be saints in heaven. Down here is where we have to work these things out.

It's so easy to say, "Well, the Lord will bring it out someday." As we used to say, "It'll all come out in the wash after a while." And we wait for the Lord to fix it when we get to heaven. That's what the Christian world is doing. They're just waiting for us all to get to heaven and the Lord will help us see all things right over there. The Christian world is confused about that scripture in I Corinthians 15: "*We shall all be changed in a moment, in the twinkling of an eye.*

For us to be righteous persons, that can't be done in a moment, in the twinkling of an eye. It has to be done in a long period of trials and testing. This is where you "*think it not strange*" as Peter said, "*concerning the fiery trial which is to try you, as though some strange thing had happened to you.*" It's not strange at all for us to suffer, for us to bear a cross. Jesus is not the only one who had to bear a cross. The Gospel is not just about Jesus' cross, about him dying on the cross. The Gospel is also about you and me dying on a cross. Jesus said, "*You can't be my disciple except you take up your cross and deny yourself and follow me."* That's where he was headed: to a cross. All that is in there, but it's glorious. It all brings forth the peaceable fruits of righteousness. There is wonderful success and power in the things of God to anybody that's willing to go through those conditions.

Brother George Wright used that scripture here a little while ago about *"The secret of the Lord being with them that fear him."* He will show them his covenant. The secret of the Lord is the mysteries that Paul mentioned so many times in the New Testament. It's an understanding of the Word of God. There's a mystery of the godhead; there's a mystery of godliness; there's a mystery of iniquity. There are all those mysteries that are opened up under the New Covenant. It's to people that fear the Lord to get to understand those secrets and enter into a covenant with him.

We don't want to just hear about the covenant; we want to make the covenant with the Lord. He's still making covenant with people because new people are being born and need to enter into the covenant that he made, the New Covenant he made with the house of Israel. New people are coming along, new generations rising up now after two thousand years. Jesus is still making a new covenant with the house of Israel as they're born and come into the kingdom and as they qualify for the covenant. Praise God!

These are special things, private things. It's a secret. There are secrets between you and the Lord. You're to have some secrets with the Lord, things he lets you see that everybody doesn't see. God doesn't show his covenant to everybody. It's to them that fear him and qualify to be in on his secrets. They get to see his covenant. They're the ones that get to enter into a covenant with the Lord, keep covenant with him and receive the benefits of the covenant. There's always a benefit to a covenant that God makes. He made a covenant with Noah when he set the rainbow in the sky.

He said, *"I'll never destroy the earth with a flood again."* That lets us rest easy. Some parts of the earth may suffer floods. Floods still come down the Sabine River. Floods still come down the Trinity and run over the dam sometimes and flood the valley down here below Liberty. Tsunami waves may wash the shorelines of the oceans in some places, but you can rest easy, he's not going to destroy the whole earth with a flood again.

That's a covenant God made with the human race. It was a covenant without qualifications, just a promise he made. He entered into that covenant with Noah and all of Noah's descendants. You and I are Noah's descendants. Noah was a man of faith. We've got a good ancestry, praise God! We ought to rejoice in our ancestry. We've got a righteous man in our family tree! His name was Noah. He found favor with God. So, we're still reaping the mercies that Noah laid up as a man of God. We're reaping those mercies today.

Then, the covenant that God made with Abraham, we're able to get in on that, in a way. We can become children of righteous Abraham by faith, believing in the same God that he believed in, trusting God like he trusted God and being willing to follow the Lord when he calls us out to move on. He called Abraham to leave his old country behind, leave his old ways behind, move out and follow the Lord into a place where he knew not. He didn't know where he was going, where he was going to end up. It's somewhat that way with us. We know we're headed for heaven! Praise God!

Well, Abraham knew that but he didn't know all the ways he would pass through to get to heaven. God has given us a destination but we don't know all the way stations along the way. We just know that we're safe in his hands. We've put our hand in his hand and he is leading us as a result of that. He's leading us to get together. God's leading his saints to get together.

This year especially is a crucial time, in that it's a significant time period. It's calling for a lot of commitment, dedication and promise just to meet the schedule that is set down for us, especially in the leadership, this year. It calls for extra effort on everybody's part and there's going to be a lot of effort called for on the part of this church in the months to come to get ready to host another convention, another great meeting of the saints of God here in our city. That will tax our energies and our patience even, sometimes, but it's what God's leading us into. There are, as I said, many benefits in the things that God does all along the way.

I listen to these new brethren. I used this thought up in Dallas last night. "God has lights…I mean light sources, people that give out light." Daniel said, *"They that turn many to righteousness shall shine as the stars forever and ever."* Jesus said to the church, *"You are the light of the world."* God has special lights that he raises up, like he raised up John the Baptist. Jesus said to that generation of Jews, *"John was a great light and you were willing to rejoice in his light for a season."* They soon got tired of his light because it was too bright. That's why they soon got tired of Jesus. *"They that sat in darkness have seen a great light."* It was too great for some of them because it blinded their eyes it was so bright. That light was Jesus.

I sometimes think we don't make enough over John the Baptist. What a great man he was! What a great preacher he was! What a wonderful prophet he was! He was so outshone by Jesus, whom he was called to introduce, that he was sort of forgotten and neglected ever since. Even the Early Church seemed to neglect John. You don't read hardly any comments about John in the Epistles. They didn't say much about him because they were not called to preach 'John'; they were called to preach 'Jesus'.

John has a right to some recognition. Jesus himself testified about him. *"There was not a greater prophet born of woman,"* he said, *"than John. He's the greatest of the prophets, even though he's the least in the Kingdom."* Anyone receiving the baptism of the Holy Ghost is greater than John because John could not have the Holy Ghost in his time, his ministry. He had to do his ministry without the *gift* of the Holy Ghost, but he didn't do his ministry without the *assistance* of the Holy Ghost. He was one of those holy men of God that *'spake as he was moved of God by the Holy Ghost'*. But he had to do it without that gift inside of him, without the new birth.

What a mighty man he was! As far as I can find, there's no other person belonging to the New Testament, prophesied and predicted in the Old Testament outside of John the Baptist and Jesus. The great apostles, Peter and Paul and John, were not directly prophesied about personally in the Old Testament, but John the Baptist was prophesied about personally and directly. His particular ministry and job was outlined for him.

If you like to talk about predestination, you can use him. He's an outstanding example of somebody that was predestined to do the will of God. Not many people fall in that kind of category. He was a great man, a great prophet. But there are great prophets and teachers and lights today. That's what I'm building up to.

God keeps light sources on hand because light is something you can't store up. It seems like, with all these lights in here, we'd get this building filled up with light and we could throw the switch and the light would stay in here; that it would take a long time for it to all leak out. But you know how it is, don't you? You throw the switch and it's gone instantly. If we don't keep producing lights, there won't be any light. We will instantly be back in darkness the moment we stop producing lights.

If all the light-givers, light sources and candle sticks passed out of the church, then one night the church would be back in darkness again. The knowledge of the glory of God would cease from the earth. But he keeps raising up lights and shining a light into our hearts. The glorious light of the Gospel has lightened our eyes. Praise God! The Gospel of Jesus Christ! It's a glorious light but it has to be kept shining in the lives of people.

That's why Jesus put it that way. He didn't say the Gospel is the light of the earth, although the apostles used it that way. Paul said, "*The god of this world has blinded their minds lest the light of the glorious gospel should shine in their heart.*" So the gospel is the light itself, but the church and the members of the church are the candles on the candlestick. They're the sources of the light, giving out the light constantly.

So, it has to be in you before it can come out. It's like where Jesus used the parable of the ten virgins. They had lamps in their hands and they had to trim their wicks. They had vessels of oil for the light. That was knowledge that was inside them. Some had more knowledge than others. Some were careless and neglected to acquire the knowledge that they needed. As soon as they burned up what they had, they didn't have anything stored up. They tried to borrow from their neighbors to keep their lights burning.

You need your own vessel full of oil. You need a knowledge of the Gospel of Jesus Christ inside of you. Don't leave it all up to the ministry here. Years ago, I heard someone around here say they didn't study the Bible very much; they just let Brother Billy tell them how it was. Well, that's not enough; it's not enough for Brother Billy to know the Gospel. *YOU* need to know the Gospel. *YOU* need to understand the resurrection. *YOU* need to have a grasp on eternal judgment. You've got to be a righteous judge wherever judgment falls your lot and you can't dodge it, can't pass it on up the ladder. There are things that arise in your life that you will be called on to judge. You have to be a righteous judge; you have to understand the principles of righteousness and holiness. Those things are necessary to everybody. To know the principles; not necessarily to be able to quote the scripture or give chapter and verse, but just *KNOW*. This is what God wants; this is what the Holy Ghost calls for.

The Holy Ghost is calling for a holy life. That has to be in your heart. If it's in your heart, then it shines out and you become a light giving off light. You can be the light of the world by just living what you know, if you know enough. Living what you know will light up the community around you.

The reason for a candlestick, as it's described in the first three chapters of Revelation is God placing a church in a city as a location for the candles. The stick doesn't give the light, but it's the candles in the candlestick where the lamps are burning that gives forth the light. He voiced that threat there that a candlestick could be moved out of a city if the city is not worthy. It might finally come time where the church would *'dust off their feet'* against that city because they weren't being received there. The darkness was too great and too gross; gross darkness has overtaken the people. Nobody would receive the Gospel in that kind of city.

Or, if the church itself proves unworthy, people show that they don't treasure the truth. Some people *'have not a love for the truth'*, Paul said. That kind of people will be sent a *'strong delusion that they might believe a lie and be damned'*. So, it's possible to lose the light out of a certain area, but God's not going to let the light go out in the whole earth. He's going to keep a light shining down here, shining in this dark world, this dark place.

As Paul said in Philippians, *"Among whom you shine as lights."* This is a dark nation, he said. You're to shine in the midst of that as lights in a dark place. God's going to keep a light burning. He's going to have some people that are going to keep their wicks trimmed and keep their lives in order and let their light shine before men so that men can see their good works and glorify their Father in Heaven. Not all the men that are glorifying the Father in Heaven will copy the good works, but they will give lip service anyway. They will be forced to it.

Some things, when you see it you can't deny it. You have to admit: those people are doing a good work. They're doing something good; they've got something special. How many people used to say back in the early days of Pentecost, after they would visit one of the revival meetings and see the people shouting and praising God and enjoying their salvation, they would stand out in the shadows and say, "If I ever get religion, that's the kind I want!"

A lot of them never did get religion. They just said that; they gave 'lip service' to it. They admitted that those people had something, but they were not motivated enough to get it themselves. The Pentecostal people were letting their light shine in the communities, in the storefront missions, down the country roads and in the brush arbor revivals. They were letting their light shine!

Men were seeing their good works and glorifying their Father which is in heaven. Praise God! I hope we haven't lost that kind of zeal. I hope we haven't lost that kind of joy of our salvation that would cause us to make an impression on the neighbors. Everybody in town ought to see that we at least believe what we say. We feel like we've got something and it makes us happy. It does something for us; it gives us a reason to live. We've got a reason to live. Amen! Surely nobody in here is contemplating suicide; nobody in here tired of living and wanting to give it up as a bad job and just quit living.

Life has got too much to offer! Sure, we have trouble. Sure, we have to solve problems. Sure, we stump our toe and we get sick and have people get mad at us and run us down, all those things. Still, life is good under the Holy Ghost! What a blessing we can get in here in the church house.

With all the burdens we brought and laid down at the door as we came in... You can lay your burdens down as you come through the door of the church house. Come in here and just lift your hands. Your hands ought to get light and go up when you come through the church doors. Praise God! There's so much good, so much to enjoy. *"At God's right hand,"* the Bible says, *"there are pleasures forevermore."* Get on his right hand and stay there! That's where Jesus is! There's lots of joy and good feeling there, happiness! Thank the Lord! Amen! Praise God!

So in spite of the problems we're facing, things we're going to have to work out, I'm enjoying the process. I'm already reaping nuggets and little encouraging truths. I so love the Word of God; I love every detail. I hate to have a verse in there that I can't set in place and explain. So, when I hear somebody say something that fits, I just grab that. You know, it's a simple thing maybe. It may not be very important, but it just *FITS*.

I heard Brother Ross say at the last meeting up in Louisville that he leaves the comma out there in Isaiah 9:6 where it says, *"His name shall be called wonderful."* The King James Version says *'wonderful,* (comma) *counselor'*, but he said to drop that comma out of there. He's a *wonderful counselor*. I picked that up when I heard him say that. I thought, "I'm going to study that out and see if he's right or not."

I had never researched that. It had occurred to me a few times when I read that. I wondered if the comma goes there, but when I turned to the books and material, the commentaries and the other versions, it really appears that he was right. You don't need a comma in there. That was punctuation the King James translators dropped in there. I noticed the Geneva Bible, which was before them, also had it there, but most of the other versions leave it out. It's a phrase instead of just a series of words. It fits with all the other expressions in that passage.

They didn't put a comma between 'everlasting and Father' or 'prince and peace'. They didn't put a comma in there. Those are phrases with modifiers, nouns and modifiers. So, it fits to use 'wonderful counselor' that same way. That's a simple thing, but I just like to get it right. It was interesting when I looked in a Jewish Bible, the transliteration of the Hebrew. They put all those phrases together there with hyphens, like it was all one word because it said, *"His name,"* (singular) *"His **name** shall be called Wonderful-Counselor-Mighty-God- Everlasting-Father."* They put the whole thing together with hyphens into one word.

Well, the Word of God is fascinating; it's interesting to people whose business it is to deal with it. I know details like that don't fascinate everybody. But, that's my business. I'm called to handle the Word of God; I'm called to teach the people. My ministry is teaching the Bible, teaching the Word, so those things fascinate me.

At the same meeting in Louisville, I heard Brother Fitzsimmons talk about the misplaced comma in the Gospels where Jesus promised one of the thieves on the cross, *"thou shalt be with me in paradise." "Verily, I say unto thee,"* our Bible says, 'comma', *"today thou shalt be with me in paradise."* Remember, the Gospel writer didn't put that comma there. Somebody preparing the English translation of it put that comma in there and some of us figured out a long time ago that they put the comma in the wrong place. It should be after the word 'today' instead of before: *"Verily I say unto thee **today,** thou shalt be with me in paradise,"* because neither Jesus nor the thief went to paradise that day, that literal day. The day is coming; Jesus made that promise *THAT* day to that thief, but the day is coming when they will be together in paradise. Amen!

I had a question a Sunday or two ago about that paradise. What is that paradise Jesus promised? Well, it's a place in God that's better than where we are right now. We're not in paradise yet, but the apostle Paul testified that one time, in a spiritual experience he had in the Spirit, he was caught up unto the paradise of God.

'*Unto*'...right against third heaven. Many other great Christians have had that same experience. Brother Sowders had it; Brother Patton had it, being caught up out of their bodies into a place up in the Spirit, a high place where it was clean and holy and to some extent, maybe frightening, even. It was so holy and pure and a pure person there was talking to them. Brother Patton said he was up there in that holy place and knew it was time to come back down here in this world with all the traffic on the streets, horns blowing and people with their spirits stirred up and to the unholy, impure atmosphere that surrounds us in a big city here. He knew he had to come down in the midst of that and he dreaded it. It felt so good and clean up there close to the Lord, right next to the Lord.

Well, they were up in a place called 'paradise'. It's not a geographical place, but it's a spiritual place; it's a condition. You can hope to get into that. You may get in that condition. It's something the Lord is going to take us through.

I was just glad to hear Brother Fitzsimmons explain that verse that way. It's the way I've been explaining it a long time, but I was just glad to have it confirmed that they were seeing it, too. I know there are still brethren among us that are not satisfied with that. They don't find that explanation satisfying; they're looking for something else. But as far as I'm concerned, it's the best thing that's come along yet to explain that verse of scripture.

I had another question that came up tonight. Somebody wanted to know how long Reuben, Gad and Manasseh had to stay and fight with the other tribes, how many years. Are you all familiar with that Bible story? How Moses led the tribes of Israel right to the gates of the Promised Land and they defeated the enemy on the east side of the Jordan River.

Moses had to die on that side of the river; he didn't get to cross over into what is called 'Canaan Land proper'. Three of the tribes liked that territory over there on that side of Jordan. They asked Moses for permission to claim that land that they had just conquered and driven the enemy off of. It was free for the taking. They said, *"It's good land for our cattle. We're cowboys and shepherds; we've got lots of stock and this would be good land for us."*

Moses threatened them: *"You think you're gonna sit here while your brethren go to war over across the river?"* They said, *"Just give us a few days here to settle our families and our stock and we'll take our weapons and we'll go across the river with our brother tribes and we'll help them conquer their land,"* which they did. They kept their promise; they went across when Joshua led the people across Jordan. They spent the next seven years, if I remember right... Somewhere in the book of Joshua it mentions that they were seven years fighting all those wars and subduing the Canaanite tribes over there. Finally, Joshua let those three tribes return to their homeland across the Jordan. They gave seven years out of their lives to helping their brethren.

Someone comments.

Does it say five? Where are you reading?

Reply: Joshua 14:10

Well, I don't think that's the right verse. This was Caleb taking his inheritance and I'm not sure how old he was at the time that he went up as a spy. This won't fit the case. Somewhere else in here it mentions seven years that they spent subduing the land. You can look that up and find it for me. The next question went on to say, "In Joshua 15, Caleb gave his daughter springs of water, the upper and the nether springs. What is it a type of?"

Well, what it signifies to me is that everybody, every church and every person needs the water of life; you need the water of the Holy Ghost. Every pastor that's giving his people their spiritual inheritance needs to give them the Holy Ghost; he needs to be preaching the Holy Ghost. Anybody that's in a church where the Holy Ghost is not being preached ought to rise up and ask your pastor about it and demand that he preach that and work that message into the assembly.

Let's be careful that we don't let anybody dry up any of our churches where we've had the Holy Ghost. It's so important! The water of life is so important! We can't make it without it; we can't survive without it. We can't go on without it. The Holy Ghost is necessary. Water, in the scripture, is a type of that Spirit of God, the Spirit of the Living God. It's called the 'Water of Life'. There's a 'River of Life' in the last chapter of Revelation. It's a source that everybody has to have. We're in a dry and thirsty land without it.

She said, "*You've given me a south land.*" That was desert land. You've got to give some water to go with it. People who try to get through this dry and thirsty world down here without the Holy Ghost are in a pitiable condition. Churches are trying to function without that, even any churches among us that don't emphasize it.

You know, we can come down so strong and strict on order that we scare people out of volunteering and yielding to the Holy Ghost. People get to where they are afraid to get up and do anything in the Spirit, afraid they'll be criticized, afraid of being out of order. It doesn't take but a few words to discourage people. It takes many, many sermons after that to get them going again. Sometimes, people ask me, "Why don't you stop certain things?"

I said, "Well, because it's easier to stop it than it is to start it. I'd hate to have the job of livening-up a dead church." A lively church was left to me; it was dropped into my hands and I'm trying my best to keep it that way. I don't want to have to resurrect a dead church.

Thank God for this lively church! We want to keep it lively! Keep it full of the Holy Ghost! We're a Spirit-filled, and trying to be Spirit-led, people. But you can't be Spirit-led if you're not Spirit-filled. We've got to be full of the Holy Ghost. Then the Holy Ghost can guide us and tell us what to do. Well, praise God!

A Brother: "Brother Brown, can I ask a question? I've always had trouble with Acts 13:46 and how to interpret that. It looks like that scripture is talking about Jesus in Isaiah 49:6. Paul repeats it and it looks like it's God's commission for him. I was just trying to... If you have any thoughts on that, I'd appreciate it. Paul uses that in Acts 13 for his commission to go to the Gentiles."

Let me look at what Paul said in Acts 13? Which verse? Verse 47: "*For so hath the Lord commanded us saying I have set thee to be a light of the Gentiles that thou shouldest be for salvation unto the ends of the earth.*"

Here's how the New Testament preachers used the Old Testament scriptures: they would quote a verse in which maybe only a part of the verse applied to what they were doing. They would use it like James brought in an Old Testament verse in Acts 15. Its context didn't really apply to his day, but it had something in it that had to start in his day. It's true that this verse in Isaiah 49 was about Jesus.

"*It's a light thing that thou shouldest be my servant to raise up the tribes of Israel and restore the preserved of Israel. I will also give thee* (Jesus) *for a light to the Gentiles that thou mayest be my salvation unto the end of the earth.*"

But Paul uses that for an excuse, a motivation, a justification to be involved in carrying the Gospel to the end of the earth. You and I could use it that way if we feel that call, that burden to go out into the missionary field. We could go on the strength of that verse, that we're called to carry the light of the Gospel to the Gentiles, to the ends of the earth. Jesus began that in his own person, but he continued it, taking it on to the ends of the earth by backing those apostles and the church ever since.

His Body is doing that right now. Jesus' body in the earth today is continuing, completing the fulfillment of that scripture. Many of the Old Testament scriptures have taken two thousand years or more to completely accomplish what was begun back there. That verse that Peter quoted out of Joel about Jesus said he was going to pour his Spirit out on all flesh. Peter used that on Pentecost, but that was just the beginning of it. In Acts

2, it was poured out on some flesh and it was poured out on all flesh that was there without discrimination that day. But ever since then, it's being poured out on more and more flesh. He's continuing to do that, and that won't be finished until there's nobody left on the earth that is not filled with the Holy Ghost. That will finally come.

Brother: "The great commission: Go ye in all the world and preach the Gospel."

Yeah, that's part of what Jesus passed on to the apostles. All right. Can we have a song to follow this? We've had some good ones to lead up to it. Let's sing a song and then we'll go.

Chapter 14

Bible History; Prophecy; the Papacy

April 3, 2005

I think we're making progress. I think we're going 'great guns'! We're making headway toward the Promised Land! I don't think we're just marking time or spinning our wheels.

You know God's people's progress in these times is typified in some ways by things that happened in the Old Testament. God made Israel an example; He chose them out from the rest of the world and made them a special people, not because they were any better than anybody else, but he just chose them to make an example of them and give them a chance to be a blessing. Israel was called to be a blessing to the world. The greatest blessing they've ever brought to the world is Jesus Christ. Jesus came through that lineage. The Israelites had a lot to do with the Holy Scriptures, the messages that God gave to humanity. They were the keepers of the covenants and promises and prophecies for a long time.

Paul said, in Romans, "*What advantage then hath the Jews? Chiefly that unto them were committed the oracles of God.*" They perfected those oracles even when they didn't understand them. They honored them enough to make copies of them at a time when they couldn't just lay a sheet of paper up on top of a machine and run a copy in a few seconds.

Men gave their lives to laboriously hand-copying the scriptures. They respected those scriptures so much that it gives us great confidence today in the accuracy of our copies of those scriptures. If we couldn't respect our copies, then we wouldn't have anything to stand on because nobody today has the first copy that Isaiah made of his prophecies. What we have are copies of the copies that people made of that original which has long since disappeared, and so with all the other scriptures. What we have are copies of copies. Inevitably, a few of what they call 'typos', typographical errors, will creep into the making of copies. That is unavoidable.

But those things were kept to a minimum, to a point where there don't seem to be any significant errors in the scriptures. Those that are in there are probably self-revealing, like transforming a 'four' into 'forty'. That was easily done in the Hebrew. When it says that Absalom waited forty years before he started his revolution it undoubtedly means 'four'. They didn't have forty years left in David's lifetime when he did that. Things like that are obvious.

The facts are that those scribes were so careful with their copying, and they so respected the Word of God, that they were hesitant to even correct the mistakes after they caught them. You know that, if for fifteen hundred years, or from David to Christ, those copiers recognized that those figures were wrong there in II Samuel about Absalom, they could have straightened it out and made a correct copy just using common sense and logic. But, they respected the copies that were handed to them too much to make the corrections. That fact is to give us confidence in the degree of honesty and application that those copyists went to in order to protect the scriptures that were given to them.

They tell us it came to the point that when a Jewish scribe was making a copy of the Old Testament scriptures and he came to a place where the name of God was mentioned, he would stop writing and go take a bath. Then he would come back and write that name and go take another bath and then come back and continue the copy. They were very, very sincere. They did their dead-level best to be accurate. That gives us confidence that nobody added anything to the scriptures.

Did you know there is a curse pronounced on anybody that would add to what God said, or detract from it either? They did not add anything to the scriptures. That helps me in trying to interpret I John 5 for example. That's a controversial passage in there where it says, I think in verse 7, "*There are three that bear record in Heaven: the Father, the Word and the Holy Ghost.*" That's not found in every one of the copies that we have of I John.

There are people that argue that doesn't belong in there; that was added by some enthusiastic copyist who was affected by the Trinitarian teaching he was raised under. He just added a little bit of his own commentary to the Word. But, knowing the respect with which those scriptures were held—and it was true in New Testament times also—I want to point out that it's a lot easier to make a mistake of leaving something out than it is to make a mistake of adding something in.

You've all had that experience of skipping over something and missing something. There have been times when I was typing copies of Brother Sowders sermons into the computer. I learned to count the lines on the page; at the end of every page go back and see if my total of lines tallied up. A lot of times, a sentence will still make sense; it will just make a different sense. You will actually be leaving out a whole line of what he said. But never do I add anything in; I don't type an extra line in there. It's just so easy to leave something out.

I'm taking the position that those copies of I John that don't have that seventh verse are the mistaken copies. Some scribe jumped over that accidentally and left it out. But, God made sure that we had at least one copy somewhere that had that comment in there. That's not a Godhead scripture; that does not establish the Trinitarian teaching. It means something entirely different. You have to read that whole passage down to the eleventh and twelfth verses to see how to fit those verses in their place.

"The Word of God is quick and powerful and sharper than any two-edged sword, dividing asunder the soul and the spirit, the joints and the marrow." It's a wonderful thing, isn't it? We have to hand the Catholic Church credit for carefully copying the scriptures, both Old and New Testament scriptures during the fifteen hundred years or so of the Middle Ages and the four hundred years of the Dark Ages in there that they were doing like the Jewish scribes of old. They respected the scriptures even though they didn't understand them. They didn't practice them; in many cases they tried to deny people's access to them.

When the Reformation began, battles were fought over the idea of making the scriptures available to the 'common Joe', the common people, ordinary people. Aren't you glad, thank God, that battle was won? Somebody won that battle for us and here you and I have it today. Do you have a Bible in your hand? You've got access to one somewhere. You can get a Bible in your hand if you want one.

That wasn't true during the Dark Ages. It was made, in many countries, against the law to have possession of a Bible. It was considered that a Bible was so sacred it belonged only to the church houses. They kept it there, chained to the pulpit in some cases, and only the educated people and the religious officials with a permit—you had to get a permit to read the Word of God. They had to get permission to come to the pulpit and study the Word of God. In those days there was a famine in the land for the Word of God. Today, we've got a plethora of it; we've got almost a glut of Bibles. There are so many different versions and copies and new translations that everybody can have all the Bibles you want.

I don't know how many dozens of them I've acquired in my library, different versions and translations. The Word of God is plentiful today. It's available. It's just that not many people have the spirit to understand it. You have to have the right kind of spirit. Elihu said, "*There is a spirit in man that gives him understanding.*" If you don't have the right kind of spirit in you, you won't have understanding of these spiritual things.

One of the band numbers had that in there somewhere, "When God's ministry steps in Jordan wide, Lord let me follow, too." That was such a special occasion when Israel crossed over Jordan. They were following the ministry. Brother Patton loved this scripture here in Joshua 3 and 4 where the people crossed over Jordan into the Promised Land after they had spent forty years in the wilderness being led of God and at the same time, judged and punished of God.

Did you know there is such a thing as punishment? We've almost forgotten that. Parents have forgotten to teach their children there is such a thing as punishment and so they don't know much about eternal judgment or punishment. But, God punished the weak-faithed Israelites, the unbelieving Israelites that did not trust him. He made them spend an extra 38 years wandering in the wilderness without a homeland, without a home to call their own.

They had to pitch tent every night and fold up the tent the next day if the cloud moved on. If the cloud stood still, then they got to rest awhile and spend a few days in their encampment. But they had no place to call their own, to plant a crop, to have a vine or a fig tree. They couldn't build a house to call their own. Thirty-eight years they had to live that way until God brought them again to the doors of the Promised Land and had Joshua lead them across.

What it tells us is that the priests, the Levites went ahead of the people because the Jordan River was overflowing. They had to cross that river at flood tide. If it had been late summer or winter time, the Jordan wasn't that much of a river. It was more like what we call a creek in East Texas where I was raised. I was raised in between a creek and a river. I fished and swam in both of them. There's a lot of difference between a creek and a river. The river was as wide as this building here. It was all I could do to throw a rock across it. I would go down there and throw a rock across it and hit Louisiana.

We threw rocks at each other sometimes. But, the creek over on the other side of the hill was not much wider than one row of these pews right here. It had cut a deep channel in a little canyon there, but when it was running low in late summer, it was just a narrow stream, or branch. We used to call those little streams 'branches'. You could jump across it or step across it in some places when it was low.

The Jordan River was about like Patroon Creek, ordinarily, but in the spring time when the snow melted on Mount Hermon up the river above the Sea of Galilee, the river ran over. There was a broad flood plain there that, every spring time, the river ran over and flooded. That's right when the Israelites crossed it. God brought them there and commanded them to cross over it in all that flood. You would have needed a flat boat of some kind, a ferryboat, to get over it.

There were several million people that God wanted the ministry to get across that river. You need to have some sympathy for the ministry and the big job they have to do. That's what that typifies. That typifies part of the big job the ministry, the leadership of God's people, has to accomplish. The way they did it, they had the priests take the ark on their shoulders.

Oh, there was lots of power in that ark! They used it different times. It was a powerful thing; it was dangerous to touch the ark. You had to handle it according to the protocol, the specifications. They had a designated way for some Levites to carry that ark slung on poles. They put the poles on their shoulders. The poor Levites, maybe at least two, would walk with it, with the chest, the ark, hung between them on those two poles.

It said, "They're to march right out into that flood water and the people are to follow." What happened was, when they marched out into that flood water, the waters split, split open, divided, dried up. The river dried up where they were. I think it implies that what happened was that God let a landslide dam up the river some miles upriver and held the water back while God's people crossed over. But, the Levites were standing there in the midst of the Jordan River holding that ark all day long while the crowd of people crossed over. As soon as the crowd crossed over and the Levites took the ark up out of the river, here came the water back down the river again. The dam broke and flooded the land again, going on down to the Dead Sea.

He said specifically, (I'll start reading in Joshua 3:15.) "... *as they that bare the ark were come unto Jordan and the feet of the priests that bare the ark were dipped in the brim of the water, for Jordan overflows all its banks all the time of harvest, that the waters that came down from above stood and rose up on a heap,* (or a dam) *very far from the city Adam and those that came down toward the sea of the plain,* (below the dam) *even the Salt Sea, failed, were cut off and dried up. And the people passed over right against Jericho."*

Now get the wording here in *verse 17*: "*The priests that bare the ark of the covenant of the Lord stood firm on dry ground.*" That's what Brother Patton liked, that idea of 'standing firm', because we use all that as a type of us facing the floodtide of public religious opinion in the end of this world. When religious opinion is going to be against us and we're having to run cross-current to it, taking an opposite stand on religious and moral and social questions, it's going to be a lot of pressure against us.

You won't be able to stand against all of that unless you are carefully taught and led by respected men, people you've got confidence in. So, the priests need to be men that know how to stand firm, take a stand and stand on it, stand on the Word of God, stand for the truth, take a stand on a controversial question, take an unpopular position because you see that's the true position according to the Word of God. Stand for that regardless of what the radio commentators and the Bible preachers in the churches are saying. Take a stand for the Truth!

Going on down in the fourth chapter, it repeats that expression. "*It came to pass when all the people were clean passed over Jordan that the Lord spake unto Joshua and said, Take twelve men out of the people, out of every tribe a man and command ye them saying, Take hence out of the midst of Jordan, out of the place where the priests' feet stood firm twelve stones.*" The priests' feet stood firm. As long as the priests' feet stood firm, the dam held and the waters stayed back! Praise God! And God's people were safe while they were crossing over!

If those priests had shifted their feet and one of them had fallen down and dropped the Ark, the flood would have come down and drowned a lot of people, but the priests' feet stood firm. You ought to be glad for that if you've got some leaders that you can count on, that their feet will stand firm even in the face of opposition, criticism and personal danger, perhaps.

It must come to that. We're all soldiers; we're to "*endure hardness as good soldiers,*" Paul said. I like that song about the army. Everybody join the army! See the world in a different light! If you join God's army, you'll see the world in a different light from what you ever saw it; it will look different to you from the way it used to look. Come on! Join the army! Be all you can be! Not Uncle Sam, but Jesus Christ wants you! Amen! Jesus Christ wants you in his army! Let's dedicate ourselves to the will of God! When we do that, we'll be taking some unpopular positions.

You have to be wise when you do that; be careful and don't go picking any fights. I know there is a scripture in the Proverbs that warns us about meddling in a fight that doesn't belong to you. Don't meddle in fights that don't belong to you. Don't pick any fights, but when you are backed into a corner and have to take a stand, be ready to take it.

Who knows what another year will bring! What an eventful year we've been through. Right now, there are changes on foot in this world, changes on foot in this body of people, the church. Changes developing that most people are not even aware of out in the church world. We're going to have another pope in a few days.

I said last night that the Vicar of Christ has not died, because there is no Vicar of Christ. Never has been! Simon Peter was not a Vicar of Christ. Jesus trained a ministry. He had twelve apostles that he placed authority on. I insist that he gave what he called the 'keys to the kingdom' to all twelve apostles. That belongs to the leadership of the church. It wasn't just one man that had the keys to the kingdom.

It is a fact that God raised up Peter and used him for the mouthpiece of those men on two special occasions, when he was opening a door, first to the Jews on the Day of Pentecost, and to the Gentiles at the house of Cornelius. Any one of those twelve could have done that. They had the knowledge to do it and they had the spirit to do it. They were capable of doing it. God honored Peter and, later on, he honored Paul as one of the great leaders, the outstanding leaders of that generation.

But, they were not popes over the church. In fact, during that time period, nobody ever dreamed of a pope being over the church. That was developed hundreds of years later. But, it's been a fact of history so long now that it's taken for granted. You know things can change radically.

In 1878, a pope died. I think it was Pope Pius, the ninth, and they elected a new pope. He called himself 'Leo the thirteenth'. While that papal election was taking place the Protestant religious commentators everywhere were speculating that "this might be the last pope." The pope was so powerless and had become so irrelevant to world affairs that "the Catholic church might not even elect another pope after he dies." That was the way things were looking in 1878.

What had happened, of course, a long string of things had happened, beginning with Martin Luther's Reformation and continuing the deterioration of the fortunes of the papacy until Napoleon humiliated the pope and they put him in jail for a while back around the early 1800's. Up until 1878, the pope had ruled over a large part of the peninsula of Italy, what came to be called 'the papal state'. It was a sizeable territory that was a nation that belonged to the pope and he was the king of that territory.

Building up to that time, before Pius died, the conquering ruler of Italy at that time took that territory away from the pope and made himself a citizen of a country that he wasn't in charge of. He became a citizen of the dictator of Italy's kingdom. It remained that way until 1929 when Mussolini, the dictator at that time, gave the pope back about a hundred acres, one hundred ten acres maybe, that came to be called the Vatican City. He made him an independent ruler of an independent state of one hundred ten acres or so, landlocked of course.

Since then they got along well with the Italian rulers and governments and have been able to come and go at will. Their power has kept growing. I want you to contrast 1878 with 2005. In a little over one hundred years, look what a drastic change has taken place. In 1878, the prophets were predicting that the pope would go out of existence and that people wouldn't bother to have a pope any more. He had lost his territory; he had been humiliated; his own members were rebelling in some countries, especially in America, rebelling against his leadership. It looked bad for the papacy. Look how things have turned around in a hundred years.

Now the pope is, without controversy, the greatest recognized man of the day and his funeral, if you watch it on the media, this is what you should pay attention to: the amount of attention it gets. And, it's all favorable attention; you don't hear criticism of the system. You may hear theologians, even Catholic theologians, disagreeing with something that John Paul taught and some positions and decisions that he made, but they don't disagree with him or somebody like him having that position.

The office has been glorified and lifted up, magnified before the world until he is one of the most powerful men in the world without owning an army. Without having an army, he has influence in everybody's army. He has servants, believers and followers in every army.

The world would say today that the American president is the most powerful man in the world because he has so much military power, military backing. He can throw his weight around and push people and countries around. But as far as having people behind him, the pope of Rome has more people that would vote for him if they had a chance than ever voted in any presidential election. A billion people would vote for him, almost unanimously. They would vote for him if he were running for office.

A lot of people have ignored the power of influence and sympathetic support. When Roosevelt was conferring with Joseph Stalin, the communist dictator, about the way the world should be run after the war with Germany was over; they were planning how to run the world after that war was ended. Roosevelt was perceptive enough to bring up the pope; we ought to consider his opinion, get his ideas.

Stalin's comments were, "How many divisions has the pope got?" In other words, "How big is his army?" He had the same philosophy that Mao of China had: "Power comes out of the barrel of a gun." He hadn't heard the old saying, "The pen is mightier than the sword." There is something that's more powerful than bullets that come out of a gun: the ideas that come out of preachers' mouths!

These are powerful weapons for good or for ill, for truth or for error. Power comes out of the mouths of people that talk. It was another Roosevelt that called the presidency a 'bully pulpit' which means a real good place to preach what you believe. He wasn't talking about religion; he was talking about politics and sociology and philosophy. Holding the office of president gave him a chance to promote his beliefs on how the country ought to be run, how it ought to be shaped.

So, every position of influence like that is a place to promote ideas. That's why the pulpits of the churches are such important places. That's why the ministers, the pastors, the teachers, the prophets are so important in the Kingdom of God. They have a chance to promote the truth, to preach the Word of God and convey to everybody what God wants.

I realize that's not the only channel that God speaks through, but it's a major one. He's not going to get through to the world by any other channel. As Paul put it in Romans 10, *"How shall they believe on him of whom they've not heard and how shall they hear without a preacher?"* That's the means God uses to get the Word out, to get the truth out, get the ideas out and win people to God's way of thinking.

We need to accept God's way of thinking. We need to hear it; we can't accept it until we hear it. It's true that after we've come in here and accepted the things that God sent to us, then he begins conveying some things to us through other spiritual channels, through the Holy Ghost itself. God can deal with you personally through the Holy Ghost, but the general order is that everybody needs a preacher to lead them and teach them and be a shepherd.

God calls every great leader a shepherd. And, us 'not so great' ones are shepherds on our level down here. The pope is a shepherd to the Catholic world and to a lot of other people. He's going to become a shepherd to a lot of other people. His word carries so much weight that you're very much in the minority and very much subject to criticism if you criticize him or his position because he has gained so much respect and support. People can't see, even people who are not Catholics, can't see how you can call a good man like John Paul II what Paul called him in II Thessalonians, "*The man of sin.*"

How can this man be a 'man of sin'? Who can point to any sin in his life? He was a good man; he was a man of peace. That's the way he is being described in the media: "A man of peace." He promoted peace. He was in a position where he could. He didn't have any armies; he couldn't do what our president is called on to do. All he can do is promote peace and work diplomatically that way.

Everybody ought to study the history of the papacy when you are reading the history in some book like <u>Halley's Bible Hand Book</u>. That's one of the textbooks of the Body of Christ; has been for generations now. We put our stamp of informatory on Halley's Hand Book back in the 1950's.

How many of you were back there? We put our approval on that and it's been in the preachers' libraries and most of the saints' libraries ever since. If you've come along lately and haven't heard about that and don't have one, maybe you ought to get one. Halley's Hand Book keeps growing. They update it every few years. There is information in it that's useful to you, things pertaining to the Bible, Bible history and church history.

There's a list of the popes in there from Simon Peter on down until now, John Paul. There are books like Fox's Book of Martyrs. That's another textbook of the Body of Christ. All of you ought to have it and read it and see what can happen to true believers, how the church can be persecuted. We feel safe and secure today because we're in a safe country; we were raised in it. We haven't had much exposure or experience with persecution, very little criticism, but it hasn't been that way very much in history, not very many years in history.

And it's not even that way in all countries today. But today, there is more freedom of conscience in the world than there ever has been before. That, too, can change as quickly and as drastically as the world's opinion of the papacy has changed in a hundred years. In much less than a hundred years, things can turn around and public opinion can turn against you.

So, you need to be aware of what the human heart is capable of. Human beings are human beings today just like they were in the days of the judges of the Old Testament, in the days of the Dark Ages in church history, in the days of the Caesars. The human heart was just like it is today. It can be trained in different ideas and habits, but the depravity is there. I don't teach total depravity, but I teach a lot of it. There's a lot of depravity in the human heart, maybe not the same amount in every heart, but some of it in every heart. We have to overcome that; we've got to be delivered from it. Depravity can take over again when it's allowed to.

The Bible prophesizes—if you don't know the purpose of this sermon or why it's relevant—the Bible prophesizes that persecution will happen again. Martyrdom will take place in the church again. Well, you may say, "That's already happening; it happens all the time in different countries in the world."

It's true that there are primitive Indian tribes in South America that occasionally martyr a missionary. But, that's not what the Bible is talking about, or only a small part of it; only a small part of it. The true church, when it ever gets the full truth and the full power that goes with the full truth will provoke martyrdom. It will provoke that kind of enmity like it did in Israel. It provoked martyrdom.

That good boy, Stephen, provoked people to kill him. How did he do it? Just by being so good, being so holy, being so right. People hate for you to be right. Yeah, telling the truth can get you punched in the nose. It can stir up a fist fight. It can turn people against you. It can drive people out of the church. The truth drives some people out of the church. It's that kind of people that Paul said, here in II Thessalonians, farther down in the tenth verse, after he has described the man of sin for a while, briefly. In verse 9, he calls him, "*him whose coming is after...*" (Meaning 'according to'), "*the working of Satan,*" (He works like Satan.) "*...with all power and signs and lying wonders.*"

I expect the papacy, the men who hold the office of pope in Rome to receive more of that kind of spiritual power. I don't believe it's questionable, impossible for them to elect a tongue-talking pope. I'm not making any predictions about what's coming up right now, but just watch the future and see what happens in this end time. Unexpected things will happen.

There are what he calls, *"power and signs and lying wonders."* How does a 'wonder' lie? What is a 'lying wonder'? Well, it's just a real wonder that is used to prove a lie. If a false teacher or false prophet works miracles, works wonders, then his miracles and wonders prove what he is teaching, but it's a lie. It can be used to prove a lie.

Just like God confirms the Word, the truth, with signs following. The false prophet, when he gets that kind of power, confirms his false words with signs following. People who don't know the difference can't tell the difference. You have to be taught the difference to know what the difference is. "*...all power and signs and lying wonders and with all deceivableness of unrighteousness in them that perish because they received not a love of the truth that they might be saved.*" You've got to have a love for the truth.

Thank God for the truth! Thank God for a love for the truth! We all need to ask God to help us love the truth, because if we receive not a love for the truth, even if we're around where the truth is preached, we still won't be saved. We've got to love the truth or otherwise, we will, as he said in the *eleventh verse,* "*... be sent a strong delusion that they should believe a lie that they all might be damned who believe not the truth.*"

I'm going to soften that word 'damned' there. It's a synonym for 'condemned'. But, ultimately, it means the same thing, "*that they all might be condemned who receive not the love for the truth, but had pleasure in unrighteousness.*" Now, when you think of unrighteousness in this context, don't think about immorality, carnal, fleshly, riotous living; but, it's religious error, religious idolatry.

Going back to this thought of who could accuse the recent pope of being a sinner. He was a moral man. He lived a clean life; he stood for morals and high principles. Like Bill Gothard said, "A man's morality tends to dictate his theology." I think Bill's personal life causes him to overemphasize some things in the field of marital relations. The Pope is in the same position; he was raised to honor celibacy in the priesthood and the ministry. He stood firm for that; of course, his own personal morality caused him to do that. He was strong on these subjects of abortion and contraception. Maybe he overemphasized some things, but it was an appeal for a high standard, a high standard of holiness and morality.

It disgraces the Protestant churches today in the degree to which they have relaxed on morals and quit preaching even the Ten Commandments in many cases. Our standards of morality have fallen low until divorce has become accepted in the churches as a means of settling, solving problems.

I heard something on the radio a couple of days ago I think we can use. Everybody knows that about a third of marriages break up in divorce. Seems like they're saying about half of them now; half the first marriages break up in divorce. That's being used in some circles to show that times are changing and that preaching monogamy and faithfulness to your mate is 'old hat', outdated, Victorian, puritan and that the world today has changed and you have to accept the change.

I heard somebody point out, after they had studied the statistics (I never heard this before) that something like two thirds of second marriages break up. Second marriages don't do as well as the first ones do in this day and time. It's because you open a door when you do it the first time. When you give in to that temptation to solve problems that way, you accept the idea that you can solve problems that way and the next time you have a problem, you try to solve it the same way. Once you give up on your first marriage you're almost giving up on the idea, the hope of a permanent marriage, a permanent relationship.

We need to preach the old-fashioned values. To a large extent, the Pope did that. There are valid reasons why he is admired. He was, in many ways, an admirable person in the world today. And some upstart preacher in a 'backwater' town like Humble is going to call him a 'man of sin'! You can understand how that is viewed in the world. But, even when you read the history of the papacy and the immorality that the papal system descended into over the centuries, don't view that as the explanation for giving them that title.

It's true that some popes were very immoral. They maintained physical relationships on the side, had mistresses and children, illegitimate children, and were criminal in their lifestyle. That's not the reason they're called the 'man of sin'. They're called the man of sin for religious reasons, religious errors, as I said a while ago. This pope who just died is as guilty of those errors and wrong teachings as the most immoral popes in their history.

Every time he proclaims Mary the co-mediatrix with Jesus, he's sinning; he's blaspheming! Amen! Every time he pronounces himself the Vicar of Christ, he's sinning! Every time he preaches that Mary was assumed body and soul into the heavens without going through ordinary death, he's sinning! Every time he promotes the idolatry of Mary and lifts her up alongside Jesus Christ, and other things they teach that way, he's promoting a sin! Every time he ordains another saint to be prayed to and encourages the people to pray to the dead saints, he's sinning! It's the Man of Sin that promotes those ideas and causes them to prevail as much as they do in the world today. Every time they hold that big, round cracker up before the crowd and pronounce that it's the living flesh of Jesus Christ, they're sinning!

It's a sin that's built into the system, not any particular man; it belongs to his office. When another man gets elected to that office, he gets elected to promote those positions and those ideas. That's why Paul called him a "*...man of sin, the son of perdition who opposes and exalteth himself above all that is called God or that is worshipped, so that he, as God, sitteth in the temple of God, showing himself that he is God.*"

That's a position that the pope claims for himself, arrogates to himself, as being the head of all Christian religion. He claims about all the authority that Jesus claimed. There have been popes in history that gave themselves the title 'The Lord God, the Pope'. I don't know how they justified that, but there's no limit to the extent of their pride. At various times, every man had his own degree and his own opportunity to manifest it. The office goes right on. Just like the presidency goes right on, the papacy goes right on. One dies and another comes to take his place.

We're standing here defending some principles. We're standing, facing the rebuilding of a system that was used to persecute and martyr the saints of God for many generations. We don't want to be deceived by it. Don't let any of the publicity or any of the natural sympathy you might feel for a good man, a good man dying with dignity and getting an honorable funeral and all that. We can give lip service to him; we can admit that he was a good man.

I went and visited the church across the street at their mass yesterday. My wife and I had to leave a little early, so we didn't meet anybody going out. But, if I had had occasion to talk to anybody, I would have just said to them, "You've lost a great leader. You've suffered a great loss." That's true. They've suffered a great loss. We're conscious of it. He was a good man; I wouldn't try to deny that. We won't try to explain to them what our position is.

But that office, some man holding that office, is again going to wield the sword someday. He's going to have armies at his command and it's going to happen as described in the seventeenth chapter of Revelation. When he describes the system he calls the beast, and a system that he calls a woman, a harlot, riding that beast, he mentions *'Ten horns'*. In Revelation 17:12, he said, *"The ten horns which thou sawest are ten kings, rulers, which have received no kingdom as yet"*, but they do receive power as kings, one prophetic hour. That calculates to fifteen years—but that's beside the point right now.

They received power as kings fifteen years with the Beast. These ten kings have one mind; ten rulers, governments, *"....and shall give their power and strength unto the beast." Then he says, "These shall make war with the Lamb."* See, they have power to make war because they do have armies. The pope himself has no army but these ten governments do have armies and when they give their power to him, or to the head of that system, then he has armies to send into battle.

Somewhat the same picture is given in the thirteenth chapter. He mentions that the dragon gave the beast his power. Let's just start reading in the beginning of chapter 13: *"I stood upon the sand of the sea and saw a beast rise up out of the sea having seven heads and ten horns."* You really can't read this without reading the twelfth chapter for a background because the dragon is throughout this chapter 12 and he was introduced in the twelfth chapter; the dragon being, at that time, the Roman Empire. The dragon in chapter 12 was the Roman Empire. They persecuted the Early Church. And, there's war in heaven described in that twelfth chapter which was war between the Church and the Civil Government. The church was preaching something different from what the civil government was preaching. It finally came to the point where the Caesars demanded to be worshipped.

The church would not worship the Caesar any more than the three Hebrew children in Daniel would not worship Nebuchadnezzar's image. Their feet stood firm on the ground they stood on; they would not 'bow, bend, budge or burn' as the song says. So, there was war between the church and government.

That dragon was the government of the Roman Empire. In chapter 13 another beast appears besides the dragon. *"I stood upon the sand of the sea and saw a beast rise up out of the sea."* It doesn't tell us where that dragon came from; he just appeared there in heaven. He didn't originate in Heaven, but he appeared there. We can find where all of these powerful governments originated back in Daniel 7 where it says, *"The four winds of heaven strove upon the great sea and up came these four beasts,"* a lion, a bear, a leopard and something like a dragon with ten horns. That fourth one was the Roman Empire which is introduced here in Revelation 12 as the dragon having seven heads and ten horns. Here, he's given his place in the whole history of civil power which began with Egypt; Egypt, Assyria,

Babylon, Persia, Greece and Rome, then the seventh one, Papal Rome here in the thirteenth chapter.

"*A beast rose up out of the sea...*" not out of the earth, but out of the sea. Back in chapter 12:9, it says, "*The great dragon was cast out, that old serpent called the devil and Satan.*" He was cast out into the earth." In verse 12, he says, "*Rejoice ye heavens and ye that dwell in them. Woe to the inhabiters of the earth and the sea.*"

The earth is one thing and the sea is another. Well, the sea is just a mass of humanity. Without taking regard to whether they are religious or not, it's the secular masses. The sea is the secular masses of humanity. The earth is the religious groupings that have a little more truth, a little more foundation.

It's "*the fool that said in his heart 'there is no God'.*" The religious person admits there is a God. He may not know much about Him; he may be totally deceived about Him, but at least he knows that much: "There is a God." So, he's got some foundation to stand on. The man that says there is no God has no foundation at all to stand on. He can't take a stand anywhere; he's got no authority to appeal to.

The dragon has come down to the earth and the sea. "*The devil has come down unto you having great wrath, etc.....*" The beast rose up out of the sea, not out of the earth. This beast didn't come along until about five hundred years after Christ and the apostles and the Early Church. During those five hundred years leading up to that, the Church was in a different guise; it was in an 'earth' condition.

That government of the papacy came, really, out of civil power, out of secular power. It was one of the Roman generals, a great military leader that established the bishop of Rome as the head of all religion. He gave him that power. That is described in the last half of the second verse: "*The dragon gave him his power and his seat and great authority.*"

There are so many details in this chapter we don't have time to explain them all. In the second verse, "*The beast which I saw was like unto a leopard and his feet were as the feet of a bear and his mouth as the mouth of a lion.*" Well, all these things are features and characteristics of world powers before then. They are what are pictured in Daniel 7 as great world powers.

This system, the government of the papacy, had features about it that resembled some things in all of those kingdoms. For one thing, it said about the bear, *"He lifted up himself on one side."* The Roman Empire did that under the popes. The Roman Empire had, by that time, two capitals, the city of Rome and the city of Constantinople. There were powerful bishops and strong churches in each of those cities.

But, the bishop of Rome took power and the bishop of Constantinople just fought his power and resisted him, split the church, split off. He did not become the head of all Christian religion. Today, there won't be near the scene on TV or in the newspapers if the patriarch of Constantinople dies as there is now that the pope of Rome has died. The system lifted up itself on one side. That's what the empire did. It got strong on one side.

That bear was the Persian Empire back in Daniel. It started out as two powers merged together, the Medes and the Persians, the Kingdom of Media and the Kingdom of Persia. They started off trying to be more or less equal, but the king of Persia kept getting more and more power and the king of Media kept getting weaker. It raised itself up on one side and became, eventually, just the kingdom of the Persians. They still referred to it as the kingdom of the Medes and Persians but, really, it was just the kingdom of the Persians by the time Esther became queen of that empire.

Then it was said to it, *"Devour much flesh."* That means swallow up a lot of people, take in a lot of territory. That's what Rome did; it took in all the territory of the civilized world at that time. It became the kingdom of Europe. Constantinople remained more or less on the outside, just a little side kingdom. The other features of the other beasts were in there. The kingdom of Greece under Alexander the Great was the leopard in Daniel.

One of the things Alexander accomplished was promoting Greek language and teachings and philosophy, including their science and mathematics. For the next thousand years or more, the Greek teachers like Socrates and Plato and Aristotle and Euclid were the authorities in the philosophical and scientific realm. Down through the Dark Ages when the popes were ruling in Europe, their theologians and scientists would just study the writings of Aristotle for answers.

It's quoted like a joke now that when they wanted to know how many teeth were in the mouth of a horse, nobody would go out to the stable and open a horse's mouth. They studied all those books that Aristotle had left behind and couldn't find it in there where he told them how many teeth a horse had, so they gave it up as a bad job, something they would never know. That's how much authority Aristotle acquired over the thinking of the western world.

It was because of the leopard, that leopard kingdom that Alexander used to conquer the world in his day. Those elements, that teaching of Aristotle and those Greeks and their philosophies were strong in the Roman kingdom, in the papal Roman kingdom.

"One of his heads was wounded to death," in the third chapter. But, I wanted to point out there that the dragon, the civil power, gave that beast his power and his seat. His seat means his location. The Roman government had already been seated in Rome for a thousand years and when that Roman general made the pope head of all Christianity and the Christian world, he gave him that seat. He chose the Roman bishop instead of the bishop of Constantinople or the bishop of Alexandria. He gave him that seat in Rome.

One of the seven churches of Asia was addressed by the Lord hundreds of years before that, in the second or third chapter of Revelation, it was *"dwelling where Satan's seat is."* Satan's seat was the Roman Empire. He wasn't just talking about the city of Rome, but the Roman Empire that was based at Rome. So, all of those seven churches were dwelling where Satan's seat was. He just singled out that one to make that comment to.

Rome became the seat of the dragon, so it became the seat of the government that the dragon approved. That pagan Roman government turned its power over to the papal Roman government and gave him great authority. Of course, the secular power didn't disappear. There were kings under feudalism, kings and lords and dukes and counts. They all exercised civil power and had their armies during the Dark Ages, but they all submitted to the pope. He could send one of them against the other and set ambush among them. Playing politics constantly between them, he kept them in subjection.

Then, there came a time when one of his heads was wounded to death. Remember that this beast had seven heads. That's because this prophecy places that government in its place in history. It was the seventh great world empire. How many remember hearing Brother Patton quote this little poem when he would be teaching on this or on Daniel 7? It begins with the picture in Daniel 7.

> *"Look to the waymarks; count them o'er;*
> *Down through the ages, past the kingdoms four."*
> (The kingdoms four are those four beasts in Daniel 7.)
> *"First the Babylonian Kingdom ruled the world,*
> *Then the Medes and Persians banner was unfurled.*
> *Then, Greece held universal sway;*
> *Then, Rome seized the scepter,*
> *And where are we today?*
> *Down in the feet of iron and clay;*
> *Weak and divided, and soon to pass away.*
> *What shall the next great, glorious drama be?*
> *Christ and His kingdom throughout eternity!"*

Amen! The trouble is we're not through with that Roman kingdom, yet. It didn't show this in Daniel very clearly; it just showed a little horn rising up to great power on that head among the ten horns in Daniel 7. But here in Revelation 13 it presents that little horn having great power as another beast, another head, a seventh head.

Pagan Rome was the sixth head on this dragon and on this beast. The papacy is the seventh head. Observe, by the way, about these heads and crowns here in Revelation. In the twelfth chapter, third verse, it describes the Great Red Dragon having seven heads and ten horns and seven crowns upon his heads. That signifies that, during the time period addressed in this chapter, those seven heads are being featured, those great empire governments.

But when it describes the next beast in 13:1, *"The beast rose up out of the sea having seven heads and ten horns and upon his horns"* (not his heads) *"upon his horns were ten crowns."* The crowns had shifted over to the horns. At that time, those horns represented the ten divisions that the Roman Empire divided into, scattered groups and scattered governments; ten divisions it broke up into. So, those are the ten horns, the ten powers. The ten crowns being on the horns, at that time, signifies that time period in history. When that breakup took place is what this chapter is dealing with, beginning with that and on down to the end of the chapter. *"And one of his heads was wounded to death."*

It's that head we're dealing with in that time period; it's that seventh head. In 1517, the papacy was wounded to death; it received a deadly wound by the sword of the Spirit which is the Word of God. For a while thereafter, Martin Luther and his successors wounded the beast. They knew they were doing it; they claimed to do it. Martin Luther said, one time, "I can't open my mouth without wounding the beast." Every time he opened his mouth another sword came out, another word that damaged the position of the papacy. From then on, the papacy was wounded. It almost died in 1878; it almost disappeared from the face of the earth it had such a deadly wound.

But after that, he said, *"...and his deadly wound was healed: and all the world wondered after the beast."* The world is wondering and admiring, marveling at the ability of that system to survive and maintain its claims as teachers of morality in the face of all the publicity they have received in recent years because of the moral problems of their priesthood. Their ministry has let them down. That's fading into the background now.

The world is wondering after the beast and they're marveling at it and admiring it. All of that unfavorable publicity caused some people among us to predict, two or three years ago, that the Catholic Church would fade as a power in America because of the scandal that they were involved in. They're not fading in power; they're still growing in power. They're being promoted; they're getting more attention, more publicity than any other religious system right now. You will see their power grow and increase yet, until that deadly wound will be completely healed and forgotten about.

Someone speaks

He said, "The President ordered the flags to half-mast." That's how much the political power of the greatest government, the greatest power in the world, is recognizing and honoring this man and his office. They worship the dragon which gave power to the beast. Don't forget the dragon when you read Revelation 13. The dragon did not disappear; he did not pass away. He gave power to the beast. He's still giving power to the beast. The beast has no power at any time without the dragon, the civil power, the civil system that gives power to it.

They worshipped the beast saying, "*Who is like unto the beast and who is able to make war with it? There was given him a mouth speaking great things and blasphemies.*" That was what Paul had against him back in II Thessalonians, the things he taught, the things that came out of his mouth. "*He opened his mouth in blasphemy against God and to blaspheme his name and his tabernacle and them that dwell in Heaven.*"

It's easy to explain those things in the way they promote the power of that church to decide when somebody is to be recognized as a saint and to receive worship and prayer. In many, many ways they exercise power. Catholics will tell you today that the priest that they confess their sins to has the power to forgive them or not forgive them. He has a lot to say about whether they get everlasting life or not. They don't talk with the modesty that Protestant preachers talk with when we're describing salvation. You can hardly find a Protestant preacher that will make the claim, "You've got to hear the Gospel from my mouth," or "You've got to have my approval to make it to Heaven." Here and there is some obscure cult figure who claims things like that. But, the entire Catholic priesthood implies that, even when they don't say it. The people have to come through their door to get to heaven. That's why they have so much power over their people.

I'm not going to try to complete this whole chapter. I just wanted to show you where we are in the scheme of things today. This wound is healed and another beast has already appeared on the scene. In the thirteenth chapter, there's another beast introduced in verse 11. *"I beheld another beast coming up out of the earth,"* not out of the sea, but this time, up out of religion. That's where Protestantism arose. It was a rebellion against that false religious system and it has grown and it has two horns like a lamb. But, it speaks as a dragon, too!

The Protestant churches thought just like the Catholic Church did when it got to proclaiming the importance of religion. Even Martin Luther and Zwingli and John Calvin taught and believed that there ought to be a state church. We in America are raised in an unusual system where our Constitution teaches that we shall not be involved in religion. There won't be one recognized, approved religion in the country. Everybody is free to choose his own religion. That's been almost unique in the history of the world. The effect prevails nowadays in the democracies of Europe, but they still give recognition to state churches. There's the Church of England and the Lutheran Church in Germany which is given special recognition; reformed churches in other countries over there. But in America, we have proclaimed a lot of individual freedom.

Still, the feeling is there among the theologians that the whole world needs to be united under one system. Already, by the 1950s, Methodist preachers were proclaiming that we ought to recognize the pope as the head of all religion again. "Let's have one world church and be all united in one system." Protestant ministers are teaching that position today.

These two horns, by the way, just represent civil and ecclesiastical power. "*...and, he exercises all the power of the first beast and causes the earth and all them that dwell therein to worship the first beast again whose deadly wound was healed.*

And, he doeth great wonders so he maketh fire come down from heaven on earth in the sight of men."

Remember that the Holy Ghost message came into Protestantism. It was a Methodist preacher that started the Bible School in Topeka, Kansas where they studied out the doctrine of tongues as evidence of the Holy Ghost baptism.

"...and deceived them that dwell on the earth by those miracles... Then he says to them that dwell on the earth that they should make an image to the beast which had the wound by a sword and did live and he had power to give life to that image of the beast." Remember—another world government. There's strong push right now for a world government.

A lot of fundamentalist preachers are resisting that, fighting it, but they're not going to hold it off forever. The trend is too strong. It's going to finally carry the day. There finally will be a world government headed by a religious leader, a powerful figure. That is when, again, *"...he causes all, small and great, both rich and poor, free and bond to receive a mark in their right hand or in their forehead."*

That means you've got to submit to that idea, that system, that order. You've got to recognize that order and fit in with it or, it says, you won't be able to buy and sell. We're talking religiously now. We're buying and selling freely here today. I'm selling; you're buying, if you believe what I'm selling. It's without money and without price, but it still costs you what you used to believe, if you used to believe something different.

So, we're buying and selling freely. We're putting out our wares here, the truth, the ideas that we have. But, the time is coming when it won't be possible to do this without the mark. You will have to get a license and you can't get a license until you pass the test and accept the principles that it takes. No man will be able to buy or sell, religiously, save he that has the mark, etc.

Now, he says in verse 18: *"Here is wisdom."* Have you got wisdom? *"Let him that hath understanding count the number of the beast for it is the number of a man and his number is six hundred, three score and six."* Well, it doesn't take a very educated person to count to 666. Where is the wisdom required? The wisdom it takes is to count the number of the Beast without counting yourself in with it. If you can count it out there: one, two, three, four, five, and so on all the way up and never point at yourself as you go by, you're a pretty smart person.

Most people can count the number, but they count themselves in with it. They count that church, and that church, this church when they're counting the thing up. We've got to be wise enough that, when we count up the elements in that system, we never count this one. This is different; this is something outside all the rest of religion. It must remain outside of all religion. It must remain different and unique in the earth or we'll compromise our holiness to God and we'll just become holy to man, holy to some system, but reprobate in the eyes of God. Amen!

All right. I may have some questions and things stirred up here, but this is what we're coming to. This is our place in history.

Question - not heard.

Yes…? In the U.N? I'm not sure. I'm haven't heard of it, but they probably do since they have a representative in every other country.

Question: "Is Ezekiel 28:2 talking about the Pope?"

Well, no. Ezekiel 28 is talking about something else. It's talking about somebody related to the Pope.

Question: "Will the pope merit a resurrection?"

Who knows? I hope he does! He could! Let me read you something that gives you hope for him. In the seventeenth and eighteenth chapter of Revelation he's calling that system Babylon. Revelation 18:21 says, *"A mighty angel took up a stone like a great millstone and cast it into the sea, saying 'thus with violence shall that great city, that great religious city Babylon, be thrown down and be found no more at all."* It's that world religious system that's going to be thrown down. *"And the voice of harpers"*, (musicians, pipers, trumpeters, etc.,) *shall be heard no more at all in thee. No craftsman of whatsoever craft he be. And the sound of a millstone shall be heard no more at all in thee."*

These are religious symbols, religious craftsmen, religious musicians; religious preachers with a true message, with the true Gospel that will be heard no more at all in her when that happens. The sound of a millstone grinding out the Word of God, the truth for people to eat, will be heard no more at all in there. The fact is, the Roman System does have some truth in it. People can get saved in there; they can have an experience with Jesus Christ. Some of the time, they are looking at one of those pictures or idol statues that are up in there, but some of those people get a real experience of conversion and accept Jesus as their Savior.

And, some truth is preached in there. "*The light of a candle shall shine no more at all in thee.*" That signifies the light of the Gospel. "*The voice of the Bridegroom and the Bride shall be heard no more at all in thee.*" That means the voice of the Bridegroom and the Bride *has been heard* in that system!

Do you know who the Bridegroom is? It's Jesus, isn't it? The voice of Jesus is still heard in that false system. The voice of people that are going to be in the Bride are going to go all the way to the overcoming life. They'll be led out of there when they do, but they are still speaking in there. So, there's a chance for those people to be in the final resurrection, those that did get a real experience with God. Those that have simply trusted in false doctrine and worshipped idols, gone around bowing before the stations of the Cross and seeing nothing there but the statue of that dead saint, they're doing all their praying to dead saints; a lot of them won't get a resurrection. Their religion is wasted; it's a false religion and it cannot save.

But, the people who are hearing the name of Jesus and turning to him in their hearts are having real experiences and becoming children of God. Their names are being written in his Book. God will start reading that book some day in the resurrection. Those names will come up.

Question: "Is it all right for a woman to be a preacher or a shepherd of a church? There are some women saying God has called them for that?"

Well, we doubt that God has called them for that, but there have been women that fell into that position and God used them there. I wish everybody could read all the things that Brother Sowders taught about women preaching. He came in contact in his ministry with women who were pastoring churches at the time he met them. A few of them may have inherited churches when their husbands died. After he came in contact with them, he would be patient and tolerant with them until they were convicted by the teaching of the Word and decided they were out of their place in that position and they would turn the church over to a man who was called of God to do that office. Women can do a lot of things that they are not necessarily called to do.

And, God actually raised up some women, at different times, to make a special point. He placed a special calling on their lives to make a statement because men were being too hard on the women. Brother Sowders mentioned Sister Amy Simple McPherson in that light. God promoted her to great prosperity and recognition and honor in the religious world back in the 1920's.

It began in the 'teens when she started as a revival preacher, a tent preacher. God caused a lot of people to get healed under her ministry. That gave her a lot of influence. She finally settled in Los Angeles and built one of the big churches, a famous temple in that city and founded a Pentecostal denomination called the Four Square Gospel. She was a major figure in Pentecost in her day. Before she became so big and well-known, Brother Sowders had her come and preach a meeting in one of his churches. This was back early in his ministry.

There were other great women preachers in the early days of Pentecost. Sister Maria Woodruff Etter had been a great revival preacher before the Pentecostal movement began. She soon came into it after it got to going. Her name gave recognition to the Pentecostal movement in its early stages. God had used her mightily; the Holy Ghost was upon her when she would preach. At her church she had rooms filled with wheelchairs and braces and things like that that people gave up and threw away because they were healed.

Brother Sowders explained that the men, at that time, were putting down women so severely that God raised up those women just to spite the men, as it were, to force them to realize that women do have something to do in the church. They do have a place in the church and they're to be respected; they're to be honored and treated with respect and deference that's due, especially to older women. They're to be treated with deference.

We're to look at all the saints of God as having special work. Let's not discount anybody. Let's not degrade and put down anybody in the Kingdom of God. There's a place for everybody. There's this order: God the head of Christ and Christ the head of man and man the head of the woman. That's God's order. Now sometimes, when things have gotten so out of order, God works out of order and does things that are contrary to His order.

He was doing that in the Old Testament. Back in the days of the judges, there was at least one female judge of Israel. A woman prophetess judged Israel. It was a time when the 'times were out of joint' as the poet said, and the whole nation was out of order. There was a lot of idolatry and men were not maintaining their place. At times like that, God will use an honest woman that's willing to be used of him.

The Lord is especially occupied today for a couple of generations in establishing a ministry and putting it in order. Even in Brother Sowders' day, he had that so well under way that when those women preachers came to his churches they would sense the government in his church. They weren't used to feeling that where they went.

Women who proclaimed themselves preachers and were used to preaching revivals would come out dressed in their white dresses and white shoes because they had seen it done that way. They would come to his church and he would let them come on the platform, but when they would try to preach, they wouldn't feel the liberty they were used to.

Sometimes, they would accuse him and his platform of men, saying, "You preachers are sitting on me, holding me down."

He would explain, "It's not us doing that. We're wanting God to bless you. We're praying for you. We want you to be blessed, but there is a government here. There is authority on these men."

So, a woman couldn't feel the authority she was used to feeling in her own ministry when she was in the presence of the God-ordained authority. Many of them recognized what was going on and would come down off their pedestals and high horses and submit to the Bible, scriptural order.

That's what we have here today. These sisters are all in order; they recognize their place under their husbands and under the ministry. We that are in the lead, husbands and ministers, recognize our duty and responsibility for the welfare of the people under our care. None of us wants to make the sisters mad or hurt their feelings. We realize a lot of our happiness and peace depends on their happiness and peace.

Not just the husbands, but the ministers, too. If you make all the women in your church mad you'll have a hard time keeping your church together. And you, as a husband, if you make your wife mad at you, she's not going to make you happy. You make her mad and then you expect her to make you happy? You married her because you thought she was what it took to make you happy. Well, she'll try to make you happy if you try to make her happy. You have to work together on that. Amen! I need a BIG AMEN on that! Hallelujah! But when all of us are doing our part, then everybody's needs are met and everybody can be happy. You don't need authority to make you happy. That's not what does it.

Question: "What is the sea in Revelation 20:13?" "The dead, both small and great stood before God and the books were opened and the sea gave up the dead which were in it."

Here's how I explain that: This is at a time when the resurrection is taking place. The resurrection takes place on an earth that is already there. There's a generation of people still on the earth at that time. There has been a great war. This is my chronology in this chapter—the great war of Gog and Magog has taken place before the resurrection and it succeeded in crushing civil power for the last time. And Satan himself, who has been put in charge of civil power, is finally destroyed in that battle.

But, that doesn't destroy every unbeliever. People are still being born at that time, during the period of the resurrection. People who have been born are still on the earth and some of them haven't got saved yet. After the Thousand Year Reign and after the Battle of God and Magog and Satan himself is cast into the Lake of Fire, there's still people that won't take the trouble to get saved. They may even believe in it and just won't do it. They won't bother to get saved; they don't want to give up their fun or they don't want to be embarrassed or something. Somebody's holding them back or they're married to somebody who doesn't believe it. All kinds of things keep people from getting saved when they might otherwise want to.

So, there's still a sea of people, humanity that's not in the Kingdom. The 'sea' is always people outside the Kingdom of God in the scriptures. The dead in them are those that are dead in trespasses and sins. That's the sea giving up the dead.

Death and Hell are conditions that people get themselves into. They come out of the graves still in those mental and spiritual conditions. Some of them are under the judgment of God when they died, but not eternal judgment yet. Death and Hell give up the dead that are in them.

Everybody comes to judgment! And everybody ends up with immortality or they end up in the Lake of Fire. And, that is the end of all things as we know it. It's certainly not the end of eternal life. God's Kingdom goes on, world without end! It's a world *"wherein dwelleth righteousness."* And, you'll be glad to be there.

Comment: "Explain the words: 'Vicar of Christ'".

I don't think the word 'vicar' is in the scriptures. It's not a Biblical term; it's a theological term that the Roman church invented. Let's see what the dictionary says about it. Vicar: a parish priest in the Church of England who receives a stipend or salary, but no tithes. That's one definition. A cleric acting in the place of a rector or bishop in the Anglican Communion. That's the idea of a vicar: he's taking somebody else's place.

He's what has been called, in some governmental situations, a 'regent'. A 'regent' acts on behalf of a higher power. Number two, The Roman Catholic Church definition: a priest who acts for or represents another cleric.

So, any religious leader can send somebody to be his vicar, to speak in his place. They don't go ahead with the application to the Roman pope, but that's what the pope means by describing himself as Jesus' vicar. He presents himself as the man Jesus sends to speak for him. The Roman pope claims to be speaking for Jesus; he's conveying Jesus' message. That's his claim. Now if he's not doing that, he's sinning when he claims that. He's blaspheming if he's not telling the truth.

A mediator is somebody who makes peace between two opposing parties. They can be two parties on the same level, or two parties on different levels. Jesus can mediate for us to God and mediate for God to us. You see that side of it there? Jesus brought God's position to us and showed us what God wants of us. And Jesus takes our requests and burdens to God and shows God what we need from him. Isn't that great to have somebody like that? We like that mediator, don't we? He's a good mediator.

Now, an ambassador is somebody that speaks for a government or power in presenting the positions of that government or power to other people. The United States government sends ambassadors to other nations. We've got an ambassador in just about every nation in the world. We've got some kind of ambassador in the Vatican City. I don't know just what his title is. He's there to represent this country and make known to the people of that country, as well as the government of that country, what the American government's positions on controversial questions are.

Paul says, "*We are ambassadors for Christ. We pray you* (or beg you) *in Christ's stead* "(We stand here in Christ's stead." He's talking primarily to the unsaved world to begin with) *be reconciled to God.*"

Every apostle and every anointed, called evangelist acts that way, representing God and the government of the Kingdom of

God to the lost world out there that dislikes God. They need to make peace with God. The preacher explains God's position to those unbelievers to help them make peace with God. That even carries over after people have made their initial peace with God. The ministry still represents God's claims, demands and positions to the people in the church that are still trying to get straightened out with God.

We've accepted him; we've submitted to him up to a point, but there are still things God wants out of us that we are not rendering to him, yet. It's a preacher's job to keep you reminded of that. You may have given up some things; God wants the rest of it. He wants complete holiness, a perfect sacrifice. Give up all of the world and everything that interferes with your holiness. Be fully submitted to God's will.

It's the preacher's job to keep the saints reminded of that. We're still begging everybody, advising everybody to be reconciled to God. You know, most of you are not fully reconciled to God because you disagree with him sometimes. Sometimes, you may disagree with him openly. We hear church people complain about something God did. "Why would God let that happen? Why did God let this person die?" That's a very common complaint. We need to accept God's will. We're not fully reconciled to God as long as we've got conflicting opinions and think he should have done something different or done it a different way.

When you really learn who God is, and what he is, you will approve of everything he does, whether you understand it or not. You won't always understand it but you can still approve everything that God does. What God does, he does it right.

All right. Praise God!

Chapter 15

Christ, the Head of the Church

February 5, 2006

Brother and Sister Zinn have gotten old working for this church, like I have. They came here when Brother Patton invited them here to take that job. They have dedicated their lives to it all this time. We appreciate the Zinn's, their labor and faithfulness. You could count on them to be on the job and get the job done. Let's give them a big hand for all they've done. (Congregation clapping.) I guess it must be time for them to retire, if that's the right word, because the Lord has dealt with a younger couple to take the burden. Brother and Sister Wyrick have been helping, learning the job and are willing to take the responsibility. That is a big responsibility. It's a big job.

Anything you do around a church of this size is a major task. It will absorb your time, keep you busy. It will make demands on you. It requires you to interact with other people. Not all those other people have patience with you to wait on you to get around to the job; to give you time to get it out.

Maybe we have spoiled them, Brother Zinn, but a lot of our people want what they want and they want it now! They don't want to be put off and told to come back tomorrow or next week or next month. Sometimes, we just have to do that because you're not the only fish in the pond. There are other fish we're having to feed and other jobs we're having to get done. In all the departments around here it's that way. We will all pray for Brother and Sister Wyrick that the Lord will give them the rest of their training in dealing with people and their personalities, their ways.

I want to thank everybody here for the good meeting, the good convention we had. We still have Brother Almanord with us. A little remnant of the convention is still here. Last weekend, we were closing out the meeting on Sunday night. So, I said last night we were having the aftermath of the convention. This weekend is the aftermath. We're glad to have Brother Almanord here from Haiti, one of the brethren of good reputation, well-respected in the work down there in Haiti. He is much admired and listened to; his words carry weight. He's been with Brother Isaac for the past week, traveling around and visiting churches, helping over there. We get the last taste here before he flies out, before he flies home tomorrow.

I just want to say again what a good meeting it was. Everybody who came helped make it a great meeting. Those that talked and sang and those that didn't do anything but say "Amen". It takes all of us being here. Brother Patton used to compare it to the notes on a piano. He said there is that top key up there that nobody ever touches very much but when the music calls for it, it needs to be there or there is a gap in the music. You never know when your time is coming. I go to meetings and don't get up. You just have to be there when the Lord does call on you.

We had some wonderful talks; a good spirit manifested, good songs sung, just a great blessing of the Spirit of God throughout the convention. I thought it was as good as we ever had. I'm directing my thanks particularly to this local church because we worked so hard for so long. People have been asking me since the meeting, "Are you rested, yet? Are you over the meeting?"

I said, "Well, I'm still unwinding." We've been wound up tight for over a year. Our spring was wound to the breaking point, especially the last few weeks and months, trying to get everything ready for the meeting and then to go through it and get all the tasks done and make everything run smoothly. I know we had lots of help. Everywhere you looked there were people from other churches filling in, being a part.

That's the way the Body of Christ is made up: All the members edify one another. Every member edifies the Body of Christ with all of us doing our part, pitching in, doing what we can, when we can, where we can and being available when we don't have a job for the moment. You never know where there will be a need that you can fill.

I've heard some of the brethren explaining the scripture about waiting on the Lord. *"They that wait upon the Lord shall renew their strength."* We may be bad to take advantage of that and sit around and wait when we ought to be busy. To counteract that, some of the brethren have re-interpreted the scripture to make it mean *"They that SERVE the Lord,"* like a waiter waiting on tables. *"They that SERVE the Lord shall renew their strength."*

But if you're going to re-interpret it that way, you're going to have to admit that, as one of the poets or playwrights said, "They also serve who only stand and wait." That's what a waiter gets to do sometimes. If he's not overloaded and overworked he gets to stand and wait sometimes. That's why he's called a 'waiter'. Initially, a waiter was somebody who waited around until he was needed to serve the table. He kept watching several tables and when somebody needed something or waved at him, he was available to go over there. Now, they keep them all so busy you can hardly get a waiter to come to your table. He's serving so many tables he can't serve any of them very well.

When you're waiting on the Lord, sometimes he will leave you idle for a while. Look at the parable of the workers in the vineyard. Jesus made up this story to illustrate several points. He said the land owner went out early in the morning and hired a crew to work in his vineyard. Then, he went back later in the morning and hired some more. A way over, just before sundown, he went back and found some people still standing around in the market place doing nothing. He said, *"Why stand you here idle all the day?"* That was a rhetorical question, I guess. He must have known what they were doing there. They came there early that morning, hoping to get hired; they were in the labor pool. The master had picked some and left them behind early that morning. They were waiting. When he said, *"Why stand you here idle,"* they said, *"Because no man has hired us." "We're willing to be hired; we wanted a job. We're ready to work but nobody called on us today."* They were still there, waiting. He said, *"All right, go out into the vineyard and finish out the day. I'll pay you whatever is right; I'll give you something."*

The result was that, when he got around to handing out the paychecks, he started with the last, first. He called those that had just worked one hour, first, and gave them a full day's pay. Those workers who had worked a long time watched that and thought, "Boy, he must be in a good mood today. He's paying good today! He'll surely have us a good paycheck. We've worked several times as long as these folks did." But, they all got their penny, their day's pay, at the end of the day.

We've made several good lessons out of that parable. One lesson Jesus made out of it was that *"many that are last shall be first and many of the first shall be last."* We've seen in there the point made that, if you work for God, if you end up your life working for God, you may have come in late in the day with not much of your life left. But, you can get everlasting life. That reward will be just as long as it is for those who have labored all their lifetime.

You that have labored all your lifetime shouldn't feel bad about that. Don't feel gypped or swindled in any way because you know you've had many blessings along the way. Most of us really spend a lot of our time feeling sorry for the people who are still out there and haven't come in, yet. But, some of you are going to get jealous of them when they do come in and the Lord begins to bless them. You'll think, "He ought to bless me more than them." The Christian spirit is to welcome everybody: come one; come all. Take in everybody that is willing to come and fall upon the Rock and dedicate themselves to the service of the Lord.

That seemed like the kind of spirit we had in this convention. It was a warm spirit, like what the old-time preachers like Roy Murrell used to call a 'come here' spirit. The spirit in which a mother says to her little child when it falls and bruises its knee: "Come here; come to Mother." That's the kind of spirit the Body of Christ tries to manifest.

Brother Patton compared it to an old mother hen that will take in all the little biddies when a thunder storm comes up and catches them outside the barn, out in the barnyard. I've seen it myself when I was a boy. When it starts raining, an old mother hen spreads out her wings and clucks. The biddies may have been half grown and when they got under her wings they lifted her off the ground. They were chirping, talking, chattering and she was clucking and spreading her wings and letting them all get under there.

What was pointed out to us was the difference in the spirit of the Body of Christ and the spirit of the Body of the Beast. Even a beast loves its own. A beast of the higher orders, the mammals at least, take care of their own children and welcome them in, but many of them will not accept a stranger, a child from another nest. Different breeds of chickens are like that. Some chickens will peck a biddy from another nest if it comes around and tries to join her brood and get under her wing.

In the old days, nearly every farm had one old mother hen. Usually, it was a Dominique, the spotted ones that would take in all the biddies, any of them that would run to her for shelter. They told us that is to be the spirit of the church of Jesus Christ. We're to have that kind of spirit and attitude. That's what Jesus himself manifested. He died for everybody. Everybody doesn't come, but if they come, they're covered. Everybody who comes in under that blood, pleading that blood, is covered.

I was reading Brother Sowders teaching on the blood of Christ, just the last few days. That's not my point this evening; it's just to recognize the goodness of the Lord and the Gospel he gave to us. "*God, who at sundry times and in divers manners spake in times past to our fathers by the prophets hath in these last days spoken unto us by his Son.*" What a teacher! What a speaker Jesus is! What a message he delivers! He has shown us the way to the Father.

Don't you appreciate the Gospel of Christ? There's a lot to it. The deeper you go in it, the deeper you can go in it. You can stay around on the surface and deal with light things, talk about the cross that Jesus died on and never mention the cross that you've got to bear. You can describe the Golden Rule and quote some of the things out of the Sermon on the Mount without ever really making it plain that it's required of us that we take on that spirit.

Like they said about the Ten Commandments; they're not just the Ten Suggestions! The commandment to love our neighbor as ourselves is not just a suggestion; it's a requirement. It is a New Testament commandment as well as an Old Testament commandment to love your neighbor as yourself. Jesus renewed it and made it new in the New Testament. He said, *"That you love one another as I have loved you."* I guess nobody had ever loved anybody like Jesus loved his disciples. One scripture said, *"Having loved his own, he loved them unto the end."*

So, He gathered them together at the Last Supper and gave them his last instructions. He began to talk to them about the things they were going to experience and go through after his departure. That begins in the thirteenth chapter of John. I was impressed by the way he introduced that long discourse of John, chapters 14 through seventeen. He began as they were closing out at the last supper.

You remember Simon Peter's profession: *"Lord, why can't I follow thee now? I will lay down my life for thy sake."* That was Peter's confession at the last supper: *"Lord, I'll lay down my life for your sake! That's how much I believe in you! That's how much I love you! That's how much I trust you! Why can't I go with you?"*

Jesus was telling them, *"I'm going somewhere you can't go yet. Whither I go thou canst not follow me now, but thou shalt follow me afterward."*

Peter wanted to know, *"Why can't I follow you now? I'm ready to go now!"*

If you go into a lot of churches today and ask, "How many are ready to go to heaven?" you'll see all the hands go up. At one place that happened and everybody raised their hands except one little boy. The preacher said, "Young fellow, don't you want to go to heaven when you die?"

The little boy said, "Oh, yeah, when I die! I thought you were making up a load tonight."

Most people know in their hearts that they're not ready to go to heaven, yet, but they don't do any more about it. They will claim they'll be ready when they die without making any further changes. Inconsistent, isn't it? There's something missing there, somewhere! They know they're not ready to go right now but they don't think they have to do anything else to get ready to go when they die. That's not logical, and it's not scriptural.

Peter didn't know where Jesus was going. That's when Jesus told him, *"You're going into something; I'm leading you into so much trouble that, before the sun comes up, you'll deny me three times. Before the rooster crows this night, you'll deny me three times."*

It goes on without any break. He didn't say, "Chapter 14," He just kept talking, *"Let not your heart be troubled. I'm leading you into so much trouble that, before the sun rises, you'll deny that you know me. Let not your heart be troubled."*

Paradoxical? No. It's hard to follow the twists and turns and the sudden changes in Jesus' subject and his approach to the subject. *"Let not your heart be troubled. You believe in God, believe also in me. In my Father's house are many mansions, etc."* We know what the mansions are, but in the third verse, He said, *"If I go and prepare a place for you, I will come again and receive you unto myself, that where I am, there you may be also. Where I go, you know; and the way you know."*

But they didn't know where he was going because they hadn't accepted it. What he was saying was, *"You ought to know. I've told you where I'm going. I'm going back to the Father."* They didn't take that seriously. He had already told them he was going to have to die and be buried and rise again after three days, but they couldn't make sense of that; it just didn't compute.

He said, *"Whither I go, you know and the way you know."* Thomas said unto Him, *"Lord, we don't know whither thou goest and how can we know the way?"* That's when Jesus said this famous statement: *"I am the way, the truth and the life."* Amen!

We were talking this morning, out at Spring about, "Who's in the driver's seat?" Somebody gave a good testimony how the

Lord impressed on her, showed her, "You're not in the driver's seat." I'm glad I'm not in the driver's seat, aren't you? I'm glad I know who is in the driver's seat!

You used to see signs and notices in cars and maybe airplanes, too: "God is my co-pilot." You had better let God be the pilot! Amen! You don't need a co-pilot; you need a pilot! Let God be the pilot and you be the co-pilot if you want to be in the cockpit! I may be the tail gunner, I don't know, but I'm in the airplane! God is piloting the plane! Praise His Name! I'm glad we know who is in charge! I'm glad I know who is head of the Body, aren't you?

Can you believe that fifty years ago we used to argue over who was the head of the Body? One of the heads would say, "A body with two heads is a monstrosity!" That's when I got the revelation that a head with two bodies would be a worse monstrosity. The whole religious world thinks Jesus is the head of all these Christian bodies! What a monstrosity that would be!

Christ is the head of his body and that's the ONLY body he's the head of! Amen! There's ONE body! Well, there are many bodies, but not many bodies that Christ is the head of! There are threescore queens, fourscore concubines and virgins without number! Those are virgin churches without number! There is just any number of them. They're without number because the number keeps changing. They spring up and die out overnight. The country is always filled with virgin churches, unorganized churches.

On that point, on that prerequisite, they meet the qualification to be the Bride of Christ. But the scripture goes on to say, *"My dove, my undefiled, is but one." "My undefiled virgin is just one!"* There is just one of them!

He said—I think it's in the end of the first chapter of Ephesians that God gave Jesus to be the head over all things to the church. The twenty-second verse says that God has put all things under Jesus' feet. By the way, that's not only in this world, but in that which is to come. Let's back up: the nineteenth verse talks about the *"...working of His mighty power which He wrought in Christ when He raised him from the dead."* That was a mighty power at work that raised Christ from the dead. Nothing quite like that had ever been done before.

People had been brought back to life, in a few cases, by the prophets and a couple by Jesus himself, but they had been brought back into this old life. Jesus, thank God, was brought back into a new life! He was dead and is alive forevermore! Amen! That was a mighty power that brought him back into everlasting life. When He raised him from the dead and set him at his own right hand in the heavenly places. That's the heavenly places up there.

That expression occurs four times here in Ephesians and twice, I think, it means heavenly places down here. We sit together in heavenly places. And twice, it means those heavenly places up there where Christ sits at the right hand of God. These heavenly places are connected with those heavenly places! That's why this is called 'heavenly places'. It's connected with that up there! The Holy Ghost is our connection! Praise God!

And it's a definite, real, palpable connection! What's another synonym? I'm running out of ways to describe our hookup with the heavens, "*Far above all principality and might and dominion and every name that is named, not only in this world, but in the world to come* (in that which is to come) *and has put all things under his feet.*" Here and there, in this world and that world, God has put all things under Jesus' feet. "*...and gave him to be the head over all things to the church.*"

Now, the church is down here. "*...the church, which is his body.*" That's down here in these heavenly places. He's head over all things to the church, which is his body. He may be the head over some things to other churches, but if they don't let him be the head over all things, then those churches are not his body! Only that church which will let Jesus be the head over *EVERYTHING* to them can qualify to be his body. "*... the church which is his body, the fullness of him that filleth all in all.*" Only that church which is Jesus' body can *BE* the *FULLNESS* of him that filleth all in all. That's the only church that can hold all of God. It's the only church that *WANTS* all of God.

All churches want some of God and all of them want some of Jesus; but we need *ALL* of Jesus. There are people trying to get around the need to come to church, the need to be a functioning member of a local church by saying, "I've got Jesus! He's my Savior and he's all I need! Jesus is *ALL* I need!"

Well, Jesus might be all you need, but you need ALL of Jesus and you're not going to get that without the church! You can't have all of Jesus without being in the church which is the fullness of Him; it contains *"the fullness of him that filleth all in all"*. The explanation for that is simply this: That no single individual can contain all of Jesus. Jesus himself is the only individual that could exhibit, contain or manifest all of God.

Somewhere else here in Ephesians, Paul says that the fullness of God might be in you. That's a plural 'you' there, not a singular 'you'; it's plural. Here in the South we would express that as 'in you all'. Where is that passage, by the way? I need to read that. Ephesians 3:19: *"To know the love of Christ which passeth knowledge that ye..."* In the King James Version, that's a plural you. We would read that as: *"...that you all might be filled with all the fullness of God."* It's got to be plural because 'you' singular cannot be the fullness of God. I, personally, cannot be the fullness of God. But, we all together can hope to hold everything that God has and does and the way he works. The whole church can manifest everything that God is. We need that. It's important that we know these things. It's important that we be educated and taught about the things of God.

There are those four major doctrines and they're by no means all of the important doctrines, but they're the foundation doctrines of the Gospel, the Christian faith. There are things in there that, if you don't know them, if you don't understand those four doctrines, you'll misunderstand God. You'll misunderstand what it is you're trying to imitate, what nature you're trying to take on and you will take on the wrong nature. You'll take on the wrong spirit.

Here in America and, I guess, throughout the world now, it's long been a statement among us that the oneness Pentecostal people have a hard spirit. There's something about their doctrine of the godhead that makes them take a hard, unsympathetic attitude toward people that don't see it their way. Oneness Pentecostals, by the way, are not the only people who have that kind of spirit; they're just noted for it. There are some of us that have got that kind of spirit. There are some of us inside this body of people that have a proud spirit about our understanding, what we think it is we understand about the godhead.

But in order to get all that straightened out, we've got to understand all these various doctrines that are in the scriptures. This is why doctrine and teaching are important. There has to be a balance in the church of the Spirit of God and the Word of God. Those four major doctrines... The doctrine of Baptisms, if you don't understand that, you probably won't get all the baptisms. You'll be satisfied with water baptism, maybe. A lot of people are, and never go on to get the Spirit baptism. Then, a lot of the people that get the Spirit baptism will not accept Fire Baptism, partly through a misunderstanding of it. I was brought up with a misunderstanding of the concept of Fire Baptism. When we read that Jesus was going to, *"baptize you with the Holy Ghost and with fire"*, we left out the second 'with', and just quoted one of them. We said, "He's going to baptize you with the Holy Ghost and Fire!" We thought they went together. Every time you get the Holy Ghost, you get the Holy Ghost and Fire! We testified like that.

My mother had a vision when she got the Holy Ghost, praying all alone in her closet. She took the scripture, *"Enter into your closet and shut to the door,"* at its word. She had a big walk-in closet, so she went in there and shut the door. She got down on her knees and prayed until she prayed through. She saw a vision of flames of fire coming down, I guess like those cloven tongues on the Day of Pentecost. After that, maybe all of her life, I don't know if we ever got her stopped from saying that. She would testify and say, "I got the fire with mine! I got the Holy Ghost and fire!" We all used that out there in Pentecost where I got the Holy Ghost. We would testify and say, "I thank God for the Holy Ghost and fire!"

When you find out what the fire is, it's harder to thank God for it, but you still need to! (Laughter) You still need to! This is one of the things that are *'sweet to the mouth but bitter in the belly'*. You start thanking God for everything, learning that you are to thank God for the hard things. Thank God for the uncomfortable things, the unpleasant things because they are doing so much good for us. They help us get out of our complacency and show us what it is that we need to be changed on. I started to say what we need to change on, but we've got so many people that think we can't change ourselves. I know we can't without God's help. But, we need to see it either way. We've got to see that we need to be changed and we will have to cooperate with the change. People resist change. That's why God doesn't get everybody changed. Some people won't change even when God is trying to change them. That is what we have to see.

All those other doctrines are important like that. There are keys and secrets in there, mysteries. Paul said, "*We are stewards of the mysteries of God, brethren.*" That's the context when he talks about the duties of a steward. To be faithful, we've got to be faithful with the Word. In fact, there's a scripture in one of Paul's letters where he said, *"Holding fast the faithful word."*

"Holding Forth the Word of Life" used to be Brother Jolly's slogan that he had on the platform wall in St. Louis, the King's Highway church. That always made an impression on me. There was a lot of the Word of God preached over that pulpit. That sign you just kept reading; every time you looked up there it said, "Holding Forth the Word of Life."

There's another place where Paul put it this way: *"Holding fast the faithful word."* That means holding onto it. As stewards, we've got to take care of the mysteries of God. Don't let them slip away! Don't let them be corrupted! Don't let them be turned into deceitfulness! Don't let them become filthiness of fornication in Babylon's cup! We've got to contend for the truth! Earnestly contend for the faith that was delivered to the saints! Have that faith in our time, in our day! I feel like we're getting close! I feel like we're seeing results! The Word of God is bearing fruit in producing a good spirit among us.

I'm going to cut it short here and make room for these visiting brethren. We're glad to have Brother Isaac, from Orange, and Brother Robinson, from Lake Jackson, as well as the local brethren here. All of us have good things we could say.

Note: "Explain what is not yet put under his feet, or what we see not yet put under his feet."

Well, let's just take a moment to put that in its context. Hebrews 2:8. It starts in the sixth verse: "*One in a certain place* (that was in the Psalms) *testified, saying, what is man that thou are mindful of him or the son of man that thou visiteth him? Thou madest him a little lower than the angels....*" That's talking about mankind. "*...Thou crownest him with glory and honor and settest him over the works of thy hands.*"

God did that in the Garden of Eden. "*Thou hast put all things in subjection under his feet, for in that He put all in subjection under him...*" That's what He told Adam—to rule over the earth. He put everything, all the animals, the fish and the fowls under his authority. "*He left nothing that is not put under him, but now...*" And, we're talking about down here under the heavens. "*Now we see not all things put under him because man lost his dominion, so everything is not under him. But, we see Jesus who is one man. He is the Son of Man, the representative man who was made a little lower than the angels for the suffering of death.*"

I wish that was the only way we were lower than the angels. That's really the only way, or the only reason, Jesus was made lower than the angels, for the suffering of death. The angels don't suffer death. We see Jesus crowned with glory and honor that he, by the grace of God, should taste death for every man. Still, we see not yet all things put under Jesus' feet for the simple reason that the project is not completed. He's still bringing things under his feet. He said, in First Corinthians 15 that "*He must reign until all enemies are put under his feet. The last enemy to be destroyed is death.*"

Jesus will reign until he brings everything into subjection. All the rebels will either repent or die off. Finally, everything that is not found written in the Book of Life because they would not come under Jesus' feet will be cast into the lake of fire. There won't be anything left that is not put under him. That's when he returns the kingdom to God, the Father.

Well, that's enough. Let's go to prayer and then turn this over to the brethren here.

Chapter 16

Man's Ways vs. God's Ways

May 12, 2006, Hurst, Texas

Welcome! We're glad you're here with us today here in Hurst. It's good to see everybody coming out this morning to see what God is going to do for us. We glorify him for this privilege we have. It is a privilege, isn't it? It's not deserved, is it? It is a privilege God has extended to us to get to know him, to have a relationship with God. You can go your whole life and go through a lot of relationships but never have a real relationship with the Lord. Aren't you glad today that he intervened in your life? I'm glad he laid his hand on me, aren't you? I want to keep his hand on me; I want God to continue to deal with me and help me with my relationship with him. I don't think the problem is on his end; I think the problem might be on my end. I'm trying to make sure that I can walk with him.

I want to tell y'all I appreciate y'all being here; and all these ministers here today. What is God going to do? I'm sure he's going to feed us with good things from heaven. We have a good spirit flowing here. I don't know, yet, what God's going to do; I certainly am a candidate for anything he is ready to do, willing to do, that he plans to do. I'd like to be ready for him.

I'm going to get out of the way. I just wanted to make sure all of you felt welcome and try to see what God's got for me. We might pray here before we go any further for those who haven't made it yet, are still traveling and for those that are in the hospital, those that may even be hurting here today. But, you came on anyway. I found that out about God; He likes for us to just keep going anyway. He likes for us to be faithful in our service and our work. We've been working for months—I don't know why we do that—we wait until the last month and then try to get everything done in that month. Maybe it's because we've got a deadline. If we started six months earlier we might not have as many people to show up to work.

We consider it a great honor for y'all to be here with us. So, let's pray for those who came anyway but are not feeling well; and for those who are traveling. Are there any special requests we need to mention here?

(Congregational Prayer)

We're all feeling after God. It's nearly always hard to be first. It's always been hard to get people up to do anything in our general meetings on the first night of a meeting. For years, Brother Giffin would do that. He had a habit of starting the meetings off. I always thought he was just trying to fill the need, fill the gap because nobody else would do it. I remember Brother Patton getting after him one time for being in a rut, always having to be the first one in a meeting. I was glad somebody was doing it; I didn't want to do it. But, we don't want to get in a rut. We want to feel after God and find his mind for this meeting.

I think this meeting is important. It seems like we've been lax in having meetings in Texas the last few years. We've been letting them get scattered and far between. Here, this spring, we're bunching everything up. We had a meeting in Houston back in the winter and just had a meeting at Brother Budd's in Sebastapol. Then, we had one over in Jackson, Mississippi that a lot of us went to. Then, this was the week of the Campground work week. There are a lot of divided loyalties right now, at this season.

Don't you wish we could be everywhere? But, you know only God, himself, can do that. And, he can only do that through his Spirit. I wish everybody could understand that part. People have magical ideas about God, his person, and how he works. But, God has a great Spirit. Thank God for that great Spirit. It can be everywhere. It's called the 'Holy Spirit' because it's the spirit of a holy God.

Every person, every sentient being has a spirit. They're not all as powerful as that one and they're not all as holy as that one. We don't call our spirit 'holy' because we're not that holy a people. We're trying to be holy people, aren't we? We want our spirits to become holy. One of the things God has provided to help make that happen is his Spirit to mingle, connect with our spirit.

Talking about the 'spirit' of the Body, we have to explain what Paul said in Ephesians 4 about *"one body and one spirit;"* there being one spirit in the Body of Christ that is separate and different from all other bodies in the earth. Many of us are confused about that spirit as just being the Spirit of God, the Holy Spirit. It's more than that. However, that is, or should be, the strongest element in the spirit of the Body. The spirit of the Body is made up of all the spirits of the members of the Body mingled together.

But, God's Spirit is the greatest and strongest of those spirits, the holiest and the cleanest. That's why you can feel holy; you can feel good in these gatherings. There is a mixture of spirits here. Some of our spirits are less than holy, polluted in some way; defiled and unclean by contact with the world. We may not have kept our garments unspotted by the flesh.

We come in here and the Spirit of God especially accepts our repentant attitude and our humility before Him and before one another; that helps cover up the evil that we have been associated with. Probably, the longer we stay here, the cleaner the spirit will feel. More of the Spirit of God will come in and take control. This is what we are striving for.

We're glad to have that much knowledge of how to work with God, cooperate with him in our own experience, our own growth. If we don't know how to cooperate with God, we can resist him; we can resist his Spirit and slow down the process by which he is trying to improve us. God is patient with us; and it's a good thing he is. He's a good example that way. We need to be patient with one another so that we can stay together and enjoy the time we spend together.

It's good to be here in this gathering in the Fort Worth area. This area has such a long history of a special work of God. This message that we love and preach is still rather scarce in the earth. You can take an atlas or almanac and consider the numbers of towns and cities in America that don't have a church preaching this message. This is a special light; it's good to have a candlestick in our area holding forth the light, the light of the Gospel, the Word of Life.

So, a lot of people in this area have been affected. I'm one of them. Amen! I was closely associated with the Fort Worth church back when I was getting my start in the ministry. I learned to love the people here, and still do. It's good that we can still be together and encourage and exhort one another "*so much the more as we see the day approaching.*" Praise God.

The song says, "I'm glad he laid his hand on me." I'm glad God touched me one time; I'm glad he didn't pass me by. I'm glad I didn't resist his touch. It's a wonder I didn't! I might have if he had waited longer. God started in on me while I was still a little boy. At first, when I was being exposed to the Gospel, I was resistant, like any eight-year old or nine-year old boy, maybe ten years old. I wasn't interested in going to prayer meeting; I was interested in playing with the boys, sitting out in the car outside the house where the prayer meeting was; carrying on and talking like unsaved boys do. Sometimes, those boys wouldn't even come to the prayer meeting. I wanted to stay home and run with them while Mother and Dad went to prayer meeting.

Thank God for a Christian mother! She would say, "You're going with us." I would argue with her, "It won't do me any good; I'm not getting anything out of it. I won't get anything there."

"Yeah, but you're going anyway."

So, I did; I went anyway and hung around those prayer meetings. The time came, when I was ten years old, that the Lord found a way to get through to my heart, also some of my playmates. He touched us, gave us an experience and led us into a real, bona fide, emotional experience of contact with God. We felt it when it happened! Amen!

I was reading the other day in some of Brother Sowders papers. He said, "If you don't know when you got saved, you didn't." He gave the example of one uncle that was the son of a godly man. But, most of that man's children didn't get saved.

He had a saved daughter who asked her brother when he was on his death bed, "Did you ever have an experience with God anywhere in your life?"

He looked up at her and said, "Florence, I don't know."

He died in that uncertain condition. "If you don't know," Brother Sowders said, "then you didn't get it." Anybody that has an experience with God knows when and where it happened. They can take you to the place and tell you the time that they met God for the first time and had an indelible impression on their soul. That happened to me as a ten-year-old boy in the fence corner of the corn field. We were just playing church and knelt to pray. God got real about the church; he made a real church out of our game.

We got saved! We went back home different. We went to that fence corner one way and came home another! We told our parents about it. Bless their hearts! They were perceptive enough to see what had happened to us. They encouraged us to proceed and ask for the Holy Ghost. We began to go to the altar in all the meetings we could get to and ask for the Holy Ghost until, one day, God gloriously and mercifully, graciously baptized us in his wonderful Spirit. He overwhelmed our spirits with his. We were glad to have it happen!

I'm glad he laid his hand on me one time! He never has fully lifted his hand from me. God doesn't like to lift his hand off people, except for tests. There's one scripture, talking about King David, that says, "*God left him for a season* (in one instance) *just to know all that was in his heart.*" There was one time God wasn't with David in his temptations. David yielded; he gave in to the temptation and went astray. God never fully lifted his hand from him permanently because David was repentant of that occasion. He straightened up with the Lord and paid his price. He suffered his penalty and made up for it as best he could. He finished his days living for God.

God doesn't want to forget and forsake any of us. He doesn't easily and lightly forsake a move that he has started in the earth. He is patient and bears long with his people. There was an incident in First Kings where King Asa, I believe, went out to battle against a great host and the Lord delivered them. A prophet met them with a message when Asa and his army came back to Jerusalem. It's one of the wonderful, glorious messages promised to God's people. Everybody needs to know it and memorize it. Maybe we ought to take a look at it right now so you don't forget it. You need to locate that. The incident I'm looking for may be in II Chronicles. Yes, II Chronicles 15.

Here's the message God gave that day when they came back from a glorious victory because they trusted God. The Spirit of God came upon Azariah, the son of Oded. He went out to meet Asa and said to him, *"Hear ye me, Asa and all Judah and Benjamin. The Lord is with you while you be with him."* There's a principle there that everybody has got to live by if you want to keep God with you; if you want God to always be with you. The principle is: You always be with him! Let's stay on his side! *"The Lord is with you while you be with him! And if you seek him, he will be found of you, but if you forsake him, he will forsake you!"*

Ultimately, finally, he may not do it right away, even then, because God is merciful and loving and patient. He keeps trying to win people back; he gives us second chances, third chances, fourth chances. He keeps offering us opportunities to straighten up our lives and get back where we used to be, if we used to be there!

Your first chance is when you get right with him the first time! If we fall away from that, He gives us chances to get back there where we used to be when we were better off than what we are now, perhaps. We can get back there where we're better off again! Amen! But, he will finally forsake people as he forsook the people of Israel. He cast them out of his sight, into captivity.

It was a long, long process of patience and dealing with those people before he did it. He said one time, back there, speaking to the Jews, he sent his prophets to them over and over, *"rising early and sending them."* That's a figure of speech, of course. God is speaking a little bit plain there. It's like getting out of bed early in the morning, getting an early start on the day, dealing with his people. That just meant he didn't let any grass grow under his feet; he wasn't idle. He wasn't lazy about finding ways and trying things to affect people's lives for the better. He '*rose early*' and sent his prophets and preachers to the people.

I think he still does that today! Glory! I think he still has preachers and prophets to send to his people. It seems to me like he's been rising early, lately. He's been pretty busy, as busy as I've ever seen him in my short life. God's been busy in the last three, four or five years gathering people together and gathering people back together that used to be together. That seems to be the plan for right now; it seems to be what the Spirit is saying to the churches in this day and time: "Come back together, unite your forces, blend your spirits and love one another. Be real Christians, the kind the world can see and know that you are disciples of Christ." Praise his Name!

So, the Lord has laid his hand on us and he hasn't lifted it, yet. He hasn't cast us out of his sight. There are always people warning us (and that's a correct warning) that there is no guarantee that God has to stay with this group of people just because he started out with us. He started us out along a certain line but he could turn away and raise up another people to do his work if we won't do it. That's all true! I just don't see that happening because we haven't forsaken him.

God forsook Israel because they forsook him and turned away to false Gods. They served other gods and quit serving the true God. There were two ways and two reasons why that happened. There is a difference between the period of the judges and the period of the kings in the Old Testament. Everybody knows what was wrong, what the key problem was in the period of the judges because it is highlighted; it's pinpointed there in Judges.

Somebody was perceptive enough to single it out and write it in there distinctly that, *"In those days there was no king in Israel and every man did what was right in his own eyes."* I'm trying to get to the end of the book of Judges here. That's the last verse of the book of Judges. It occurs somewhere else in there; I think it's written twice in Judges. "*...every man did what was right in his own eyes.*" The evil result of that was, people drifted away. There was no strong leadership.

By saying there was no king in Israel it was saying there was no central government, no strong leadership over Israel during that period. The twelve tribes sort of got scattered and localized. They didn't fellowship very much. You can tell how little fellowship they had between the tribes in the incident where the Manassites had war with the Ephraimites. The Ephraimites went across Jordan to fight with the half tribe of Manasseh over there. The Manassites whipped them and when the Ephraimites were trying to flee home, every man for himself, the Manassites took control of the fords over the river. Every time a stranger came by wanting to cross over the river, they would stop him and examine him; they had a test they gave him. "*Say now, 'shibboleth'.*"

If you and I were there, we would have said 'shibboleth'. We wouldn't have any trouble with that. But peculiarly, the Ephraimites had lost, had forgotten how to make the 'sh' sound. They had stayed so separated from the rest of the tribes that their language changed that much; their pronunciation changed and they didn't use the 'sh' sound anymore. They had changed it into just the 's' sound and would say 'sibboleth'; they couldn't say 'shibboleth'. That way they knew the person was an Ephraimite and would take him and put him to death right there. That shows how separated and scattered God's people were at that time.

They weren't having enough meetings; they weren't going up to the place of God's presence three times a year like they were commanded to do in the Law of Moses. They weren't mingling that much; they didn't have much to do with each other. So, it was almost twelve nations, twelve tribes scattered. This was the meaning of that incident where the Levite took his concubine who had been abused and murdered, divided her into twelve pieces and sent one piece to each tribe throughout all twelve tribes of Israel. He was making a statement with that action; he was calling the people's attention to how divided they were, how un-unified they were.

The point was: if we can't get together and do something about a crime like this, then the Body of Israel is divided and scattered and sure to die as this woman's body. The Body of Israel is as divided and scattered as this woman's carved-up body if we can't get together, unite and take action against a problem like this. To their credit, they did! At that time, they did come together and deal with the problem.

The weakness of that day in time was that they didn't have a strong central government. It doesn't mean they didn't have any leadership available, but the leadership was not strong most of the time and they didn't follow it much. They did have the priesthood during that whole period. The tabernacle was there at Shiloh. The Ark of the Covenant was there that whole time. Some people were continually going to it but a lot of people quit going to it. Some of those who went to it went to other churches too, other denominations. They tried to mix their idol worship with their worship of Jehovah.

God kept sending revival, raising up strong leaders for brief times, judges he called them, and would call the people back and bless them again. But after that strong leader had passed away and nobody filled his shoes, they would drift back into their idol worship and stray from the truth. That was a period somewhat empty in Israel's history; not much progress was made under those conditions.

The time came for a change and God yielded to the demands of the people and gave them a strong central government because they wanted it. It needs to be noted, though, that they didn't have much better results in that period, either, another four hundred years or so under the kings. They still kept going astray. The difference was, under the kings it wasn't just a family here, a family there, a scattered group here and there gradually drifting away. It was the whole nation being led wholesale into idolatry by backslid, apostate kings and governments.

That kept happening over and over and over. In the period of the judges every man did what was right in his own eyes because he was free to do that. Many times he did what was right in his own eyes but not what was right in God's eyes. Under the period of the kings they weren't really free to do what was right in God's eyes all the time. Many times, they were forced to do what was right in the king's eyes, which was not right in God's eyes. So, it just transferred the blame and responsibility from the individual to the central government. It had worse results in the end.

The period of the judges came to an end with one of the greatest prophets and leaders Israel ever had, the prophet Samuel. There was a great restoration under his ministry and it ushered in the kingship under good conditions, under good auspices. But the kingship had its ups and downs and finally resulted in the whole nation being destroyed and cast out of God's sight into captivity.

Government is not the answer, is it? Government is useful for some things; and, God gives government. We need to note that he called even his backslid, apostate, rebellious kings 'shepherds'. They were still shepherds that he placed over God's people. Many of them didn't work right, didn't turn out right. God kept giving them government until he was through with that period and lesson in their history.

Some good examples are in here of men working for good and working for evil and men that made mistakes. There are lessons for all of us: Don't give in or give up over a mistake. You can always repent. God will give you another chance. He will do something else. He will give you something to work for.

Hezekiah is another example. We've already mentioned David. I wanted to say some things about the life of Hezekiah. He was one of the best kings over Judah in that period of the divided kingdom. He started a revival. His father had been an idolater and had brought trouble upon the kingdom. Hezekiah, to his everlasting credit, turned things around, started a revival and got people coming back to the temple. He even invited the neighbors from the northern kingdom, many of which had already been scattered into captivity. He invited the remnants of them to come down and take up the worship of the true God again. Many did. He got results out of that.

Then, one of the outstanding responses to prayer was when Judah was being invaded by the king of Assyria, one of the great, destructive, powerful, destroying nations of ancient history. They destroyed everybody they invaded except Judah. They invaded Judah, took a lot of the cities and were poised to capture Jerusalem when Hezekiah took the letter the Assyrians wrote into the temple and knelt and read it before the Lord. *"Look here what they are saying about you."* They had made slighting remarks about the God of Israel. *"Do you think your god is going to deliver you? Which gods of any of the nations have been able to deliver their people out of our hands?"*

You know, God responds to things like that when his reputation, his name is challenged. Both Hezekiah and Isaiah put it to him straight. God sent Hezekiah a message promising him that they, the Assyrians, were not going to capture that city. He would send them back to their own land in disgrace. What happened was, he sent a destroying angel among the Assyrian army one night while they were camped outside Jerusalem. One hundred, eighty-five thousand soldiers *'woke up dead'* the next morning. Of course, there must have been more than one hundred, eighty-five thousand there. The few that were left over woke up to see the others dead. It does say something like that. *"When they arose in the morning, they were all dead bodies."* It almost says *"they woke up dead that morning."* So, God delivered Hezekiah and the nation of Judah because they trusted in him.

The next important thing in his life was, he got sick. God told him to get ready to die. Now, ever since then Hezekiah has been an example to all of us who are not ready to die; who don't feel like we're ready to go. I've heard a lot of people asking for fifteen more years. I remember, but can't think of the brother's name now; he built a little shack on the Ten Acres and lived there till he died—Brother Chase Tucker. He had cancer and asked for fifteen more years and got it! He lived another fifteen years or so, maybe more. People are always using that for an example. It's hard for me to evaluate whether this is that good an example or not.

God did hear his prayer. I think that is noteworthy. It's worth considering the value of prayer. It says, *"Hezekiah turned his face to the wall and reminded God how good he had been."* Don't try that unless you have been pretty good! Hezekiah had been pretty good! He had served the Lord; done a lot for him; done a lot for God's people. He had some things to point to. He had followed the Lord from his youth up. He hadn't done anything to cause God to criticize him. The prophet had just left his bedside after telling him, "Get ready to die. Set your house in order; make out your will. Get the lawyer and get things straightened up. It's time for you to die."

Before the prophet had got out of the courtyard God spoke to him, *"Go back in there and tell Hezekiah I've heard his prayer."* Isn't that good when God hears your prayer? *"I'll add to his life fifteen years,"* which He did. I'm not sure that fifteen years bore good fruit. It was during that fifteen years of Hezekiah's life that he had a son who turned out to be, possibly, the worst king Judah ever had. It might have been better for the people of God if Hezekiah had died when God decided for him to. Of course, we don't know what other person could have taken the throne and how he might have turned out. That one didn't turn out so good, we know that much. Still, it is a good record of an answer to prayer prayed in the right spirit.

Prayers have to be prayed in the right attitude to get a favorable answer from God. Another thing that happened to Hezekiah was, he got *'lifted up with pride'* the Bible says. That's a sad case, a sad story. The history of lives in the Bible is full of them. It's so common for great, successful leaders, blessed of God, to get lifted up with pride and get in the wrong spirit. That happened to Hezekiah in II Chronicles 32:24, 25: *"But Hezekiah rendered not again according to the benefits done unto him for his heart was lifted up. Therefore, there was wrath upon him and upon Judah and Jerusalem."* When there is a strong central government and wrath comes on that central government, it comes, to an extent on the whole people; the whole group suffers. I like this next verse: *"Notwithstanding, Hezekiah humbled himself, both he and the inhabitants of Je-*

rusalem so that the wrath of the Lord came not upon them in the days of Hezekiah."

Repentance has results, doesn't it, if we make a mistake, if somebody does get lifted up with pride and can see the results of it? The way Hezekiah saw it was he was willing to listen when somebody told him; somebody pointed it out. He didn't wait until the trouble came. That might have convinced him he had taken the wrong spirit if God had sent wrath upon him but he didn't wait for that. So, it didn't have to happen in his day. He let somebody tell him that he had missed God. He was willing to consider; he was approachable.

That's what James says about *'true wisdom';* that it is *"easy to be entreated."* Christian people need to be *'easy to be entreated'*, especially anybody who has any authority, responsibility in the church. They need to be easy to be entreated so that people who are working under them look up to them and respect them. People will feel different about approaching you with a complaint or criticism. We need to be 'easy to be entreated' so that people will find it easy to come to us, bring things to our attention that we might otherwise overlook. We might overlook mistakes we're making or there might be information they can give us that will help us with other cases.

Preachers can get so exalted, so authoritative, so lifted up on a throne of worship and glory that people don't feel free, don't feel at ease about coming to them about anything. It may be hard to maintain that kind of contact with people. Your attention gets divided as the congregation grows. A lot of people I knew were slow even to go to Brother Clyde Patton. He was my example. No one ever called him unapproachable, but people just honored his position and reputation so much that they were intimidated by him.

People would tell me, "I don't know how to talk to him," because he was, frequently, cautious about giving an answer, especially when he wasn't sure how the answer would be received. He sometimes wouldn't give an answer; he might ask them a question. They would be telling him a problem and he would turn, walk away and shake hands with somebody like he had been suddenly distracted and forgot he was talking to you. That was a trick he used.

I don't know if I knew it instinctively or if I figured it out, but I learned how to go to him when I had a problem that needed his attention. I learned that I could go visit him, start talking to him and he would do me like he did others. He would answer two or three phone calls or maybe go feed the chickens and dogs. He would start another conversation along another line of thought, then when there was a lull or lag in the conversation, I would bring my problem up again; I would call his attention back to my subject. Eventually, he would usually tell me what to do. I finally realized what he was doing. A lot of that time, he was studying the problem while he was talking to other people and doing other things, putting me off. He didn't want to make a snap judgment. He was studying, praying in his heart, feeling in the Spirit and he would give an answer when it came to him.

We like to have instant answers. Somebody comes to us with a question and we want to tell them immediately, like we know everything. Nothing fazes us; nothing challenges us. But, we're not that smart! We need to get things through the Spirit; we need to feel the mind of God. We need to feel the mind of the Spirit! We need to be cautious about giving quick answers; not be too fast to move and answer just according to our opinion.

Sometimes, you get a chance to repent for a mistake you made. Whatever the reason for the mistake, it could have come from pride; it could have come from hate; it could have been what we call an honest mistake. Is there such a thing as an 'honest mistake'? What is that? Anyhow, what we mean when we say that is that we were doing the best we could. We were trying to do right; we thought we were doing right, so that's what we call an 'honest mistake'. Even an honest mistake can have bad results if God doesn't cover up for you. I think He covers up for us a lot of times because He saw that we did have the right spirit. He makes a lot of things work out that shouldn't have. We weren't that smart but he saw that we had what they call 'an honest heart'.

So, Hezekiah recovered himself from his error, came back to God and finished his life. His young son that was born during that period—something went wrong in his upbringing. You know he heard about the way God answered Hezekiah's prayers. You know he heard talk about the time God healed his father when he was about to die. You know he heard about the time God killed all those enemy soldiers and delivered the land from the invasion. You know he heard about the great revivals and the great times they had gathering people out of all the countries round about for big conventions in Jerusalem and what a glorious time it was. You know he heard those things!

What happened? Something went wrong in that boy's upbringing. He was only twelve years old when he was anointed king and had to take over the throne. That's too young. Maybe he didn't have good advisers while growing up into manhood. It says he reigned fifty-five years in Jerusalem. I can't think of any other king that reigned that long. What would have been the result of fifty-five years if he had been a wise, righteous, holy king? He was the worst thing that ever happened to Jerusalem! It says, *"He did that which was evil in the sight of the Lord,"* II Chronicles 33, *"like unto the abominations of the heathen."* It lists all the wicked things he did. Verse nine says, "*So Manasseh made Judah and the inhabitants of Jerusalem to err.*"

This is the danger of central government. If it goes wrong, it takes the whole group with it; everybody goes wrong, almost. There are just a few people who hide, who are in the underground, like that seven thousand in Israel who were so hid away that Elijah didn't even know about it. A few people have to hide out to serve God and do what's right in God's eyes at the jeopardy of their lives and freedom. *"He made Jerusalem to err and do worse than the heathen whom the Lord had destroyed before the children of Israel. And the Lord spake to Manasseh and his people."* Get that now! As wicked a man as he was, God spoke to him! God kept speaking to him!

If you've never looked at this before, this will surprise you. In reading the story of Cain and Abel, when Cain got mad at his brother before he killed him, God kept talking to him. God was talking to Cain; He called him a prophet. God linked him with the prophets in the Old Testament! He was a religious man. He was seeking after God and God was seeking after him. Even after he killed his brother, after he committed murder, God again talked to him. God still dealt with him and even protected him. God protected his life from suffering the capital penalty.

God's loyalty, God's mercy, God's patience, God's love for his erring children! God spoke to Manasseh and his people but they would not listen. "*Wherefore the Lord brought upon him the captain of the hosts of the king of Assyria,*" the very nation God had delivered Manasseh's father from. "*...which took Manasseh among the thorns,*" I guess they found him out in the thorn patch, captured him, bound him with fetters and carried him to Babylon. They carried him into captivity in a foreign country.

Note this: another case of repentance. "*In his distress he sought the favor of the LORD his God and humbled himself greatly before the God of his fathers. And when he prayed to him, the LORD was moved by his entreaty and listened to his plea; so he brought him back to Jerusalem and to his kingdom. Then Manasseh knew that the LORD is God.*" I wish we had that prayer. We've got a couple of Hezekiah's prayers; we've got a prayer or two of David's and Solomon's. I wish we had Manasseh's prayer, a prayer that got that kind of result. Somebody said his prayer was written somewhere in the records back in those days, but it's lost now; we don't have a record of it. I would love to read the kind of prayer that man prayed. As wicked a life as he lived, when he finally woke up he turned to the God of his fathers and prayed a prayer that God listened to and responded to. God brought him back to his kingdom and placed him on his throne again. That's about as great a miracle as when he brought Nebuchadnezzar back from among the wild beasts and placed him on his throne again.

"*Then Manasseh knew that the Lord, or Jehovah, he was God.*" It took that much to convince him. His problem, like other people in his day who turned to idolatry, was because they were confused. There wasn't a clear message in those days, enough to convince people. A lot of people just didn't know who the true God was. As Elijah said, when he put his challenge to the nation and gathered the prophets of Baal and the prophets of the groves together for the contest, he said to the people, *"Make up your minds. If Baal be god, then follow Baal; but if Jehovah is God, follow him!"* The people said, "Well, that makes sense," and stayed for the results of the contest. They finally saw who was God!

God kept having to prove himself to every generation like that. I guess it's still like that today. Children don't learn much from their parents; there's not enough to keep them stable. Children have to have their own experience with God. What my parents received from God would not have helped me if God had not dealt with me in the corn field. If I hadn't received the baptism of the Holy Ghost on a berry-picking expedition I wouldn't be here today. We had to have our own experience, our own contact with the Lord.

People kept falling away before having those experiences. Some of them had to get into bad shape like Manasseh did. He was in *BAD* shape! His life was messed up! He was worse off than people who come to us nowadays with their homes broken up. Different things, drug addictions get hold of people. They think, "I'm too far gone; it's too late for me. I've missed my chance."

You can get in that frame of mind if you don't watch out. Manasseh's life was messed up *BAD*, but when he prayed the right kind of prayer from the right heart—a broken and contrite heart God will not despise in any day in time, any generation! It's good for us to be together, knowing that the Lord is still dealing with us. He's still speaking to us! He's still got things to say to us.

So, I'd like to leave Manasseh on a high note; I'm glad he got saved. The tragedy I still have to point out is, even though he got saved, he could never undo all the harm he had done. He could not erase all the evil he had committed. There are a couple of comments in II Chronicles 33:18, *"The rest of the acts of Manasseh and his prayer unto his God, and the words of the seers that spake to him in the name of the Lord God of Israel, behold, they are written in the book of the kings of Israel."* (But, it's not that book we've got called Kings.) (19) *"His prayer also and how God was entreated of him, and all his sins, and his trespass, and the places wherein he built high places, and set up groves and graven images, before he was humbled; behold, they are written among the sayings of the seers.* (20) *So, Manasseh slept with his fathers, and Amon, his son reigned in his stead."* His son took over, but he didn't follow his dad's example in the last part of his life. He followed his example in the first part of his life, a bad example. Isn't that disappointing when your children don't follow the example you are setting after you got saved, but they thought too much of that example before you got saved and follow that one? It is so disappointing.

The results here that didn't work out—I'm trying to find the verse where it says that *"later on God would not forgive the innocent blood that Manasseh shed in Jerusalem."* I'm not sure now whether that is in Chronicles or Kings. It's in there somewhere that things were going wrong in Israel again after Manasseh was dead. It was pointed out that all the wicked things Manasseh had done and the blood he shed in Jerusalem God would not forget. He kept *'treasuring them up against the day of wrath'.*

Like an individual person, a nation or group having generational history can treasure up things against the day of wrath. It finally becomes like Jesus said about the generation he was born into, *"The day is coming that the blood of all the righteous men that have been slain from righteous Abel to Zechariah, son of* Barachias *whom ye slew between the porch and the altar is going to be required of this generation,"* Jesus said.

That blood has already been required several times, most of it. You know Abel's blood was required in Noah's flood. It lets you know that when God finally judges a world, he goes all the way back to the beginning of the world. I think the same thing is going to happen to this world. It happened to the Jewish world back there; the blood of all the martyrs and prophets, beginning with righteous Abel on down to Dennis McClure who they may kill on the streets of Cisco or Fort Worth if it gets worse before his hair gets any whiter! His name may be added to that list. All of these will be totaled up and required of this generation.

Even though you repent of your evil deeds, you can't erase the consequences. They bear consequences in other people's lives. You may be able to escape the consequences in your own life, but they still bear consequences in other people's lives. It's important that we keep the right attitude, keep the right spirit and listen to the Lord and his prophets, his leaders. Listen to the people he raises up as mouthpieces to speak through.

That is primarily in the New Testament, Jesus Christ, himself, but he has prophets and teachers and apostles under him. We still have something like that, some remnant of that today. We must be willing to hear when God speaks through an anointed minister or any other person that he anoints at the moment. Let's not go back to the period of the judges where we just do what's right in our own eyes.

I teach a lot of freedom. That's why I describe the judges a lot of times. That was an era of freedom, something God loves. God likes that. He set it up that way. That was God's order and they rejected that order when they desired a king. There's something to be said for people to be free enough to do what's right in their own eyes but they are not to exercise their freedom to the point of using liberty for *'an occasion to the flesh'* as Paul said.

Back in Deuteronomy 12, God, speaking through Moses, told them, "*When you get into the land, you shall not do like you are doing here in the wilderness, every man doing what's right in his own eyes.*" Right there, camped on the plains of Moab, before they crossed over Jordan, God said to Israel, "*You shall not do according to all the things you do here this day, every man doing whatsoever is right in his own eyes.*" Note that they did have some government in Israel then. Moses was an outstanding and very visible leader.

Aaron and his sons, the priesthood, were strong and visible. Then, they had seventy elders and captains of thousands, captains of hundred, etc. So, there was leadership in the land but it was not oppressive, tyrannical. People were given a high degree of freedom. It was like a frontier society, a pioneer society. People could do pretty much what they wanted to if it didn't cause too much trouble. So, every man was able to do 'whatsoever was right in his own eyes'.

God said, *"Don't do that when you get in Canaan's land."* That's advice that carries over to us in our day: "Don't do that!" In other words, don't just do as you please! We want you to be free enough, we want to have the kind of order that makes people able to do as they please, but we want people to be well taught enough to do right! When people please to do right, when people know what's right, then they can do what's right in their own eyes, if what's right in their own eyes is what's right!

The problem in the judges was that, what was right in their own eyes usually wasn't right! When a man fell away to idol worship it was because that was right in his own eyes! He thought that was the right thing to do! They weren't listening to the right voices; they weren't listening to the right people, the right leaders, the right preachers and the right God!

The solution to that problem—let's look at 13:18: *"When thou shalt hearken to the voice of the Lord thy God to keep all his commandments which I command thee this day to do that which is right in the eyes of the Lord thy God."* That's everybody's answer! That's everybody's solution! Do that which is right in the eyes of God! If you can find out what is right in the eyes of God, then try to do that! When you try to do that you may find it sometimes difficult.

God has given us the power to do it! This is why Jesus came to this world and died for our sins and sent back the Holy Spirit in his place. He sent back the Holy Spirit in his place when his physical presence left here. He said, *"I will give you another comforter that he may abide with you forever."* Praise God! The Holy Ghost has been with me now for sixty-two years! It has never left me! I haven't always been what we call 'in the Spirit', but the Spirit has always been in me!

It's still here today, thank God! And, it's as good as it ever was! The Holy Ghost is an experience everybody needs! It will help you! It won't do everything for you, but it will help you do what you ought to do if you cooperate with it and be led by it, guided by it. The Holy Ghost will help you! Jesus gave us that for the power we need to do what's right in the eyes of God.

Everybody in here ought to be able to do what is right in the eyes of God! First, you have to know that! Jesus said, "*The Holy Ghost, the comforter will guide you into the truth.*" He spoke that to those twelve men, eleven of them, actually. I'm sure the Holy Ghost did guide them after they received it and kept laboring and studying, talking and discussing there in Jerusalem for several years.

When the problem came up about how to feed the widows in the church, they didn't want to be distracted by that. They said, *"It's not sense that we should leave the Word of God and serve tables,"* that is, that they should do natural things like ushering and serving meals. There are plenty of people out here that can do that. The twelve apostles devoted themselves to the word of God and to prayer. In Acts 2, that Spirit they had received kept guiding them into truth. It didn't guide them there all at once in one big step, one giant step. They didn't see everything that was meant by the word of God.

That is proved by how hard it was. I use that word 'hard' symbolically. I don't know how hard things are for God. He said one time, *"Is anything too hard for me?"* That suggests some things might be hard, but not too hard! Some things are harder than others. One of the hardest things, I think, is for God to get people to cooperate with him. He has to go to some trouble; God has to take time out, sometimes, to argue with people. He sure did it with Moses. That argument Moses had with God took up part of two chapters back there in Exodus before God finally got the last word, which he will! Don't try to argue with God! Don't try to out talk God! Don't try to 'Jew' God down! Let him set the terms! It will turn out best that way.

The Lord was trying to get Peter to go to the house of Cornelius, a Gentile, and open the door; to use the keys the Lord gave him and open the door to the Gentiles. He gave him a vision of all kinds of animals, wild animals and unclean things, things that were not permitted under the Law of Moses. Peter was hungry. Remember how that got started? He was fasting and told them to cook for him. He went up to the upper room and lay down to take a nap while they were preparing lunch. While he was lying there hungry and napping, he had a vision of a vessel, a container, filled with all kinds of meats. A voice said, *"Rise, Peter, kill and eat."* Kill a chicken, kill a rabbit, kill a squirrel and eat it. He kept saying, *"Not so, Lord."*

That's what we say, sometimes, when we ought not to be arguing with the Lord, "Not so, Lord." We don't want it that way. That happened three times and he said, *"I don't eat things like that."* Each time, the voice would answer and say, *"That which I have cleansed, you quit calling it common and unclean."* When he woke up he realized there was a message in that somewhere. There's a lesson in there somewhere. What does that mean?

Did you ever wake up from a dream in the night and wonder, "What was that about? Why did I dream that? Was that from the Lord?" Well, he understood that was from the Lord. While he was thinking about it, Cornelius' messengers were knocking at the door asking for a man named Simon Peter. They invited him to go home with them to the house of Cornelius, a Gentile.

Peter felt moved of the Spirit to go with them, *"nothing doubting."* He took some brethren with him and went over to Cornelius' house and went in, much against Peter's previous practice. Peter didn't just go into Gentiles' houses and sit down at their dining table and have coffee with them. He was a Jew. He was too holy, too clean to do that.

But, God had given him a lesson in the Spirit, so his heart was open. There was something different, something peculiar about this occasion. He was still wondering what it was. He came in and said, "Well, I'm here. If you know anything about Jews, you know it's not lawful, it's not normal for us to enter the house of a Gentile, but you sent for me. I felt impressed to come. Here I am. What do you need?"

They began to ask him for the message from God. So, with the preparation God had given him, he did what he might not have done without that preparation. He began to preach to them the Gospel of Jesus Christ. He didn't get to the point about the Holy Ghost being sent from heaven. Maybe he was just fixing to talk about that when the Holy Ghost fell from heaven on that group of people. The Lord sanctioned his words and made the Holy Ghost fall on those Gentiles*!* Right there the door was flung open and nobody has ever got it closed again! Thank God! That's our salvation! That's our benefit! Nobody was able to close the door after God opened it through Peter!

He knew he was in for a struggle when he got back home to the rest of the apostles; he knew they wouldn't understand. They hadn't seen that in the scriptures, yet. What I'm telling you is, the Holy Ghost had not yet guided them into all truth. This was several years down the road! It takes a while to get all the truth.

People come in here and hear some of these revelations. They like some of what they hear and say, "Tell me all of it! Tell me the rest of it! Give it to me straight! I can take it! I just want the truth!" But, you have to be careful about how much truth you give them. They may not be able to take it all, yet. There are some things they think they are ready for, but they're not. I remember Sister Janie Lee. She was one of Brother Patton's first saints in Houston. She said she began to hear remarks about a particular Bible subject and she sensed that there was something in there she wasn't catching, so she went to him and began to ask him about it. She wanted him to make it plain to her, tell her.

Brother Patton kept going around the bush, beating around the bush, avoiding a direct answer. Finally, she pressured him until he just opened up and gave it to her. She said she went away and for the next three days there was a lump in her throat she couldn't swallow. She kept trying to swallow it. She had thought she was ready, but that one was hard to take.

All of us found some things hard to swallow when we got here. I did! Amen! We all think we're ready for the truth! We all think we want the truth! We all think we love the truth, don't we? Amen! We're afraid not to love the truth! We're afraid we'll be sent a strong delusion; be sent a lie and be damned!

Someone speaking

Did y'all hear that? But, we don't love them, do we? Let's be careful we don't love any lies. What I'm saying is, you have to learn what is a lie and what is truth before you can make a decision. It has to be pointed out some way. God had to point things out to the apostles and they pointed those things out to the flock, to the congregation and to the rest of the ministry. They gave out those truths and revelations.

Peter brought a revelation home to Jerusalem when he came from the house of Cornelius. He came with a revelation and it was challenged. It wasn't easy; it wasn't popular, but he had too much evidence to his credit. He was reputable enough; he had a reputation and they had to listen to him. They might not have given everybody a chance to even give their testimony after something like that. But, God used a man that had enough prestige among the group that they would at least listen to his testimony. He explained how it happened and had it confirmed by witnesses. He said, "It wasn't something I did. I went there and broke the rules. I ate dinner with them. When I was talking about the Lord Jesus to them, the Lord sent the Holy Ghost from heaven just like he did on us. I didn't have anything to do with that. There was nothing I could do about it. It wasn't me; it was God!"

That's a real good hiding place when you need it! If you can say, "It wasn't me; it was God! I didn't decide that! I didn't do that! That was something God did and I couldn't help it!"

He hid behind God when he was explaining to the people. They finally had to accept it and said, "*Well, evidently God has granted repentance to the Gentiles. We didn't think he was ready to do that, but it looks like it happened without us doing it. Without us being much involved, God has decided to do something.*" When God decides to do something, we have to let him do it! We have to cooperate with him; go along with it! It's going to bear good results in the long run.

It caused some troubles, yes. There was conflict in the New Testament church after the house of Cornelius over how to deal with the Gentiles, how they were to fit into the church and how much of the Law of Moses they needed to practice, how they were to relate to the Jewish people who had it first. There was lots of conflict over different doctrinal questions and practical questions. They had to work those things out. But, it had good results in the long run. It has done more good than evil. It's done more good than harm to the church! Praise God!

They had to get over the problems and difficulties but it strengthened the church in the long run! Eventually, that Jewish church faded out and mostly disappeared from the earth. Those great apostles and prophets from back there were martyred and went to their reward. The Jewish church faded out. Fewer and fewer and fewer got saved as the church period went on. But the Gentiles kept on following the truth, following the leadership, following God.

Always, throughout those dark years, the years we call the Dark Ages, right in the middle of the Middle Ages when things ...(skip in tape)...none of those words would fall to the ground. The two witnesses, even though they lay dead in the streets they prophesied, clothed in sackcloth, and their prophecies came true. They *"had power to shut heaven that it rain not in the days of their prophecy."*

Even though there was not a visible church that people could find or point out, there was a noticeable group of people living those things. Still, the truth was chained to the pulpit. The written letter was there and that written word kept coming through whether anybody believed it or understood it. Many things were not understood well enough to be believed during that period. But, the prophecies kept coming through; world events kept falling into place. The Reformation finally broke out; the restoration process finally set in.

Then finally, God called William Sowders to preach *HIS GOSPEL!* Preach the real, true, New Testament Gospel. *"This gospel of the kingdom must be preached in all the world and then shall the end come!"* Praise God! We've got to respect the message and, to some extent, respect the messenger.

It's sad when messengers let us down, like David, Solomon, Hezekiah, and Manasseh. People have let God's people down. Leaders, ministers, kings and rulers have let God's people down. But, God doesn't give up. He keeps bringing things out and taking people on. There's a destiny, a destination; there's predestination, if you want to call it that. There's a plan God intends to fulfill; he's going to make things happen. He's going to get enough people to work with him that it will come to pass.

We don't want to give up over personal problems. Don't lose faith in the message, the vision, the Body, the Church over things that happen to us individually in the church. I admit you can get hurt in here. If you get hurt in God's house—stay in the house! You'll be better off there than anywhere else. You will finally get healed in God's house. Things can be worked out.

Leaders rise and fall; great men live and die but the church moves on. We can always find somewhere that God is working and cooperate with that. We need to respect the men of God whom he is using at any moment in time without worshipping them or honoring them to the point where they could lead us astray. It would have been better for all the people during Israel's history if they had refused to be led astray by men like Ahab and women like Jezebel. There are a few people who refused to be led astray during that period. The leadership was out of order; the leadership missed God; they were leading people wrong but there were people that didn't give up God. Probably very few of them ever got to see the temple in Jerusalem, but they stayed hid away in their homes, read and studied what they could get of the scriptures and communed with one another.

It's in times like that when men who think upon the Lord speak often one to another. It may be privately, somewhere in their houses because they don't have a public meeting place. It's in times like that that people need to *'speak often one to another'* and keep one another encouraged. There is always somebody around like those seven thousand that God reminded Elijah of. *"I've got at least that many in Israel that haven't bowed the knee to Baal or kissed his image."* God was watching over them and Elijah was supposed to be watching over them. God asked, *"What are you doing down here, Elijah?"*

Elijah was looking for God. He went off down there where God used to be, trying to find him. A man that had just been met by God, the day before yesterday, experienced a mighty move of fire falling from heaven and consuming the sacrifice, and then an answer to prayer, rain coming from heaven after a three-and-one-half-year drought. All that great move of God and this man flees for his life and goes off down in the desert trying to find God! Well, God was merciful and met him down there but he sent him back to where he belonged.

Elijah said, *"They're trying to kill me up there. I'm the only one left and if I stay around, they will kill me and there won't be anyone left."* God said, *"I've got seven thousand left up there just like you. They may not be publicly visible like you are. But, you go back up there and finish your ministry; finish your job in those dangerous conditions! I can watch over you and guard you."*

Jezebel never did get Elijah, did she? He went back up there and she never did catch him! She never did get to make his life like one of those prophets that he slew there in valley of Gidron. She threatened his life but God took him out of this life when his time was to go. He didn't go by Jezebel's sword!

We want to work, today, in a way that God can work with and get glory out of. I don't want to puff up the ministry and overemphasize the value and power of the ministry, but we can't afford to ignore it, either. They are there for a purpose. When God calls somebody to an office, he does it for a reason. It's not to reward that person that he calls. The reason is, there are people out there that need that; they need what that man's got. If God puts somebody over you it's because you need what that person's got. They may not profit by their position very much, but the church is supposed to profit by it.

Let's make sure the church can profit from it. We want to respect and honor men like that, men like George Bragg, here.

God has brought him to our rescue in this condition, this location right here. We appreciate all the men of God and the saints of God in this area and are just glad God is moving us back in the direction of being together again. Amen! Working together! Brother Bragg was needed here in this peculiar position, this dangerous, exposed place. He's working wisely and being guided by the Lord to fit in with the work of God. As such, as a man of God, his words carry some weight. He's to be considered.

Even though we want everybody to be free to do whatever you please, we don't want to be free to ignore the minister and feel like he has no authority. Several people criticized me (and some to my face) not long ago down there in Houston because we had had an outstanding song. I just knew that another song right at that time wouldn't fit; it would be a let-down. What happens in our church, a lot of times, because we like singing and music, we can get a spirit of song going. Because one song blesses, someone else will think, "Well, my song will fit in right here. Songs are blessing tonight and I want to sing my song."

A person stood up and asked permission. He was wise enough to ask permission, "Can I sing a song right here?" Since he asked, I tried to give him wise advice, "Let's wait on that. We've just had something special and it would be hard to fit another song in right now. A song is not what we need right now."

Other people resented that and objected to it, so they started popping up and singing their songs. One wrote me a note to explain why she did it. She felt sympathy for that brother, felt like, you know, we need to be free to volunteer when we feel led. I agree. When you feel led, you need to be that free. But, you need to be free enough to ask for direction and advice because somebody with more responsibility than you is present who is responsible for the feeling of the whole crowd.

Those people who were criticizing me weren't considering that I might be led of the Spirit or I might be speaking from long experience and have reason for the decision I made. I guess they felt like I was just there to open and close the service. None of the songs went over after that. The service went on and we had a good service. At the close of the service I called on that brother that I had turned down earlier and said, "Bring your song up here, now. We need one right now."

He came up, sang his song and it blessed! It brought a blessing. There is something to be said for recognition of authority, God-given, God-placed authority. And cooperate; this is the main purpose of government and will always be in the kingdom of God throughout the ceaseless ages of eternity, the need for coordination, keeping a group working harmoniously together. When everybody is doing what he pleases, people are not working together. There's no teamwork; there's no team spirit in that condition when everybody does what's right in his own eyes, or does what pops into his head, what he feels like doing.

There needs to be some government, some coordination, some direction, keeping things running and keeping all the needs supplied. One of the jobs of the ministry is to see after the needs of the people in the church. If somebody is not watching closely, needs will fall through the cracks. People will be lost and their cases ignored because nobody is paying attention, nobody sees. But, somebody in authority feels responsible for all that.

So, God raises up men like Brother George Bragg and gives him the care, the position of a shepherd to take care of the flock. I admit we don't compare to Jesus as a shepherd. He's the Good Shepherd; we may be assessed as half-good ones, but we are doing as good as we can; we're being the best we can be. And, he's making us get better! We're all supposed to become like Jesus! Let's be working at that! The more you become like Jesus, the better off we'll all be and the better we'll all get along together.

Chapter 17

Different Kinds of Love

July 1, 2006

Some of us are in danger of what Jesus complained about in the second chapter of Revelation, about that first church there of the seven churches, the church at Ephesus. He said, "*...have left your first love.*" He wasn't talking about that feeling you had when you got up from the altar and you could hug and kiss everybody in town, not just everybody in the church. You would have been glad to hug everybody in town.

You had affection. You had affection at that time that you just loved everybody in an affectionate sense. Jesus knew that wouldn't last. You don't keep that kind of feeling continuously. That comes and goes and builds and fades. But there is another love that's constant. Many times that's what the King James Version of the Bible calls charity. But, it doesn't always translate it that way. Sometimes it's called love and you have to know the different kinds of love that it's referring to.

Most of the time throughout the New Testament, the word 'love' is what's described as charity in I Corinthians 13. That's the love that God had for the world in John 3:16. "*God so loved the world that he gave his only begotten Son.*" He wasn't talking about affection there. God had that goodwill. Goodwill is a good way to translate it. God had goodwill, so much goodwill for the world that he gave his only begotten Son. He had goodwill for all the sinners in the world. He'd like for them to get out of sin and live forever, so he gave his only begotten Son to die for their sins. "*Whosoever believeth in him should not perish but have everlasting life.*" That's a great manifestation of love and that is also called your '*first love*'. You got a dose of charity at the altar, but it's not an affection that is dependent upon your feeling, how you feel at the moment.

The reason you can still love your wife or your husband when you're mad at them is because you do have an element of charity in there. The people that can't do that can't stay together because their affections are not a reliable uniting force. The goodwill that the Bible commands us to have for one another is exactly what's he's talking about when he commands husbands to love their wives.

He's not talking about affection; He's not talking about romance. He's talking about goodwill, charity. We need that at home as bad as we need it in the church, don't we? And conversely, we need it in the church as bad as we need it in the home. We need that committed, determined, goodwill that says: "I will bear with you. I will put up with you. I will do you favors if you let me. I will watch out for you, watch for chances to help you. I will help you if I can." That's charity. That's godly love. That's the main love in the New Testament.

There are just a few scriptures about brotherly love and kindness, filial love as it's sometimes called. And God is capable of that too. God does have affections. That kind of love is what we call liking people. You know you wouldn't use that on your wife or your husband, but that's really what it means when you say "I love you". You're saying I like you; I like to be with you. I don't have just goodwill for you, I have desire for you; I desire to be with you.

And it's a similar kind of love among friends, brothers and sisters, family members. And this is one big family, isn't it? We've all got some brotherly love in here. But brothers and sisters can get mad at each other. Husbands and wives can get mad at each other. Parents and children can get mad at each other, but if they've got charity, they can get over being mad and go on being a family. You can quit being mad after a while and keep on being a family if you've got the right kind of love. Part of our reward for keeping that kind of love is that we can have, permanently and continuously, that other kind of love that we like.

We like to be liked, don't we? We appreciate goodwill, but we all want to be liked. And we want God to like us, don't we?

One of the old time preachers used to have as one of his favorite slogans "May the good Lord take a liking to you". Well if he was talking about charity, you'd answer "The Lord has always loved us; he's always had charity for us. Even before we got saved God loved us."

That doesn't mean he liked us. God doesn't like the sinner. One scripture says *"He's angry with the sinner every day." "Angry with the wicked,"* I think it said. God loves the wicked in the charitable sense. They are included in the world that he gave his Son for. That doesn't mean he likes them. And he may not like every Christian. He doesn't always like what we do is why. But may the good Lord take a liking to you. May you live in such a way that God can take a liking to you. We want God to like us because he can.

He's capable of emotions. In John 5, Jesus said the Father loves the Son and that was the word he used, that family type of love, that affectionate love.

God has affection for his Son. You don't blame him do you? I hope we all have some affection for Jesus. I'm afraid we don't have very much because we don't love him well enough. We've never seen him.

And we have enough trouble having affection and even goodwill for each other. John raised this puzzling question: *"If we can't love one another whom we can see, how do we think we can love God whom we don't see?"* It's hard to love people that you've never seen. But you might be able to do that if you learn enough about them. I've heard of people falling in love with people because of something they heard about them. Maybe they saw a picture or... This may be a fable, but I did hear about a woman that fell in love with the author of a book. You can fall in love with a concept you have, what you think a person is.

Whatever good you think about Jesus, he's better than what you think, and so our affection for him should grow and increase. The closer we get to him, the more we associate with him; the longer we live under his care, the more our affection should grow to him. It should manifest itself in a lot of gratitude, a lot of praise and thanksgiving and also a lot of faithfulness in these services, and in our service to him in every way of living right, serving one another.

So, I'm just saying that we've found something that satisfies. God has made my life worthwhile. Jesus Christ has made my life worthwhile. It's worth the things you suffer to be in church. It's worth what you suffer, the criticism and the exposure that you feel sometimes. You feel exposed as a Christian before this world, knowing that they deride you and they ridicule you for the way you live, for not *"running with them in the same excess of riot,"* Peter said. They think it's strange that you run not to the same excess of riot; they speak evil of you.

But what is excess of riot. We don't think of ourselves as rioters, do we? Rioters are people on the streets out there demonstrating, fighting the police. Rioting has an overtone of just partying, living it up, having a good time. That's how James is using it there. We don't run to the same excess of having a good time that the world does. All that they can think of is having a good time. This is a pleasure-mad world.

That's a common theological expression there: Pleasure-mad world. The populace of this country is bent on having more fun, having more pleasure, enjoying life. Even church people, they mostly want to hear a message on prosperity and blessings and the goodness of God and how God will forgive you and let you get by. They make it so easy to live for God that you don't have to go to any effort, go to any trouble or make any sacrifice. There is no mention of a cross in the prosperity message.

Jesus didn't preach a prosperity message. He preached a cross message, a sacrificing life. That was his challenge to people who are looking for something worthwhile. The way of the cross is worthwhile. He followed the way of the cross because it was worthwhile. AMEN! And he has reaped his reward. He's still reaping his reward for the things that he suffered and endured. Well I'm glad we're here tonight going on with God, carrying on this message.

Bro. Albert Cantor: Could you delve into that word "love" a little further, in this respect: Is it because iniquity shall abound, the love of many shall wax cold? Then over in II Thessalonians 2:10-11 he said 'because they have not a love for the truth, God shall send them a strong delusion that they may believe a lie and be dammed.'

Bro. Brown: Yeah, those are good scriptures to put with that one in Revelation 2 that talks about the man of sin he mentioned in verse 3. In verse 8 he calls him *'that wicked'* or lawless one and in verse 9 it's *"even him whose coming is after* (according to*) the working of Satan with all power and signs and lying wonders.*" Notice that. The man of sin comes with power. He has a lot of power and signs that make it look like he's really got something. A false prophet, a false leader, an antagonist to God can have enough success to make it look like he's got something, like he's got something from God.

Bro. Albert Cantor: I don't want to take you away from the thought I want you to deal with. Can you couple that with what it says about the two-horned beast in Revelation 13?

Bro. Brown: Well yes. All three of those beasts, you might say all four of them in *Revelations 13* have special power, but it mentions the two-horned beast that had power to call fire down from heaven and do wonders in the sight, or in the presence of, the first beast because he's building him up or building the image to the beast. He made an image that's just like it and he had power, he said, to give life to that image that it should both speak and cause all that wouldn't take the mark of the beast to be killed. So that's a power that is in the false system that is deception. And it deceives people that don't love the truth he says here in II Thessalonians.

Bro. Albert Cantor: Now couple that with Matthew 24.

Bro. Brown: Yeah. All right, we'll start with Matthew 24, just work through these. Which verse is that?

Bro. Albert Cantor: It's near the beginning of the chapter.

Bro. Brown: Where it says "*the love of many shall wax cold.*"

Bro. Albert Cantor: "Because iniquity shall abound".

Bro. Brown: Verse 12. Jesus is talking about deceptions that arise in religions. They affect the church. In verse 9 he said,

"They shall deliver you up to be afflicted and shall kill you and you shall be hated of all nations. Then shall many be offended, (He means many of you in the church shall be offended) *and shall betray one another and shall hate one another."* It's sad when a spirit like that gets in the church. Many false prophets shall rise. They rise up in the church. Even that great false prophet called the man of sin in II Thessalonians rose up in the fallen church in the latter days after it went into the wilderness. But he arose in the church after it became a false church. False prophets shall deceive many Christians, and because iniquity shall abound at a time like that in the church among church people, the love of many shall wax cold. This is a warning to you and me. We don't want to let our love wax cold.

Bro. Albert Cantor: Would that be a love for the truth?

Bro. Brown: Yes, it's a love for the truth. It's a love for the church.

Bro. Albert Cantor: For the vision?

Bro. Brown: Yeah, love for the vision.

Bro. Albert Cantor: Also, go back to verses 4 and 5 in that same chapter.

Bro. Brown: Verse 4 and 5: *"Jesus answered and said unto them take heed that no man deceive you."* Men are going to try to deceive you. *"For many shall come in my name saying I am Christ."* I take that to mean they're saying Jesus is Christ. It's just like the religious world out here today hollering Jesus is Lord. There are all kinds of movements out there proclaiming Jesus Is Lord. And you think, well they've got something. They're admitting and professing Jesus is Lord, but most of them that are saying that don't even have the baptism of the Holy Ghost.

That's the kind of people Paul said somewhere else; in *I Corinthians* wasn't it, that no man can say Jesus is Lord but by the Holy Ghost, meaning they can't say it truthfully? They're lying when they call Jesus Lord because they won't let him be their Lord. They won't even accept the Spirit that he died for them to have. *"If any man have not the spirit of Christ he's none of his."* The Holy Ghost is the spirit of Christ just as it's the spirit of the

Father. Christ gave us the spirit of the Father. So, it's the spirit of Christ. You have to have that before you can even be called one of his. Converted people are not his in that sense. They have been able to see the kingdom. They've got an opportunity to go through the gate into the kingdom, but that's another experience.

So, let no man deceive you and don't let your love wax cold for the truth and for the church that the truth is producing. Don't let your love of the church and its mission, its goal, wax cold. The Church at Ephesus, according to Revelation 2, had left their first love; they had let it fade. They no longer had the zeal that they had. That's what he's calling their first love. They loved God; they loved the truth; they loved the church. They loved the experience they had in the Spirit and they wanted to promote that; they were zealous for it.

Bro. Sowders himself warned us that after you have the Holy Ghost about twenty years, your zeal begins to fade if you're not careful, if you don't watch out and take measures to keep it alive. I thank God for these services we have here where people can pray through again and get an experience in the Holy Ghost frequently. You need to get it frequently.

I've never forgotten (I've vowed never to forget) the condition I got into and was into already when I came to the Body of Christ. I'd had the Holy Ghost about ten years when I got here and I had been out of church because my church went down, the church I was brought up in, and I went away to college. (Dangerous place! a good place to get away from church!) There wasn't any church, the kind I was used to at college and so I drifted away in the spirit. And I lost my—what is it that you have?—the enthusiasm, spirituality and zeal for the Holy Ghost? All that faded in me when I was there.

I came here with a cold spirit, so cold I could not pray through and talk in tongues. I don't know how many years it had been since I'd talked in tongues when I came to this church. And there are some of you here tonight maybe in that same condition; you haven't talked in tongues in five years or ten years. If you get that way, you're getting cold. You're in a bad condition.

I knew I was in a bad condition. I was singing in the boy's quartet. I was faithful in church. I was committed to this. I believed it. I loved the truth. I was rejoicing in revelation, but I couldn't break through in the Spirit and talk in tongues. And I got desperate. I was still married to my first wife, Hazel, at that time and I sort of shook her up about it one Sunday. I was talking to her about how I felt and she got the impression I was so discouraged I might quit church if something didn't happen.

I wanted to pray through. I needed help. I was discouraged. And so that night, that Sunday night, in the church service, we had one of those praying services, shouting services, and I got down to the front to pray through, got brethren around me to help me pray through.

I don't remember who all was around me. Brother George may have been one of them at the time. I can remember Tom Wilkerson. I know he was one of them. And old Brother John Kilough and Joe Singletary, those men were around me, trying to pray me through to get me to talk in tongues again. My wife told them, "You'd better pray him through tonight or it'll be too late; he's gone. You'd better get him through". So they stayed with me and worked hard with me and I was working hard. I tried to do what they told me just like a beginner down there praying for the Holy Ghost.

They'd tell me to say "Jesus!" Say "Hallelujah!" and holler "*GLORY!*" I did everything they told me. I was trying to get it again; I was having to pray through again. Brother Kilough wanted me to holler real loud. I never have had a holler. I don't have much of a holler. I holler as loud as I can and it sounds like I'm just putting on. But I was trying it, doing my best. They'd say, "Holler louder." Bro. Kilough would say, "You can do better than that! You can do better than that!" I'd holler as loud as I could. I just wouldn't come out loud.

Finally I heard him tell the others, "The boy can't holler." They gave up on that. Try something else; there's got to be some other way. But finally, thank God, I broke through that barrier and I could talk in tongues again. I made up my mind right there and then on the spot: "I'll never get in that shape again!" And I never have, thank God. I've stayed close enough to the Lord and frequent enough in the Spirit that I can pray through. I can touch the Holy Ghost. I can yield over. I can give up control of my tongue and let the Spirit use it. Thank God! So, you want to be careful about losing your first love. It's hard to get back your first zeal and enthusiasm. Now where were we?

"*In vain they worship me teaching for doctrines the commandments of men; for laying aside the commandment of God you hold the tradition of men as the washing of pots and cups and many other such like things ye do.*" That was part of their law. That was their interpretation and development, customs they derived from the Law of Moses, putting cleanliness and holiness on ritual. We don't want to make the mistake of proclaiming that a clean face on a sister is holiness. That does not constitute holiness, but it is a common result of holiness. A clean face is a reflection of holiness.

We don't want to make the mistake of thinking that the motions we go through, and certain dress standards that we hold, constitute holiness. They are signs of holiness. Signs can be counterfeited and copied and have no reality behind them. But if you have the reality, you ought to have the signs. So those are some of the things that we use to show our love, our zeal, our trust, appreciation for the Lord. Praise God! Well I've said enough tonight. I would like for somebody else to say something.

Mark 7:6: "*He answered and said unto them: well hath Esaias prophesied of you hypocrites, as it is written, this people honoreth me with their lips, but their heart is far from me.*"

Well anybody can get in that condition and it's true that's where the Pharisees were. Remember the Pharisees were in the church when Jesus got here. "*He came to his own,*" and some of his own were Pharisees. Some of his own were Sadducees. A couple of his own were high priests over that religious group. Caiaphas and Annas were some of Jesus' own. They were just the part of his own that wouldn't receive him. "*He came to his own,*" John said, "*and his own received him not.*" But a few of his own did receive him. Zacharias and Elisabeth were his own. Joseph and Mary were his own. Peter and John and Peter and Andrew, John and James, they were his own. Lazarus and Mary and Martha were his own and they received him. "*To them he gave power to become the sons of God.*" And here we are tonight. We're some of his own, thank God, and we've received him

So our heart is not far from him. We are honoring him with our lips but also with our heart. We're putting our heart where our lips are. Sometimes we put our money where our lips are, don't we? And we're putting ourselves into this. We're not just talking about it. We're trying to do it. We're living this. We're living this message. We're promoting it. We're sacrificing for it; suffering for it in some ways. But it's real, it's valuable. It's worthwhile.

We've always looked for ways to define charity. And all we've been able to do is describe it. But, goodwill is close as you can get in a Bible definition. If I've got a new thought, it might be just which scripture to apply to it like the one in Revelation 2. I don't know if we all understood which kind of love that applied to previously. I was trying to make something clear there: The difference between affection and goodwill or benevolence. Benevolence is another word that's a synonym for charity.

One of the points I like to make is that we all want the other kind of love. You know you enjoy being affectionate. You enjoy being in love. Young people especially get carried away with being in love, but we all enjoy a feeling of love. You don't always enjoy charity even when you're on the receiving end of it. If you know that you're on the receiving end of it, you may resent the very idea that "*they're having to bear with me, and suffer long.*"

There's no way you can really make up your mind to always be affectionate. You've got to make up your mind to stay together when your affections are strained and you don't feel affectionate. So don't build your marriage, or any other relationship, on just affection alone. But affection is one of the benefits you can have if you stay together on this other foundation of charity, kindness, forbearance, tolerance, putting up with people. If we can put up with each other, we can have a lot of affection at different times.

Brother Tom Peach: I'm thinking and wondering about two questions. I'll ask them both and you can answer them. If we're in a church or a marriage where the main thing that holds us together is charity, then it looks to me like we're in danger of having the kind of love that we're ultimately striving for. I know charity like you're explaining it, is vital and necessary, but I guess the second part of my question hooks on to it: What kind of love does an evangelist have for unsaved people? Have you thought of it in those terms?

Brother Brown: Well, yes, it's the kind of love God had for the world. It's charity. It's not affection for even a preacher that looks out over the people and weeps over their condition like Brother Sowders did in his early days. He was weeping over the condition of the people of God. He would look out there and think, "Those are God's people," and he would just break up and cry. But that was not brotherly love at work; it was charity at work, goodwill, and a desire for their welfare. A concern for their welfare, that's what an evangelist has. He sees the lost. They need God. He knows they need God. He knows God can help them, and he gets his feelings involved in it, but it's not what we call brotherly love because you have to know somebody to have affection for them. Some stranger that you have an abstract love for, that's charity. Do you see the difference?

Brother Albert Cantor: First of all, along this idea of love, the Biblical definition of love, how would you relate that to what John said in his epistles? You know he talks about loving God and then loving your brother.

Brother Brown: And then he said God is love.

Brother Albert Cantor: Yes

Brother Brown: That's I John. I think we can get all of this in the fourth chapter. Get all of these thoughts out of the fourth chapter, starting at verse 7. *"Beloved let us love one another."* That's charity he's advocating. *"For love is of God, and ev-*

eryone that loveth is born of God and knoweth God." That's mainly the kind of love God has for the world of people. Now, he has a different love. He has that kind of love for his Son, but he has a different kind of love also for his Son. But we don't get to experience much of that until we get pretty close to him.

We've got to start out here where we are. So let us love one another in this charitable sense. *"For that love is of God and everyone that loveth that way is born of God and knoweth God. He that loveth not, knoweth not God, for God is love."* He said that twice in this chapter. God is charity. That's what that's saying. It's not saying, *"God is affection, or God is brotherly kindness,"* but it's saying God is charity with all of the things that charity means. *"In this was manifested the love* (or charity) *of God toward us because that God sent his only begotten son into the world that we might live through him."* What a reward! What a blessing!

What if God hadn't loved us that way? What if God didn't have charity? Where would we be? *"Herein is love* (or charity) *not that we loved God, but he loved us."* We didn't know anything about God until somebody told us. But he already knew about us and loved us and *"sent his son to be the propitiation for our sins. Beloved if God so loved us we ought also to love one another. No man has seen God at any time. If we love one another* (in a charitable sense) *God dwelleth in us and his love* (or charity) *is perfected in us."* His goodwill is perfected in us. We have goodwill. *"Hereby know we..."* and everybody ought to look at all the occurrences of the word *"know"* in I John. The operative word in I John is "*know*".

There are so many things you can know. He told us how we know. Here's how we know that we dwell in him and he in us: *"because he hath given us of his Spirit."* His spirit is a spirit of love. The love of God is *"shed abroad in our hearts by the Holy Ghost"* he's given to us. *"And we have seen and do testify that the Father sent the Son to be the savior of the world."* Isn't that poetic? That's beautiful!

"Whosoever shall confess that Jesus is the Son of God, God dwelleth in him and he dwells in God. And we have known

and believe the love, (the charity*) that God hath to us,"* He said that *"God is charity and he that dwelleth in charity dwelleth in God and God in him. Herein is our charity,"* I'll keep reading it like that, *"made perfect that we may have boldness in the day of judgment because as he is, so are we in this world."*

Don't get confused by that now; don't lose sight of how he is. How is God? God is love. Back to verse 16: *"As God is, so are we."* God is love, or charity. We're supposed to be charity. We're supposed to manifest so much charity that people think that's what we are made out of. *"As he is, so are we in this world."* And if we're like that we can have plenty of boldness, be full of boldness in the Day of Judgment, because we won't be doing anything to offend the judge. We're friends with the judge. You can have boldness in the Day of Judgment.

There is no fear in love. Let's get the real meaning of that. He's not talking about fear of rattlesnakes, or fear of tigers, or fear of criminals with guns and knives in their hands. He's talking about fear of judgment. There's no fear of judgment in love because love doesn't do anything to offend. Love doesn't do things to offend God. Perfect love casts out fear of judgment, not fear of ghosts in the dark or heights, or whatever it is that you're afraid of. Perfect love doesn't cast those out. You have to do it some other way; that has to be dealt with another way. But perfect love casts out your fear of the judgment of God. You don't have to be afraid in the Day of Judgment. Fear has torment. He that feareth is not made perfect in love. He that fears the judgment of God is always afraid God is looking down his collar. "God's on my trail. I'm afraid God's going to get me."

I heard a quartet song on the radio one time. It was a real rhythmic and attractive sounding song but it went like this, "God's gonna get you for that, for that. God's gonna get you for that." All some people ever hear about is what God's going to do. He's going to get you for what you've been doing. As long as you're living in the fear that God's going to get you for something, it's because you're not made perfect in love. If you love God enough not to offend him, there's nothing for him to get you for. All you can sing is, "God's gonna bless you for that." Hallelujah! Amen! God's gonna bless you for that, for that; God's gonna bless you for that." Glory!

We love him because he first loved us, don't we? He's still talking about charity. God first had goodwill for us; now we've got goodwill for him. We *will* to please him now. We've got enough goodwill for him to try to please him. *"If a man say I love God and hates his brother he's a liar,"* because his brother belongs to God; his brother is a child of God. His brother is somebody that God loves. How can you love God and hate somebody that God loves? That's too contradictory. *"He that loveth not his brother whom he hath seen how can he love God whom he hath not seen? And this commandment,* (We'll reduce it now to a commandment) *have we from him that he who loveth God love his brother also."* That's a pretty good commandment, don't you think? Makes sense!

Brother Albert Cantor: I'd like for you to deal with the Song of Solomon. We have a picture of a relationship, it's my understanding, between Christ and his bride. It mentions love in many, many different passages, in fact all the way through the whole book. What I had in mind in one verse was "My beloved said unto me, arise up my love, my fair one and come away for the winter is past, the time of the rain is ceased and the time of bird singing is at hand, the voice of the turtle is heard in the land." Not necessarily only that scripture; I just happen to think of that particular one. But the description of the affection and the beauty that the bride sees in Christ, or her lover, and also in the beauty that Christ sees in his lover, or the bride, is all the way through.

Brother Brown: One of the problems of the Old Testament is it doesn't have these different words for love, so we fall back into the same difficulty we have in English where the same word means different things. But obviously, in the Song of Solomon, it is a romantic setting. And so affection is what's being described here. However, I'm having a hard time finding the word 'love' in the Song of Solomon as a verb. Most of the time in there, it's a noun. It's calling somebody 'my love'. That's a title you apply to somebody you're very affectionate toward, isn't it?

This person is my love; she is my love. It's obviously talking about affection there. I did find the verb somewhere here in the first chapter and I've lost it again. Yeah, "*The virgins love thee.*" I found '*loveth*' somewhere in there also. Most of the time, it's using it as a noun. What we're faced with, confronted with, in the Song of Solomon is an affection being taken as a type. It may be debatable whether it's a type of affection but I'm ready to admit that Christ is going to have affection for his people. There is going to be some affection between us and Jesus, but there's got to first be affection between you and me.

Brother Albert Cantor: That was my point in bringing this out, was the fact that all this that's been spoken in the New Testament, the object is to create an atmosphere where there can be a true affection between the bride and Christ, and Christ and his bride.

Brother Brown: Right. In the Song of Solomon the emphasis is not on duty; it's on pleasure, enjoyment. The enjoyment we feel in one another's company. Don't you enjoy this tonight? We're not just having to endure this, are we?

Brother Mark Riley: John 15. This has always intrigued me, verse 15, where he seems to make a transition from no longer calling him servant, but calls him friend. Is this the same principle we're talking about tonight, being able to enter into a deeper relationship?

Brother Brown: Yes. That is the principle we're talking about. In John 15:14-15, he said, "*You are my friends if you do whatsoever I command you.*" But then he said, "*Henceforth, I call you not servants for the servant knoweth not what his lord doeth, but I have called you friends.*" Notice who it is he's talking to here. He's not talking to everybody in the church. He was talking to those twelve men that were the closest to him. Do you realize some people in here are closer to God than others are? Can you accept that? Do you think we're all on the same level; that all have the same degree of relationship? Some people are just closer to the Lord than others are. Even among those twelve apostles, some of them were closer to Jesus than the rest were.

One of them apparently was closer to him affectionately than all the others were. John was the one, the disciple Jesus loved. Everybody knew him that way. That was his nickname: the one that Jesus loved. But I do want to recognize the principle that you can get closer to the Lord and have a closer relationship with him. Before Jesus finished that speech, he said, *"The Father himself loveth you."*

There's an interruption in the middle of chapter 16 where the disciples argued among themselves. But Jesus went back to talking to them again and in verse 27, he said, *"The Father himself loves you* (twelve apostles) *because you have* (affectionately) *loved me."* That's talking about affection in that verse; instead of charity, that's affection. Probably, mostly what we feel for Jesus is charity because we just have never been as close to him as those apostles were. But if you can develop an affection for Jesus, the Father can develop affection for you. Some people are going to affectionately love the Lord.

It's worth noting that that's not what the commandment calls for. You can't be commanded to have affection simply because you can't make yourself have affection. Affections are developed. You can make yourself have charity and that's why you're commanded to do it. Where are we now?

Brother Zinn: When you're talking about the commandments, Deuteronomy 5:29 could apply to us too as it did back in that day.

Brother Brown:_There is one where he said there was such a heart in them that they would fear me.

Brother Zinn: Yes, "such a heart in them that they would fear me and keep all my commandments always that it may be well with them and with their children forever." That could apply to us too, couldn't it?

Brother Brown: Can you feel the heart's cry in that first phrase there? Oh, that there was such a heart in them! He's saying, *"Oh, I wish that there was such a heart in them."* That's God talking. The previous verse says, *"The Lord heard the voice of your words when you spake unto me and said we can't stand to listen to this. The Lord said unto me I've heard the voice of the words of this people which they spoke unto me; they've well said all that they have spoken and oh how I wish there was such a heart in them that they would fear me and keep all my commandments always that it might be well with them and with their children forever."* And that's how it will be with us if we obey God.

Brother Greg Turner: Didn't Paul command that husbands have affections for their wives?

Brother Brown: No, that was my point. He wasn't talking about affection there. He's commanding you to have goodwill for her when you get to where you can't have affection anymore. If we do things right, we can have the affection that we crave. The affection we desire, that's a reward. It can be developed. Two great commandments; and again we're talking about goodwill. "*Thou shalt love the Lord thy God with all thy heart,*" but the word he used there was the word for charity. You shall have charity with God with all your heart. That's the way it comes down to us through the Greek, "*and your neighbor as yourself.*" Again, the commandment is for charity. The reward you'll get out of it, finally, is brotherly love, affection.

Chapter 18

Unity; the Soul That Sins Shall Die

August 18, 2007

The Lord doesn't have trouble talking; he just has trouble getting people to listen to him. There is a scripture in Habakkuk 2:20 that says, "*The Lord is in His holy temple, let all the earth keep silence before him.*" That doesn't mean quit praising him; it means quit arguing with him; quit talking back. Let him have his say; let him have his way. We honor the Lord tonight. We want to let him have his say in our midst. We respect and join in with his effort to unite a people in his name.

We keep having to prove to people that unity is important. Some of you remember that I've been saying, for years, and getting flack over it, that the unity of the Body is more crucial than the purity of the Body. I say that as a way of emphasizing the unity of the Body, not denying the need for purity in the Body. I'm just showing how crucial unity is. In the Lord's Prayer—I mean the one in John 17—this is the prayer Jesus prayed on his own behalf. The one in Matthew 6 is the one he taught us to pray for ourselves. He prayed this one for himself, but it was about us.

What he prayed for the most in there was that his people would be one. He started praying for them in the eighth and ninth verses and in the eleventh verse, he said, "*I am no more in the world, but these are in the world and I come to thee, Holy Father. Keep through thine own name those thou hast given me that they may be one as we are.*" And in the twentieth verse he said, "*Neither pray I for these alone,*" talking about the twelve, or just the eleven at that moment, who were still with him, "*but for them also who shall believe on me through their word.*" We fit in under that covering. We believe on him because of the word, the testimony, the witness, the preaching that those apostles did.

Verse 21: "*That they all may be one as thou Father art in me and I in thee, that they also may be one in us, that the world may believe that thou hast sent me.* "

Verse 22: "*And the glory thou gavest me, I have given them that they may be one even as we are one.*"

So, he was laying heavy emphasis on that 'oneness', the unity of the disciples. That's what creates a church, disciples getting together. The town can be full of disciples staying home, scattered, going about their business, never getting together. You don't have a church that way. But when the disciples get together and support one another in worshipping and serving God, then you have a church.

That was Jesus' vision. We talked about that today in the meeting up at Goodrich. The church was built on the foundation of the solid rock, Jesus Christ. He said this about it: On this truth he was calling a rock, he said, "*I will build my church.*" That was Jesus' intent, his plan, his purpose to build a church. But that church has to be together. If it's not together, it's no longer a church, it's just a scattered flock of disciples that are not a flock anymore; they're just members of the flock.

Something in that first song we sang was about "Though I stumble o'er my trials and tests, please hear me when I call, for you know I want to go all the way." Yes, it was about pressing on.

Jesus was praying here, not to keep us from stumbling; he wasn't praying for our purity, directly, although he did make this point in there that he was wanting God to keep us from the evil that's in the world. That has to do with purity. But, he didn't dwell on that like he dwelt on the thought of oneness, unity. The point is, we can stumble and still be together. We can fall and get up again; we can sin and repent again and still be together and be a church.

But when we decide to divide up and stop being together, we quit being a church. We might become two churches or three churches or five churches or no church because nobody is coming together. Some churches get scattered to the wind because there are not any groups of them or any splinters of them anymore. The unity is the basic part of the identity of a group of people that constitute what we call a 'body'.

The apostles, especially the apostle Paul, developed that analogy because it's the most apt example of the unity of a group of people united under a head. That's what the church is; it's a group of disciples united under the headship of Christ. Christ is the head of the church. And those disciples, that church which is under his headship, becomes his body by being under him as the head. So, we're the members of his body.

Consequently, when you are talking about the church, you are talking about the Body. It's the same thing; those are just different descriptions of it. We have come to use heavily that term 'body' in our times because it so aptly describes the cooperation that's called for from us. Every member of the body contributes to the welfare of the body; every member of the body has something to do for the rest of the body.

That's the way the church of Jesus Christ is. The term 'church' doesn't convey that aspect. Even calling it a 'family' doesn't convey that aspect as clearly as calling it a 'body' does. Maybe we do overuse the term, but it's because it's such a useful term. It says more than any other term identifying the disciples of Jesus Christ. I'm glad to be a part of those disciples tonight. Praise the Lord!

We had a good meeting promoting the unity of the Body of Christ up in Goodrich today. Brother Pedro Reyes, the pastor up there, Brother Emmons here, the overseer. We appreciate Brother Emmons. He surprised us with a visit tonight. It's an honor to have him on the platform. His ministry, his encouragement, his help are blessings. Brother Gadbury came and helped with the meeting. And, we had a lot of our Spanish language group up there; the two Rodriguez families and the Cortinas were there. Sister Cortina got blessed and ran the aisles and started a trend. Little Sister Rosie was there with her flute, playing in the band. I tell you, that Goodrich band is coming along; they are learning fast. They have got to the point where they provide the needed music for that church. That's always been one of the weaknesses of that little, new church. It's still a relatively new church. They've had to grow their own music. They had to plant it, sprout it, water it and grow it, but they've finally grown a nice little band with their young people. They can play and help bring in the Spirit. Praise God!

Brother Alonzo was a home-run hitter today. He really got in the channel. He got up and preached and brought the power down. He got hooked up and really put the word over! We were all in a spirit of unity; we all had the same purpose. We were working on Jesus' work.

We're doing Jesus' work in the earth. Paul said, "*We are ambassadors for Christ.*" That means we are representing him and speaking for him. If we don't speak the right things, we'll misrepresent him. If we speak the right thing but don't have his authority to do it, it will be wasted. But, we're speaking for Christ when we say to the whole world, "*Be ye reconciled to God.*" We say it still to people in the church that are not fully reconciled to God.

If you're not submitted to the will of God, you are not fully reconciled to God. You don't have complete peace with God as long as you're arguing with him. He may be there in his holy temple and you may be there too, but you may be disagreeing with what God is doing and saying. It's just not natural for the natural mind to approve and like what God decides and what he calls for, but it is pleasant to the spirit. It's pleasant to the soul that's in the Spirit.

It's necessary that we get our souls into the Spirit and out of the flesh, otherwise, when the day of our death comes... Here's what Solomon says happens in the day of death. "*The body returns to the dust from whence it was taken and the spirit returns to God who gave it.*" That means you give up the spirit when you die. Now, that means a lot of things. It means some things that some of you never thought of before.

One thing it means is that some of you think you have to have this Holy Ghost to get a resurrection and you think you are guaranteed a resurrection because you've got it. You've got the Holy Ghost that resurrects; that is the power of the resurrection. You are that right about it, but you've forgotten one crucial point there; that is, if you die short of perfection and you're not ready to move into a new body, then you give up the ghost.

Remember, Jesus gave up the ghost. That means you give up the spirit. When you give it up, you don't have it anymore. When you die and your spirit returns to God who gave it, you don't have it anymore. Your Holy Ghost is indestructible; it doesn't die. It goes back to God who gave it. But if it doesn't take you with it, you've lost it. That's why I keep making this point on the resurrection: It's not *the Holy Ghost you've got* that will bring you up in the resurrection, it's *the Holy Ghost God has* that does that job.

God doesn't die! His spirit doesn't go anywhere! (ha, ha, ha!) He keeps it! It stays with him! He's always got the Holy Ghost! HALLELUJAH! I don't know how many tongues he can talk in, but he talks in all of them! Praise the Lord! He's the origin, the source of the Holy Ghost! That feels good, doesn't it? The Spirit doesn't die.

But, to get back to our description of ordinary, mortal death when the spirit returns to God and the body returns to dust, Solomon didn't even bother to mention what happens to the soul, where it goes. The body goes to the graveyard; the spirit returns to God. Where does the soul go? You know we're not *just* a body; we're not *just* a spirit; but we're also a soul. In fact, that is what we *are* and those other things are things that we *have*. You are a soul living in a body; that body is your house.

The Bible calls it your house, your tabernacle, because it is just temporary, but when you get a permanent one, we'll call it a 'mansion'. Jesus said, "*In my father's house are many mansions. I go to prepare a place for you,*" there in that house where those mansions are. So, those mansions are new bodies that you can get. You can get one and I can get one; nobody can get more than one. There's enough for all of us that qualify; there's enough to go around.

But if you're not ready for that body, you can't make the transition. Then what happens when you give up the spirit of life, give up the ghost and the soul dies? Well, the body dies. You know what becomes of the body when it dies. It deteriorates; it crumbles away back to its atoms. It turns into other chemicals and goes back to the dust, the ground that it was made out of. Your body's made out of ground, just like Adam's body was.

Adam was made out of the ground, initially, but after that he had to eat things that were made out of the ground to keep his body alive. We got here a little different way than he got here, but we're in the same condition. We have to eat things made out of the ground because that's what we're made out of. Things that come out of the ground are what keep our bodies alive. Finally, nothing will keep our bodies alive; they wear out and crumble away, back to the dust they were made out of.

But, what becomes of the soul? You can drive up and down the freeways on Sunday mornings and see the signs on the marquees, "Come and hear Dr. So-and-So preach on 'WHERE ARE THE DEAD?' How many remember hearing Brother Patton say, "Silly, they're dead."? But, people don't believe that, so they preach sermons about where the dead are. They don't believe what the Bible said, *"The soul that sinneth, it shall die." "The wages of sin is death."*

When a soul dies it doesn't go anywhere because it's not made out of anything. The soul is the process of being conscious. It's the total mental processes of a person. I compare it to the flame of a fire. You know what a fire is made out of, don't you? It's made out of fuel and air. Those are analogous to the body and the spirit. When the fuel and the air get together and start combining in a chemical reaction, it's an ongoing process that creates a flame. You can't stop the process and hold the flame in your hand. When you stop the process the flame quits being there. And so, the fire goes out.

Nobody preaches sermons about where the fires are that have gone out. Where are all the fires that have gone out? They're not anywhere. They're just out. They're not outside; they're not just out of sight. They're out of existence, that's where they are. They went out of existence; they no longer exist.

That's what happens to a soul that goes out. The soul is a living process and when it quits living, it quits being, just like the fire. When the fire quits burning, it quits being. That's why

Solomon didn't tell you where the soul goes; it doesn't go anywhere.

What the Bible says about the dead is: *"They are NOT!" "Rachel weeping for her children because they ARE NOT!"* They *ARE NOT* in heaven; they *ARE NOT* in hell. They are not anywhere; they are not anything! They *ARE NOT*! The soul *IS NOT* until God starts up that living process, again.

You know, you can light a fire that's gone out, if you can believe it's that same fire. Once it's burnt up the fuel, it might not be the same fire. But, God can start up the same fire again. He can start up the same soul again. That's what he does in the resurrection. In the New Testament, Lazarus lay down and died one day. Lazarus, the brother of Mary and Martha, got sick and died. His fire went out; his soul went out. They took his body to the graveyard to let it return to the dust. His spirit had already returned to God who gave it.

But, the Son of God came along and stood in front of that tomb and called that man's name with a God-given authority and the spirit came back from God who gave it! He gave it again and healed that dead body! It came alive and Lazarus' mind started working again; it came into existence again. God *'lit him up'* again but he didn't bring him into everlasting life; He just brought him back into the natural life he had just left. Sooner or later, he had to leave it again.

There's going to be a resurrection and God's going to bring people up and they're never going to die again! He's going to light their fire and they will burn forever! Praise the Lord! That's *his* power that does that! It's not the power he gives you! It's the power he reserves to himself! You don't resurrect yourself! God resurrects you!

Now, there is a little theological controversy over the resurrection that we call 'getting saved'. That's really what happens to you, at least when you get the Holy Ghost. You get resurrected out of trespasses and sins. The Bible says we've been dead in trespasses and sins and had to be resurrected.

But, the people who think man is so depraved...(end of tape; skip in dialogue)...can a dead man assist at his own resurrection? Well, not in any ordinary sense. However, the scripture does say this: *"Awake thou that sleepeth and arise from the dead,"* (That sounds like something for you to do) *"and Christ shall give thee light."* So, in that sense, the man that is dead in trespasses and sins can assist at his own resurrection. And, he can prevent his own resurrection.

A similar case to the one we describe in the case of Lazarus, Luke 8:52. It is worth noting there how Jesus handled that situation because he was in the midst of unbelievers. I think he carried three believers in with him when he went in to raise that girl from the dead. He was confronted with a houseful of unbelievers. The girl had died and they had already got the funeral party there. They hired people, and others volunteered, probably, to come and weep. They had professional weepers, professional mourners that helped supply the mourning for funerals in those days.

Everybody was in the house, weeping. Verse 51: *"When he came into the house he suffered no man to go in save Peter, James and John and the father and mother of the maiden."* But, there were other people already there at the house and they were all weeping. Verse 52: *"And all wept, and bewailed her; but he said, Weep not; she is not dead, but sleepeth."*

He put out this challenge to the crowd of people to get them to admit she was dead because he was fixing to bring her back from the dead and he didn't want them to say, "Oh, she was just asleep all the time; she wasn't really dead." So, he beat them to the punch; he suggested, *"She's not dead; she's just asleep." "They laughed him to scorn, knowing that she was dead." (Verse 53)* They laughed off Jesus' suggestion that she was just asleep.

Jesus put out all the unbelievers. He didn't put out Peter, James and John, or the father and mother. But, he put out the unbelievers that were making fun of him. Then, he took the little girl by the hand and called, saying, *"Maid, arise." (*Get up!) *"And her spirit came again."* She had given up the ghost but when he said that, her spirit, her ghost, came again and lit her fire. The process of living began again in her body and her brain, her thinking processes started working again and there was that soul! That's the same thing he said about Lazarus, *"Our friend, Lazarus, sleepeth."*

The disciples said, *"Well, that's good. He's been sick. If he's sleeping he will probably get well. He must have taken a turn for the better."* Jesus had to tell them plainly: *"Lazarus is dead. He's sleeping the sleep of death."*

Just like when you take a match and strike it, you have a flame there and you give a puff of air and blow it out. It's gone! It didn't go anywhere; it didn't leave; it just quit existing. But, you can touch another match to it and light that same matchstick again, have it burning again. God lit up that little 'matchstick' and her flame was alive again! We don't know what her future held; we hope she got saved; we hope she got in the church after the day of Pentecost. She was twelve years old at that time and Jesus hadn't finished his ministry. Maybe she heard some of his sermons after that.

She had been brought back into life for the rest of her opportunity to qualify for one of those new bodies. She wasn't ready for a new body. She hadn't died and gone to heaven, like the preachers all say. She had just died and hadn't gone anywhere. Her fire went out.

But, there was a possibility of her getting in a condition that when her body died, her soul would not die. Read Matthew 10:28. You can't do without that one. You'll never understand moving out a live soul without Matthew 10:28. This is Jesus talking: *"Fear not them which kill the body but are not able to kill the soul."*

Most of the religious world takes that to mean it is true of everybody, everybody's soul: *"Don't worry about anybody getting killed because nobody can kill the soul."* That's not what he's saying; he's talking to believers. You believers out here, if you're in the right place with God, all the way in Christ, people can kill your body but still cannot kill your soul.

That's not what happens to most people when they get killed. When unbelievers get killed, it kills their soul because their soul is dependent on the body. But if your soul is no longer dependent on the body, if it's living by the Spirit, then people can kill your body and your soul won't die. That's what he's saying here. That means, 'move out a live soul'. They are not able to kill the soul.

Somebody's gonna get in that condition! How about you? How about me? Let's qualify! Let's get all the way in Christ! Let our lives be hid with Christ in God! Hallelujah! Let me read you again the condition of the people that are in Christ. In Colossians 3:1: *"If you then be risen with Christ..."* already! He's talking about where we are ***now***. We've been buried with Christ in baptism; we've been resurrected with Christ in that Holy Ghost resurrection out of trespasses and sins. So, we are risen with Christ since we got the Holy Ghost.

"If ye then be risen with Christ..." That's your resurrection. That is your first resurrection. That is what the Bible calls the first resurrection. It doesn't mean when that happens to you that you are the first person who ever got 'lit up' again. It means you got 'lit up' into everlasting life*! "He that believeth on me,"* Jesus said, *"hath everlasting life."* Now, beware that you don't lose it!

But, when you got the Holy Ghost you did get everlasting life. Adam had everlasting life one time. *"If ye then be risen with Christ, seek those things which are above where Christ sitteth on the right hand of God."* Quit seeking these things that are here below, things of the earth, things of the world, carnal, natural pleasures. Because they will cause you to lose your everlasting life; they will lead you into sin.

"Set your affections on things above, not on things on the earth," because you are dead, already! You're already dead! You died in Holy Ghost baptism, buried with Christ in baptism. And, your life is *"hid with Christ in God,"* already, if you will keep it there. Don't let anybody find it! Don't pull your life out of God and show it around to this world that's liable to take it away from you. Keep your life hid with Christ in God! Nobody can get in there to get it away from you!

I got that revelation from C.N. Patton. He said, "If your life is hid with Christ in God, how can anybody get in there to take it away from you?" If anybody takes your life away from you it's because they were able to find it. It wasn't hid in God. It was out here in the world somewhere, where they could find it.

Question—not heard clearly

Well, in a way, yes. He said that about himself when he said he laid down his life. No man was able to take it from him but he gave it up voluntarily. He wasn't saying there that he committed suicide. It just meant he was in a condition where he could live forever. But, he laid that down and took our sins upon himself and died. He died in our place! He died for our sins! He who needed not to die; who had no reason to die! The wages of sin is death but he had never sinned! He hadn't earned the wages of sin! But, he took it for us. He made the way for us to get in the condition that he was in where we don't have to die, either!

After you get the Holy Ghost, if you let it do everything for you it is capable of doing, then you don't have to die again. You've already died and been resurrected. *"Blessed and holy is he that hath part in the first resurrection; on such the second death hath no power."* How does it feel to be in that condition? Glory! Well, I'm going to leave that with you.

We're glad to have Brother Emmons here tonight. We want to leave some room for him. I just wanted to testify about the meeting up at Goodrich today and what a good time we had. I know that it's important that we consider people's language problems. A lot of people are saying that the Spanish-speaking people and all the other immigrants need to learn English and get it over with. But, you can't do that instantly.

Furthermore, while this group here is learning English, there are new ones coming in across the border all the time. Some of them are already Pentecostal people when they get here and others become Pentecostal soon after they get here. So, there's going to be a steady supply of people in this country that can't talk English who need to hear the Gospel in their language.

The Book of Revelation tells us that there are going to be people before the throne of God 'out of every kindred and tongue'. That means language and nationality. Hallelujah! So, we're doing everything we can; we're experimenting; we're praying; we're seeking God; we're trying things to meet the needs of God's people. I want everybody's needs to be met. We have to find a way. God has to show us how to meet everybody's needs. He meets a lot of our needs through these ministers.

Thank God for the men on the platform who have the call of God on their lives and have dedicated themselves to serving God and serving his people. They are all worthy of honor and we want to honor people that God honors.

Let's go to prayer here before we go further.

Chapter 19

Mercy; the Power of the Air

January 13, 2008

I'm glad for the Lord's mercy. We, I guess, need to be reminded, or remind ourselves of our need for mercy, lest we forget. We can forget how much we need mercy and take on the wrong spirit. It's so easy to take on the wrong spirit and hard to keep the right spirit. We have the Word of God, but it's hard to live it. It's very interesting to talk about it, but it's hard to live it.

The proudest man I ever knew could give a good Bible lesson on humility. He just didn't see that he didn't have any. He knew how to talk about it; he just didn't know how to have it. There are two hundred, sixty-one verses in the Bible that use the word 'mercy'. The first one is in Genesis 19 where Lot was delivered from Sodom. The last one is in Jude. Both of them pertain to life, mercy with life. In Genesis 19:19, Lot said to the angel that was trying to get him out of the city, *"Behold now, thy servant hath found grace in thy sight and thou hast magnified thy mercy which thou hast shown unto me in saving my life."*

If somebody saves your life, that's magnified mercy. That's great mercy; that's bountiful mercy to save your life. Mercy can be shown in lesser ways. And, we are to be full of mercy; we are to be a merciful people, continually showing mercy. But, these are outstanding measures of mercy. This is the mercy God has measured out to us to save our lives. That scripture in Jude mentions Jesus and the mercy he has bestowed upon us. Jude, verse 21, *says, "Keep yourselves in the love of God, looking for the mercy of our Lord Jesus Christ unto eternal life."* That word, 'unto' means 'the results of'. The mercy of the Lord Jesus results in, or produces, eternal life.

That's how great his mercy is! It's magnified! Jesus' mercy is magnified unto us to produce eternal life. The angel gave Lot mercy enough to save his natural life, his temporary life. Jesus gave his life in mercy to give us eternal life. So, it's a human subject. We're dealing with a race of people that needs mercy. Every human being has need of mercy.

Now, I was just wondering, Brother Phillips, if they ever talk about mercy in heaven. Do the angels ever talk about that? There's no mention of mercy connected with the angels except when they are bringing it to us. The angels don't need mercy, at least not now, so it's not a subject that's even relevant to them; they are not in need of mercy. But, all human beings are in need of mercy.

It's possible to forfeit mercy. We need to know how to obtain mercy. "*Blessed are the merciful,*" Jesus said, "*for they shall obtain mercy.*" You get mercy by being merciful. James said, "*He shall have judgment without mercy that has shown no mercy.*" See, mercy is connected with judgment even though it is not a function of judgment. It is something to balance judgment. Somewhere, it says, "*Mercy rejoices against judgment.*" Mercy can nullify, or set aside, judgment at the discretion of the judge. Only a judge can give mercy.

So, when you're giving mercy, when you are being merciful, you are acting, in some measure, as a judge. You are deciding or concluding that somebody is wrong. The only person to give mercy to is somebody that needs it. They need it because they've done something wrong. Whoever does an offense to you, commits an offense against you, you can show mercy to that person.

Jesus included that in the Lord's Prayer: "*Father, forgive us our trespasses as we forgive those who trespass against us.*" This is an act of mercy; it's not an act of judgment. Condemnation is the act of judgment but forgiveness is the act of mercy. We can get condemned. Let's see, how did somebody put it in the New Testament that "*we should not be condemned with the world*"? Is that in First Corinthians where Paul was talking about "*judging ourselves that we should not be condemned with the world?*" I need that one. Let's find that.

He said, back in verse 31 that, if we judge ourselves then we wouldn't have to be judged. We would already be judged if we judged ourselves. But when we are judged because we didn't judge ourselves, we are *"chastened of the Lord that we should not be condemned with the world."* All this is function of judgment.

Chastening is an act of judgment but it is short of condemnation. We're *"chastened of the Lord"* so we won't have to be condemned along with the world. God doesn't chasten the world, he just condemns it. That's the ungodly. *"The ungodly shall not stand in the judgment..."* Judgment doesn't really apply to them; they are already under the judgment that was passed upon Adam.

All this began in the Garden of Eden, as far as the human family is concerned. Really, we're not given much information about the angelic world and what may have happened in the distant past there. But we do have, we're confronted with an evil spirit in the Garden of Eden, an evil being. That was that spirit that came upon the human family because of a temptation and a deception. The tempter, sometimes he's called a tempter and sometimes he's called a deceiver.

Those are two ways we can be trapped. Adam was trapped one way and Eve, the other. Eve was deceived by the deceiver, but Adam was tempted by the tempter. He was presented, indirectly, with a temptation from that evil spirit. That temptation came in the form of his wife, but the temptation was to disobey God in both those cases. But Eve was deceived; she was deceived by false doctrine. This is what shows the importance of doctrine to the church.

It's significant that we've all been nailed in place in the Body of Christ by doctrine. And, if we don't have an interest in doctrine, if it hasn't taken hold in our minds and our vision, then we're not really *'fastened in a sure place'*. We may drift out. Not everybody can get fastened in the church because they don't comprehend the doctrines; they don't take them seriously.

It was false doctrine that brought the first deception to the human race. That deception succeeded in producing a temptation to the person who was not deceived. Adam couldn't be deceived; he had too much truth. Somewhere in the New Testament it says,

"*...the very elect would be deceived, if it were possible.*" What keeps it from being possible is the very elect know too much to be deceived. But, they still have to guard against temptation.

"*Every man is tempted when he is drawn away of his own lust and enticed.*" Don't forget 'enticed' there. But, he can't be enticed if he doesn't have lust. Every man is drawn away of his own lust when he is enticed by something that appeals to that lust. He may not be deceived; he may know he's doing wrong. Therefore, he gets the greater condemnation.

Adam was held responsible more than Eve was. The serpent was held responsible more than Adam was. But, there is a history of that relationship: he is a more ancient figure than Adam. This brought the need for mercy into the human family for what happened at the Garden of Eden.

The children of Adam, his first two sons, were godly men in the sense of being religious men. Both Cain and Abel were religious. One of them had the right spirit, the other didn't. The wrong spirit can only produce false religion. It takes the right spirit to have true religion.

Abel had the true religion and God had respect to him and his works; his sacrifice was his works. God had respect to him because his works were righteous and his brother's works were evil. But Cain had a knowledge of God and, up to that point, a relationship with God. It seems that God communicated with those boys. There's no hint that God ever communicated with Adam again after he threw him out of the Garden of Eden because God did not apply mercy to Adam. God applied judgment to Adam.

The law that He had pronounced was, "*In the day that you eat thereof, you shall surely die.*" When he ate thereof, the judgment was pronounced and he was driven out of the Garden lest he should partake of the Tree of Life and live forever. So, his judgment was pronounced and no mercy extended to him. But, mercy was extended to his sons because they had not committed the deed. They had not received the law the same way Adam had and had not rebelled against it in the same way. So, they were not held accountable for the whole race.

So, God was dealing with those two boys. And, they were having church, in a fashion. But Cain did not have the right spirit, so he did not have the right works. When God tried to correct him, he was not correctable. This didn't all happen instantly, but there was time for reasoning and prayer and consideration and meditation to take place.

In the fourth chapter of Genesis, it says, *"Unto Cain and to his offering God had not respect and Cain was wroth, very angry."* Second mistake! First mistake was offering the wrong sacrifice; the second mistake was getting mad when it didn't work! When we do the wrong thing and don't get the right results we get mad, usually, if we've got the wrong spirit. See, that shows the wrong spirit to begin with. If he would get angry because God would not respond to him the way he wanted him to, who was he mad at? God!

He was mad at his brother too, but he was mad at God. Cain was very wroth and his countenance fell. That means his smile turned to a frown; a cloud came over his face. And the Lord said to Cain, *"Why are you angry? Why is your countenance fallen? If you do well, won't it be accepted?"* In other words, if you do right, you will get the right results just like Abel did. It wasn't predestined that Cain would fall and receive a curse. He had a chance to avoid that. *"If you do well, you will be accepted."* If you don't do well, sin lies at the door. You're just about in danger of doing something worse than what you've already done.

"Sin lies at the door and unto thee shall be his (or, its) *desire."* Remember, there's no word for 'it' in the Hebrew language; there is just a pronoun. So, sin is considered a masculine noun and gets a masculine pronoun. *"Unto thee shall be his* (or its) *desire and thou shalt rule over him."* We are to rule over that desire to sin. We were born with a desire to sin, a desire for selfishness.

Evidently, Abel had gotten control of his sinful desire already and was obedient to God. He was in the right spirit; he was keeping his sinful desires in check. Cain was more wayward, more independent, willful, strong-headed. So, he didn't take God's advice. God told him what to do.

If God judges people, it's because he has given them a law and they've broken the law. God laid down the law to Cain, here, *"Do right and you will get the right results. Don't let sin get control of you; you get control of sin."* But, he didn't take that advice. He came to talk with Abel, his brother, and it came to pass that when they were in the field, Cain rose up against his brother. A fight broke out and he slew him; he killed his brother. Curiously, the Lord kept on talking to Cain. He got his attention with this question: *"Where is your brother?"*

This is one of God's significant questions. It's worth studying God's questions to people in the Bible. The first one we find is where he asks Adam, *"Where are you? Adam, where are you?"* That means, *"Why aren't you here where you're supposed to be? I'm looking for you. I expected you here. Why aren't you here? Where are you?"* Here, he says to Cain, *"Where is your brother?"*

Cain was supposed to know where his brother was. His cynical response, showing his attitude, *"Am I my brother's keeper? Am I supposed to know about my brother?"* Well, from the context, it's clear that God does expect him to know about his brother! He expects us to know about each other! He expects us to help take care of each other! I *am* my brother's keeper! We *are* to be responsible to each other! We *are* to take an interest in each other!

God said to him, *"The voice of thy brother's blood cries to me from the ground."* Now, he says, *"You are cursed from the earth, etc."*

Cain said to the Lord, *"My punishment is greater than I can bear."* He's looking for more mercy. *"Behold, Thou hast driven me out this day from the face of the earth and from thy face shall I be hid."* Isn't that a clue that he had a relationship with God? He hadn't been hidden from God's face up until that point. He was used to having some relationship with God and feeling accepted in the church services, but from now on, he knows that God won't respond to him anymore. God hides his face from him.

So, God's mercy is not automatic; it's not a function of law. There's no Law of Mercy. Mercy is at the discretion of the judge. But when we find ourselves in the position of judge, Jesus warns us that if we don't commonly apply mercy, then when we're on the other side of the see-saw facing our judge, he may not apply mercy to us.

Mercy begets mercy. *"Blessed are the merciful for they shall obtain mercy."* We're all going to need some more mercy. We need mercy from each other; we need mercy from God. Since we need mercy from each other that gives us all a chance to practice mercy. I need mercy from you; you need mercy from me. When I see you need mercy from me I have a chance to give mercy because it's at the discretion of the judge. The person who needs the mercy doesn't get to decide whether mercy is applied, or not. The person who is in the position of the judge is the one who gets to decide whether we use mercy in this case, or not.

This is one of the problems we have in civil judgment today. The legislatures keep trying to write laws that nail everything down and have specified penalties for every detail and don't leave any judgment up to the judge. I guess the reason for that is we're dealing with human, fallible judgment. We don't trust them to administer justice or mercy fairly. The lawmakers try to make the law cover everything. You can't make the law cover everything. Not even God could do that.

That's why he had to have judges. He recognized that in the Law of Moses, as detailed as it is, six hundred, thirteen commandments and that's a trivial number, a drop in the bucket. But that was a detailed law in its day, the Law of Moses, all of those commandments. God recognized in there that you couldn't cover every case with the law. There will always be a new circumstance cropping up. So, he told them through Moses in Deuteronomy that when you have a case that's too hard for you... He had already told them to have judges; they were expected to have judges and elders in all their cities. But, he said, *"When you have a case that's too hard for you in your hometown, your locality, and you can't figure it out, then,"* he said, *"you are to take that case to a higher court, up to the place which the Lord shall choose."* God chose places in Israel throughout their history where judges would reside.

When they got into Canaan's land, it became Shiloh. They put the tabernacle at Shiloh for four hundred years. People came there where the high priest was to get their questions settled and to get problems dealt with when the local elders and judges couldn't work it out. Later on, the seat of authority was moved to Jerusalem when David established the capital there and brought the Ark of the Covenant into that city.

His son, Solomon, finally built the temple there in that city, Jerusalem. That became the place the Lord had chosen to put his name. All hard cases came to that territory. But there are always cases that you can't decide just on the basis of law what you should do. So, sometimes we have to pray about things, don't we? How to handle any case and what kind of decision we're going to make about it and how much mercy to apply and has mercy been exhausted, yet?

Some people may exhaust our mercy. We apply mercy over and over until it becomes evident that the person is incorrigible, not going to change. There are examples throughout the scriptures where God did not extend mercy because mercy had already been surpassed. Adam was one of those cases. Cain was another. It appears God had disowned Cain, disfellowshipped him although He did not take his life right then. It's interesting to note that God did not allow anybody else to take vengeance on Cain.

They had not established the death penalty in human judgment, yet. Before the flood they did not exercise the death penalty. Cain was the example of that. He was the first test case. God did not exercise the death penalty upon him and forbade anybody else to do it. That's why He set a mark upon him. He set a mark upon him lest anybody find him and decide to kill him because of what he had done. Seven generations later, one of Cain's descendants used that fact to justify his act in self-defense.

He killed somebody in self-defense. That was Lamech who had his two wives, Adah and Zillah. He said, *"I have killed a young man for wounding me, hurting me.*" He was pleading self-defense. He said, "*If they would take vengeance for Cain sevenfold, if anybody tried to judge him, surely they would take vengeance for me seventy fold.*" What he was saying there was, "I had more right than Cain did. If Cain got that much mercy, I will surely get seven times as much mercy for what I did because I was justified by self-defense."

That's the principle of legal self-defense. But after the flood came, God made it a law in Noah's family: "*Whoever shall shed man's blood, by man shall his blood be shed.*" That has been God's principle in dealing with the human race. It's something he requires of us, a guideline he's given us. The death penalty is justified if we can administer it justly. The reason I'm having trouble now with our use of the death penalty here in Texas is it's becoming evident that our justice is not reliable. Our ascertainment of guilt is not dependable. We may be passing a death penalty on people that don't deserve it.

That's why I'm hesitant, now, to back the death penalty. But, it is a righteous principle that God honors when it is administered properly. But, when you have any kind of penalty there is an opportunity for mercy. There are various penalties short of the penalty of death for breaking laws. For breaking God's laws there are penalties short of death. There is chastisement and there are judgments that God passes that are time-limited. You can serve your time and get free again, be considered liberated.

This is called the 'Law of Liberty'. Isn't that what James called it: "*the royal law of liberty?*" That's in James 2 or 3. We do have a law. James 1:25? "*Whoso looketh into the perfect law of liberty and continueth therein.*" So, we do have a law, but it's a law of liberty. Chapter 2:8? That may be the one I'm looking for. Yes, if you fulfill the royal law according to scripture, "*thou shalt love thy neighbor as thyself.*" That's what he called the royal law, the kingly law. That's the highest law. "*Thou shalt love thy neighbor as thyself.*"

But, where is the one that says, "*You shall have judgment without mercy?*" Yeah, 2:13. Just before that he mentioned the law of liberty in verse twelve. "*So speak ye and so do as they that shall be judged by the law of liberty."* The law of liberty is a law that has liberated us. Romans 8:2 helps explain that: *"The law of the spirit of life in Christ Jesus has liberated me from the law of sin and death."* That's where our liberty is. We are liberated from that law of sin and death. We're not necessarily liberated from the law of God, any of the rules of conduct that God has given to the human family. We're not liberated from that law, but we are liberated from the law of sin and death.

There is no law in my members anymore that can make me sin. The law may still be there but I'm not subject to that law anymore, the law that Paul was talking about back in Romans 7:19. He said, *"The good that I would, I do not and the evil that I would not, that I do. Now, if I do that I would not, it is no more I that do it but sin that dwelleth in me."* In other words, sin is making me do things that I wish I wasn't doing. *"I find then a law..."* That's the law he's describing there, that law of sin that's in me that makes me do things I wish I wasn't doing. Evil is present with me. Evil is always present with me; it's part of me; it's in my nature.

"For I delight in the law of God after the inward man." When I read Matthew 5, 6, and 7 (and I agree with all that) I say, "That's wonderful. That's how I ought to live." That's after the inward man. *"But I see another law somewhere else in me, in my members, warring against that law that my mind gives assent to, bringing me into captivity to the law of sin which is in my members."* He's describing the condition of every person without the Holy Ghost.

This was the condition of every person in the Old Testament trying to live by the Law of Moses. They had another law in their members which was defeating the Law of Moses they were trying to obey. It was keeping them from obeying the Law of Moses which was the Law of God. *"...bringing me into captivity unto the law of sin which is in my members. Oh, wretched man that I am,"* he said. In that condition, *"who shall deliver me from the body of this death?"* (Because the wages of sin is death) *"I thank God there is a deliverance through Jesus Christ our Lord".*

"So then, with the mind I, myself, serve the law of God, but with the flesh, the law of sin." As long as I'm having to walk in the flesh I will serve the law of sin. *"There is now no condemnation to them which are in Christ Jesus,"* There is no condemnation because we're not breaking God's law anymore when we're in Christ Jesus. *"...who walk not after the flesh but after the Spirit"*. We've been liberated from the flesh to walk in the Spirit. *"...for the law of the Spirit of life in Christ Jesus has made me free from that law of sin and death."*

We still have this law of liberty that liberated us from the law of sin and death but it doesn't have the penalty of death in it. The law of liberty doesn't deal with death; it deals with life. Jesus Christ has *"brought life and immortality to light through the Gospel."* Praise God! That gospel is the law of liberty. We are to obey the gospel. Somewhere in the scriptures it speaks of obeying the gospel. The gospel is something you obey; it's not just something you receive the benefits of by faith; just accept it by faith. You accept it and obey it!

The gospel has these things in it: *"Blessed are the merciful for they shall obtain mercy."* The gospel has in there: *"Blessed are the pure in heart for they shall see God"*. The gospel has in there: *"Forgive us our debts as we forgive our debtors."* The gospel has in there: *"Love your neighbor as yourself."* It has all those admonitions about how to get along in the kingdom of God, how to live in the kingdom of heaven. He's made us sit together here in heavenly places where we practice living like we're in heaven. We're to practice in the church acting like we're in heaven.

If we don't want to go to church, maybe we don't want to go to heaven! The church is like heaven! People fall out of the church, just like some people fell out of heaven! Amen! Some people fell out of heaven the same way we fall out of the church. Heaven will not include people that cause trouble.

"Blessed are the peacemakers for they shall be called the children of God." Troublemakers are not called the children of God. They are the children of the devil. In Luke 10, Jesus said, *"I saw somebody fall from heaven."* Get the context of that! In

Luke 10:17, the seventy preachers Jesus had sent out *"returned again with joy, saying, Lord even the devils are subject to us through thy name."* The devils there are the demons, the evil spirits. These were preachers Jesus had sent out to preach. He commanded them to heal the sick but he didn't command them to cast out devils. He had given that commandment to cast out devils to his twelve apostles when he sent them out. He didn't tell these to cast out devils.

So, when they went out they probably weren't expecting to cast out any devils. They hadn't been authorized. But, they had seen devils cast out; they had seen Jesus cast them out and watched the apostles cast them out. They ran into them out there! If you go out on a mission field you will run into them! In fact, if you stay home in church you're liable to run into them.

Naturally, when the devils are standing in your face and giving you opposition you want to do something about it. So, they tried! They decided to see if they could cast out a devil and found out they could! Through the name of Jesus the devils were subject to them! There is so much power in the name of Jesus! *"Devils are subject to us in thy name!"* They were happy about that! They were thrilled to discover they had power to cast out devils! They hadn't expected that!

He said unto them, *"I beheld Satan as lightning fall from heaven."* He's commenting on what they've just said. That's connected with what they said, *"Devils are subject to us through your name."*

"I saw Satan as lightning fall from heaven." (Satan, the chief devil) *"I saw the main devil fall from heaven as lightning." "Behold, I give unto you power to tread on all these devils."* See what he calls them: *"serpents and scorpions."* Those are two different kinds of demons. Serpents are deceivers; scorpions are tormentors.

Some spirits come to deceive; some come to torment. Some cause sickness, mental sickness, even. They just upset things. Others come with doctrine. Paul mentioned people who were receiving doctrines of devils, doctrines of demons. Those are serpents that bring false doctrine like the serpent brought the false doctrine to Eve. There are others that come just to make trouble, cause pain and suffering. They are tormentors, he called them. *"I give you power to tread on serpents and scorpions!"* Tread on serpents and scorpions! You can walk right on top of them! You can step on them! Step over them! They can't stop you! You've got authority over them! *"...and over all the power of the enemy!"*

The enemy here is the devil. That's not the only enemy, but it's the main enemy. It's the enemy he's talking about in this passage. This enemy is the Devil. *"...and nothing shall by any means hurt you."* Well, swords and crosses and stones did hurt them, from a physical standpoint. They could knock the life out of them, that is, out of their bodies. But, they couldn't knock the life out of their souls. Jesus said in Matthew 10:28, *"Fear not them that kill the body...they can't hurt you...,"* He didn't say that part there, but you connect this with it: Fear not them that kill the body because they can't hurt you when they kill the body if you are in the condition he's talking about.

He was producing some people that couldn't be hurt by killing their bodies. That is a special race of people; that's not ordinary human beings! Those are human beings who have become children of God! They've had a new birth! They are new creatures! These old creatures can be hurt by killing the body, but those new creatures that are living up to their privileges can't be hurt by killing the body.

"Nothing shall by any means hurt you." Notwithstanding, in this, *"Rejoice not just because the devils are subject to you."* There is something greater than that you've got. Your names are written in heaven, which theirs are not. Those devils don't have their names written in heaven. You can tell that they know they are going to be destroyed. They know their destiny is destruction because they have received judgment without mercy. We don't know the history of that judgment, whether they ever had a chance for mercy. We just know the conclusion of it at this stage of things; there's no mercy for evil spirits. They're upset about it; they're bitter about it; they're unhappy about

it. They are living in fear of the end of their lives just like most human beings live in fear of the end of their lives.

That's something Paul was saying in Hebrews 2:14, *"The children..."* The children he's talking about are mentioned in verse 13, *"...again I put my trust in him; again, behold I and the children that God has given me."* He's quoting verses from the Old Testament that are prophetic of Jesus. That's the verse where Jesus said, *"I and the children that God has given me."* God gave children to Jesus.

Jesus, in John 17, praying to the Father said, *"Of these that you gave me, I have lost none except the son of perdition."* That had to happen. Another place, he said, *"The Father which gave them to me is greater than all and no man is able to pluck them out of my hand."* So, the people that came to Jesus and stayed with him were people that God gave him.

Now, talking about these people here in Hebrews 2:14, *"Forasmuch then as the children are the partakers of flesh and blood...."* All the people God gave to Jesus are partakers of flesh and blood. Since that is true, he himself likewise took part of flesh and blood; he took part of the same. *"...that through death he might destroy him that had the power of death, that is, the devil, and deliver them who through fear of death were all their lifetime subject to bondage."*

Every living being born into the world has to live in fear of death. That fear keeps them in bondage; it's the bondage of fear. Jesus came to deliver us from that fear of death. *"Rejoice because your names are written in heaven!"* Since they are written in heaven, they are written for God to remember you. The reason God writes things down is to remember them. Of course, he writes them down on the tables of his mind, on the tablet of his mind. But, he's got them written down so he can remember you. God will remember you when you go down in death if you're not among those in Matthew 10:28, if you don't move out a live soul. If your name is written in heaven, that's all it takes for God to remember you when the resurrection day comes.

He will call your name again. The result of him calling your name will be the same as Jesus calling Lazarus' name when he was standing in the graveyard. He cried out one name and one grave opened; out came a resurrected person because his name was written there. Praise God!

So, we're to be able to tread on serpents and scorpions, both the deceivers and the tormentors. We don't want to be deceived by the deceivers and we don't want to be tormented by the tormentors, do we? We've got power and authority over those. These are a special class of characters themselves and they have a special character as a leader, a prince.

Help me find that scripture in Ephesians where he spoke of the '*prince of the power of the air*'. That's in Ephesians 2: "*You hath he quickened,* (or enlivened) *who were dead in trespasses and sins, wherein in times past you used to walk according to the course of this world, according to the prince of the power of the air.*" That prince is the spirit that now worketh in the children of disobedience.

Well, we know we can see that the power of the flesh is working in the children of disobedience but there is a prince called the 'prince of the power of the air', not the power of the flesh. To identify the prince of the power of the air, you've got to identify the 'power of the air'. What is he calling the 'power of the air'?

Going back to the first chapter of Genesis and dealing with creation, there were three classes of the animal creation: one in the waters, one on the land and one in the air. The waters brought forth both the moving creatures in the waters, fishes of the sea and fowls. Genesis 1:20: "*Let the waters bring forth abundantly the moving creature that hath life and fowl that may fly above the earth in the open firmament of heaven.*"

So, as a result of that God created "*great whales and every living creature that moveth which the waters brought forth abundantly after their kind,* (talking about the fishes of the sea) *and every winged fowl after his kind. And God saw that it was good. And God blessed them saying, be fruitful and multiply and fill the waters in the seas and let fowl multiply in the earth where they fly in the heavens.*" So, they inhabit the air.

The fishes inhabit the water. In verse 24, He said, *"And let the earth bring forth the living creature after his kind, cattle and creeping thing and the beast of the earth after his kind. And it was so. And God made the beast of the earth after his kind and the beasts of the earth after their kind and everything that creepeth upon the earth after his kind. And God saw that it was good."*

In that same environment, God brought forth man: *"Let us make man in our image after our likeness and let them have dominion over the fish of the sea and over the fowl of the air and over the cattle and over all the earth, over every creeping thing that creepeth upon the earth."*

But Adam lost that dominion when he was driven from the Garden as a sinner; he lost his rulership. But there remains what is called a *'prince of the power of the air'*. There's a power of the air. There's a power of the sea; that's simply the creatures that inhabit the sea. The power of the land is the creatures that inhabit the land. The power of the air is the creatures that inhabit the air.

But, there's a *'prince of the power of the air that now works in the children of disobedience'*. That leaves us to speculate a little bit, study and wonder, "What else lives in the air that can influence human beings?" We have to ask ourselves, "What category do we put evil spirits in? Do they belong among the fish of the sea? They drove a herd of swine down into the sea and drowned them but what became of the evil spirits? Did they join the fish of the sea?"

The 'power of the air': How do evil spirits behave? They are spirits and so they are not subject to gravity; they don't have to walk on the ground. They probably can pass through the water but that's not their element. They can float above the earth; they drift around in the air, the firmament between earth and heaven. That's the power of the air. We've found a power that lives in the air; evil spirits live out here above the earth, just in space. They can travel through space like any angel. They are not bound by gravity; they don't breathe air; they don't eat foods; they don't need anything that pertains to the earth. They can float around in the air better than the birds of heaven. The birds themselves have to alight somewhere to sleep at night. But, evil spirits never have to alight anywhere.

Someone asks question—not understood

It doesn't say. We're just finding something that it hasn't given us the origin of. The reason I went back to Genesis was to show the three places where a power could be. But, what's called the 'power of the air', I'm showing here that it wasn't anything that could be described there in Genesis. What he's calling the power of the air, we're not going to say that's the birds that fly in the air, that they're the 'prince of the power of the air' working in the children of disobedience. It couldn't be that. There is something else out in the air called 'the power of the air'.

Question—not clear

Well, it's something more than words; words simply describe it. Words themselves are not substantial, but they describe substantial things. What I'm going to say is, the power of the air is evil spirits because that is where they dwell. They can pass through the air as easily as any bird. That's their dwelling place when they are not in a human being. They are not physical; they're not corporeal; they're not bound to the earth by gravity.

What I want to show by that is that man himself cannot be the power of the air. He's not free to float through the air. He has invented ways to get up there, but he has to come back down. Man is a power of the ground; he lives on the earth; he's part of the beastly creation.

So, the power of the air is not the carnal mind; it's not false religion; it's not the birds and bees; it's not the U.S. Air Force! It's evil spirits! The power of the air is the kingdom of evil spirits. That will help us locate the prince of the power of the air. The prince of the power of the air is not a human being; it's not the mind of all human beings. But it's the leader of the evil spirits, what the Jews call Beelzebub. Jesus called him the prince of devils. He's the prince of the power of the air. He's the prince of the serpents and the scorpions; he's the chief one of them.

Every kingdom has a king, a leader, a government, regardless whether you place them under the control of God. That's where you place the kingdoms of this world, under the control of God, also. But, they have governments here in the earth; there are empires, leaders and governors that God manages and exercises a certain control over. But, he certainly does not identify with the kingdoms of this world and is not to be held accountable for all of the evil that is done in the kingdoms of the world.

Neither is God to be held responsible for all the evil that's done by the kingdom of evil spirits. This is a common error that's being made in explaining evil spirits, that they are just sent of God. We have examples of them being sent of God, just like we have examples of evil men being sent of God. That doesn't make them totally willing tools in the hands of God.

Pharaoh was a tool in the hand of God but he wasn't a willing tool; he wasn't willingly serving God. God was just manipulating Pharaoh and making him do his will against his own will. He was making Pharaoh do God's will. Pharaoh didn't have it in mind to do God's will, but every time he refused to let Israel go he was doing God's will. *"For this cause I have raised you up so I can show forth in you my power."*

Those are examples we can go by to let us know that we're not to hold God accountable for everything that's done by evil spirits. If it were that way, we would be in rebellion by casting one out. But, we are in authority of Jesus Christ to drive away and drive back the evil spirits because they are in opposition to the will of God. They are doing things against the will of God. They are trying to prevent the will of God from coming to pass.

Question—not clear

In the sixth chapter? Yeah, once you see this, you can see that *"We wrestle not against flesh and blood."* Regardless of how you symbolize the powers of this world, there is still flesh and blood. The kings of this earth, the magistrates, the religious leaders are flesh and blood. But, they're really not in charge. If you can identify the 'prince of the power of the air' then you can see him as the spirit of the dragon; the spirit that is in the dragon. The prince of the power of the air is working in the children of disobedience and he's the spirit that is working in the dragon.

That is why the dragon can be called *'that old serpent called the Devil and Satan'*. It's because that old serpent called the devil and Satan is in charge of the dragon. That is exactly what he admits to Jesus in Matthew where he said, *"The kingdoms of the world are given unto me. If you will fall down and worship me all these things I will give to you because they are given unto me."*

That brings up the question of who gave them to him. Obviously, it was God that turned them over to him. You see God exercising control of that prince in the first two chapters of Job. It's the same person in operation. *"The sons of God came together and Satan came also."* The sons of God, in that passage, evidently are the angels. See, not all the sons of God are in the earth. There are sons of God in heaven. This was a gathering of heavenly creatures, supernatural creatures. At this stage of the game, the sons of God could come together and Satan could come also.

Now, that may no longer be true! There's a scripture in Revelation 12 where the dragon is called Satan. One of the verses, after there is war in heaven...I admit this is a different heaven that the war was in. But, it says this down in the *tenth verse* of Revelation twelve, *"I heard a loud voice saying in heaven, now is come salvation and strength and the kingdom of our God and the power of his Christ for the accuser of our brethren is cast down which accused them before our God day and night,"* past tense, like he can't do that anymore. He's lost some of that access that he used to have.

Accusing the brethren before God is exactly what Satan was doing in the first chapter of Job. He was there at that meeting accusing Job before God. Here in Revelation 12:10 it says that guy who used to accuse him before our God day and night has been cast down. He doesn't have the same power to do that anymore. Verse 12: *"The devil has come down unto you having great wrath because he knoweth that he hath but a short time."*

The devil is somebody that can know something. He knows he's got but a short time. You can't say that about the spirit of the flesh; you can't say that about civil power; you can't say that about any human agency or any abstract quality of the human agency. This is an intelligent person who can know his time is about up; his chance is about to run out.

Where were we? Back here in Ephesians 6: *"Put on the whole armor of God that you may be able to stand against the wiles of the devil."* Not the wiles of civil power; not the wiles of the flesh, but the wiles of the prince of the power of the air, the leader of the kingdom of evil spirits. *"For we wrestle not against flesh and blood,"* which is what we would be doing if we were just wrestling with Nero or the president of China. That's flesh and blood.

But, we wrestle against principalities, powers, rulers of the darkness of this world, spiritual wickedness in high places. Now, that's a description of human conditions because evil spirits are working in humans. Satan is the head of the kingdoms of the earth. He has his agents operating in all these government circles and centers, including religious circles and centers. But, the real authority in all of that is Satan himself.

Where does it say, *"Satan, himself"?* That's an expression. Satan has a self. I can't think of the verse now, how it uses it. *"Wherefore...,"* Well, that's as far as we need to go with that. We've explained spiritual wickedness in high places. That's human beings committing spiritual wickedness in high places because they are inspired and deceived by demons. It all traces to the devil.

Satan himself is transformed into an angel of light. That's in II Corinthians 11:13. That describes false apostles, deceitful workers, transforming themselves into the apostles of Christ. *"It is no marvel, for Satan himself is transformed into an angel of light."* He's not calling the false apostles 'Satan', but they are doing the same kind of things that Satan does. Satan himself is transformed into an angel of light. That's how he deceives people: promising to bring them light when he's bringing them darkness. *"Therefore, it is no great thing, no marvel, if his ministers, his servants, also be transformed as ministers of righteousness whose ends will be according to their works."*

While we're in II Corinthians 11, we ought to, if we have time... We're about to use up our time. I will deal with this verse and close.

"Would to God you could bear with me a little in my foolishness, and indeed try to bear with me," Paul says, *"for I am jealous over you,"* talking to the church, *"I'm jealous over you with godly jealousy for I have espoused you to one husband, that is Christ, that I may present you as a chaste virgin to Christ. But I fear, lest by any means, as the serpent beguiled Eve through his subtlety, so your minds should be corrupted from the simplicity that is in Christ."*

For years, I've heard that verse quoted like this: *"The serpent beguiled Eve through his subtlety, so your minds could be corrupted."* "See there, it was all in her mind!" How many times have you heard that said? But, let's look at the case he's applying it to. He's making an example out of Eve and applying it to the church, particularly that local church there in Corinth. *"Just like the serpent beguiled Eve through his subtlety, I'm afraid your minds could be corrupted from the simplicity that is in Christ."*

Now, how was he anticipating that their minds could get corrupted? Explain in the next verse: *"For if he that cometh preacheth another Jesus..."* *"He that cometh"* is any visiting preacher that comes by preaching false doctrine. They had visiting preachers coming by, just like we do. We've got some this weekend. Some of them will be at Humble this evening. If they preach false doctrine they could corrupt our minds from that simplicity that is in Christ.

The brethren we have today, I don't think they will do that. There are false preachers spreading false doctrine around and corrupting people's minds. My point here is he's not saying it's all in your mind. He's saying somebody is liable to mess with your mind and mix you up. That's what happened to Eve. He said somebody messed with her mind and mixed her up. The same thing that happened to Eve could happen to us.

The same thing that sometimes happens in the churches today is what happened to Eve. A false preacher mixed their minds. That's how Eve's mind was corrupted. Now, some of the brethren have seen that hook-up there and have got around it by identifying Adam as the person that messed with Eve's mind; that Adam deceived Eve and corrupted her mind and talked her into the sin. That's an ingenious artifice to explain that.

The reason I don't accept that is because the Good Book just don't tell it that way! Go back and read *Genesis 3* and see if it looks like Adam deceived Eve, if he talked her into the sin. Which one tempted the other? In Genesis 3, it tells us that Eve tempted Adam, not that Adam tempted Eve. You can follow that through very easily. Every detail falls into place when God begins to question them. He started by questioning Adam in the eleventh verse: *"Who told thee that thou wast naked? Hast thou eaten of the tree of which I commanded thee that thou shouldest not eat?"* The man said, *"The woman you gave to be with me, she gave me of the tree and I gave in; I ate it."*

He's telling the truth. God didn't question him any further. He turned to the woman and said, *"What have you done?"* She didn't say, "Adam lied; he talked me into it." What she said was, *"The serpent deceived me and I ate."* She was telling the truth. God didn't question her any more.

You know, if she had said, "It wasn't me; it was Adam!" and one of us was having to judge, we would go back and forth between the man and the woman: "What did you say?" and, "What did you say?" and have an argument between the two. They weren't blaming each other. He was blaming her and she was blaming somebody else, *"The serpent beguiled me and I did eat."*

Question or comment—not clear

But, you can't define it that way in the context here; they didn't have that kind of argument. If the serpent had been Adam, it would have been just a "he said—she said" argument. God didn't question her any further because she was telling the truth. He didn't question the serpent; he just pronounced judgment on the serpent.

There are three judgments pronounced here: the first one on the serpent in verse 14: *"Because thou hast done this, thou art cursed above all cattle and above every beast of the field. Upon thy belly shalt thou go; dust shalt thou eat all the days of thy life."* That is a symbolic way of saying, "You will suffer defeat at every turn." It's our job to help fulfill that scripture, make the devil suffer defeat at every turn.

Question: Are you saying that Eve got into trouble by listening to another voice instead of her husband?

Well, yes, that's what it means; she listened to another voice instead of her husband. Then he pronounced a judgment on the woman in the sixteenth verse. This is the second judgment, the second person: *"I will greatly multiply thy sorrow, etc."*

Then, he pronounced a judgment on Adam in the seventeenth verse, the third person judged: *"Unto Adam he said, 'Because you've done this the ground shall be cursed for thy sake."*

Three persons, three curses. Very clear, very easily explained, isn't it? But, it's not easy to prove to somebody that doesn't want to believe it because we don't have statements of the origin of the serpent. That's not given to us, so we can't claim what is not given to us.

Question: "If someone would've inserted that word 'so also' your minds..."

How's that again?

Repeating: "...as Eve was corrupted, so could we be corrupted by false doctrine."

Well, that is what he said; that is the import of his words. It is implied. Whether it's written or not, it is implied.

Comment: "I was just saying if that word 'also' was written in there...."

No, it's evil spirits. There are demons and all they do is torment. That's mostly what we've dealt with, the kind we've cast out. We've been casting out tormentors. But, there are deceiving spirits; they come with doctrines, doctrines of demons.

Question: Can spirits that work in a person torment other people?

Well, they will have that effect. A tormented person can't help but be a tormentor. I've been singing the song of Moses and the Lamb.

Chapter 20

What Time is It?

March 18, 2008

Well, we're planting seeds, aren't we? It's always gratifying to see those seeds sprout right away, see the results of your message or teaching or desire. Sometimes, you have to wait years to see those words bear fruit. Words are seeds. Jesus was the sower that went forth to sow in Matthew 13, in the parable of the soils. But, he left us carrying on that job. We've become part of the harvest from the seed-sowing, ourselves. Every one of us is here because we've had seed planted in our hearts. We are to plant it in others and keep the harvest going on until we come to the fullness, the completion of the harvest.

The Bible says, "*...the fullness of the Gentiles must come in.*" The question a while ago asked, "What time is it?" There are a lot of different ways to answer that. To start with, it's approximately 8:16 P.M. on March 18, 2008. That figure, '2008', should call our attention to spiritual timing because it's a very significant figure. It means it's around two thousand years since our Savior was walking in this earth. If we were trying to be exact about exactly how long it's been since Christ was here, we would have to be able to agree on which period of his life we were going to measure from.

We know we're in that time frame. We're in the time frame of around two thousand years since Jesus was here. That time was around four thousand years since the creation of Adam, the father of the human race. That adds up to six thousand years of human activity that are pretty much behind us. We're at a change-over, in other words.

To measure God's time and his calendar, you want to start with his words about the Sabbath. That began in the first or second chapter of Genesis. Second chapter: "*Thus the heavens and the earth were finished and all the host of them and on the seventh day God ended his work which he had made and he rested."* Then in *Exodus 20,* God reminded Moses and the Israelites of that fact when he was giving out the Ten Commandments. Exodus 20:8: *"Remember the Sabbath day to keep it holy. Six days shalt thou labor and do all thy work but the seventh day is the Sabbath of the Lord thy God. In it thou shalt not do any work."*

Verse 11: *"For in six days the Lord made heaven and earth, the sea and all that in them is and rested the seventh day. Wherefore the Lord blessed the Sabbath* (or the seventh day) *and hallowed it."*

In the New Testament, in II Peter, he told us that when God is measuring or experiencing time he said, *"To God, a thousand years is as one day."* II Peter 3:8: *"Beloved be not ignorant of this one thing that one day with the Lord is as a thousand years and a thousand years as one day."* I don't think that means that the six days of creation were thousand-year days and that God rested for a thousand years after he finished creation. I just think he's typing these thousands of years that we've been here as being six days that God has given man to work. Those days are about up! We're living in the sunset of that sixth day.

The seventh day belongs to God. Now, to develop that point, I'd like to turn to Hebrews 4 where he talks about rest and connects it to the Sabbath day. *"Let us therefore fear lest a promise being left us of entering into his rest...."* That's God's rest he's talking about, *"...any of you should seem to come short of it."* He doesn't want us to come short of God's rest. *"For unto us was the Gospel preached as well as unto them."* He had been talking about Israel in the wilderness, *"...for the word preached did not profit them not being mixed with faith in them that heard it."*

There's a Revelation right there! We've got to have faith mixed with the Word that we hear or it won't profit us, either! If we don't believe what God said we won't get anything out of it! They may have believed what he said when he said it but they couldn't put in practice in their lives. They didn't see what it meant when he reminded them of the times he had worked miracles on their behalf to set them free from Egypt and feed them in the wilderness. They had to admit, "Yeah, all those things happened." They believed that much but they didn't believe he would do it the next time! That's what faith constitutes.

How many times has God delivered us? How many times has he come to our rescue? Look at the history of this church, this Houston area work. It's been something God's been in from the beginning. If he hadn't met our needs in many ways, many times, we couldn't have survived this long; we wouldn't be here today.

I like that song; I can't sing it without thinking about Brother and Sister Kilough. They had sung that song that says, "Just look out yonder where I might have been; He brought me in." They were new, visiting, and they sang that song the night they were visiting. He said they were driving home that night, real quiet, through the dark, down the highway, when all at once, she hollered out, "JUST LOOK OUT YONDER!" He said, "WHAT? WHERE?" She was still thinking about that song, "Just look out yonder where I might have been," and she was mad because she knew they were singing about where she had been—out yonder—and still was, if she didn't get in, get out of it.

Every one of us ought to consider what it means for the Lord to bring us in to where we know something about what time it is. We're still working on understanding some of the details of God's timing. His plan has timing built into it. There are certain times when God does things. "*When the time was fully come, God sent forth his son, made of a woman, made under the Law.*" That couldn't happen until the time was fully come.

When the Day of Pentecost was fully come, then the sound came from heaven like a rushing, mighty wind and cloven tongues sat on each of them. That couldn't happen until the Day of Pentecost was fully come; and it had to be that particular day of Pentecost. They had been having days of Pentecost for fifteen hundred years and that didn't happen. But, that day of Pentecost was the one that God's timing was wrapped up in.

We want to know what time frame we're in now. To begin with, we need to keep faith mixed in our understanding of the Word so that we live what is our portion; we live in the *present truth*, as Peter said.

Hebrews 4:3 goes on to say, *"For we which have believed do enter into rest."* Now, he's just been quoting, in the previous chapter, a verse out of Psalms 95 where God said, *"I swore in my wrath they shall not enter into my rest."* We need to turn back there and read that Psalm, at least the last part of it. It's a short one, anyway. We could read the whole thing if we want to.

What is relevant to us right now is in the eighth verse, beginning there, Psalms 95:8 where he says, *"Harden not your heart."* Good advice to everybody! Don't let your heart be hardened; keep a tender heart, especially tender toward the things of God. That includes the people of God. Be tender toward the people of God. Also, be tender enough for God to write things on your heart, write his word on your heart.

"Harden not your heart as in the day of provocation, as in the day of temptation in the wilderness when your fathers tempted me, proved me and saw my works." They saw God work! Paul explained in Hebrews that the word that was preached to them and even demonstrated to them was not linked with faith in them that heard it. So, he goes on to say in verse 10, *"Forty years long I was grieved with that generation."* God was grieved with those Israelites in the wilderness, with their lack of faith and their constant complaining. God, help us to quit complaining!

"It's a people that do err in their heart." They go wrong in their heart. *"...and they have not known my ways."* They saw his works, it says in the *ninth verse,* but God said, *"They don't know my ways."*

If you know God's ways you can partly predict what God is going to do. Do you feel like you can predict what God is going to do? Well, your first answer is going to be 'no', we can't predict God. But, if you don't feel like you know something about the way God acts, you will be afraid to trust him with your life. You want to at least be able to predict that much, that he will take good care of you. You need to be convinced you can predict God this much: He will take good care of me. I can safely trust in him.

There is no risk to trusting in God. I wish everybody could get that revelation, get that written in your heart; believe it with faith. We need to know his ways so we can predict him that much. We can predict that he will do right. There are other things we can predict because of what he's let us know by way of prophecy.

He said, "*They have not known my ways. Unto them I swore in my wrath,*" God got mad! Got mad at those unbelieving people! "*I swore in my wrath that they should not enter into my rest.*" Now, if you know Bible history from that time period back there, the exodus and the crossing of Jordan and the subduing of Canaan Land under Joshua, you will immediately think he was talking about the rest they got when they finally got out of the wilderness, quit traveling and settled down in the land of Canaan. That was a good rest. For one thing, it represented them being delivered out of slavery, the hard labor they were under in Egypt. They were brought out of that into the rest of Canaan.

Going back now to Hebrews 4: Paul makes it plain that it means more than that. It wasn't just talking about that rest they got back there when God said, "*They won't enter into my rest.*" There's a rest that God is still in. He says we can enter into his rest. God is not still creating the world; He got that job done. Hebrew 4:3: "*We which have believed do enter into rest, as he said, as I have sworn in my wrath, if they shall enter into my rest: although the works* (God's works) *were finished from the foundation of the world.* (5) *For he spoke in a certain place of the seventh day on this wise, 'And God did rest the seventh day from all his works.* In this place, again, the one we just read in Psalms 95: "*...if they shall enter into my rest.*"

Hebrew 4:6: "*Seeing therefore it remaineth that some must enter therein,* (that is into God's rest) *and they to whom it was first preached entered not in because of unbelief.*" They entered into Canaan, finally, but they didn't enter into God's rest even though that generation got to go into Canaan. (7) "*Again, he limiteth a certain day, saying in David, Today, after so long a time; as it is said, Today if ye will hear his voice, harden not your heart.*"

(8) "*For,*" (Now Paul argues here) "*if Joshua....*" (It may say Jesus in your Bible, but that's just a New Testament form of the name 'Joshua' and it's talking about that Joshua back there that led them across the river into Canaan's Land.) "*If Joshua had given them rest,* (the rest God spoke about) "*then he would not afterward have spoken of another day.*" That was four hundred years later that David said that, in Psalms 95. "*There remains, therefore, a rest to the people of God,*" that God is promising that people of faith can enter into, "*for he that has entered into his rest...*" Here he gives you an understanding, a revelation on what kind of rest that is that God gives, "*...he also hath ceased* from his own works *as God did from his,*" when he rested back there after the creation.

What he's telling us there is we're going to get to cease from the works of the flesh! Are you tired of them? It's slavery! The lusts of the flesh bind you; they drive you, they make you serve sin and self! We're going to get to cease from those works! And in fact, he said we're to that place right now! I want you to know what time it is! For two thousand years, now, we've been at this time where you can cease from your labors and just do the works of God. That doesn't mean you don't do anything; you just don't do your own works! You cease from your own works! So, we're doing God's works after this.

That's to be done forever! That's what we're going to do forever and ever! We'll never go back to serving self again! We'll never go back to the bondage of the flesh again! We've been given a power to subdue the works of the flesh! Praise God!

Now, hooking that to the time of six days that man was given to work, those six days are about up. It's time for God to work! This next seventh day is known as the Day of the Lord, the Lord's Day. Jesus is going to take control of this earth. He's going to work and show what he can do.

Brother Sowders used to say, "God has given man six days to show what he can do." Well, he's done a lot, but he hasn't done anything that lasts! He hasn't given anybody everlasting life! You've lived in a time when we've seen man's best works. God bless Henry Ford! Thank God for the Wright brothers! We've seen a lot of good things come out of man's labor. But, Henry Ford is dead now; the Wright brothers are in the grave. We will be in the grave, pretty soon, if we don't enter into this rest and cease from these works of the flesh.

God is going to show what he can do and it will produce *"a world wherein dwelleth righteousness!"* Carnal minded men have dreamed about that, but they've never been able to build a world like that. Jesus Christ, the son of God, and his helpers are going to build a world wherein dwelleth righteousness. People can live in peace forever and ever, live on and on. We're living right at the end of six days and the beginning of the seventh. It's about time for the sun to rise on the seventh day.

That's one framework of time. Now, there are other scriptures that use other metaphors and narrow things down a little more. Let's turn, for example, to Matthew 24 because there is some timing in there. That represents one of Jesus' 'goodbye' messages to the disciples just before he left this world. He spent most of that chapter describing to them the things leading up to the end of the Jewish world in which they were living at that time. That was the main thing they asked him about. In the beginning of the chapter, verse 3, he had just told them that the temple was going to be torn down and not one stone left on another. They were bragging on that temple, what a nice building it was.

Verse 3: They said, *"Tell us when these things shall be, the things you were talking about. What shall be the sign of thy coming and the end of the world?"* They thought all of that came together. The time he was describing, when the temple would be torn down *must* be end of the world! Well, it was the end of that world, the end of that Jewish world.

There was more to that. It wasn't the end of the church world and, it wasn't the end of the Gentile world. So, there were several parts to the question but most of it was pertaining to the end of that world until you get to verse 29. Verse 29: *"Jesus said, immediately after the tribulation of those days..."* He then describes the tribulation that happened in A.D. 70. If you want to read, literally, about that tribulation, get the copy of Josephus' book, The Wars of the Jews. You will find a detailed description of it. It's horrible to read, but it's fulfillment of prophecy. It was what Jesus predicted: the end of their world would come.

Immediately after that tribulation, Jesus says, *"...the sun shall be darkened and the moon shall not give her light."* He's talking spiritually here, symbolically. The sun represents the New Testament, the Gospel, the Word of God. The moon is the Old Testament, the Law of Moses. *"The stars shall fall from heaven."* That's preachers and religious leaders that fell out of their pure place, their pure condition in God. They fell down into a more carnal state of mind because *"there came a falling away in those days."*

Let me show you; we'll keep our hand here in Matthew 24 and digress over to II Thessalonians, momentarily, to see how Paul described that time period. This is after the tribulation of those days. II Thessalonians 2:3: *"Let no man deceive you by any means for that day,"* that they were asking about, the day of the coming of the Lord, the return of the Lord, *"shall not come,"* he said, *"except there come a falling away first."*

You may have heard preachers explain that 'falling away' happening down here because it seems like every religious movement that starts off in a high place in God gradually falls away. This was a greater 'falling away' than any you have seen in your day! What happened after that Early Church period back there, after those apostles died, there was a great falling away of that church! *"...there shall come a falling away first and that man of sin be revealed, the son of perdition who op-*

poses and exalteth himself above all that is called God or that is worshipped so that he, as God, sitteth in the temple of God, showing himself that he is God."

That's radical language, but it happened! It has already happened! However, that man is still around. He's still here. It's not a particular man; it's an office of a man. It's like the president of the United States. We've had a president for over two hundred years. There is a different one every few years but we keep a president, somehow.

The man of sin has kept being replaced generation after generation. We still have a man of sin sitting in that office and making those claims! If you were listening to it! Most of the world is not listening to that today. They don't believe that; they don't accept that anymore.

Here is a mark you can put on your spiritual calendar: We're living in the last days of the man of sin! His time is about up! These are the last days of the man of sin. He is going to have one more big fling and then it is over for him and he will end up in the Lake of Fire.

Back to Matthew 24. We talked about the stars falling from heaven. That was the great 'falling away'. *"Then,"* sometime after that, he didn't say how long. It's been almost two thousand years since then. *"...shall appear the sign of the Son of Man in heaven."* He didn't say, *"There shall appear the Son of Man in heaven."* Read the language there; stick to the grammar!

*"Then shall appear the **sign** of the Son of Man in heaven and all the tribes of the earth shall mourn."* I believe that, after the ***sign,*** they shall see the Son of Man, himself, coming in the clouds of heaven. Do you know what 'clouds of heaven' are? Are they cumulous? Are they cirrus? Are they stratus clouds?

Paul says, *"Now, we are compassed about with so great a cloud of witnesses."* Who are we compassed about with? We're compassed about with Enoch, Elijah, Moses and Abraham. We're compassed about with them. They are a 'cloud of witnesses'. They tell us something. Everybody needs to listen to Abraham's words today. Everybody ought to be listening to

Abel's words today. Admittedly, there is some more blood that '*speaks better things than the blood of Abel,"* today, but we all need his message, too.

Jesus said, at the end of that age, (and I think that applies to the end of every age; it will to this one) "*... shall all the blood of the martyrs that has been shed from righteous Abel,"* to the last martyr that dies just before that prophecy comes true. All that blood will be required of this generation. That happened back there; a lot of blood was required of that generation. It's going to happen again, though, and you can say it in the same words. It will just be a longer list of martyrs, this time. You will start with Abel again and all those martyrs' blood will be required of *THIS* generation when there is another martyring of the saints of God.

So, I hope you've already seen the *SIGN* of the Son of man. You haven't seen the Son of Man coming in heaven, yet, but you may see him coming in the CLOUDS of heaven. Do you understand what those clouds are? There are some more witnesses forming. Jesus is coming to this earth in a church before he comes in person. He is going to come in person! But first, he's got to come in a church and judge this generation like that church back there judged that generation.

When he went away, he left the church behind to judge that generation. Before he comes to appear to this world, he's going to have a church to judge this generation. His coming then will be to establish his kingdom in that seventh day. He will start the seventh day. Praise his Name!

We can find ourselves in Hebrews 4; we can find ourselves in Matthew 24. Now, help me find that one in Luke (I think) where he gave the four watches; where he said, "*You be watching like a man who is watching for his master to come from the wedding. If he comes in the evening watch* (I don't believe he said the evening watch) *or the midnight watch or the morning watch....*" That's in Luke 12:35, *"Let your loins be girded about and your lights burning..."* Having your loins girded about just means having your belt on; be fully dressed, ready to go to work.

Men sometimes run around the house with their trousers but no belt on because they just haven't bothered to put one on. But before you get out there to follow that lawnmower, to make sure your britches don't fall off, you'll put that belt on! (Laughter) Let your loins be girded about! Don't run the risk of losing your trousers while you're serving God! Your light is burning! Don't run out of light!

He is talking about the night time, now. We've been comparing it to day time, these six days. But now he is comparing it to night time, while we're waiting for the Lord to return. *"You, yourselves be likened unto men that wait for their Lord when he will return from the wedding, when he cometh and knocketh, they may open unto him immediately."* He's telling us, "Stay alert; stay awake because it is night time," when people are liable to go to sleep. Lots of Christian people are going to sleep. They're getting sleepy; they're getting tired of serving God. They're getting tired of coming to church; they're getting tired of overcoming the flesh, tired of resisting temptation, tired of giving up the pleasures of the world! They are relaxing and going to sleep.

Keep your lamp lit and stay awake! Watch for the Lord to come! You don't know when he is going to get here. *"Blessed are those servants whom the Lord, when he cometh, shall find watching. Verily, I say unto you that he shall gird himself,"* he will tighten his belt up, *"and make them sit down to meat and come forth and serve them."* What would you think if Jesus was the waiter at your table? *"And if he shall come in the second watch or come in the third watch and find them so, blessed are those servants."* Let's stop and chew on that verse for a little while. This is a good place here to chew the cud.

In the first place, why didn't he suggest he might come in the first watch? Well, it's because that church he was talking to had the first watch. The first watch is the evening watch. Literally, the evening watch ran from about sundown up until about 9:00 p.m. at night. The second watch ran up until midnight. It was called the 'midnight watch'. Then, there was the cockcrowing watch that reached from midnight till three o'clock. Finally, the morning watch was from 3:00 a.m. until sunup. They had four watches.

Now, Jesus didn't even suggest he might be back in the first watch. He wasn't coming back in the period of the Early Church. They might not have caught that point the day he said this, but they probably remembered it later when their watch was about drawing to a close and he hadn't come back.

Paul wrote the first and second letters of Thessalonians to a brand new church he had just planted, to correct the impression they had picked up that Jesus might *'come back any day now before morning'*. He gave them to understand there were some other things to happen before Jesus would come back. It would be a long time period. Jesus wasn't going to come back in the first watch. He didn't even suggest that. That first watch was the period of that Early Church and it included the period of the Falling Away as the night got darker and darker, going into what we call The Dark Ages. That term was made up by historians but it has spiritual significance. The church went into a dark age.

"But if he shall come in the second watch or come in the third watch..." The second watch reached up until midnight, the darkest hour until the cockcrowing watch started. That was really the period of the Dark Ages, the darkest ages. The second watch was the midnight watch and reached till the time of the cockcrowing. We understand that the cockcrowing began with Martin Luther and those early reformers. That was when they began to wake up the church again!

The long night was drawing to an end and light was beginning to dawn again. Roosters began to stand up and crow and announce to people that, "Jesus is coming again! Get ready! The Son is going to rise!" Amen! *"The Son of Righteousness shall arise with healing in his wings."*

Well, looking back on it from our vantage point, the church passed through the evening watch; it passed through the midnight watch and it has been through the cockcrowing watch. We've had several hundred years of cockcrowing, advancement of the Reformation, the restoration; a rising out of that wilderness darkness. "Coming out of the wilderness" is another picture we use to describe it. It's from another scripture. The Song of Solomon says, "*Who is this coming up out of the wilderness leaning upon her beloved?*" The answer is it's his church, his bride, his wife, coming back out of the wilderness!

How did it get in the wilderness? You will find that in Revelation 12 where it says the woman that represented the church, "*To her was given two wings of a great eagle that she might fly into the wilderness where there was a place prepared for her where she was nourished for a time, times and half a time.*" Twelve hundred, sixty years the church was in that dark wilderness but it was fed and kept alive so that there was a church to preach to, a church for those Reformation 'roosters' to crow to! There was somebody to hear them when they started crowing. Everybody hadn't gone deaf; everybody wasn't sound asleep.

The point I want you to get out of verse 38 is: "*If he shall come in the second watch...*" In other words, in the midnight watch, "*or come in the third watch, the cockcrowing watch, blessed are those servants....*" He just wasn't telling them which watch he was coming in. He knew he wasn't coming in either of those two watches, let alone the first one. He wasn't coming in the second or the third one but he didn't let them know it. He warned them: "*You be ready at any time. You don't know when he's coming; just be ready!*"

That command applied to the sincere people of God during those dark years, the Dark Ages. There were people there who took this admonition seriously and they did their best to be ready for the return of the Lord. Some of them may be under the altar, under the golden altar in Revelation 6, right now, because they were ready. They kept their lamps burning; they kept their belt tightened. They were ready to work any time the Lord called for them. If he had returned, they would have gone up in the Rapture.

Question: "Can we use Matthew 25?"

Yeah, you can use that. We're talking about the parable of the virgins, the wise and the foolish. That is talking about that same time period when the lord returns from the wedding. The wise virgins were ready and the foolish virgins weren't.

Here in this parable, Jesus is just condensing it and talking to his men, saying, "*You be like men, not virgins, but like men that are servants in the household waiting for the lord to get through with the banquet he has been to and come home. You want to welcome him home when he gets here. When he gets here, he will set a feast for you! He's been to a feast and he will set a feast for you!*" I wanted to make this point that people were told to be ready in those watches when he didn't come. I think that we can assume some obeyed the commandment and were ready.

He stops the parable there and didn't go on to mention the fourth watch, but the implication is still there. If he didn't come in the second or the third watch and you are still here in the fourth watch, he's still to come! He is still going to come! He didn't come in the first, second or third watch! We're in the fourth watch! What time is it? It's the fourth watch! It's almost daylight, time for the Son to rise with healing in his wings! That gives us an idea of what kind of time we live in.

Question: "Brother Brown, just to add something to this, isn't that about the time when Jesus actually resurrected from the tomb? Wasn't it in the early morning, the twilight just before...?"

We can't prove that. It makes a good description but there is no scripture that actually says what time during that night he woke up and came out of the grave; he just beat the sunup. He was up when the new day dawned.

I want to look at another time frame in Revelation 12. This is a calendar of events in Revelation 12: "*There appeared a great wonder in heaven, a woman* (the church) *clothed with the sun* (the New Testament) *and the moon under her feet,*" (the Law of Moses for a background). Don't forget that the only scriptures that New Testament church had was the Old Testament. They wrote the New Testament, but they didn't have it to build the church with. It was written toward the close of their labors. They built a church on top of that Old Testament. It was the foundation under their feet.

"And on her head a crown of twelve stars, (twelve great, powerful preachers! They were a crown, the authority over that church. The twelve apostles were the authority over that New Testament church. *"She being with child* (it was a pregnant woman) *cried, travailing in birth and pained to be delivered."* The church is supposed to give forth children! Bear seed! A lively church, a lively woman is to bear children! This church that was back there in that New Testament period was *'with child'* and being delivered of overcomers! That was the purpose of the church: to produce overcomers!

"There appeared another wonder in heaven, a great red dragon (an empire, a powerful government that gave that church trouble, persecuted them) *"...and his tail drew the third part of the stars of heaven and cast them to the earth."* That's a little picture, a reminder of the falling away. The dragon stood before that church which was ready to be delivered of a child. The dragon wanted to devour her child as soon as it was born.

Most preachers today explain that child as being Jesus who was born of the woman Israel, but this is more to the point: Israel didn't have the sun for clothing. They had the moon, all right, but it wasn't under their feet; it was their clothing. It was their coat. They didn't have that crown of authority on their heads.

This is the church that came out of the upper room and worked such great wonders during the pages of the Book of Acts. The dragon wanted to devour those overcomers that the church was producing, like Stephen. Stephen was the first martyr. He was the first one of those overcomers. The enemy killed him, stoned him to death, tried to devour him. However, what happened was, verse 5: *"she brought forth a man child who was to rule all nations with a rod of iron."* That does sound like Jesus, doesn't it? You just need to learn that it includes everybody that is in Jesus. *"...and her child was caught up unto God and to his throne."* He wasn't destroyed! The dragon didn't get to devour those overcomers! Cut their heads off! Stoned them to death! But, their souls moved out and went up to God! They had new bodies to move into.

The woman fled into the wilderness in verse 6. "*...where she had a place prepared of God.*" That was just the wilderness, a place outside of Canaan, outside of the Holy Place of God. They left their Holy Place and went into a more carnal condition. That's where the wilderness is, the wilderness of ignorance. They lost their perfect understanding of the Word of God. That's why there is so much argument over what the Bible means today. The understanding has been lost and hardly anybody has it anymore. So, they were in darkness in the wilderness.

"*The woman fled into the wilderness where she has a place prepared of God and they feed her there a thousand, two hundred, three score days.*" That represents 1,260 years. Now, it mentions war in heaven and that's repeating the history of the conflict between the church and the world back there. It mentions that the dragon, the civil power, lost its power over that Early Church. Again, it repeats in verse 14, "*The woman was given two wings of a great eagle that she might fly into the wilderness.*" That's not another wilderness. The woman didn't go into two wildernesses. It's just a repetition of what was said in the sixth verse. The fourteenth verse is just a repetition of verse six.

She went into the wilderness where she was nourished; into her place where she was nourished for a time, times and half a time. Compare that with verse six: a thousand, two hundred and three score days. That's how long a time, times and half a time is. So wherever you find, elsewhere in here, time, times and half a time, remember it's 1,260 days and each day stands for a year, prophetically.

"*The serpent cast out water as a flood after the woman that he might cause her to be carried away of the flood.*" He tried to destroy the woman with a flood of persecution, but it says, "*The earth helped the woman and the earth opened her mouth and swallowed up the flood which the dragon cast out of his mouth.*" We see that as Protestantism that finally broke the power of the persecuting element in the Dark Ages.

Here is where we come in. Here is where we are right now. See yourself here in verse 17: "*The dragon was wroth with the woman and went to make war with* (not the woman, but) *the remnant of her seed."* That's the rest of the man child. The whole man child wasn't born back there. There are some more of it to be born after that wilderness period. That's where we are today. We're trying to produce some more overcomers! We want to have a perfect church like the Early Church! We want to restore the church into the New Testament condition! There can be overcomers for the dragon to make war with. When he makes war with them, the results will be the same as they were back there. He will kill their bodies but cannot kill their souls. Their souls will move out under the altar. Here's where we are in this calendar. This is another of God's calendars here.

There are other scriptures we could use like that. I want to wind up with one in Romans which is totally different, if I can remember which one it was. Yeah, Romans 13, beginning with verse 11 says, *"Knowing the time...,"* I hope we know this much about the time. What time is it? *"It's high time to awake out of sleep!"* Time to wake up! *"For now is our salvation nearer than when we believed."*

I believe it was Brother Dyal over there at the meeting the other day that got to talking about examples of how we read verses and emphasize some words in the verse and ignore others. Because we think we are seeing the main point, we miss another big point that was covered up in some of those other words. He used John 3:16 for an example: *"God so loved the world that he gave his only begotten son that whosoever believeth in him should not perish but have everlasting life."*

That 'everlasting life' captivates our attention right there! Everybody focuses on that and never gives much thought to the idea of the opposite of what he delivered us from: *"whosoever believeth in him should not perish!"* That has to be pointed out to you before you can see what that means. There is a deep revelation in that word 'perish' that helps you understand major doctrines in the word of God.

This is sort of like that here. Romans 13:11: *"Now is our salvation nearer than when we believed."* Most people read scriptures about salvation and think, "Well, I got that salvation a long time ago. When I believed, I got salvation."

"Believe on the Lord Jesus Christ and thou shalt be saved." Everybody thinks they get the salvation that's promised in that scripture the day they believe on the Lord. We need to look at Paul's words here: *"Now is our salvation nearer than it was the day we first believed."* Salvation is a *longer* subject than most people give it credit for. You get saved from *some things* the day you believe.

Let's see if we can find that one in the fourth or fifth chapter that speaks of being saved from sins that are past. Which verse is that? Somebody find that for me, the fourth or fifth chapter, I forget which. It speaks of being delivered from sins that are past.

Romans 3:25, that's where it is. Back up to verse 23: *"For all have sinned and come short of the glory of God. We, being justified freely by his grace through the redemption that is in Christ Jesus whom God has set forth to be a propitiation through faith in his blood to declare his righteousness for the remission of sins that are past through the forbearance of God."*

You can emphasize righteousness and remission of sins and forbearance of God and overlook that word 'past'. *"Sins that are past."* What does it do to those sins that are not yet past, in other words, future sins? The day you believed and got saved, you got saved from your sins that were past. Your past sins were forgiven. But, God doesn't forgive you for things you haven't done yet. You can't even repent for things you haven't done yet. You know, you might not ever do them. We hope you don't do some of those bad things that you are going to be tempted with. But all those sins that you do commit in the future, they need to be forgiven, too! We need to be saved from them! That's one reason we're not fully saved on the day that we believe. We're saved from those past sins.

We need to be saved from any ***tendency*** to sin before we're ready to go to heaven. We've got to be saved from any ***likelihood*** of sin because God doesn't want any sin to happen up there. He doesn't want it to happen down here, either, but if it's going to happen, this is where he keeps it. He's going to make sure it stays down here and doesn't get up there.

So now, our salvation is nearer than when we believed because we're growing up in God and approaching maturity. Now, that's the time that we are living in. It's high time to awake out of sleep and get out of this lethargy that a lot of us have fallen into, not being dedicated and faithful to the services, not really serving God, not really witnessing to the lost. We've become lethargic and lost our first love! It's time to awake out of that sleep because, for one reason, the time is drawing near to an end. The salvation that we've been waiting for is for the Lord to come back from heaven with his reward in his hand and give us our position in everlasting life, a position of rulership in the world of the future. That's when our salvation is complete. It's finished then.

Somebody made a good point the other day about—it came to my attention real forcefully. Maybe I read this in a book somewhere about what Jesus said on the cross when he said, *"It is finished."* What a powerful statement that was. Now, you can use that in finishing a carpentry job or baking a cake or in getting dressed for church: "I'm finished."

When Jesus hung on the cross in all that pain and said, *"It is finished!"* A lot of preachers think he meant everything is finished; all the work is done and we don't have to do anything. He did it all! Well, what he finished that day was his work! That wasn't your work! He finished his work but he didn't finish your work! You've got to do your work now in overcoming sin by taking advantage of the power he put in your hand to overcome sin and learn to live above it so God will trust you with everlasting life. Amen! He's got to have some people he can trust!

So, here's what time we're in: *"The night is far spent; the day is at hand."* We're living in the days of the coming of the Lord Jesus! *"Let us therefore, cast off the works of darkness,"* Cast off the works of the Dark Ages and the wilderness period, *"and let us put on the armor of light!"* Where are you going to get that light? Out of this Book, right here! I'm trying to light it up for you tonight! "*Let us walk honestly as in the day time, not in rioting and drunkenness; not in chambering and wantonness; not in strife and envying.*"

We've got to get rid of all that! It's day time! Day time is dawning upon us! We've got to leave all that strife and envying back in the darkness of the wilderness! "*And put ye on the Lord Jesus Christ and make not provision for the flesh to fulfill the lusts thereof.*" Glory!

Scriptural References

Scripture references appear bold, page numbers appear italic.

Biblical Characters & Terms

Index